I0332090

MORE TO LIFE
THAN POLITICS?

Richard Alston

Connor Court Publishing

Published in 2020 by Connor Court Publishing Pty Ltd.

Copyright © Richard Alston

Not to be reproduced without the permission of the Copyright holders.

Connor Court Publishing Pty Ltd.
PO Box 7257
Redland Bay QLD 4165
sales@connorcourt.com
www.connorcourtpublishing.com.au

ISBN: 9781925826753

Cover Design by Maria Giordano.

Printed in Australia.

Contents

List of illustrations	*v*
Foreword by Henry Ergas	*vii*
Preface by Ziggy Switkowski	*ix*
More to Life than Politics?	*xi*
1. Early Years – Family, Fun and School	1
2. University Days	19
3. Life and Times at the Bar	31
4. The Long and Winding Road to Canberra	47
5. Life in the Bubble	71
6. Leadership	107
7. Communications, IT and the Media	139
8. The Arts	175
9. Indigenous Art	201
10. Whose ABC?	223
11. Life beyond Politics – Before and After	257
12. London – My Duty	297
13. My London – a Tribute	321
Acknowledgements	345
Index	349

List of illustrations

After page 106

With Megs at Government House, Canberra, after being sworn in as Minister for Communications and the Arts, March 1996

With Amy and Nick, Sydney, 2001 (top)

Sheila and Bob Alston picnicking in car park at Flemington, 1970s (bottom)

MV *Gudrun Bakke*, a general cargo vessel whose crew I joined to sail the Pacific (top)

Gudrun Bakke's pop-up swimming pool (bottom)

With Nelson Mandela at inauguration of Thabo Mbeki as President of the Republic of South Africa, Pretoria, 1999

Sartorially threatening Gough Whitlam at the Sydney Opera House, 1994 (top)

Valued correspondence: *Dear Richard . . . Regards Gough Whitlam*, September 1994 (bottom)

With John Howard at Lord's, First Ashes Test, July 2005 (top)

John Howard launches the Liberal Party's Arts policy, *Arts For Art's Sake*, during 1996 election campaign (bottom)

At RAAF Memorial, Reykjavik, Iceland, 2002, with Helen Williams, Secretary, Department of Communications, Information Technology and the Arts, and David Quilty, Chief of Staff

Customer feedback from John Anderson, Deputy Prime Minister, August 2003

Mother Teresa's self-described business card which she gave to me at her Home for the Dying in Calcutta, 1993

At North-West Frontier Province, Peshawar, Pakistan, 1991

Goat tree, Marrakech-Essaouira Road, Morocco, 2016

Inimitable warning signs, Bollywood film studios, Mumbai, 1998

Painting of porter in souk, Doha, Qatar

MORE TO LIFE THAN POLITICS?

After page 222

David Hockney in his studio in the Hollywood Hills

With David Hockney and Peter Goulds, his agent

David Hockney, "Two Red Chairs, March 1986"

David Hockney, "Green Grey and Blue Plant, July 1986"

David Hockney, "The Studio March 28th 1995"

In my study: major Aboriginal works by Long Jack Philippus and Clifford Possum and "one small upright bear" from Whistler, British Columbia

Stella Gimme, Balgo artist, untitled

Jack Dale, Kimberley artist, "Wandjina Woman"

Wilma Ross Ngala, Ampilatwatja, untitled

With Dr Brian Kennedy, former Director, National Gallery of Australia (left) and artist Michael Jagamara Nelson (centre)

A soumak (flat woven tapestry) from the Caucasus

Persian silk carpet purchased in Tehran, 2006

Foreword

Henry Ergas AO

By and large, Australians do not hold politicians in high esteem. Some earn a grudging admiration; a few, a measure of genuine affection. But a child who expressed an interest in a career in politics would no doubt be dispatched to the school counsellor, if not the psychologist, and advised to consider more respectable options, such as becoming a pole dancer or the neighbourhood dope peddler.

That may not be entirely unfair. The Periclean democracy was a glorious thing, but there are good reasons to believe it had its fair share of strivers and stragglers, temporizers and time-servers. As for Australian democracy, when it shines, it shines all the more brightly for being cast against a backdrop that is at times so unedifying. Its evolution into a playground, if not a battlefield, for budding careerists, whose ambition is dwarfed only by their superficiality, does not improve the picture.

It is, however, possible to do things differently. And in these memoirs, Richard Alston shows how. There is an element that is strikingly old-fashioned in the path he took. As had been the case for many of the outstanding ministers of an earlier generation, he entered politics after already having had a career in the law and pursuing a wide range of interests, notably in development assistance. Aristotle, in the Nicomachean Ethics, tells us that "A young man is not a fit person to attend lectures on political theory, because he is not versed in the practical business of life from which politics draws its premises and subject matter." As is apparent in the pages that follow, that experience of the "practical business of life," in which illusion after illusion is scraped away by the pumice-stone of experience, left a foundation of sturdy common sense that contributed greatly to the success of the Howard Government.

There is, however, a modern element that is every bit as striking. Having set his attention on communications policy, Alston prepared for it not merely by meeting with stakeholders and reading widely; he enrolled in a postgraduate degree and took a course in it on the economics of telecommunications. Whether what I covered in that course ultimately helped or hindered is for others to judge. What I can attest to is how seriously he approached the course and how probing—indeed, forensic—he was in testing every contention I advanced. And there is no doubt that the material we covered was very much in his mind as he dramatically reshaped Australian communications during his years in office.

To say that is not to suggest that everything went to plan in the reform program. There are, as Machiavelli put it, no safe options in politics: only ones that are more or less unsafe. Inevitably, some of those risks go bad, and clearly some did. Whether those outcomes could have been avoided is contentious; what is not is that the overall gains the Alston reforms yielded were large and enduring.

Politics cannot, and should not, hope to endow the life of the community with splendour and greatness. But for all of its flaws, it remains its vital task to provide a framework which gives all Australians opportunities to pursue the good life, and, more important still, that ensures that fools and knaves do not make its pursuit impossible.

To that extent, it is a truly noble calling. Moreover, engaged in with conviction and maturity, it can be a deeply rewarding one, all the more so to those as well-rounded as Alston is. It is an error to believe that all political careers end in failure: on the contrary, they can, and in this case did, lead to a well-merited sense of having served and achieved. There are, as one would expect from a man one of whose many passions is reading and collecting all the books that make it into the final selection for the Booker Prize, many fascinating pages in these memoirs. And, yes, they certainly prove that there is far more to life than politics. But they should also make us hope that that child will stick to his or her ambition and ultimately contribute, with judgment and determination, to the unfolding saga that is Australian democracy.

Preface

Ziggy Switkowski AO

The election of the Howard Government coincided with the emergence of the Internet and there followed a critical decade of policy reform covering telecom competition and Telstra privatisation, the era of the media moguls, the dotcom boom and bust, and building the foundations of today's digital environment.

Richard Alston was there – crafting the telecommunications and media policy architecture for the 21st century, engaging with the media moguls and new age entrepreneurs, shepherding far reaching legislation through Parliament, and leading the public debate about the new world on the Internet and of digital services.

More to Life than Politics? vividly describes the arc of a career that bookended this period and more. It illustrates a lifetime of public service of a brilliant politician who was in exactly the right place when the Internet arrived. The experiences covered in this very readable book will be of interest to policy wonks, political tragics, and everyone else trying to anticipate the next turn in our digital lives and the world of Google, Facebook, Amazon, Alibaba, and our ABC.

x

More to Life than Politics?

Politicians' careers are often defined by their time in the public spotlight – their fifteen minutes of fame. This is unsurprising as a person's public image is usually a reflection of their public activities. Whilst my time in politics has undoubtedly been the highlight of my career it should nevertheless be seen in a wider context. It was very important, but not to the exclusion of family and outside interests, and certainly not so intrusive as to interfere with my overall enjoyment of life. My diversions included sport, painting (both modern and Indigenous), music, notably grand opera, and, above all, literature, with a preoccupation with the Booker Prize.

There is always a degree of luck and/or good timing, fortuitous or otherwise, in a political life, and perseverance is required. My path into politics was not straightforward. My attempts to win Liberal Party pre-selection for a House of Representatives seat were not successful. Eventually I secured the Party's nomination to fill a casual vacancy for the Senate just when I least expected it.

My apprenticeship in the Party organisation, culminating in a period as President of the Victorian Division, gave me the time and opportunity to shape my political philosophy. In my early adult years my primary concern was for the poor and underprivileged in third world countries and I devoted almost a decade to this cause in non-government organisations.

But in the developing world, I eventually came to the view that spending ever more money was unlikely to provide a sustainable, long term solution to problems of poverty, many of which stemmed from structural deficiencies including, not least, endemic corruption. I realised that not only were these most effectively addressed by political action, but that politics was a very important business which required serious study, attention and experience. As my interactions with government at multiple levels increased, I was inexorably drawn to politics as the main place to achieve permanent and effective change.

My Jesuit upbringing taught me that we were not put on Earth just to have a good time – it is the duty of all who are able to do so to strive for the betterment of others. Politics is potentially the most fruitful and effective means to accomplish this vital task. A life well lived is a rounded one, which must be founded upon solid ethics and principles. This does not mean virtue-signalling or ostentatiously supporting worthy causes, but rather pursuing practical and durable solutions. Politics offers a conspicuous avenue for doing so.

My family history of small business inclined me to the philosophy of the Liberal Party, which I saw as positive and pragmatic. The Australian economic model has been a long running success story, fundamentally on the right track. But, change is constant and regular reappraisals and upgrades are essential. John Howard's approach to the 1996 Federal election, which, as Deputy Leader of the Party in the Senate, I observed at very close quarters, was an important case study in philosophy and advocacy tempered by pragmatism – repairing the Budget deficit, getting the national debt under control, addressing (and funding) some sizeable environmental challenges – these were sensible commitments with which Australians readily identified. Most of the media, by contrast, much preferred colour and movement and saw Howard's practicality as pedestrian.

Politics is often viewed as a brutal blood sport and high wire act, not to be pursued by normal people. But its importance has been underlined by Pulitzer Prize winning journalist, Charles Krauthammer, in *Things That Matter*:

> While science, medicine, art, poetry, architecture, chess, space, sports, number theory and all things hard and beautiful promise purity, elegance and sometimes even transcendence, they are fundamentally subordinate. In the end they must bow to the sovereignty of politics.

Politics is not for the fainthearted but it has a magnetic attraction for those who yearn to participate in the great and noble task of nation-building. It opens many doors and can lead to a variety of adventures. But it is the inner life, the politics of the soul, where some of the greatest challenges and satisfactions lie. The life of

MORE TO LIFE THAN POLITICS?

a politician can be 24/7, exhilarating and, for some, very reward-ing. I spent ten years in Opposition – a hard and at times a lone-ly grind, but the thrill of the chase never waned. Many leave the stage, voluntarily or otherwise, with regrets for what might have been, even when they have had a good innings. I left Parliament and ministerial office without any regrets, only many rich memo-ries and profound gratitude for many rewarding opportunities.

Three years after entering Parliament, I was first appoint-ed Shadow Minister for Communications, then a low rank-ing portfolio, mainly concerned with media issues but on the cusp of the information revolution. For me, having just complet-ed an MBA with a major thesis on telecommunications, it was the jackpot.

Most aspiring Cabinet ministers will take any portfolio they are offered, irrespective of their knowledge, experience or aptitude. I was handed the one I most coveted. The Arts, when it was added in 1994, was the cream on an already splendid cake.

Information Technology was the most stimulating component of the brief – meeting, reading about, and being inspired by the ac-tivities of entrepreneurial, often breathtakingly young, leaders in the tech business. This encouraged me to think creatively, not an inherently natural instinct for a person trained in the law but look-ing for ways to do things differently was highly stimulating.

I thoroughly enjoyed the cut and thrust of my political career and the wonderful opportunities it offered to do worthwhile things. I took particular pride in extending high quality telecom-munications services to regional and rural Australia and for ena-bling Indigenous art to generate jobs and income in many remote communities which would otherwise never have been available to them.

I had the great good fortune to be around during the Howard ascendancy which many now regard, rightly, as a golden era. After nearly eighteen years in the Senate I had been on the front bench for nearly fifteen years and Deputy Senate Leader for ten – a good innings, but when to declare? As the years raced by, my thoughts started to turn to life after politics. All politicians have to adapt to the afterlife at some stage and I decided it would not be a very sat-

xiii

MORE TO LIFE THAN POLITICS?

isfying transition if, because of frequent absences, the family had become indifferent and I was left with few outside interests or qualifications.

I have always seen politics as a vital profession, indeed, a high calling, in a well-functioning democracy. So it was probably not surprising that on returning from three years in London as High Commissioner that I was still attracted to politics but this time to giving something back and ultimately serving as Federal Liberal Party president. Because of my admiration for the Federal Treasurer, Josh Frydenberg, I served for ten years as chair of his Kooyong Federal Electorate Conference, an achievement which Josh seems to regard as the pinnacle of my political career. The reality is that it gave me a unique vantage point from which to admire both his remarkable people skills and his peerless writing capabilities.

It is a considerable personal satisfaction that I left politics of my own accord – well, with a little prompting from my wife. I could have changed portfolios but I concluded it was better to leave as a one trick pony. Little did I realise I would be entering new fields – almost every company board position and later activity came from people I knew, but in fields I did not. Breaking new ground gave me a much wider spread of interests than merely doing what I had done during my many years at the Bar and then in Parliament and Government.

I am now on my fourth career: barrister, politician, diplomat and company director. In each I have found both great challenges and immense satisfaction. In particular, the business phase has not only been a great learning experience but it has provided enjoyable opportunities to strike a more even work-life balance – more time for reflection, reading, travel, collecting, investing – and more time for friends, wife and children, especially grandchildren, a source of endless pleasure.

1

Early Years – Family, Fun and School

Although I was born at St John of God Subiaco Hospital in Perth, I have no recollection of my first, and relatively fleeting, acquaintance with my birthplace. But in later years I often visited Perth in the course of my duties, and it proved very useful, when some local Sandgropers grumbled about "what would someone from the eastern states know?", to be able to say: "it's nice to be back home again".

As my father never spoke of his upbringing or, like many of his generation, of his war service; his late pre-war movements are uncertain. It seems that my parents (always known as Bob and Sheila to their three boys), both from NSW, married in Melbourne before they headed for Perth with his best friend, Robert Linton, son of Sir Richard Linton, politician, businessman, philanthropist, Victorian Agent-General in London and, most importantly, in 1923, founder and benefactor of the Linton Cup, an interstate junior teams tennis competition.

Bob and his best friend were both of Scottish heritage, my proof of lineage being a medallion which I found in my father's belongings inscribed:

Robert Alston of Scotland

DUNFERMLINE

February 23rd, 1844

gained local medal

from

Grand Caledonian Curling Club

The medal allowed me to definitively establish my line of genetic inheritance, although it is unlikely that it would have inadvertently made me a dual citizen!

This Robert was probably the father of my great-grandfather, Robert Andrew Alston (1853-1906), the first Alston to come to Australia in about 1870 and who, family legend has it, died after being hit on the head by a hatbox of bowling balls which fell from an overhead compartment in a train. He and his successors were all first named Robert until I came along; I only scored Robert as my third Christian name.

Neither of my parents had a tertiary education. In fact, my father barely had a secondary education, leaving school aged 15 when his mother died. He had already won a scholarship to Fort Street, the legendary and prestigious Sydney selective high school, but was forced to abandon such ambitions: as the oldest of six young children he was required to help his father, a master builder in the small but pretty river town of Corowa on the New South Wales side of the Murray. Not long before my father was born in 1910, the town had played a significant part in the Australian nation's coming of age: the Corowa Conference held in 1893 to discuss a proposed federation of the Australian colonies.

His subsequent career demonstrates that he could have been a successful university graduate, but it was not to be. I am not sure of my father's occupation in Perth. He may have been transferred there by The Irish Linen Company for whom he had worked in Melbourne, but he was certainly still there when I was born, 12 days after the bombing of Pearl Harbor.

When I was about six months old my parents decided to return to Melbourne – why I'm not sure, as neither had been born there, nor had they any relatives down south. They never regretted it and lived together in Melbourne for another fifty or more years after Bob returned in 1945 from the Pacific campaign.

Army service

Shortly after returning to Melbourne Bob joined the Army. Twelve months later he was promoted to Lieutenant. His war service record shows that in August 1943 he was recommended for promotion by a Lieutenant Colonel whose report said of him: "A very fine type with a strong confident personality. Worked well". It

EARLY YEARS

was a relief in some ways to come across such a positive and, in my experience of him in later years, an accurate character assessment.

Bob saw out the Pacific War as a Lieutenant on Morotai, an island off Borneo, now in Indonesia but then part of the Dutch East Indies. In 1944-45 it became the strategic base of the Allied forces, from which they attacked posts in the Philippines and Borneo in the fight against Japanese forces during the Second World War.

Bob never spoke about these experiences, other than to say that he was there when Allied forces from the USA and Australia, under the leadership of the supreme commander for the South West Pacific, General Douglas MacArthur, landed on Morotai's southwest corner. MacArthur saw this as the most strategic location for a counter invasion to recapture the Philippines from the Japanese, who had been in occupation since early 1942. Allied troops quickly settled on Morotai, where MacArthur constructed a number of airstrips over the rough coral ground. At one point Morotai was said to house no less than 60,000 soldiers, a large 1900-bed hospital and a busy naval base.

The island continued to be a strategic site for staging attacks on the Philippines. The Battle of Morotai 1944-45 erupted when the Japanese Army unsuccessfully tried to stop American forces constructing three large airfields there as a springboard for the Liberation of the Philippines. The island's base facilities were further expanded in 1945 to support the Australian-led Borneo Campaign.

The formal surrender of the Japanese military was accepted by General MacArthur on board USS *Missouri* on 2 September 1945. Bob once spoke proudly about meeting MacArthur and being there when General Sir Thomas Blamey accepted the formal surrender of the Second Japanese Army at Morotai a week later. Morotai hit the headlines again in 1974 when a lone Japanese soldier emerged after hiding in the jungle for nearly three decades, unaware the War was long over.

Bob brought home with him a splendidly embossed Samurai sword, with a curved, single edged blade, a squared guard and a long two-handed grip. This treasured wartime memento lay around the house for some 45 years until he became permanently incapacitated following a severe stroke and Sheila surreptitiously disposed of it as she didn't like reminders of the War.

Although he never attended RSL activities or marched on Anzac Day, Bob did join the Naval and Military Club and remained very actively and generously involved in Legacy and its work in support of some 65,000 war widow(er)s and their dependents. He even recruited me, by then a Senator, to address a Legacy lunch more than forty years after the War's end.

Bob returned home relatively unscathed from the War, although I do remember that he was entitled to a small part pension because of some, presumably, relatively minor war injury. As a proud self-made small businessman, he refused to accept it and, as he worked full-time until a severe stroke left him totally disabled at the age of 80, he never received the age pension. It was not uncommon at the time for those who could afford to do so to choose not to take government handouts. In later years the Labor Party in government convinced many that they were entitled to claim benefits irrespective of financial need.

Back to Melbourne

Once we were back in Melbourne, Sheila moved the two of us into a comfortable and refined, if somewhat tired, flat, one of a number in a mock Tudor complex, in Marne Street, South Yarra (Moore Abbey, as it was known, still stands today). It exuded an air of genteel poverty. My earliest recollection is of being rebuked for putting pieces of coke (the coal derivative variety) into the petrol tanks of neighbours' cars – a harmless prank to me, but no doubt an annoying and potentially engine-wrecking activity to others.

When Bob finally returned from the War he became a commercial traveller with The Irish Linen Company. We moved to a respectable two storey timber and brick dwelling in Middle Brighton. My bedroom was a small, glassed-in upstairs balcony, overlooking the street corner – very cold in winter, with no heating. People were encouraged to be as self-sufficient as possible: to keep hens for eggs, and to grow their own vegetables at home. We did our bit.

In due course I acquired two brothers (a third later died shortly after birth), but I was also particularly fond of Pip, our half Kelpie, half Cocker Spaniel who, in keeping with the slower paced languor of the times, was able to survive to a ripe old age, despite often lying in the middle of the T intersection outside our house, while cars went around and sometimes over him. It was a classic feature of those now-forgotten times that there was very little traffic around, by today's standards. We often played street cricket and there was always plenty of time to carry the box, which served as the stumps, safely to the side of the road when a car appeared.

Pip was a wonderful childhood companion. My brother Ian, accompanied by Pip, was wont to walk, past Melbourne's iconic foreshore bathing boxes, the 3-4 kms to our prep(aratory) school, enabling him to pocket the tram fare, which could later be used to purchase "sweets". The faithful hound would often walk slowly up the dirt path alongside the playground, where the entire school was assembled, as though he was inspecting the troops, before making his own way home, without any traffic concerns. He was never on a lead – we didn't own one – and he was always there when we needed him, especially when he was quietly ensconced under the dinner table and more than happy to accept surreptitious offerings of lamb's fry and tripe, which, for reasons known only to herself, our mother somehow thought would be good for us.

I very much doubt that anyone in the surrounding streets had anything like a secondary, let alone tertiary, education. A likeable Italian family, the Auditoris, lived a few doors away but spoke little or no English. Mrs Auditori seemed to spend most of her time running down the street screaming "Johnny", in pursuit of her wayward little boy. On one occasion she entered our backyard screaming: "where's my Johnny?" and, having spotted him cowering near the coal box, proceeded to break off a big branch from our oleander tree and raced after him brandishing her lethal weapon. Perhaps not surprisingly, her husband, Frank, the gentlest of people, spent most of his time pursuing his occupation as a fisherman, and he often took us out on his little boat, launched at the end of a nearby slip rail. Opposite us were a very friendly, elderly pensioner couple, the Peebles, of very good working class stock, while around the corner lived Dave Bland.

Dave had a brief but extraordinary career of 36 games in VFL football with St Kilda. In 1955, injuries and suspension (a regular feature of his playing style) limited his season to just seven league games, yet he won the Grosvenor Trophy for St Kilda's best player and finished third in the club's best and fairest. In his spare time, he played football with us in the street. He went on to play interstate football for South Australia.

Our street had a number of workmen's cottages, behind which towered a huge gas works. The grounds were officially closed to the public but easily accessible, after hours, to enterprising youngsters, for whom it was an escape into another world. Every aspect of this massive brick and steel construction was a potential danger to life and limb, yet we survived quite comfortably.

Not far away were the Middle Brighton baths, an open air, salt water, quad-shaped enclosure, with a very high broadwalk surrounding it, and live mussels clinging to every upright. In those days of endless summers, we all headed for the baths early morning and spent the days lying on the concrete, getting maximum exposure to the sun's rays – resulting in deep tans and sometimes serious sunburn, but never giving a thought to the potential dangers to which we are now all constantly alerted.

Church Street is now a thriving up-market strip shopping centre, unrecognisable from the 1950s when its main feature was the Dendy cinema. Saturday afternoon was a must – double features, often Westerns, with Tom Mix a special favourite, and sometimes an electric piano or a hurdy gurdy churning out plastic music.

What is now a solidly middle class enclave was a largely lower income working class area and our house, very modest by today's standards, but with a respectable backyard, was probably one of the better ones. I have a clear recollection of the late 1940s system of rationing essential food items, such as meat, butter, sugar and tea and a large outdoor paint cupboard around the side of the house with a sticker proclaiming, "Property of the Department of Supply".

Our childhood days were relatively carefree and enjoyable, if not without the inevitable mishaps and injury scares. Bob could be a hard task master and took particular exception to idle students who preferred to watch TV and supposedly work with their brains rather than their hands. A constant outdoor worker, he would often ask us to help him in the garden. Unfortunately, what this really meant was "come and watch me in action". Inevitably this palled, so that when I got up at my 21st birthday party and said: "I've always been a do it yourself man – when my father asks for help in the garden, I say 'do it yourself'," this attempted comedy line went down like a lead balloon, leading to a prolonged patriarchal sulk.

In those days, before refrigerators became commonplace, an ice box was an essential kitchen item. Daily visits from the horse drawn milk and ice carts were standard fare. One day, while I was assisting the iceman, I managed to fall from the driving bench on to the roadway, only to have the vehicle's iron clad wheel run over my leg, resulting in significant hospitalisation, followed by twelve months wearing an iron calliper. The fact that I cannot remember which leg it was suggests I made a full recovery!

A new car was a big deal as the country emerged from post-war austerity. My mother, brothers and I were all filled with nervous excitement when our father came home one night with a brand new Ford Customline, predecessor to the Fairlane, and we were in seventh heaven as he took us for a drive around the block. This probably led to an enthusiastic over reaction on my part, as a few of my under age schoolboy cronies and I took it in turns to "borrow" our parents cars, usually starting the motor with the aid of jumper leads in lieu of car keys, in order to go on midnight cruises. Fortunately, we came to no harm as there was nothing like the volume of today's traffic or police vigilance to challenge us.

Although Bob had had virtually no secondary education, like many post-war strivers he was keen to ensure that his offspring had every opportunity. He had been brought up as a Presbyterian but deferred to the obligations of his wife's Catholic religion, which required that all children of a "mixed" marriage attend Catholic schools.

Xavier College

Xavier College, founded in 1878, was and remains the leading Catholic private school in Victoria, so I was fortunate to be enrolled at its recently established preparatory school, Kostka Hall, at Brighton Beach. Set in the ti-tree lined grounds of an old private mansion, it was perfectly insulated from the real world. My class brought together a diverse group of some twenty students – four went on to University, indeed, one to be dux of the senior school, two to gaol, one to win a Commonwealth Games gold medal and another (Peter Williams, best man at my wedding) to play cricket for Victoria.

The gold medallist was Ken Roche, an amazing all round athlete, excelling in the high jump at Victorian schools' level and later internationally in 400m hurdles. His father ran a very successful family civil engineering and contract mining company, and it was the social highlight of our primary school years to be taken each year to the West Melbourne stadium for the Saturday night boxing and wrestling.

My initial immersion in primary school was somewhat fraught, as I apparently did not take quietly to authority. Matters came to a head when, having been ejected from the classroom for setting fire to a pencil sharpener, I then proceeded to spray a fire hose back through the open class window. The reward for such high jinks was a year's "leave", which I served at St James Primary School, Gardenvale.

It must have had a salutary effect as I soon found myself filling the role of altar boy at the adjoining parish church and, for the next few years, rising at 5.30 am in order to ride my bike nearly two kilometres in time for 6.30 mass – quite a challenge in the depths of winter, often through heavy fog all the way.

I was eventually able to resume my studies at Kostka, where I also thoroughly enjoyed playing cricket and football, the main sporting options in those days. My studies seemed to proceed uneventfully, thanks in large part to some excellent teaching from both clerical and lay staff.

In due course I ascended to the senior school in Kew, an hour away from my Brighton home. It was not uncommon to hitch-hike a lift from city bound car drivers, fortunately free from any unwanted advances, which were unheard of in those days.

In many respects I had been very fortunate – a stable family home life if not without the competitive tensions inherent in a family with three boys. My father's strong work ethic, pulling himself up by his bootstraps, had enabled us all to be the beneficiaries of a high quality private school education. We were classified as a bit above average, although Philip, the youngest, who went on to become a long standing and internationally respected professor in the human rights field, clearly had the most academic potential.

In those days, what we now call years nine and ten were subdivided into four streams on the basis of someone's judgment about perceived intellectual capabilities. I started life at the senior school in sub-intermediate A, but I was definitely not in the top half of the class. I probably coasted, doing the minimum required and cramming intensely as end of year exams approached.

Xavier was good to me. Founded by the Jesuits, "the Society of Jesus", it was one of the original six (now eleven) in the APS (Associated Public [read Private] Schools) – boys only, but open to both day students and boarders. It had an impressive spiritual ethos, which has since remained with me and helped me to cope with the "slings and arrows of outrageous fortune" which at times beset us all.

The sub-intermediate class was divided into four groupings – A to D – supposedly on the basis of merit. I managed to get into A but did disastrously in first term arithmetic, scoring a miserable 19%. I was somewhat jolted and embarrassed by this effort, so I applied myself more diligently in term 2 to record 81. This heroic turnaround was not universally applauded, however, as the teacher took the opportunity to tell the class that I must have cheated and asked me to apologise. When I protested my innocence, I was hauled out the front and given "six of the best" with a quite lethal looking black strap.

Despite this bracing episode, the senior school immediately felt like a truly adult experience and there were so many more things to do. Unfortunately, joining the school cadets was one of them – this one compulsory. It wasn't that I disliked the concept, although it was certainly far removed from my hitherto sheltered upbringing.

My paternal grandfather had been a crack rifle shot at Corowa on the Murray, where shooting rabbits and foxes was everyday sport. But even little-league army exercises were a reminder of the big and potentially dangerous world beyond. But for one reason or another I was constantly at odds with authority figures – not in a nasty way, but rather in testing them and frequently pushing the boundaries.

Not that I am especially proud of it now, but I recall that a very good friend, Michael O'Sullivan, who later became secretary of the Federated Clerks Union and a big wig in the industry superannuation funds sector, shared with me the record for the number of consecutive defaulter's parades. Punishments for our rather mild brand of insubordination included wearing cadet uniform to school on a normal day and detentions of one form or another.

Other inglorious episodes included orchestrated disruptions of a performance of *Hamlet* and a session of Alliance Francaise. These transgressions culminated in my appearance before the Rector who advised, in stern tones, that it was only my father's generosity of spirit which had saved me from expulsion. It was unclear whether he was referring to my father's nature or his wallet, but either way I was very grateful.

Bob was a bit of a martinet, so I guess it had become my instinct to rebel against authority – perhaps a sign of immaturity but, looking back, I wondered whether being a contrarian or risk taker could sometimes be a key to later career success.

It had never occurred to me to become a prefect. I was quite happy being an outsider. Years later I became aware that Tony Street had been captain of the school at Melbourne Grammar, while his classmate, Malcolm Fraser, was not even a prefect. Yet it was the outsider who rose to the top in later life. For me this was a validation of my instinct that those who felt comfortable being close to authority figures were less likely to challenge the status quo and perhaps more inclined to settle for second best.

Dick Pratt once showed me a framed message on his desk. It read: "All progress depends on the unreasonable man." I later discovered this was a shorthand version of an aphorism attributed to George Bernard Shaw: "The reasonable man adapts himself to the world: the unreasonable one persists in trying to adapt the world to himself. Therefore all progress depends on the unreasonable man". Another useful epigram is from John Dyson, a legendary inventor and father of the Dyson bagless vacuum cleaner: "Failure is interesting – it's part of making progress. You never learn from success, but you do learn from failure."

Most of the teachers at Xavier were priests, with a few laymen making up the numbers. Nowadays, with the decline in clerical vocations in most Western countries, priests as teachers are an extinct species. The quality of teaching at Xavier was variable – no doubt not unusual.

We had first class teachers in English, Latin and History. Mr Ludwig Van Baer was a kindly, dedicated and, at times, eccentric English specialist. It was a memorable day in his Matriculation English class when he announced that I had won the Edward Ryan prize for Modern English Literature. This was met with widespread guffawing from my fellow students, but I had the last laugh. The prize, then worth £5 (today about $250), allowed me to select my own classics and, amongst others, I duly chose Cervantes' *Don Quixote, The Imitation of Christ* by Thomas à Kempis, *Crime and Punishment* by Dostoevsky, Goldsmith's *The Vicar of Wakefield* and *The Collected Works of Henry Lawson.*

I struggled a little with Latin, but was thereafter forever grateful for having studied it, as it inculcated invaluable English roots into my vocabulary and set up a lifelong fascination with the English language. There were two history subjects: Modern, which was essentially European – largely Italian Renaissance; and British, which alternated between true English and Australian. There was no risk of missing out on one strand as in those days nearly everyone did two years Matriculation.

We also had a very good Maths teacher in Leaving (today's Year 11). His favourite trick, when he espied an inattentive student, was to suddenly shout, "Smith, what are you doing?" The answer was invariably: "Nothing, Sir", to which he instantly replied: "Well get out, you can't come in here and do nothing."

I will never forget our Geography teacher. After bumbling his way through a subject about which he clearly felt both uninformed and uncomfortable, I had the good fortune to mention my predicament to a Shelford girl who lived nearby. She expressed surprise at my ignorance of several key topics – "after all", she said, "it's all in James". When I asked who James was, she quickly retorted: "the compulsory textbook, of course."

Naturally I pursued the matter of our non-use of James with our teacher. He initially brushed off my concern but, when pressed, he finally conceded that he had forgotten to put in an order for the key text book until it was too late. The class struggled on, unaided, but I was able to borrow the redoubtable James from my friend and ultimately managed to be one of four students out of about forty to pass the subject. There were no parental threats or complaints in those days, so this disaster presumably remained buried.

Father Thomas O'Donovan (universally known as Tod) was the Prefect of Studies and a legendary figure – no nonsense, enough to strike fear into the hearts of the bravest student. He had us all bluffed, but he ran a very professional show. Years later, when I had been invited to Riverview, Xavier's sister school in Sydney, to say a few words, I was pleasantly surprised when he greeted me warmly. Despite the grief I had given him in earlier years, all was apparently forgiven, as he seemed to derive some satisfaction from my subsequent progress through life. For my part, I had always retained great respect, verging on admiration, for the leadership he had provided.

Sport at Xavier was taken very seriously. The school motto was *Sursum Corda* (Lift up Your Hearts), but there is no doubt the Jesuits were also firm subscribers to another Latin maxim, *Mens sana in corpore sano*, usually translated as "a healthy mind in a healthy body", a recognition of physical exercise as an important, even essential, part of our mental and psychological well-being. All students were required to play in a football team. Unless my memory is defective, I can recall that Denis Hart, who recently retired as Catholic Archbishop of Melbourne, played in the Eighths.

On the sporting field

My sporting career was most enjoyable but relatively undistinguished. Perhaps the highlight was winning the day students' table tennis championship two years running. Even so, I was understandably shocked when it was condescendingly described at the annual prize night as "one of the minor sports."

I have always enjoyed playing and watching all manner of sporting events. I was somewhat better at (Aussie Rules) football, managing to play almost a season with the Old Boys in the A grade Amateurs. Once, at Olympic Park, I played in the first Amateur game ever televised. I was wearing number 55 and the commentator, dual Brownlow Medallist Roy Wright, expressed amazement that someone could have such a high number – nowadays it is commonplace.

A highlight of my brief career at the senior level was playing alongside some seriously good footballers. Tony Capes, who went on to be a GP and President of the Footscray VFL team, was one of those extremely gifted all-rounders, probably in the class of Bob Cowper, if not quite C B Fry. An excellent golfer and squash player, he could have played VFL had he applied himself. It was his standard practice at the half-time break to skip the coach's pep talk, preferring to stand aside and listen to the races. One day one of our key centre players went down, writhing in agony with what was believed to be a badly injured ankle, but medico Capes remained standing at centre half-back. He was eventually prevailed upon to examine the patient, which he did, somewhat cursorily, before pronouncing: "Yeah, I think it's broken. Better rest him in the forward pocket."

Above all, I much preferred the grace, statistics and drama of cricket. The best I could do was get a game with Riversdale in eastern suburban B grade matting – shades of Gideon Haigh. In later years I played some competition squash and later, in Parliament, I almost always managed to beat various staff members; whether they felt obliged to lose was another matter. Neither of my brothers was much better at sport, so I think we can safely blame the genes. Bob assured us he had been a respectable country week cricketer and he played a bit of golf and bowls in later life, but I don't remember seeing any trophies. Perhaps, like me, he preferred to claim that he had put his career first. Sheila claimed a modest distinction at tennis, but her since-childhood deafness probably put an end to that. Otherwise she was totally uninterested in all sports, except horse racing, which was almost an obsession.

Melbourne has always been a sports mad town. Aussie Rules has long been the religion. In the post-war years, except for the minuscule number of members of Keith Dunstan's Anti-Football League, everyone had to follow a side. When asked which team she supported, Sheila always said Fitzroy, where her husband's business was located, but I have no doubt that she did not know the name of a single player.

In my first year, the school first XVIII won the APS football premiership, but generally it was a long time between drinks on the sporting front – last won the cricket in 1924, thanks to boy wonder Karl Schneider; last won the Head of the River in 1948 with (later Sir) James Gobbo on board; and who knows if they had ever won the athletics.

The school's football prowess had improved dramatically by the 1990s, when our son, Nicholas, managed to play right through primary and secondary schools, culminating in membership of the APS premiership side, without ever playing in a losing team.

And it wasn't just the schoolboys. For the last several decades the Old Xaverians have been a footballing colossus in A grade Amateur football, winning more than 10 premierships.

My parents played significant, but very different parts, in my career development, mostly by example. Sheila had attended Normanhurst, a leading Catholic girls' school in Sydney and lived in a succession of fine hotels during her family's glory years as graziers and race horse owners, until her father was wiped out in the Depression. Her love for the horses never left her and many happy Saturdays were spent at the races; she only ever admitted to winning or breaking even, a feat very few have accomplished.

She also retained a strong Catholic faith, of the conservative bent. Like many wives of her era, she never pursued paid employment, but was indefatigable in her charitable activities. A lifelong smoker, who only gave up in her nineties due to puncturing several lungs in an accident, she managed to remain in total denial

EARLY YEARS

about the health consequences of smoking, aided and abetted by my mother-in-law, who also defied the odds by smoking till her death, aged 90.

The Alston family home in John Street, Corowa, which Bob's father, Bert, had also built, was a large rambling timber house with multiple chooks and dogs. He was a keen rifle shooter, often travelling widely to compete in organised events, resulting in a number of medallions strewn around the house. Following the death of his first wife, Bob's mother, his second wife, Peg, was very kind to us, so we always looked forward to our visits. No doubt Bob enjoyed the trips but while he was proud to have played cricket for Corowa in country week, he never spoke much about his home town or country life.

Bert, from a long line of Robert Bruces, was a successful builder, with a number of notable town buildings to his name, but he also presumably had an alcohol problem, as his death certificate gave "cirrhosis of the liver" as the principal cause of death. This may explain why my father felt the need to leave town to make his way in the world. It is likely that he came to the big smoke to escape the small town mentality, which he had already outgrown.

Bob's business career

There can be little doubt that Bob's time in the Army had a major character building effect on him. When he returned to Australia he was in his mid-thirties, married with one child, no job, no inheritance and a lot of income earning ground to make up. He spent years on the road and was a proud member of the Commercial Travellers Association of Victoria, then in its glory days, with a number of country facilities where fellow sales representatives could compare notes and share a quiet beer. Founded in 1880, it closed its operations and its prestigious city premises in 2014, by which time history had finally overtaken both him and it.

He possessed more drive and determination to better himself than his two brothers, who both struggled with psychological issues in their later years. He was determined to lift himself up by his bootstraps. A fervent disciple of Dale Carnegie, on several occasions he presented me with a copy of the phenomenal best seller, *How to Win Friends and Influence People*, which is still both inspirational and available.

He later became a manufacturer's agent for a number of Australian shoe makers, such as Whybrow and overseas stalwarts like Clarks until, in 1960, in a major career breakthrough, he was appointed as the Victorian and Tasmanian agent for Bata Shoes, at that time the largest private company in the world. I remember this critical moment very clearly. I was working as a deckhand on a cargo ship in the days when the only affordable means of communication with home was by post. Having arrived in port I opened an aerogram to learn of this happy news, little realising that he was about to embark on a very successful and rewarding period of his life. Bob never spoke to us about money, occasionally confiding that "it hadn't been a bad year", but more often blaming the weather for a bad season.

He later proudly told me that the Calcutta plant made one million pairs of Bata shoes each week and that there were Bata shoe shops in over 90 countries. The Australian operations were located at Seaford, outside Melbourne, which imported vast quantities of Bata Scouts for boys and Bata Ponytails for girls, later branching out into heavy duty industrial footwear.

As he gradually became immersed in the Bata world, from never having been outside Australia until he was fifty, save for war service, he and my mother began attending Bata Conferences around the world on a regular basis. He was so well regarded that at the age of 78 he was offered and accepted the big NSW agency but, unfortunately, at the age of 80, and still running a successful small business with some eight employees, he suffered a major stroke from which he never recovered, spending his last six years in a semi-conscious state.

In the post-war years manufacturing was seen as vital for national development so the pre-war protective tariff arrangements, together with import licensing restrictions, stayed firmly in place until the 1960s. By that time manufacturing's share of GDP and employment had reached historic heights. This encouraged the trade unions to take advantage of developing labour shortages and plentiful profits to press for better wages and conditions. They were a powerful force and there was constant strife with management. It was in this context that dramatic changes were starting to wrench the footwear industry. It was increasingly apparent that guaranteed all-round protection meant that businesses did not need to keep up with the latest technology and were making easy and largely unearned profits in the absence of serious competition. This led the Federal Government to question the cost to consumers of continuing to prop up local shoe manufacturers, who were increasingly uncompetitive by international standards.

By the time Gough Whitlam and Jim Cairns decided in 1973 to cut tariffs by 25% and increase the value of the currency by a similar amount, Bob was beside himself. I had only recently joined the Liberal Party and was studying part-time for a commerce degree. This made me quite sympathetic to macro-economic arguments in favour of competition and effectively oblivious to the human consequences for those left behind – most Australian shoe manufacturers and their employees, for many years the backbone of our family business. It had probably enabled my father to send his sons to a leading private school. But the rapid decline of the Australian shoe manufacturing industry led to heated father-son debates – me arguing the case for national interest efficiency and he fiercely defending the once highly protected but hitherto successful industry. Bob's increasing involvement with Bata had been a very farsighted move, as they were better able to compete with a previously pampered local industry.

Whilst he was at times a hard taskmaster with a sharp temper, he worked hard and honestly throughout his life to support his family and set a standard which made his sons as proud of him as he was of them. For someone who started out with absolutely nothing he became an exemplary role model and his work ethic undoubtedly played a major role in forming my ultimate political philosophy.

Mother and Brothers
In her own way Sheila was quite a contrarian who rarely accepted conventional wisdom at face value. She cared deeply for us all, but was no sentimentalist, rather a kind hearted and no-nonsense

realist. Her Catholic religion was always very important to her and, once her children were off her hands, she devoted herself almost full time to helping others less fortunate. Most particularly in the last six years of his life, she made daily visits to the nursing home to be with her husband despite his inability to recognise her. Thereafter, she was fiercely determined to remain self-sufficient in her own home until a series of blackouts forced her to spend her last five years amidst the mindless boredom of the nursing home.

My two brothers each lived away from Australia for more than forty years, but she never complained and was delighted when my wife and I had the opportunity to spend three years in London, which gave us the chance to spend some serious time with my brother, Ian, who has lived in London for nearly fifty years. Now a retired schoolteacher, he practised law for a few years before deciding that helping children was to be his preferred vocation. He continues to teach on a part-time basis and has also kept himself busy as Chairman of the Edmund Burke Society for the last ten years.

My other brother, Philip, has been a leading international scholar for many years, holding professorial posts at Harvard, the prestigious European University Institute, the Fletcher School of Law and Diplomacy and, in recent years, at New York University, as John Norton Pomeroy Professor of Law. He wrote the founding international human rights handbook a long time ago and has also worked closely with the United Nations, as Special Rapporteur for Extrajudicial Killings and, currently, for Extreme Poverty and Human Rights.

While my brothers went their separate ways in their twenties and have essentially lived overseas ever since, they both kept in regular contact with Sheila, making trips to see her whenever possible.

There is no doubt my brothers and I were very fortunate. Our parents made every effort to assist us in our careers and provide guidance and advice when required. They did not see it as necessary to give us any significant financial assistance, which was entirely consistent with their self-support ethic and I think we have each been the better for it.

2

University Days

As a relatively normal teenager, I was both fascinated and semi addicted to television (black and white, that is – colour was almost twenty years away) when it reached Australia just in time for the 1956 Melbourne Olympics. The new medium was dominated by an unrelieved diet of Americana and, amongst *The Saint*, *Sergeant Bilko*, *I Love Lucy* and *77 Sunset Strip*, there was the incomparable *Perry Mason*.

The television version of the US justice system allowed all manner of leading questions when examining one's own witnesses and was certainly, even in real life, replete with theatrical objections, a feature which I later observed when attending a famous love triangle murder trial in Los Angeles in 1961. I also vividly recall the trial judge chain smoking his way through the proceedings with his feet up on the bench.

All this intrigued me, but I cannot claim that I felt an inherent destiny for the law. No one in our broader family network had been anywhere near a university, let alone a law school. The reality was that I had already been steered in this direction, almost by default. There was no such thing as careers counselling at Xavier College in the 1950s, but the high-principled Jesuits had been quick to advise that, as arts was for priests and teachers, and commerce was "a bit grubby," the only way to go was to enter the professions. There was not much choice. For one who struggled with maths and science but had managed to win the school prize for literature and pick up a few low honours in history, the humanities dye was probably already cast.

I thoroughly enjoyed my years at law school despite usually leaving serious study until late third term and, even then, allowing group swotting sessions to turn into extended card playing marathons. There was a very low entry threshold, enabling many with mediocre matriculation results to join the throng. Of about

440 entrants in my first year at Melbourne Law School, only 110 finished in the minimum four years. There were no penalties for laggards, and one fellow law student was notorious for spending ten years in desultory attendance at lectures while spending most of his waking hours running a successful SP (starting price) book-maker's business.

I did not drink alcohol in my first year, a deficiency for which I made up later. I had no interest in political activities or the machi-nations of the student union, and the Vietnam War essentially passed my cohort by. We followed the news reports, but studies and social life were the main game.

My involvement in committee activities was confined to being secretary of the law faculty football team, which allowed me to self-select, alongside some serious VFL players such as Bob Miller, later godfather to our son Nicholas, as well as Labor MP for the Victorian state seat of Prahran, and play against the likes of John Elliott, a 300-gamer for Carey Old Boys and John Benetti of Carl-ton, and later Victoria.

In those days it was standard practice to spend the Christmas holidays in gainful employment to fund the necessities of student life for the rest of the academic year. I had a number of semi-inter-esting work stints: from carting crates of bottles and fruit picking to working in an insurance office and working as a "slushie" in an army camp. Most memorable, for its aftermath, was working with some fellow law students as a labourer on a new swimming pool at Scotch College. We turned up at the advertised starting hour of 7.30 am only to be told it was "no ticket, no start"; in other words, you had to be a union member.

But just as we were heading home, the site foreman called us aside and said: "We're all full today – don't ask me why, but I'm sure there'll be a few vacancies tomorrow". It turned out that one of the perks of the trade was that if you worked until lunch-time you were entitled to a full day's pay. Accordingly, a number of the workers headed off for a very long pub lunch and were not seen again till next morning, when they arrived to claim yesterday's wage. It did not make sense to us, but who were gilded youths to question the ways of the working class? So we paid our subs and settled in for several months of intermittent back-breaking toil until we had to stop as the nominal starting date for resumption of studies was fast approaching.

The whole experience quickly faded from memory until, about twelve months later, an ominously worded letter arrived from the Builders Labourers Federation (predecessor of today's CFMMEU), headed in bold black type, **Notice of Intention to Prosecute**, in respect of alleged outstanding member's fees. I immediately rang the Secretary, Paddy Malone, who turned out to be somewhat more civilised than his successor-in-title, the legendary, nay notorious, Norm Gallagher, who subsequently went to gaol, not for holding builders and building owners to ransom, which he did, but for the slightly lesser offence of using other people's money and labour to build himself a nice little holiday home!

Paddy explained that the threatening headline was a ploy designed to get attention: "don't worry about it, mate – it's just our way of keeping track of people." Then still in my salad days, I nevertheless realised that such a threat had no legal force, but I admired his inventiveness.

An unforgettable Pacific adventure

My first year at law school was relatively uneventful, as we joyfully adjusted to the notion of unlimited freedom after years of non-oppressive, but often ineffective, school discipline. But nothing prepared me for the momentous end-of-year adventure that was suddenly to eventuate. Out of the blue I was asked if I would like to work for four months during the upcoming university vacation as a deckhand on a Norwegian cargo ship on its regular voyage around the Pacific. Not only that, but I could bring a friend with me.

My godfather, and my father's best friend, Robert Linton, was not only one of Perth's leading eye surgeons but also owner of the biggest chicken farm in the West. Although it was close to twenty years since my father had returned from Perth where they had been great mates, they had kept regularly in touch. But my godfather's main claim to fame, as far as I was concerned, was that he was also Australian agent for the Norwegian Knutsen shipping line and, as such, came to play a pivotal role in my life's journey.

The Knutsen line, founded in 1896 and still going strong to-day, operated cargo ships, known as the Bakke boats. Most of them were, somewhat disparagingly, known as tramp steamers. The officers and crew were mainly Norwegian and the galley (kitchen) crew Chinese. Very few, except officers, spoke even a smattering of English. As a result of the strict operation of a long standing scheme to protect local workers from foreign competi-tion, known as cabotage, merchant ships with foreign crew were only allowed to land at one point on the Australian coastline, in our case, Fremantle. So, accompanied by my school friend, John Little, this was where our voyage began. We were quickly assigned very different duties – me outdoors as a deckhand, a modest role which suited my modest labouring talents, and John indoors to the engine room, which probably suited his advanced scientific instincts, having been dux of Xavier College barely a year earlier.

We arrived at "Freo" in the middle of an industrial dispute which delayed our departure for several weeks. I was assigned to keep guard over the loading of the vessel, which sounded like a routine assignment, but turned out to be anything but. It wasn't long before I was watching with amazement as the crane driver deliberately smashed a crate marked "fragile" against the side of the hold. When I asked what was going on I was quickly told: "you don't understand – those bastards mark everything 'frag-ile' to stop us opening the crates". I then noticed that, although it was the height of the summer season, dockers were wearing huge lumber jackets into which they were putting whatever they could. When I saw one stuffing toys into his pockets I was naive enough to ask how many kids he had. He looked at me as though I was a complete idiot and simply said: "none – we'll be flogging these quick smart down at the pub".

Our vessel, the *Gudrun Bakke*, was approximately 150 metres in length with a deadweight (maximum carrying capacity) of 10,000 tonnes. My duties were to keep the ship's walls and decks clean and tidy, with occasional attendance to the needs of up to twelve passengers – any more required a doctor on board. On the out-ward journey to Singapore I was also required to look after sev-eral thousand live sheep, accommodated in makeshift pens on the deck. As we all know, sheep are intensely socially gregarious with other sheep but not so responsive to humans, and I frequently found great difficulty in persuading them to clear a pathway. I had always fancied the effectiveness of my dog whistle and, sure enough, this ploy worked a treat, with sheep falling over themselves to accommodate me. Unfortunately, on one occasion, their enthusiasm to jump out of my way went too far and several went right overboard. This resulted in a stern warning from the captain, a back of the envelope assessment of the cost of turning the vessel around, and an assurance that we would certainly not be undertaking any sheep rescue operations.

Every place we visited had an exotic flavour. First port of call was Singapore, then a poverty-stricken Asian backwater. The captain's initial decision was that, as crew, we were required to stay on board while in port. This would have been catastrophic for our chances of foreign exploration, but fortunately he relented and, thereafter, we were permitted to go ashore as soon the ship docked.

Bugis Street, with its nightly gathering of transgender denizens, was an irresistible tourist attraction, while the world famous Raffles Hotel, well before its later makeover, was notable as much for the smells emanating from the open sewer running alongside as for its legendary drink, the Singapore Sling.

Hong Kong just oozed unique aromas and Far Eastern mystique. The old Kai Tak airport, located in the heart of urban Kowloon, was surrounded by skyscrapers and mountains, its only runway jutting out into the harbour. It provided a dramatic and potentially dangerous experience, as I later discovered on my way home from London in the mid-1960s, when my plane seemingly narrowly avoided collision with nearby tenements. In 1961, the harbour was twice as wide as now, thanks to a subsequent multitude of land reclamation projects. Our vessel was not permitted to dock (or maybe it was too expensive), so we weighed anchor mid-harbour and went ashore on motorised lighterage barges. Cable car to the top of Victoria Peak, eating at the live fish restaurants in Repulse Bay, climbing to the mid-levels – it was all very exciting, especially in the days before global brands dominated shopping

MORE TO LIFE THAN POLITICS?

strips and quaint local mementos were readily available, with which to impress friends on returning home.

Thence on to Japan, through the marvellous tranquillity of the inland sea. First port of call was Yawata, a steel town constantly fire-bombed by US superfortress B-29s during the Second World War as the site of the Japanese Imperial Iron and Steel Works, which manufactured about a quarter of Japan's wartime steel needs. Next was Kobe, a major port and manufacturing city, where a drunken crew member delayed our departure by holding customs officials captive for several hours before coming on board and threatening us all with knives and broken bottles. He was eventually subdued, put in the brig and later offloaded on the west coast of the United States.

Then Yokkaichi, an ancient city now a centre for the chemical industry, was one of the first cities bombed by the United States during the Second World War. On to Nagoya, a manufacturing and shipping hub, Shimizu, largely a tourist port, with magnificent views, on a clear day, of the sacred mountain – and dormant volcano – of Mt Fuji and, finally, the port of Yokohama – very grimy, but very busy – and Tokyo, an emerging Asian supercity. Absolutely no one spoke English – my most abiding memory was wandering into a bar in the blazing neon-lit nightclub district of the Ginza and finding that one of the bar girls knew the words of *Waltzing Matilda* – presumably from earlier encounters with roisterous Aussie visitors.

From Japan we headed north-east, following the warm Gulf stream via the Aleutian Islands to Vancouver, en route negotiating a savage four day storm, with constant pitching and rolling which confined us to our cabin day and night, except for brief visits to the galley. Meals were served on a fixed wooden table, with four raised sides and a large metal tureen anchored on a large wet towel. The trick was to hold on to the table with one hand and ladle a shallow portion of soup into a bowl with the other. The gales were so strong that it was not possible to walk around the ship for fear of slipping on the icy metal planks and being thrown overboard let alone work on deck, as even a gloved hand would immediately stick fast to metal. I tried working in the hold but its artificially warm atmosphere immediately induced seasickness.

The west coast of North America, with stops at Vancouver and Seattle, was relatively uneventful. We were permitted to leave the ship in San Francisco, where we met a complete stranger, Dr Bob Gilbert, a medical practitioner, who generously escorted us on a tour of the city and then invited us to his home, where he and his fiancée treated us like royalty. From there we caught a Greyhound bus and, together with some hitching down State Highway 1, we made it to Los Angeles, where John had a distant relative married to the deputy mayor of the city, and he arranged ringside seats for us at a celebrity murder trial.

From LA we crossed the Pacific to Cebu in the Philippines, but before we did so John and I changed roles as we had agreed at the outset, so that he could enjoy the fresh air and I could get a taste of sea life below deck. Unfortunately, at least for John, the captain wouldn't have a bar of this arrangement, insisting that we had both been trained for specific roles and his decision was final. Accordingly, I had the pleasure of being "on watch" on the bow, more for insurance requirements than for any worthwhile safety precaution. My duty hours were 4-8 am and 4-8 pm. The best part of the day was spent gaining a very impressive suntan in and around a pop up, above-ground, canvas swimming pool. The very early hours of the morning were quiet and peaceful, which lulled me into thinking that my turn at the ship's wheel only required an occasional adjustment to stay broadly on course. To my acute embarrassment, my meanderings left a permanent recorded footprint, leading to another well-deserved rebuke and, by now, an acute awareness that I was not cut out for the life of a sailor.

By the time we reached the Philippines the "stir crazy" frustrations of the crew, induced by more than three weeks at sea, led to a three-day orgy. By the time the vessel was ready to sail I was about the only sailor capable of standing upright. We were already several weeks late for the resumption of studies, so we were given leave to fly home.

This adventure made an indelible impression on me. From a sheltered middle class upbringing I had suddenly come into contact with people from very different cultures and economies, both rich (United States, Canada and Japan) and poor (Singapore – pre-Lee Kuan Yew's ascendancy, Hong Kong and the Philippines). Not only did it open my eyes to people, places and activities I might never have otherwise experienced at home, and jobs and lifestyles that I could have hardly ever imagined, it made me aware of Australia's relative isolation and appreciate that I needed to acquire a more outward-looking world view beyond my domestic comfort zone. It also gave me some sense of being an outsider, especially since on my return to campus none of my friends seemed more than perfunctorily interested in my exploits or the world beyond our shores. This no doubt led to my later involvement in internationally oriented non-government organisations and the international aid field, together with a growing awareness of the importance of politics.

The experience also introduced me to several potentially pernicious habits. The first was smoking, long before it acquired pariah status – in this case, tasty, unfiltered Pall Mall cigarettes, irresistible at 10 cents a packet. The second was alcohol. Having gone through first year at university without needing the stuff, perhaps a legacy of the Pioneer abstinence pledge which Xavier had actively promoted, my first taste of the demon drink was in the form of aquavit, a legendary Scandinavian spirit distilled from grain and potatoes, flavoured with a variety of herbs.

Passing exams

Despite my fascinating international diversion, and my continued somewhat lackadaisical approach to my studies, I managed to pass all my law subjects and graduate in the minimum four years. I later discovered that this was an achievement accomplished by only about a quarter of the original intake, for which, in those days, there was no quota.

Yet, at the time I was acutely aware that I could and should have worked much harder. I still cringe at the memory of a group of us, probably in third year, convening after lunch each day in the last weeks before the exams, ostensibly to revise the course but, in reality, spending virtually the whole afternoon playing an undemanding card game called, in its polite form, "Oh, Hell". This meant that when I got home I found myself working feverishly after dinner until the early hours of the next morning, with the aid of a full packet of Peter Stuyvesant cigarettes – and no time for any exercise!

The young believe, or at least assume, they are invincible. One Saturday, playing football with the old boys in the Amateurs, the captain and our best player turned up for the game in their dinner suits, having been out all night at a ball. Needless to say they both played well.

Once my playing days were over, I realised I had a choice to make: simply put my head down and focus on career and family, or endeavour to combine both with a determination to stay fit and find the time to do something worthwhile.

I have especially fond memories of the law school moots program. It was conducted by the legendary bon vivant, P D Phillips, QC, a veteran of the Western Front in the Great War, before excelling at law school and heading for the Bar. Despite becoming involved in a very wide range of organisations and flirting with conservative politics, his legal career had flourished. As a leading silk, he appeared for the Commonwealth in the famous Bank Nationalisation case. When he retired from active practice in 1960, Menzies appointed him to the prestigious post of Chairman of the Commonwealth Grants Commission, but he spent most of his later years at the law school. A larger than life character – both garrulous and self-important, he was very knowledgeable and worldly wise – and quite intimidating for mere students.

As PD's moots were usually followed by protracted alcohol-sodden lunches, it was perhaps inevitable that, a short time later, he was appointed to head a royal commission into the Victorian liquor industry and was thus responsible for liberalising Victorian liquor laws and ending the notorious "six o'clock swill."

The law course was conducted by some outstanding academics, such as Zelman Cowen, David Derham, Harry Ford and Robin Sharwood. Zelman, as Dean, was absent for one term out of three, while moonlighting as a visiting professor at Harvard. This earned him the somewhat unfair nickname of Seldom Seen Cowen. However, we were all suitably impressed when, on his return, he told us that Harvard regarded Melbourne as one of the world's top three law schools.

We were also fortunate to have as guest lecturers such leading barristers as Jim Gobbo, Murray McInerney and Cliff Pannam. These visiting lectures were conducted out of normal court and student hours, which inconvenienced some of the lazier students like myself, as they interfered with more urgent matters, such as football practice or recovering from the after-effects of late night socialising.

One of my more inglorious achievements was effectively to boycott 8.45 am twice-weekly Conveyancing classes, because of what then seemed to a callow youth to be an ungodly hour. Towards the end of the academic year a fellow student, Paul Guest, a champion rower and later a Family Court judge, approached me mid-morning and breathlessly informed me that I had better break my duck and attend the next lecture as the lecturer, Rosemary Balmford, subsequently the first woman to be appointed to the Supreme Court of Victoria, would be outlining the upcoming examination paper.

I fell for this ruse hook, line and sinker, and turned up at the appointed hour, only to discover the lecture had been cancelled. Sheepishly, I proceeded to the law library where I was met with gales of laughter by all who had been dutifully briefed. I cannot now remember whether my embarrassment caused me to make a guest appearance thereafter but, suffice to say, I satisfied the scorers when it mattered.

Off to London

This was the era before gap years, so the next best thing for many recent graduates was to head for London and the Continent as soon as funds would allow. Although, unlike today's student generation, we worked at odd jobs through the long summer vacation, most still found it necessary to work in serious employment for a year or so before heading abroad.

I do not now recall whether any parental funds were on offer but, in any event, I thought it made sense to complete articles (a form of apprenticeship in the law) first and be admitted to practice before heading off. Articled clerks, however, only received a pittance – £10 a week from memory – so I needed to ply my trade as

UNIVERSITY DAYS

a solicitor for another year in order to accumulate sufficient funds. It was not until a few years later that my younger brother, Philip, appalled at the manifest exploitation of neophyte lawyers, led organised protests to achieve a living wage for articled clerks.

My articles year was not short of drama. My father had kindly arranged for me to do articles at Mallesons, then Melbourne's most illustrious law firm, courtesy of one of his close friends who was a senior partner. By then I had all but decided to go to the Bar on return from my proposed "Grand Tour." So, when I was told on my induction at Mallesons that my articles year would be split between conveyancing and company law, I decided this was unlikely to be relevant preparation for advocacy, and that I should try elsewhere. Looking back, this was a momentous decision, both foolhardy and brave, as it effectively determined the course of my legal career.

Fortunately, my father was sympathetic and immediately arranged a transfer to a small firm, run by a racing friend of his, which did a lot of motor vehicle (or "running down" as it was known) litigation. After spending all of one week at blue blood Mallesons, Davis, Cussen & Co was the polar opposite – headed by Albert Davis, a big, burly and impressive sole practitioner with a large and florid facial birth mark and an encyclopaedic knowledge of the practical side of the law, especially relating to horse racing.

But just as I was getting into my stride in the litigation department, Mr Davis suddenly dropped dead. The Law Institute had to step in as administrators in the absence of any qualified practitioners. After being in legal limbo for some months, the practice was eventually acquired by Moorhead and Moorhead, a slightly larger firm with whom I remained for a further year.

During my first year as a qualified solicitor I learned the advocacy trade by doing the rounds of the Courts of Petty Sessions (later called Magistrates Courts) and completing an Arts degree. Football and its attendant social life remained key pre-occupations, but by then I was more than ready to depart for foreign climes.

After a very pleasant but exhausting cavort on the cruise ship *Fairstar* with some school friends, I finally arrived in London only to discover that the local legal profession were world experts when it came to restraint of trade practices. Whilst a law degree from a Commonwealth country was, in theory, automatically acceptable, there were many and varied strings attached, all designed to protect the incumbents from "unfair" competition at the hands of foreigners, as even Australians were regarded.

Not only was two years of practice required (I only had one), but it was necessary to sit for, and pass, a considerable number of examinations before being eligible to practice. The unpalatable alternative was to work as a lowly and poorly paid law clerk, an option I quickly rejected. The next best was to audition for a role as a film extra but, alas, my talents were not sufficiently compelling.

That was the beginning and end of my London legal career. I subsequently reached new heights in repossessing television sets and supply teaching in London; my exploirs in these fields are recorded in chapter 13. At this time, however, my head and my heart were increasingly drawn to my original career choice as a barrister.

By mid-1967 I had flown home, stopping over in Hong Kong, where I witnessed young Chinese activists, presumably members of the student paramilitary social movement known as the Red Guards, then in thrall to the Cultural Revolution, jump-marching around the Hilton hotel, with copies of Mao's *Little Red Book* held high, against the backdrop of a vast array of burning flares.

A brand new chapter was about to open up.

3

Life and Times at the Bar

In some states of the Australian Commonwealth a fused profession exists, with no separate Bar. The Victorian Bar, however, remains separate and distinct, with a special kudos. This mystique has faded somewhat, as solicitors have discovered that they can often extract the same fees premium hitherto reserved for the masters of the Bar. Nowadays, most advisory and litigation work seems to be subsumed under the rubric of "commercial", a field in which highly competent solicitors can often play equally as well.

Unlike today, when I signed up there was no threshold requirement to become a barrister – anyone with a practising certificate could join the club. Whether they prospered or not, or chose to be elegant part-timers, did not matter, as long as they paid the rent. Almost everyone was required to reside in the one building, owned by Barristers' Chambers Ltd. Nowadays, larger numbers require more flexibility. As a result many barristers make other arrangements, official, like Owen Dixon West or Aickin Chambers, or unofficial, in a private office, or maybe even from home.

By July 1967 I had signed the Roll of Counsel and was firmly ensconced as a reader to a leading common law barrister, Geoff Colman, at Owen Dixon Chambers, 205 William St, Melbourne. Geoff was a very kind, helpful and informative teacher – my obligation for the next six months was to follow his every move, both in and out of court. In this time I was not allowed to accept briefs, but part of the deal was that the reader helped his master with his paperwork (known as "devilling"). The role of "master" (mentor) was an ancient one, inherited from Britain, but of inestimable value to all new arrivals at the Bar, especially someone like me, with virtually no previous exposure to the, at times, delphic practices of the barristers' guild.

It was a very exciting time, as it also provided an opportunity to drop in on prominent trials and watch masters of the art, particularly cross-examination, in action. At the Bar I learnt many skills of great use in my later career in politics. Knowing the law, or at least the relevant parts, was not enough. Mastering a brief was clearly an imperative, but there were many less obvious skills that needed to be acquired.

Dealing sensitively with clients, many of whom were almost entirely ignorant of the ways of the law, was invaluable training in people management skills. Knowing when to go for the jugular, after setting the witness up, was also critical in demolishing credibility.

Being able to address a jury for well over an hour, often deliberately forsaking notes, was perfect practice for political speech making. Being vigorously interrogated by a crusty judge or responding quickly and cogently to a point of order, developed the art of thinking on your feet, an essential tool of trade for a politico. Preparing and presenting final submissions required clear and precise thinking, and the ability to marshal and prioritise the best arguments, not just all of them, was a vital part of the armoury in terms of effective persuasion.

Judgment was also critically important – knowing how and when to advance or retreat or, as Kerry Packer several times reminded me, knowing when to hold and when to fold. I would sometimes return to Chambers complaining that my opponent in court had completely missed the point or, worse, only to be told that I should be grateful to have fools around me, as it made me look relatively good.

When I arrived

When I arrived in the late 1960s the Bar was quite small – around 400, about a quarter of today's complement, and compact, all in one or two locations, compared to nearly twenty today. It was also proudly insular, verging on the self-important – totally unrecognisable from what it is now. There were virtually no women, and the commanding ethos was determined by older men from "good schools", characterised by their sense of dignity and authority. There were very few divorcees and no known gays. It also had a very collegiate atmosphere – a recent arrival could walk into the room of almost any senior barrister and seek advice, as I often did.

It also had a number of very interesting characters such as Neil McPhee, who came to the Bar with a glittering track record, having been a Major in the Korean War, won a Military Cross and topped the law school as a mature age student. His legal skills were legendary, as one of the most lethal of cross-examiners, but he played hard, too. I remember being junior to him in a licensing court application for an expanded night club business. It was quite a big deal, and several witnesses had come from the United States. He arranged a conference for 9 am at his chambers but, at the appointed hour, and for quite some time thereafter, he was nowhere to be seen. He finally showed up wearing dark glasses, ignored the customers and beckoned me to come inside. His first question was: "Got a (cigarette) light?" We then had a brief conference before he decided that a view [inspection of the premises] would be necessary. He and I agreed to meet there on the following Friday evening. As he had to attend a dinner that night he would call when he was free.

I duly went home to await his call. When midnight arrived without disturbance, my wife and I decided he was a "no show" and it was time for bed. Lo and behold, sometime after 1 am the phone rang – no apology, just: "Are you ready to go?" When I pleaded weariness, he calmly said: "No worries, I'll just mosey on down by myself."

As I became more politically prominent, I had a sense that a number of judges, and probably some senior barristers, regarded politics as an inferior occupation, certainly not a profession. Nevertheless, they all undoubtedly had a political world view, mostly well concealed but in evidence when there were important issues up for general or formal consideration.

One such historic occasion in 1975 was a heated, and at times rancorous, debate with no holds barred, over whether to support the appointment of Lionel Murphy to the High Court. Murphy had been a barrister specialising in labour and industrial law and was a silk before being elected to the Senate in 1961. At the time of his nomination to the High Court he was the Federal Attorney-

General, with radical social views which made him a controversial and polarising figure. Many at the Victorian Bar did not consider his legal credentials to be anywhere nearly sufficient to warrant such an appointment, which they regarded as purely political, rather than one based on legal merit. Not surprisingly, as I recollect, the Bar were inclined to disapprove but it made little difference. I found the exercise a fascinating one, which gave me some valuable insights into a number of my colleagues

On the lighter side, I had the pleasure of having a bit part in a film called *Carson's Watermelons* – no idea now what it was about. But John Walker, QC, one of the finest of criminal barristers, was involved, as was another barrister, Ben Lewin, who subsequently left the Bar and went on to considerable glory in Hollywood.

The Bar had its ups and downs. As Philip Dunn, QC, a doyen of the Melbourne Bar, has rightly said: "Life at the Bar is not for the fainthearted. You don't get paid every week and everything you do is uncertain. You walk on shifting sands". The strain on families can be considerable. My wife, Megs, a trained lawyer herself, was very supportive of my chosen career but was understandably anxious that we could afford to give our young children the education they deserved.

The Bar was certainly very competitive. Every case was there to be won or lost or, indeed, settled. It was often said that "you are only as good as your last case." A barrister is effectively a sole trader, forbidden to belong to a partnership or to shelter behind the corporate veil. Physical misfortune can be insured against – for a price – but serious injury or illness can bring a promising career to a speedy conclusion. At the time there were no barriers to entry, no entrance tests or suitability interviews and, even now, no retirement age. But it was somewhat daunting to observe that while many were called, not all were chosen. It was very sobering to see silks, who had in theory reached the top of their profession, suddenly bereft of briefs, having priced themselves out of the market, or reached the limits of old age. In those days they could not even advertise or promote their areas of expertise.

The Bar had the great luxury of allowing members to take time out whenever it suited them – to mind the children, tend to a sick

LIFE AND TIMES AT THE BAR

relative, play golf, travel abroad, pursue a hobby, take a sabbatical, or simply recover after marathon litigation.

This flexibility was invaluable for those with political inclinations. When I became State President of the Liberal Party in Victoria at the relatively tender age of 37, despite the incessant demands of the role, it in no way impaired my ability to practice or earn a respectable income, but it no doubt affected my capacity to attend promptly to my paperwork.

In later years, as more women signed the Roll of Counsel, those with children must have found the ability to leave work early a great benefit. But, as demand for their services increased, such spare time would usually diminish dramatically, giving females without immediate child-rearing responsibilities a significant advantage.

The civil (non-criminal) Bar was informally divided into common lawyers (jury types) and whisperers (equity types) – a rough but meaningful distinction between *viva voce* and the written word.

Common lawyers as a class were more flamboyant, with greater emphasis on personal presentation. The pre-eminent jury performers were a class above Rumpole in terms of mastery of both oratory and points of law – being "quick on your feet" was an art in itself. Some, like Bill Crockett, QC, were giants. He deliberately cultivated a "jury accent", whereby aitches were dropped with monotonous frequency and interspersed with broad use of the vernacular, in an often successful endeavour to appeal to the average jury member, who tended not to come from the professional classes.

Before police interviews were recorded, it was standard practice for barristers, often for good reason, to make ferocious attacks on police interview methods. I had several experiences of such police excesses, known as "fitting up" the accused, "verballing" him (never her) by putting words in his mouth or obtaining a forced confession by beating him up. A leading silk and notable Bar wag, "Woods" Lloyd, QC, was wont to characterise such alleged assaults as "over interviewing."

A classic formulation, which I encountered a number of times in police records of interviews, went roughly as follows: "Did you assault X?" "No sir." "Are you sure you didn't?" "Yes, sir." There was then a short pause before the accused said: "A man's an animal, I'd like to tell you what really happened." There were no prizes for guessing how many of these recantations were voluntary.

But, as the famous 1959 case of Rupert Maxwell Stuart amply demonstrated, this was no laughing matter. Stuart, an illiterate, itinerant, alcoholic, Indigenous Australian, was alleged to have admitted having had "sexual intercourse with the deceased", when it was blindingly obvious that he would never have used such refined terminology. Yet he was convicted of murder and, despite a number of appeals, the conviction stood. The case became a *cause celebre* in political agitation to protect and secure prisoners' rights.

One of the most effective criminal barristers was Jack Lazarus, a small but intense man whose sister, Joan Rosanove, was the first woman to become a QC in Victoria. I well remember being given a brief to represent one of a number of young louts accused of participating in a gang rape. Having read the brief I could see no way out, so I approached Jack, who was acting for one of the ringleaders, and asked if we were all pleading guilty. He gave me a withering look and said: "just stick with me", and in due course they were all acquitted. This taught me some valuable lessons. Jack could read a jury's mind and he had a fervent belief that all police were crooks. His intensity was a great asset and he refused to accept defeat. I realised that when the chips were down it was important to hold your nerve. Instructing solicitors appreciated such courage, as any fool could recommend a guilty plea.

Although I took my Bar career seriously and enjoyed it greatly, it was never my sole concern. Inspired by the life changing experience in my early student days as a deckhand on board a cargo ship around the Pacific, I had started to take a keen interest in international affairs. Accordingly, I became increasingly involved with several internationally focussed non-government organisations. This also provided invaluable, albeit low level, experience of organisational politics and, in due course, I became Federal President of the United Nations Association of Australia and National Chairman of the Australian Council for Overseas Aid, which represented more than one hundred locally based aid organisations.

LIFE AND TIMES AT THE BAR

These roles inevitably brought me into contact with leading politicians on both sides of the fence and, as I was already quite actively involved in the Australian Institute of Political Science, my appetite for political matters increased.

Court life

My early days in practice followed a well-worn path – do the rounds of the Magistrates' Court and get some real life and practical legal experience, before aspiring to move to higher ground. I was very fortunate that a number of solicitors with whom I had been at Xavier or Law School were happy to give me a go, particularly Alan Burnes, an employee solicitor with John Cain, later Labor Premier of Victoria, and who, at that time, had a thriving practice in Preston in the northern suburbs of Melbourne. Alan, an entertaining knockabout with a good legal brain, had an instinctive empathy for the large blue collar working class in the northern suburbs and had quickly built a large and loyal following. As a result, plenty of briefs came my way from the outset, providing invaluable experience in petty crime, maintenance disputes, various driving offences and motor vehicle collisions, commonly known as "crash and bash."

The Magistrates' circuit was a lot of fun for a new arrival. Often, while waiting for your case to be reached, it was difficult to avoid the many glimpses of the extraordinary detritus of the human condition. Because the volume of business was often beyond the capacity of a single already over-worked magistrate, in a time-honoured practice, matters of relatively minor importance were heard "out the back" by untrained volunteer Justices of the Peace. In theory, they took advice on the law from the Clerk of Courts, who was, however, also usually lacking in any training in the law. Not surprisingly, this led to some manifest injustices and I was not surprised when eventually their jurisdiction was severely curtailed.

A classic case was a plain vanilla speeding matter. In those days the police used a contraption which measured a car's speed between two tapes, 88 feet apart. In order to prove their case they had to produce documentary evidence that the machine was approved and in proper working order. When they were unable to do so, I submitted: "no case to answer." The learned justices conferred amongst themselves for a few minutes before the presiding member announced that, although I had made some interesting points, they had to find the driver guilty because, "after all, he was speeding." I immediately said that my client would appeal (to a higher court). They again conferred, momentarily, before announcing "appeal dismissed"!

One of my most interesting and exotic assignments was to represent in a series of cases a likeable rogue, whose very lucrative main line of business was smuggling valuable and highly protected bird species to various offshore locations. The contraband was hidden in a variety of elaborate false cages, concealed behind regular cages containing legally saleable specimens. His undoing usually came from random checks by inspectors who were quick to detect muffled bird noises.

I cannot even remember the precise defences we mounted, but I certainly remember appearing before the County Court on an appeal when the presiding judge suddenly asked if there was any relevant case law on the subject. This was a thunderbolt, as the only authority in the Victorian Law Reports concerned an earlier, very similar episode involving my client. I mumbled something like: "nothing that would be helpful, your Honour." Whether his Honour got the hint I do not know, but he did not pursue the matter, to my great relief. This was, however, only temporary, as he quickly proceeded to send us down the river.

On another occasion I had the somewhat dubious pleasure of representing a waterside worker. When he was, in due course, convicted, the judge took it upon himself to say: "Well, I suppose he's got the usual string of priors", which was, to say the least, both politically incorrect and legally improper. When I quickly informed His Honour that my client was, in fact, a cleanskin, his reply was: "I thought in his profession a few convictions was a requirement of employment."

I soon became aware that a number of Magistrates expected Counsel to have a drink either during the lunch break or at close of business. It was not even unusual for the Clerk of Courts to hand you a note saying: "the magistrate would like you to join him for a [liquid] lunch". Other magistrates would ask you to drive them home, with frequent stoppages, in what was then known as a "pub crawl".

Difficult as it now is to believe, in those days, before .05 and random breath tests, driving home in a semi-liquid condition was not particularly hazardous, as there were less vehicles on the road and the police often took quite a tolerant view of drink-driving.

It is hard for today's generation to conceive of long boozy lunches, let alone the crowds that flocked to the hotels in the vicinity of Owen Dixon Chambers, well before 5 pm most days. I have vivid memories of silks lying on the floor in the Four Courts Hotel, and the behaviour at the nearby Metropolitan was little better. Fortunately we have come a long way since then. Barristers these days are more at risk of dying from overwork, but in the 1960s and '70s it was almost impossible to go on circuit to country towns and avoid consuming several bottles of wine before the night was out, which was often not until the early hours. My partial solution was to go for a long run before dinner, so at least I was not consuming large quantities on an empty stomach.

I soon realised that after-hours socialising was not the road to success, nor conducive to domestic harmony, so I made a conscious decision to improve my health and broaden my knowledge by resuming studies part-time. In those days the law course required passing two Arts subjects, so it was not difficult to obtain an Arts degree with, as I recall, four additional subjects, which I had completed before going abroad. So I then embarked on a commerce course at Melbourne University – another career-defining move, as it opened my eyes to economic concepts, which became very useful in both law and politics. It also encouraged me, later, to undertake Master's studies in Law and Business Administration.

A certain success in the lower courts led to briefs to appear in the higher courts, starting with criminal matters in the County Court – rapes, break and enter, injurious assaults and one unforgettable and very sad case involving the death of a young boy from hypothermia, a consequence of being placed in a manure pit by an illiterate quack. The eminent silk leading me (Phil Opas, who had represented Ronald Ryan, the last person to be hanged in Australia) chased international experts all around the courtroom in a desperate attempt to discredit their evidence that no one in their right mind could have contemplated administrating such treatment – all to no avail, and the defendant was duly convicted of manslaughter. Another case involved my client buying a very small quantity of drugs at the request of his roommate. Whilst putting him down for supplying a prohibited substance was probably in order, the Supreme Court also convicted him of trafficking, which, in my view, was over the top.

Having a good room was a matter of some pride and convenience – for many years I occupied a second floor room overlooking William St, ideally located for a last minute dash downstairs. It was next to the room of David Cross, a wonderful man, an invaluable mentor and an excellent insurance company advocate who, in his spare time, wrote a series of very amusing law-related books, such as *The Mug Gardener's Handbook* and *I'll Plead Insanity*.

Later I moved to the twelfth floor where I "shared" a comfortable and spacious room overlooking Port Phillip Bay with the rarely sighted Bill Snedden, QC, MP.

In time, I graduated to even more serious matters in the Supreme Court. These included kidnapping, armed robberies, gaol breaks and two murder cases. The first, which I conducted on my own, was the trial of a psychiatric patient whose hospital records said, "marked homicidal and suicidal tendencies." Despite this ominous warning, he was somehow released, and three weeks later killed his wife. I successfully pleaded insanity.

In the other, I was junior counsel to the universally revered Dick McGarvie, then a leading silk, later a Supreme Court judge and Governor of Victoria.

Deep in preparation, we had been labouring in chambers late one Sunday evening. The next morning Dick told me that in the course of a taxi ride home the driver asked where he had been until such a late hour. When Dick politely informed him that he had been working back as a barrister the driver immediately said: "You can't fool me. I was once on a jury and I know you bastards only work from 10.30 am to 4.15 pm Monday to Friday."

The McGarvie magic eventually secured an acquittal for a woman who successfully pleaded provocation on the basis of a long history of physical and mental abuse, involving frequent hospitalisation. The case broke new ground as, hitherto, provocation had to stem from actions immediately preceding the fatal attack whereas, in this case, she had waited up late for her drunken husband to come home before stabbing him to death. This propitious outcome vindicated Dick's long held belief in "the wisdom of juries."

As well as personal injury cases which had proved both interesting and lucrative, especially on circuit, I deliberately decided to broaden my practice to include commercial and administrative cases in order to gain wider experience. Having already been admitted to practice in NSW, a relatively straightforward matter, I was offered a brief in the Supreme Court of South Australia. Each State then made its own arrangements. South Australian practitioners were clearly terrified of any interstate competition, so I was required to attend in person for a preliminary interview, followed a few weeks later by a more formal application – a relatively costly and time wasting anti-competitive charade. To rub salt into the wound, having completed all the necessary formalities, the client then decided not to proceed.

I steadily developed a worthwhile administrative law practice involving disciplinary proceedings against real estate agents, pharmacists and other errant members of professional bodies. I also undertook a number of interesting Freedom of Information cases. The most significant of these involved confronting, head-on, the Victorian Labor Government, for its refusal, under Freedom of Information legislation, to release some public opinion polls which were being paid for by the Government, that is, the taxpayer, instead of by the ALP. I appeared for Mark Birrell, then an Opposition frontbencher, who was later a senior Minister and Leader of the Government in the Legislative Council in the Kennett Government.

Cain and comrades claimed that the opinion polls were "Cabinet in Confidence" documents, a claim rejected by the Administrative Appeals Tribunal. The Government then promptly issued a regulation proclaiming that a Cabinet document was anything declared to be so by the Cabinet and, for good measure, made it retrospective.

Not surprisingly, the AAT, and, on appeal, the Supreme Court, took a dim view of this blatant subterfuge. The Government, for its part, refused to lie down until finally their application for leave to appeal to the High Court was refused.

In later years, once I had entered the Senate and before elevation to the front bench, I made a number of pro bono appearances in the Commonwealth Administrative Appeals Tribunal on behalf of parliamentary colleagues seeking access to various documents of political significance. A very unusual piece of political litigation arose out of the extraordinary result in a Legislative Council seat in the Victorian Parliament at the 1985 Victorian State election, where, out of 130,000 odd voters, the outcome was tied and only resolved by the returning officer pulling a name out of a hat. I was retained as junior counsel to Alan Goldberg, QC, later an eminent Federal Court judge and one of the finest people I have ever met. Thanks to Alan's diligence and legal acuity we comfortably won the case.

I still did some personal injury cases, including a number of medical negligence suits, in one of which I was briefed by a young James Gorman, later the most senior Australian ever on Wall St and still serving as CEO of the venerable Morgan Stanley investment bank in New York.

My practice manifested plenty of variety, one of the great joys of the Bar: migration cases, licensing court applications, town planning matters, a dual citizen application and industrial court proceedings. The latter was a confusing mix of law and pragmatism – one case I fondly remember concerned a union official who was secretary of both the Victorian and National arms of the Hospital Employees' Federation No 1 branch.

Under the organisation's rules, a State secretary had to seek permission from his federal counterpart for all international travel. He duly approved his own application. Heartened by this success, he then wrote back to himself seeking to take a cash payment in lieu of the fare, as he was by then too busy to take the trip. This application was also approved.

Notwithstanding this flagrant misbehaviour, he received barely a wrap across the knuckles. No one seemed to bat an eyelid when I further objected to his practice of convening board meetings at extremely short notice at some obscure Gippsland hamlet at around midnight.

On circuit

For those practising in the common law jurisdiction, as the majority did in that era, there was the added, principally financial, attraction of circuit work in leading country towns. Most cases, usually personal injury ones, settled at the door of the court, delivering a bonanza to the barrister who reaped a full brief fee, even if the solicitor had undertaken the bulk of the settlement discussions. I was fortunate to make regular visitations to the prosperous Victorian south-western district town of Hamilton, which then proudly proclaimed itself "the wool capital of the world."

Defendants, often insurance companies and their solicitors, commonly delayed settlements until the last moment to keep maximum pressure on plaintiffs, many of whom were almost nervous wrecks by the time their matters came to court, making them highly susceptible to a last minute offer. Eventually the practitioners and their insurance company clients worked out that they could settle earlier for pretty much the same figure, but without incurring the barrister's generous full fee, with additional circuit fee attached. As a result, the circuit bonanza gradually became more of a hard slog, as only intractable matters ended up proceeding to court and the inevitable trial.

Whilst many of these cases were "running down" actions, there were also a number of large property partnership disputes, as well as contested will bequests, known as testators family maintenance claims. Some of these estates were very substantial, as the Western District was a by-word for prestigious properties and prosperous farmers and graziers. When such a case was settled at the door of the court, in the time honoured manner, a barrister could be sometimes heard grumbling to his sympathetic opponent: "What a shame – another magnificent estate squandered on the beneficiaries." As the stakes were often high, it was not uncommon to have silks all round – all parties being represented by Queen's Counsel, who fortunately required the invaluable assistance of juniors such as myself.

Rural Victoria has some of the most fire-prone areas in the world and Hamilton often experienced scorching summers and raging bush fires causing untold damage to persons and property. Litigation usually followed against instrumentalities such as the State Electricity Commission of Victoria or the Electricity Trust of South Australia who were responsible for maintenance of poles and wires, often the prime suspects. I was fortunate to be involved in a spate of bush fire cases involving property damage, personal injuries and death.

The last big case in which I was engaged before heading to Canberra arose out of the 16 February 1983 Ash Wednesday bush fires, which swept across Victoria and South Australia, killing 75 people. Years of severe drought and extreme weather combined to create the deadliest bushfires in Australian history, until the Victorian Black Saturday bushfires in 2009.

Over 100 fires started on that day, including one in the shire of Ballangeich in south-western Victoria, where 50,000 hectares were burnt and nine lives and nearly 900 buildings were lost. I was engaged as a junior to Michael Dowling, QC, who did a superlative job on behalf of the defendant shire, skilfully cross-examining a series of expert witnesses on the science of bush fires, as well as the various actors in the drama.

The shire was the owner of a road roller, which had a defective spark arrestor and was seen driving past a scoria heap at about the same time that the fire was subsequently estimated to have begun in the vicinity of the site. The plaintiff was the owner of one of about 30 properties which were severely damaged, and the action was regarded as a test case for the others. The case went for seven weeks with silks on both sides and experts from around the world summoned to give their opinions as to the most likely cause.

The plaintiff's claim was that the circumstantial evidence pointed to the road roller as the likely culprit and therefore the shire was negligent for not ensuring that the spark arrester was properly serviced and maintained. However, we adduced evidence on behalf of the shire demonstrating that there were a number of other equally plausible explanations: an unidentified person and possible arsonist seen in the vicinity of the scoria heap at the relevant time; sparks caused by the clashing of overhead power lines; a faulty electric fence or fierce rays from the sun, inducing refraction from nearby broken glass; and other manifold ways of setting fire to tinder dry natural vegetation.

The jury ultimately decided that they were not satisfied that the shire had been negligent; perhaps they were aware of local newspaper reports prior to the trial that, if the shire was found responsible, it would be bankrupted and property rates for all landowners (presumably including some jurors) would need to increase substantially to cover the deficit (as I had helpfully informed them).

When we had finally won the case after seven long weeks spent at Warrnambool in western Victoria, in the time honoured tradition of the Bar, Michael Dowling generously presented me with a blue silk bag, designed for carrying courtly possessions.

After my long involvement in organisational politics, I was very happy to move to Canberra, but I have always looked back fondly on my years at the Bar. This fondness was accentuated a few years later when I calculated that I had earned more in seven weeks in the bush fire case than I did in my first eighteen months in Canberra. But very few go into politics for the money, and I never had the slightest regret about the direction of my new career. In fact, after spending my first ten years in Parliament in Opposition, I did once reflect on whether I had made the right decision. I quickly concluded that being a Senator was a privilege accorded to very few, with unique thrills and spills and never a dull moment. Even if we had never made it to government, it would still have been very worthwhile.

4

The Long and Winding Road to Canberra

For more than four decades politics, public affairs in general and Parliament in particular have been central to my life. I have always thought of myself primarily in political terms, even at the Bar where, busy as I was, my main pre-occupation was increasingly the state of the nation and the accompanying politics. I well recall sitting in my chambers listening, transfixed, to the real time dismissal of the Whitlam Government. On one occasion during my term as High Commissioner in London I told a gathering at Stoke Lodge, the High Commissioner's residence, that, although currently on diplomatic assignment, I remained at heart a politician. This earned me a stern rebuke from the senior Foreign Affairs official present, so I was quite gratified not long afterwards to read that Robert Hill, formerly the long-serving leader of the Liberal Party in the Senate, and by then Australia's Permanent Representative at the United Nations, had recently said pretty much the same thing. You can take the boy out of politics but ...

Anyone with experience in Parliament, particularly at the higher levels of Government and Opposition, remains acutely aware of the primacy of politics. In its deepest sense politics is about the advocacy of ideas, building organisations and networks to advance those ideas, and seeking to win electoral support for their achievement. A critical challenge is to come up with enduring solutions to real problems, not just looking for a quick fix or a cute line to win the day's news cycle.

I had my fair share of idealism but no burning desire for revolutionary change. A succession of 20th century revolutionaries, from Lenin, Hitler and Stalin to Mao and Pol Pot, had demonstrated the folly of seeking to radically change society, usually by revolution, against the will of the people. I preferred to look for steady improvement in the lot of humanity and that took the form, in my case, of a strong concern for the welfare of those living in less for-

47

tunate countries than Australia and the benefits and shortcomings of foreign aid or, to use the jargon, "overseas development assistance". The zealotry which characterised the political activity of those who, a few years later, were preoccupied by the Vietnam War and conscription battles, post-dated my formative experiences.

My journey into politics, the main story of this chapter, followed three paths. My earliest pursuits beyond the law centred upon international aid and development. These activities led to my increasing involvement in organisational politics and an ever greater involvement with the Liberal Party, culminating in my becoming State President of the Victorian Division, when Malcolm Fraser was Prime Minister and Dick Hamer was Premier of Victoria.

But politics essentially meant Parliament so, during the early 1980s, I started looking in earnest for a seat, which resulted in a number of highly unsuccessful tilts at marginal House of Representatives seats, for which I should be grateful I failed. On reflection, given my background in the organisation, the Senate was probably right for me, as it better suited my interests and my temperament. When I finally cracked the code and landed in Canberra, Labor Senator Robert Ray immediately dubbed me "the member for Melways," after the leading Melbourne street directory, an allusion, not without wit, to my search for party endorsement for a seat which recognisably fell into the "winnable seat" category.

Life in the world of NGOs

My international travels, including my tour of duty as a deckhand plying my trade around the Pacific and twelve months in London, Europe and the Middle East (chapter 13), had made me very much aware of the poverty and disadvantage suffered in many parts of the world. It was not long after my return to Australia that I became involved with organisations with a clear external orientation. It was only some twenty years since the end of the Second World War and there were still high hopes in many quarters that the United Nations would somehow come to play an important, even pivotal, role in securing world peace. So I joined the Victorian branch of the United Nations Association of Australia, and later became Federal President. This role exposed me to significant policy debates as well as some memorable experiences.

The key international financial institutions, the IMF (International Monetary Fund) and World Bank, have largely been forces for good, based as they are on what is now mainstream economic dogma. To the extent, however, that they generally follow the Western-inspired Washington Consensus reform package, promoted for crisis-wracked developing countries, they still attract frequent criticism from many emerging economies who resent economic strictures and to whom "austerity" is always a dirty word. Similarly, key specialised agencies such as the World Health Organisation and the United Nations High Commissioner for Refugees have made significant contributions to the alleviation of sickness, poverty, hunger and disease, especially in the most deprived regions of the globe.

But, just as the League of Nations, despite the soaring rhetoric of Woodrow Wilson, was brought down largely by the concerns of the United States, that it would involve a critical loss of sovereignty of its members, so the UN quickly became pre-occupied with its own self-interest. The General Assembly was designed as the main deliberative, policy-making and representative organ of the UN. But its "one country, one vote" rule, enabling a group of micro-states to outvote even the richest nation state, has distorted its influence and diminished its power. By 1975 the General Assembly was happy to equate Zionism with racism, an offensive resolution repealed some years later. Other specialised agencies such as UNESCO and the UN Commission on Human Rights have likewise lost their way.

As the number of member states of the General Assembly grew from the original 51 to its current 193, the balance towards the developing countries became increasingly oppressive. Senior positions have long since been allocated by region, not merit. The organisation was bogged down by internal politicking and the division of spoils, long before Shirley Hazzard wrote *Defeat of an Ideal* in 1973, presciently sub-titled, "A Study of the self-destruction of the United Nations".

As its reputation became more tattered, my interest and commitment waned. I concentrated instead on issues concerning alleviation of poverty involving countries then collectively known

MORE TO LIFE THAN POLITICS?

as the Third World, but now referred to as "emerging economies." Poverty and economic stagnation were rife, particularly in Africa and many parts of Asia, but despite the mega millions thrown at them, they made conspicuously little progress. This has not deterred poverty activists like Bob Geldof from simply demanding ever more and measuring "progress" by how much wealthy nations contributed as a percentage of their GDP.

Meanwhile, the People's Republic of China has rescued hundreds of millions from abject poverty and transformed itself into a super power, all without any significant overseas aid assistance. There is still a valuable role for foreign aid to play in humanitarian assistance and some development projects, but it does not provide a fast track out of poverty for individual nations.

I became increasingly convinced that more money was not the answer, particularly when it was obvious that many African autocrats were little more than kleptocrats. It was quality rather than quantity which mattered, and effective solutions lay much more in stamping out corruption and building enduring economic structures and institutions.

My confidence in this approach was strengthened by my studies in commerce and economics and, later, in business administration, so that by the time I arrived in Canberra I was much more an "economic rationalist" than a "bleeding heart liberal", in the pejorative jargon of the time. It was not a matter of making binary choices – it is perfectly possible, indeed desirable, to be economically competent, while exhibiting compassion and concern for those in need.

People can be economically conservative and socially progressive or, indeed, vice versa. They can also have a libertarian streak. It is also true to say that nearly all people develop a distinct set of values and beliefs – not necessarily equally coherent – enabling them broadly to self-define their politics. This is a very common experience and is evident in board rooms, football clubs, non-government organisations and in political parties around the world. The balance may vary but it seems to be an instinctive feature of human interaction for people to take sides on issues or rally around a thought leader.

World Conference on Women, Mexico City, 1975

The UN General Assembly had proclaimed 1975 to be International Women's Year and, accordingly, I was invited with my wife to attend the first UN World Conference on Women in Mexico City in June that year. The two weeks-long Conference was attended by over a thousand delegates, including Elizabeth Reid, who had been appointed in 1973 as Australia's and the world's first adviser on women's affairs, and Margaret Whitlam, wife of the Prime Minister of Australia and a keen feminist.

Other prominent Australian participants included Germaine Greer, whose 1970 book, *The Female Eunuch*, had become an international bestseller and an important text in the feminist movement. It was followed closely by *Fear of Flying*, Erica Jong's 1973 feminist tract, and *The Women's Room* by Marilyn French. *The Feminine Mystique*, published in 1963, a trail-blazing work by Betty Friedan, had been widely credited with sparking the second-wave of feminism in the United States. I had read all these path-breaking texts and found the emerging second wave very thought-provoking. Since that time there had been increasing interest in women's issues and the Mexico world conference was a milestone of the new movement.

It was somewhat bemusing to be so greatly outnumbered by the other gender, but the experience was very exciting. It was full-on at times, with plenty of strident rhetoric, but it was a great example of a people's movement in action. Especially stimulating was Warren Farrell, an American educator and activist, who provided a distinctive counterpoise with a masterclass on men's issues.

Visiting Mexico City, the second most populous city in Latin America, with a population then believed to exceed twenty million, was eye-opening. Resting on a lake bed, the city is a geological phenomenon, with its soft base collapsing, a consequence of over-extraction of groundwater. Since the beginning of the 20th century, the city has sunk as much as nine metres in some areas. One of the most important cultural and financial centres in the Americas, there was, nevertheless, plenty of poverty on display.

We stayed for several weeks at the Mayaland, on the outskirts of town, a modest two-star hotel serving scrawny chicken morning, noon and night. Only when we finally visited the upmarket Zona Rosa in the central area did we discover that the city also had some very fine cuisines.

A greater treat was in store after the conference. With a number of other Victorians, Megs and I embarked on a seven-day tour of Cuba. It was a country frozen in time, largely as a result of the US trade and diplomatic embargo imposed following Fidel Castro's 1958 coup. The Havana Hilton had become the Havana Libre, with all air conditioning units ripped out, and free public access to its swimming pools. 1950s gas-guzzling "yank tanks" abounded. The regime claimed there was a single wage rate but, locals told us, surreptitiously, that there were quite diverse pay grades.

Likewise, there was not supposed to be any private enterprise activity but, in rural areas, it had been quietly allowed, in order to incentivise production. It turned out that tourists were allowed, but all, including us, had to follow exactly the same program – staying at the same hotel, travelling outside Havana to the same seaside resort and being escorted around town by officials – nevertheless, it was a revelation and one of life's great experiences.

In about 1976 I visited Papua New Guinea, as a delegate of the Australian Council for Overseas Aid, to inspect some Australian sponsored aid projects. One meeting was with the Governor-General, Sir John Guise, a charming and immensely dedicated servant of his people. In the course of discussion he mentioned that a number of his former parliamentary colleagues often brought home minor souvenirs such as shampoo, soap and toothbrushes from their travels. Rather cheekily, I asked whether he had done the same, to which he replied: "Certainly not. My constituents were very poor and insisted that I only bring home important things like towels and blankets".

Norfolk Island lies about 1600 km north-east of Sydney and occupies a unique and colourful place in Australian history. Discovered by Captain James Cook in 1774, it served as a British convict penal settlement on and off from 1788 until 1855. In 1914 the UK handed it over to Australia to administer as an external territory, and it has remained so ever since.

It had been largely left to its own devices in running its domestic affairs until a Royal Commission in 1976, headed by Justice Sir John Nimmo, somewhat tentatively recommended that the residents be given voting rights in the federal electorate of Canberra and that the Norfolk Island Council be replaced by a watered down Assembly. Shortly thereafter, all hell broke loose. In 1979 the United Nations Association of Australia published a report arguing that, as Australia was firmly committed to the UN and the internationally recognised principle of self-determination, it should grant this right to the people of Norfolk Island.

This somewhat provocative stance certainly aroused the ire of the Minister for Home Affairs, Bob Ellicott, QC, who rang me to register a vigorous protest, accompanied by dark mutterings that the UNAA's meagre annual federal grant might be at risk. I quickly decided that I had better go and see for myself, so I spent a week on the island canvassing opinions before making further representations to the Government. In 1979, twelve months after the release of our report, a limited form of self-government was granted under which the Norfolk Island legislative assembly elected a government to run most of the island's affairs. But the principal threat of political incorporation into the mainland had only been temporarily averted.

In 2010 the island's Chief Minister announced that the island would voluntarily surrender its tax free status in return for a financial bailout from the Federal Government to cover significant debts. As a result, in 2015 the Australian Parliament abolished self-government and established a new Norfolk Island Regional Council to govern the island as a local government area, subject to the laws of NSW. It also appointed an Administrator, advised by two local residents, to maintain authority on the island. Australian personal and corporate tax arrangements as well as levies, Centrelink and Medicare facilities, now apply.

In 1978 I became chairman of the Australian Council for Overseas Aid, the peak body for all Australian aid agencies, with a membership in excess of fifty organisations, both home grown and those with international connections. Shortly afterwards, when the Fraser Government granted tax deductibility for donations to approved overseas aid organisations, the membership doubled overnight. I soon found myself attending meetings of the International Council of Voluntary Agencies in Geneva and participating in official overseas aid delegations to East Africa and the Indian subcontinent, including Bangladesh. These visits involved speechmaking and high-level meetings with senior officials of various countries, a very important opportunity for learning to converse in depth on a range of policy issues, as well as a good primer on the art of diplomacy.

In 1979 I attended a meeting in Manila of the UN Commission on Trade and Development, where I had a number of interactions with the leader of the Australian Government delegation, Vic Garland, Minister for Special Trade Representations, who, after the 1980 election, was appointed Australian High Commissioner to the UK. I subsequently came to know him much better in London when I followed in his footsteps a quarter of a century later.

Soon after returning home I was approached to run for the position of State President of the Liberal Party in Victoria. I had only been on the State Executive for two years, but I had been chairman of the powerful Constitutional Committee for several years. There was no outstanding candidate, so I agreed to run. On reflection, I realise how fortunate I was to succeed as, in the weeks leading up to the State Council, where the vote would be held, I was in Hamilton, in western Victoria, working hard on the legal circuit and unable to meet delegates or make very many phone calls.

Fate, as it happened, came to the rescue of a relative political neophyte. As is common in politics, groups quickly formed in order to decide which candidate to support. Philip Russell, a Western District grazier, had previously been State President but his wife, Alethea, was actually a much more formidable operator. She arranged for me to address a substantial group of prominent, mostly female, delegates from both metropolitan and country Victoria. They must have been reasonably impressed. An invisible political force went into overdrive, while I busied myself on circuit, blissfully unaware of the organised operation behind me. Fortunately, on the day, I made quite a good speech, for eight minutes, without notes, and this would have considerably helped my cause.

My tortuous path to Canberra

The first few years of my emerging political life had been spent, mainly at local level, progressing from secretary of the Fawkner Park branch in the then Labor stronghold of Melbourne Ports (now McNamara), held by Labor stalwart Frank Crean, through to branch president and ultimately chairman of the federal electorate committee.

Having become a delegate to the Party's supreme governing body, the State Council, I started to move in wider circles and a few years later I was elected to the State Executive and appointed chairman of the legal and constitutional affairs committee, where I subsequently spent considerable time re-drafting and updating the Party Constitution. Two years later, with the active support and encouragement of John Elliott, I was elected State President.

John had been metropolitan vice-president for some years and the top job would have been his for the asking. He took a keen interest in policy debates and party matters, but his extensive business commitments as the highflying managing director of Elders IXL made his further party advancement not feasible. He deserves considerable credit for popularising the important economic concept of privatisation, which the ALP, aided and abetted by the media, managed to turn into a notion to be feared. John's business success had persuaded him that government business enterprises were much more likely to be efficient and effective when run in the private sector. In fact, he was then also actively looking at taking his own public company private.

There was one classic occasion which I will never forget. Dick Hamer, a Premier for whom I had the highest regard, had adopted the generous practice of inviting members of the State Administrative Committee (successor to the State Executive) to meet the Victorian Cabinet on a monthly basis. On this particular morning he confided that later in the day he would be announcing an extension of the remit of the State Insurance Office, a policy decision of which he was very proud.

But instead of adulation he had to withstand a withering blast from Vice-President Elliott, who vehemently argued that governments should be going in the opposite direction – they had no business to be competing with, let alone crowding out, the private sector. I was very sorry that John's career ended in the way that it did because, at his peak, he was a very impressive and imposing leader who would have had a great deal to offer in public life had he not so spectacularly self-imploded.

Seeking pre-selection

It took me a number of unsuccessful attempts at pre-selection before I finally made it to Canberra. In part this was because I somehow thought that policy was more important than people – the vice of intellectuals. In my naivety, almost verging on intellectual arrogance, I assumed that I only needed to go along and demonstrate that I was on top of all the key policy issues. My light bulb moment came after I sought pre-selection for the federal seat of Hotham, which had been held by Don Chipp for the Liberal Party for many years. Disaffected after having been dropped from the Ministry following the election of the Fraser Government in 1975, he decided to run for the Senate after forming a new party, the Australian Democrats.

It was assumed that the seat would remain a Liberal stronghold. It transpired, however, that Chipp had, perhaps deliberately, discouraged new members from joining up, so the current membership was pretty long in the tooth, and the branches were in very poor shape. As it transpired, the Liberal Party held Hotham for only one more term before it changed hands and became a Labor stronghold. So, with hindsight, I was glad that I didn't win.

The pre-selection convention commenced with a round table event, at which each candidate would rotate between tables of ten delegates for a Q & A session. When I arrived at the first table I was told: "We don't have any questions for you". I said: "Well, would you like me to address you?" The response was fast and brutal: "We don't care what you do, because we're not voting for you". I hoped this was a one-off, but a few tables later I got the same message: "You're not a local, and one look at your CV tells us that you will not be interested in local issues, so we suggest you go elsewhere."

This heavy bucket of cold water should have taught me a very important lesson. I had not made it my business to meet and cul-

THE LONG AND WINDING ROAD TO CANBERRA

tivate the local delegates, confident that my speech on the day would do the trick. Being involved in too many things at once was part of the problem. This was a naive and, in this case, a fatal mistake. It is true that, unlike the Labor Party, where the numbers are all tied up beforehand, many Liberal delegates can be open to persuasion, but why should they vote for a blow-in whom they did not know and who might not have anything much in common with them? In my defence, at that time in 1977, I had just been elected to the then State Executive, an unwieldy 57-member body, and I was still green behind the ears. Two years later I was State President, so I should have been a fast learner.

I had yet another stumble in 1980 while I was State President. I decided to run for what was then the safe seat of Chisholm following Tony Staley's retirement. But, before I could even start to do the rounds, I received a call from the Chairman of the Chisholm Electorate Committee, warning me off, saying that I was not entitled to speak to any delegates. This was intimidating rather than accurate, but it was clear that I would be pushing uphill, as proved to be the case. There was also some resentment that I was the incumbent State President and should have been focused on that role alone. It was, indeed, a liability, because it limited my time and opportunities to canvass support.

Even in late 1982, when my term as State President had expired, I had no greater success. One of the Liberal Party's finest sons, Phillip Lynch, had been forced to retire suddenly, suffering from what turned out to be a terminal illness. This opened up the seat of Flinders, another formerly safe seat, which was to change hands at the 1983 election not long afterwards. Again, I was an outsider looking for a safe seat or, as the locals probably characterised it, a carpetbagger.

This time there was an organised campaign to stop me. When it came to the pre-selection convention, each candidate was entitled to be asked three questions in a five-minute period. My first questioner was determined to speak for as long as possible. After he had deliberately rambled on for well over three minutes, without being urged to hurry up by the similarly hostile chairman, I complained, but it did me little good. The purported question had been a mini-diatribe about my international aid activities.

57

The whole exercise was a complete disaster, and I finished a distant third. Perhaps there was also another factor at work. I was known to be a practising Catholic, who had attended Xavier College, the leading Catholic private school of the day. In this regard I was following in the footsteps of Phil Lynch who had also attended Xavier and lived in the same suburb of Kew and had come down to the Mornington Peninsula seeking a safe refuge.

Phil was a class act – a natural politician and a very effective one. He succeeded in gaining strong support from the locals. But a few days after the convention all hell broke loose when some blue bloods belatedly realised that he was a Catholic and this led to resignations, strong criticism from his predecessor, and much local unhappiness. I have no idea whether this continued to be a factor in my application but, on one occasion, a stalwart from the area, also a very senior member of the Liberal Party's State Executive, unwittingly showed me a piece of paper listing the candidates for an upcoming State election with the notation: "NB number of RCs." When I asked what this was about I was told: "Well, of course, I have no objection to Catholics, but a lot of people like to know this information". A quick count told me there were all of four out of about eighty!

The successful candidate in Flinders in the 1982 contest was a local, Peter Reith, who went on to become an outstanding member of Parliament and a senior Cabinet minister, and whom I have always counted as a good friend. I felt no animosity towards him – I presume he found himself pushing against an open door.

Lessons learned

Such are the trials and tribulations that many confront just to obtain endorsement for a relatively marginal seat in Parliament. Even the holder of an ultra-safe seat can be at risk in a boundary re-distribution. The lesson is that the prize of a safe seat is not just waiting for some high flyer to turn up. Even Malcolm Turnbull in 2004 had to pursue a monumental branch stack to wrest the seat of Wentworth from the hapless incumbent who, like himself, also happened to be a Rhodes Scholar.

These experiences have particular relevance when the relative

THE LONG AND WINDING ROAD TO CANBERRA

paucity of women in the Federal Parliamentary Liberal Party is being debated. It is easy to "enjoy the problem" and simply lament the numbers reality. It is much harder to fix the problem if you aspire to have the best team on the park. Success in politics generally requires a long gestation period of careful preparation. Most women who succeed in politics do so because, as for men, it has been a long-term ambition. Not everyone has a burning ambition to succeed. Many do not, which is probably just as well for our collective community sang froid. In politics it is necessary, not merely desirable, to have at least some warrior mentality – it is not enough for a successful chief executive, male or female, to think that a political career would be "nice to have". It has to be a "must have". Having a "baton in the knapsack" can be a healthy character attribute.

Many women, especially those with young families, instinctively shy away, perhaps thinking that one day they might have a crack. But that is not how it works in any pressure cooker environment where the stakes and the rewards are high. There are many activities, such as attending branch meetings, which an aspiring politician-in-a-hurry might think are boring chores, but which serious contenders know are essential prerequisites. Politics can also be a very fragile business, leaving many ambitions unfulfilled. Most fall from grace not because of policy ineptitude but because of an electoral loss or some personal failing: rorting expenses, conflict of interest, public drunkenness, swearing in public, rudeness to staff. Some of these transgressions can be little more than peccadillos, but the media and Oppositions will always endeavour to have a field day and, where possible, make a mountain out of a molehill.

As Federal President in 2016 I commissioned a formal inquiry, with specific instructions to identify what structural impediments could be removed and what needed to be done to encourage quality women to become involved and seek pre-selection, especially in safe seats. I had already learnt on a visit to the UK that it was much easier for women without children, such as Theresa May, to prosper. Even in Australia, Julia Gillard and Julie Bishop are but recent high level examples. Politics can be a brutal and all-consuming activity, without any guarantees of success.

Suffice to say, the Federal Executive report identified no silver bullet. It emphasised the need for mentoring and giving prospective candidates some sense of what would be required to prevail. From my observation, there is little or no hostility to women candidates, rather a perceptible frustration that not enough serious candidates are prepared to come forward; this, fortunately, seems to be quickly changing. In Victoria, ever since the formation of the Party in 1944, there has been a constitutional requirement for equal numbers of male and female delegates to State Council, State Assembly and the Administrative Committee, the principal governing organs of the party: since I stepped down as State President at least four women have assumed the role. This is a legacy of the Australian Women's National League.

Knowing how to behave in public is very important. As Minister for Communications I had direct responsibility for the ABC, and many of its staunchest defenders were very ready to take serious offence at any reflection on the organisation, however well justified. On one occasion I stopped my car outside a shop to pick up a sandwich and, when I returned, after no more than three minutes, I was rudely accosted by someone who proceeded to tell me, in a very officious tone, that I was stopped in a "no standing zone." I said: "who are you? You don't look like a parking inspector". He immediately said: "I take strong exception to your treatment of the ABC, and you have just committed an offence". I thanked him for the free advice, got into my car and drove away. Shortly afterwards I received a phone call from the local police asking me to come down for a chat. They were very sympathetic and said that, in normal circumstances, they would not have proceeded with the matter but, as the complainant was clearly a zealot intent on making trouble, it might be wise to go quietly and pay the $100 fine, which I duly did.

On another occasion, outside the parliamentary offices in Sydney, I returned to the Commonwealth car to find a protester with a placard proclaiming an environmental message blocking the path of the driver, who was not prepared to confront him. So I got out of the car and went around and stood directly in front of the obstructor. Holding my arms up high so I could not be accused of hitting him, I proceeded to use my chest to push him out of the way, allowing the driver to exit, and we left without further incident.

Some weeks later a federal police officer informed me that he had witnessed the episode and thought I had handled it well. He then proceeded, no doubt with his tongue firmly in his cheek, to give me some pithy advice: "What you do is you walk up, as you did, and push with your chest. If he does not respond, you step firmly on his foot and, if that doesn't work, you raise one leg so as to cause him some slight discomfort in the groin area. It usually does the trick." I promised to reflect on this professional wisdom, but it did not take long to decide that, on balance, it might be a disproportionately career-limiting solution.

The politics of politics

For all successful politicians, the laser focus must be on the politics of politics, at all times a very serious business and, all too often, a deadly game of winner take all. This means that outside interests must be subordinate and, at best, avocations. It requires being constantly on the job.

In fulfilling my London duties I was appalled to host a dinner with some leading Conservative politicians then in opposition, several of whom later held senior Cabinet positions as Secretaries of State. I had read that one Conservative Party chairman had disclosed that he held no less than eleven corporate appointments. This was despite the fact that the Party Chairman is almost always a serving MP and, unlike in Australia, a member of Cabinet.

Moreover, I had been told on several occasions that the then Shadow Chancellor, Oliver Letwin, had a senior position with investment bankers, Rothschild's, which meant that he usually did not enter the political fray until after lunch. His direct opponent, in Tony Blair's Labour Government, was Gordon Brown, an intense, verging on the morose, bruiser, and a potentially lethal operator with a fanatical work ethic, renowned for firing off emails to all and sundry in the middle of the night. Brown was never off the field. After the 2005 election *The Times* reported that, having increased his majority locally, Letwin had requested a less onerous role than his former Treasury brief so that he would have more time to pursue his career in the City. Truly a gentleman politician, but stuck in the wrong century!

I asked the dinner guests why it was that many politicians jeopardised their political careers by preferring to have well-paid outside interests, often with leading corporations. Their response was that I needed to understand that many had young families and politicians' pay was manifestly inadequate. Consequently, they needed significant outside income to pay for such things as mortgages and school fees.

My immediate response was that there was no level playing field here – a group of part-time, amateur, political operators (the Conservatives) were happy to compete against a full-time, ideologically committed, professional outfit (the Labour Party). My protests were to no avail. In due course they lost the election and it was not until the arrival of Lynton Crosby, previously Federal Director of the Liberal Party, as Conservative Party Director that they sharpened up their act.

My deep involvement in international NGOs, particularly in the international aid field, led to me becoming chairman of the national peak body for five years, and throughout my term as State President of the Party. This led me to focus more on social issues. In my early years at the Bar I had written a number of articles on issues such as a bill of rights (which I then favoured) and trial by jury (which I still favour). I had also prepared a series of factual papers for a major debt collection agency, as well as contributing to some fringe publications, but it is fair to say that while my Catholic religion gave me conservative instincts on moral issues, my social dispositions were generally left of centre.

With greater experience I came to appreciate the importance of combining both in-depth knowledge and practical experience. I realised that "lifetime learning" was more than just a slogan – indeed, more likely the key to sustained success. I obtained four additional degrees on a part-time basis, studying at night for at least ten years. This, combined with the increasing tempo of a busy legal practice, caused me to have a greater appreciation of the need for serious research and a deep understanding of policies, without simply relying on advocacy skills.

The Bar was a very good training ground for politics. Addressing a criminal court jury for over an hour without notes was not

THE LONG AND WINDING ROAD TO CANBERRA

only a good test of memory, but invaluable training in the art of assembling logical and persuasive arguments. It certainly helped me to handle the bear pit of Question Time without too many nerves or fears. Being on top of the brief was essential at the Bar, as well as a sine qua non for political success. The ability to do so quickly separates the sheep from the goats.

The question of what skill sets are required to be a successful parliamentarian is not easily answered. It is often asserted that private sector experience is very helpful and, whilst I would generally agree with the proposition, it does not follow that someone who has been successful in business is likely to succeed in politics. In business a CEO can sack a subordinate, almost always without repercussions. A generous golden handshake usually does the trick, sometimes accompanied by a well-financed "non-compete" or "keep quiet" agreement. After all, most of those moved on will be looking for another career opportunity; spitting the dummy in public could be fatal. None of these softening factors exists in politics. A sacked minister will usually go to the back bench to bide time, and often be ready to conspire with others for a return to prominence.

In business, as in most other walks of life, problem-solving and minimising dissension are part and parcel of success. In politics such skills may be necessary, but they are certainly not sufficient. Malcolm Turnbull was a classic example of a leader keen to minimise political differences in the hope of being rewarded for his transactional competence. But politics does not work in that way. Very few voters closely study the detailed merits of policy issues. They have their own lives to lead, families to care for, careers to pursue. They get their political fill from the headlines and the issues du jour.

The more controversy around an issue the more the punters are likely to notice. I recall several striking examples. As Shadow Minister for Superannuation in the early 1990s, in close consultation with industry leaders, I beavered away for several years devising a detailed and comprehensive policy. It went down a treat with the stakeholders but, because it was probably too arcane a subject, the ALP left it alone and there was hardly any media cov-

63

erage. Or, as Paul Keating once famously said: "If it's not on page one or page three, it didn't happen". As a result, it presumably swung very few votes.

The same thing happened years later when I was Minister for Communications. I spent many long hours crafting a policy to facilitate the uptake of venture capital and private equity in Australia. Labor did not respond, and a good policy sank without trace. The irony was that, as Telstra privatisation was stuck in the Senate, I did not need to spend much time thinking about it, as the issues were clear cut. Yet this did not stop the media from writing almost daily on the subject. Which issue would the average voter think was important?

Politicians have a need to be different – product differentiation is vital, and controversy often helps, not hinders. Many in the media and elsewhere pretend to deplore conflict, although their livelihoods often depend on it. They urge politicians to close down a subject, frequently aided and abetted by the inane cry that "business needs certainty" or "strong leadership." The business community has to deal with uncertainty on a daily basis. That is what planning for the future is all about. Business needs good policy outcomes from government much more than certainty, which is often a mirage.

The culture of parliamentary life is fundamentally different from that of business. Sure, in business there is always jockeying for position and it is perfectly understandable and acceptable to have the ambition to succeed, but it is not a dog eat dog proposition, as political life often is. If a firm has a product to sell it would be unheard of for all its competitors to come out immediately with heavy criticism. Yet this is what happens in politics on a daily basis. There is no clean air, everything is contested, and because the stakes are so high – the honour and prestige of running the country – it will be forever thus, and it is naive in a robust democracy to long for a quieter, gentler discourse. It should not necessarily be open slather, and standards of debating decorum should always be encouraged. Notwithstanding, politics remains a vigorous contact sport and not for the faint-hearted.

Most politicians believe they are deserving of higher duties – often immediately, if not sooner. Frustrated ambition can cause the disgruntled to create havoc by leaking sensitive or embarrassing stories, attempting to curry favour by backgrounding journalists or simply bad mouthing colleagues. Those who believe time has passed them by can threaten to leave the party or suddenly discover a cause which is an open sore to their side of politics. The media loves to exploit disaffection of this sort.

When a Cabinet colleague was once asked how he enjoyed political life, he replied that he was not in politics, he was in Parliament. This was a most unusual reaction, implying a distaste for the endless sparring that goes with the trade. Normally a politician seeks to make a policy difference and thereby advance the national interest, but also knows that it will, on frequent occasions, involve a fight to do so. Those there simply for career advancement do their country a disservice. They could not be in Parliament without the support of the organisation which nominated them. They therefore owe a duty to assist the cause. This does not mean "whatever it takes," but that they should have a strong commitment and belief that the values of their party are superior to those of others and very much to be preferred and pursued in the national interest. Members of Parliament must be prepared to devote a lot of time and energy to persuading the voters to agree, which is, after all, the essence of democracy.

There are some great prizes in politics but there are also some unpleasant chores. Political life is certainly not just a bowl of cherries, more a constant struggle against the odds. I once met Phil Lynch, when he had just got off the plane from a meeting of the United Nations in New York. When I asked where he was going, he said to a branch meeting. The bathos of this contrast forcibly impressed me – in every job you have to take the good with the bad – best to embrace both with equanimity.

The media is quick to encourage the view that parliamentary standards are abysmally low and that politicians rank below real estate agents and used car salesmen in public esteem. After all, controversy and outrage is core business for most media organisations. Another view would be that, because the stakes are high in the Canberra colosseum, the gladiators should be allowed considerable latitude to pursue their bloody contest.

Few democracies are in more robust good health than

MORE TO LIFE THAN POLITICS?

Australia's. We run no risk of coups (notwithstanding the laments of Kevin Rudd and, latterly, Malcolm Turnbull), secession is not an issue, our elections are free and fair; our politicians are overwhelmingly not corrupt – much of what passes as corruption is very minor. Defeated parties leave government disappointed but not outraged. We can always do better but, in a wealthy and prosperous country, with low unemployment, more than a quarter of a century of continuous economic growth, low levels of income inequality, a well-balanced welfare safety net, safe borders (for now) and relative social and community harmony, the ingredients for prolonged civil unrest are simply not there. As a community we are generous in support of charitable organisations and hospitable to both immigrants and those who arrive courtesy of our world's best per capita refugee intake.

A successful political leader needs to have close ties with the party organisation and a genuine empathy with its members. Long-time, often life-long, supporters can have quite forthright views and prejudices, whereas the leader usually has to adopt a more nuanced approach. But this does not mean that the members of the organisation should be sidelined, let alone disregarded. They provide a useful sounding board for understanding broader community attitudes. It is often asserted, usually by those with no skin in the game, that it is important to reach out beyond the base. This is often code for ignoring it.

But a leader who does not carry the base is asking for trouble. A classic example was Malcolm Turnbull's ill-timed superannuation announcement on the eve of the 2016 election. The policy had been too generous in some respects and needed to be changed. During the campaign I received a call from a supporter complaining that we were plundering the $50m in his self-managed super fund. But to announce poorly explained changes to a matter close to the hearts – and pockets – of many Coalition supporters, right at the beginning of an already highly charged campaign, was courting trouble. And Turnbull certainly got plenty of it, as the issue dogged him throughout the campaign.

Gorton, Hewson and Turnbull treated the organisation as, at best, a necessary evil, and paid the price accordingly. More recently, Howard and Morrison came through the NSW Division

THE LONG AND WINDING ROAD TO CANBERRA

and respected its values. The organisation is the glue that holds the show together. It is responsible for selecting and de-selecting candidates, so MPs must ensure they retain local support. It also provides forums for important speeches, funds the campaigns and arranges volunteers to serve on polling booths on election day – all essential for the parliamentary party's well-being and electoral success.

David Kemp, an eminent Professor of Political Science before entering the Federal political arena in 1990, is a shining example of someone prepared to acknowledge the importance of the organisational wing. When he could have gone straight from Federal politics back to the commanding heights of academe, he chose instead to give three more years of Party service (having previously been State Director) as State President.

Another critical organisational link is the relationship between the Liberal Party and the National Party. Menzies was acutely aware of the critical significance of this arrangement, given the close shared values, and never thought of going it alone. Neither did Howard, even when he had the numbers to do so. As the National Party has progressively lost seats in regional and rural Australia, to the extent that Liberal members now outnumber them in their heartland, there have been calls to merge the two parties.

Even National Party leaders such as Doug Anthony have seen merit in the idea, but Howard has always pointed out the likelihood that this would simply lead to emergence of another more conservative force, such as Pauline Hanson's One Nation, which was founded in Queensland, the very state where the Liberal and National parties have in fact merged. This then requires the new entrant to distinguish itself from, and therefore criticise, the combined Liberal-National entity, with whom it would otherwise have a considerable affinity.

Canberra at last

Arriving in Canberra in mid-1986 after a substantial apprenticeship may have been frustrating in the short-term, but with hindsight it probably enabled me to hit the ground running. It was four years after my term as State President had expired and, in that time, I had seriously wondered whether politics was ever going to be my career. It is such an unpredictable business, and a very inexact science.

After my spectacularly unsuccessful attempts to gain pre-selection in some marginal House of Representatives seats I had finally come to terms with the reality that I was probably unlikely to gain pre-selection for a relatively safe House of Representatives seat. With hindsight I was also very grateful that I had not been successful, as my chosen seats had all been very vulnerable to shifts in the electoral tide, and most did subsequently change hands.

The Senate, in contrast, is much more accessible for someone who has spent a lot of time in the organisation, has been State President, and knows many of the likely delegates.

My problem by 1986 was that the only upcoming vacancy was a convention to fill the shoes of Dame Margaret Guilfoyle, the former Minister for Finance, who was retiring. As she had been the only sitting female Senator on our side from Victoria, the overwhelming likelihood was that her replacement would also be a woman, as it was – Kay Patterson.

But, by one of those quirks of fate only too common in politics, Senator Alan Missen, who had only been in the Senate for ten years and had given a lifetime of valuable service to the Party, suffered a heart attack and died suddenly, at the tender age of 60.

I realised that this was likely to be my last great opportunity, so I promptly rethought my strategy. My emphasis had always been on policy matters but, in the process, I had neglected to understand that politics is a people business, first and foremost. Accordingly, I decided that my Senate preselection speech should be divided into three parts: an outline of my background, family and values; followed by a strong commitment to the importance of the Party organisation; and, finally, an indication of my position on some key policy issues.

I took three weeks leave of absence from the Bar (the ability to do so at will being one of its great attractions) and travelled around Victoria, meeting every delegate. This was critically important, as it enabled me to have relaxed, in-depth discussions with a wide

THE LONG AND WINDING ROAD TO CANBERRA

range of people, and, at the same time, understand their widely differing experiences, values and concerns.

The task was much easier in the mid-1980s, as there were only about 120 delegates. My new, more people-oriented approach stood me in good stead as, from memory, there were 26 candidates and I won on the first ballot. Unlike in the House of Representatives, where a vacancy must be filled by a by-election, for the Senate the Constitution requires that a member of the same party as the retiring or deceased senator should be pre-selected and then approved by the State Parliament. And so, within a matter of several weeks of being preselected, I found myself in old Parliament House, ready for a whole new life.

My somewhat tortuous path to Canberra had a fair share of setbacks but ultimately I was once again reminded of the wisdom of James Dyson, British inventor and entrepreneur extraordinaire: "Failure is interesting – it's part of progress. You never learn much from success but you do learn from failure". I realised that if you can keep your feet on the ground and embrace Jordan Peterson's recipe for success in life – a job, intimate relationships, and family – you are well on the way. I also think my Catholic faith helped enormously in dealing with inevitable setbacks. Most of my Cabinet colleagues were in safe seats, having won pre-selection at their first try. My path was different, but the experience probably helped to make me more grounded than if I had had similar early success. The main thing is that perseverance got me there.

70

5

Life in the Bubble

After nearly two decades of operating out of sedate law chambers, Old Parliament House was a dramatic change of pace. The building was full of history and charming ambience, but it was no longer fit for purpose. It had a number of temporary Members' and Senators' offices dotted around the outer perimeter. My office was the size of a very small dog-box. I shared it with a staffer and, whenever I had to see a constituent or visitor, there was no room for the staffer.

In the two years that I was there, before the move to the new Parliament House, my abiding memory is of having breakfast in the dining room. It was generally very sparsely populated at that hour, with the exception of Labor's Finance Minister, Senator Peter Walsh. Possessed of a razor-sharp mind, he was also a fearsome warrior who appeared to hate all Liberals, including me.

Each morning he would studiously ignore me and fail to respond to any of my salutations. I came to recall this ostracism as very poignant because, a few years later, when I had become Shadow Minister for Child Care and he was no longer Minister for Finance, he started to call me and send questions for me to ask the responsible Labor minister. Particularly after he went to the backbench in 1990, he became convinced that Labor's spending was excessive and out of control. I am sure he well understood that Labor's costly policy to significantly increase the number of child care workers, under the guise of a very expensive and unnecessary accreditation scheme, was more about boosting union membership than helping families. This was particularly so as the new regime simply pushed the price of non-unionised private child care through the roof, while making the extensively unionised and subsidised community child care sector correspondingly more attractive.

Life and work in the new Parliament House was transformational in many ways, but at the expense of the warmth and closeness which had brought all the inmates into regular contact with each other. There was no separate ministerial wing in Old Parliament House, so I often found myself bumping into many of the leading players. In stark contrast, the new place was canyonesque, with the House of Representatives and the Senate effectively "miles apart". The distances to anywhere were much greater. For the requirement to attend the chamber for voting the time allowed from the ringing of the bells until the doors were closed was accordingly extended to four minutes, compared to three minutes in the old building.

A new Parliament House "gym junkie", one of my greatest athletic achievements was to be on the squash court when the bells rang, but still manage to run to my ministerial office at the other end of the building, get changed and make it to the Senate chamber, with seconds to spare. I trust this record still stands. I should also confess that there were several occasions when I didn't quite make it, providing a field day for my political opponents, especially on one occasion when it proved necessary to have a re-count. Labor's Senate leader, Senator John Faulkner, even claimed that I once turned up to a division in a jacket covering my gym gear. I don't recall doing so, but it is too good a story to deny. The last word on the subject came from my hitherto good friend, Senator Rod Kemp, during my valedictory. He had the cheek to suggest that I held the record for the number of divisions missed and called on me to apologise to the Senate. He also unearthed several trivial, but perhaps notable, statistics about my parliamentary performance: that I had put out 1,722 press releases and chalked up 1,753 interjections. The significance of the latter achievement, trivial as it may seem to outsiders, is that interjections are only recorded by Hansard if the speaker responds – proof positive of my powers of attracting retaliation.

One undoubted attraction of the new building was the epic-scale Great Hall, with its expansive tapestries designed by Arthur Boyd, depicting a bush scene in the artist's own Shoalhaven River, and hand woven at the Victorian Tapestry Workshop. One of the largest tapestries in the world, it measures twenty metres wide by nine metres high, and is the focal point of the native timber-clad Great

Hall. Over the years it has hosted many visiting dignitaries, including the Queen and various heads of state. Budget night is another very big occasion for visitors, and there are always endless numbers of school groups wandering around during a sitting week.

It didn't take long to work out what made the place tick. I soon realised that the weekly party room meeting during sitting weeks was one of the most important institutions. It provided the opportunity to speak on the issues of the day and upcoming legislation, but it also contained some traps for young players. Reporting on local issues is an important source of information for colleagues, and useable feedback for ministers, but it is not likely to enhance a reputation for being able to think about the big issues. It also became clear that talking on procedural, or other matters of lesser importance, was usually not smart.

My legal training stood me in good stead, as it helped to ensure that my arguments were concise and to the point – no need to say how much you agreed with other speakers – carve out a distinctive position with which others could agree. I was reminded of the truism that anyone can be an expert on the cost and colour of pencils, but very few could debate the cost and merits of the purchase of submarines. A sense of humour and the use of persuasive language, with some memorable phrases, were other very desirable attributes of speechmaking. Creative thinking and new angles on old problems were also highly valued.

To be able to sharply distinguish the merits of our policy position from those of our political opponents was also very important. After all, the major reason we were there was to win government and do what we believed was necessary for the advancement of the nation. A politician prepared to make the case on issues of political contention and take on political opponents in public was much more likely to attract the attention of the leader and approbation of colleagues. The path to preferment was certainly not a matter of waiting for "Buggins' turn," whereby appointments are based on rotation and longevity rather than merit.

We were engaged in a very big battle and the stakes were high, with no quarter given. In many respects, politics will always be a lethal blood sport, highly competitive and full of pitfalls, with political reputations constantly on the line, but ultimately it is a system based largely on performance, both actual and potential. Gender, regional and State-based considerations need to be taken into account, but prime ministers are loath to promote someone unlikely to be able to handle the policy subtleties of important debates or survive the often difficult media cross-examination. Indeed, in my experience, the politicians who rose to the top were usually those prepared to tackle political opponents in the daily media head on, not just put out a press release or write a newspaper article. The critical target market, especially in the lead-up to an election, must be middle Australia, whose denizens don't have much time to read thoughtful opinion pieces and generally get their news from headlines, radio and TV and, increasingly these days, from social media.

Almost by definition, politicians and journalists are engaged in a relationship of mutual dependency and distrust, with competing priorities and agendas. It is generally advisable to endeavour to stay on side with the media, but not at the expense of compromising one's political position. Leaking, or briefing journalists off the record, is not a winning strategy long term. Apart from being disloyal, it runs the serious risk that a number of scribes cannot be relied upon to keep a confidence. Whilst they might not directly name their source, they are not above engaging in loose talk, which can have the same effect.

There are particular pitfalls when a journalist is seeking to get, or stay, on side with the Prime Minister's Office in the search for scoops. Exchanges of political gossip are a stock in trade for most players, so it is unwise to spend too much time bagging others; word quickly gets around. It started to dawn on me that, when I read in a newspaper that someone was "highly regarded", "influential" or "very promising", it could often mean that they were the likely source of the journalist's story.

I had always enjoyed writing, so it was not long before I was penning articles for journals on topics of current importance. And, as I developed this habit, I took to sending items of interest around to colleagues, which Bill Hayden had frequently done in his upward progression. Most colleagues were not likely to have the time or inclination to read my pearls in depth, but at least they would become aware that I had done some hard yards on matters of policy importance.

Sitting in my office when my first Budget session came around, I started to devour the Budget Papers in detail. I soon realised, however, that most of this acquired knowledge was superfluous to my current requirements, as, at that stage of my embryonic career, there were no opportunities for me to argue the case in any detail. It was actually more important to have a broad understanding of key initiatives, which could as easily be gathered from ministerial press releases and newspaper commentary.

Accordingly, when the next Budget came around, I spent most of my time immersed in writing papers and articles that were of interest and immediate relevance to me, and hopefully others. In my first year in Parliament I was also in the throes of completing a Master of Business Administration degree, which involved putting the finishing touches on my thesis on telecommunications. This had introduced me to the fascinating concept of cross-subsidies, which I soon found to be everywhere. If a hotel imposed a separate charge for attending the gym, it was user pays but, if the cost was built into the room price, then non gym users were cross-subsidising users.

I had become absorbed in telecoms, both the issues and the technology. Thanks in large part to the urgings of that amazing guru on everything, Henry Ergas, I realised that around the world new technologies were transforming communications and boosting economies. Looking back, I think that having a passion for the subject matter is key to mastery of an issue.

A classic example of the pace of technology-driven improvements was in the field of fibre optics, where it had become possible to transmit 100,000 simultaneous voice conversations on a single glass fibre smaller than a human hair. Such breakthrough technologies were leading to very complex policy debates, certain to be of direct relevance to Australia. Most of the concepts had not hitherto been part of political discourse, except in the context of privatisation.

I also came to appreciate the pivotal role that leading-edge communications services could play in building a modern economy.

My chosen subject was therefore squarely in the mainstream of the economic debate. "It's the economy, stupid", widely attributed to Bill Clinton, was not just a cute slogan – it was a piece of priceless wisdom.

After reading various books on the privatisation experience in other countries, I decided to approach the then Leader of the Opposition, John Howard, to ask if I could establish a backbench committee on privatisation, a subject which I knew was also of great interest to him. He sensibly suggested that I should consult the Shadow Industry Minister for his agreement but, unfortunately, this was not forthcoming. After licking my wounds for a while, I made another approach, this time to advise him that I had recruited several other interested colleagues, including John Hewson, whose career was then very much on the rise. This time the Leader's view was: "if someone is as determined as you are, it's probably not a bad idea to accommodate them."

I proceeded to write articles on the Commonwealth Bank and Qantas, then big government business enterprises, as well as what I thought was a persuasive piece on privatising Australia Post. Unfortunately this latter work was regarded as politically incendiary by the powers that be, so it never really saw the light of day.

The 1987 Election

Meanwhile, the 1987 "Joh for Canberra" election came along – a double-dissolution election ostensibly about the proposed Australia Card. The Coalition had been split asunder by Bjelke-Petersen's intervention and we did not do well. As is often the case, it took some weeks following election day to conclude the Senate count. I will never forget, after some twelve months, going along to a Collingwood pre-match lunch. The Club President, Allan McAlister, announced that he would like to welcome a new senator. Very chuffed at this thoughtful gesture, I was was about to stand up and take a bow when he named the "new senator" as John Halfpenny, a well-known rabid unionist and ex-communist who was on the Labor ticket and, at that stage of the count, in with a real chance. Unfortunately for him, and the Club President, the final spot went to the Liberal candidate, Dr Kay Patterson.

The 1988 Constitutional Referendum

Since 1901 there have been 44 referendums and only eight have been successful. The Referendum held on 3 September 1988 went down to an ignominious defeat, with the lowest "yes" vote count for any Australian referendum. Peter Reith was the Shadow Attorney-General at the time and we worked closely together to defeat the proposals. I authored the No Case in an official booklet and Peter spruiked our case far and wide, and with great effectiveness.

The Hawke Government presented the proposals as being a considered response to a report by the Australian Constitutional Commission, which had been set up in 1985 to review the Constitution. Headed by Sir Maurice Byers, a former Solicitor-General, its membership consisted of eminent political and legal representatives, including Gough Whitlam and Dick Hamer. Most were of a "progressive" inclination, so from the outset it looked like a stacked deck.

There was no attempt to explain why the questions were suddenly being raised at that time. In the five years the ALP had been in power there had not been one whimper from the Prime Minister or any of his senior colleagues that their ability to govern in general or manage the economy in particular was being hampered by any lack of constitutional power. The proposals did not result from a recently exposed flaw, or a series thereof, which had recently emerged in the courts or the wider community. Nor were they in response to a clarion call from some group of distinguished lawyers. They were largely derived from the musings of a group of constitutional activists, among them Senator Gareth Evans, who had briefly been Attorney-General, 1983-84.

What gave the game away, and exposed the whole exercise as little more than a stunt to distract attention from more pressing problems, was the fact that the Constitutional Commission chairman, Sir Maurice Byers, and his colleague, Gough Whitlam, were suddenly wheeled out to pontificate about why they now supported four-year terms for both Houses, without explaining why their own Commission had not long before recommended a four-year term for the House of Representatives but a Senate term of eight years.

The Commission well understood that the constitutional

framework provided that Senators would be elected for terms of six years, and that, except where there was a double dissolution, half the Senate would be elected each three years. This arrangement, and adaptation of the counterpart provisions in the Constitution of the United States, was intended to ensure a measure of continuity, residual experience and stability in the membership of the Senate and, implicitly, the Parliament as a whole. Except in the case of a double dissolution, this would be significant when a government was swept from office. Moreover, it injected a degree of autonomy and independence into the structure of the Senate. The proposal supported by Byers and Whitlam was not a variation on the parliamentary scheme contained in the Constitution but a fundamentally different concept at odds with it.

The referendum consisted of a series of separate questions on a range of disparate and unrelated issues:

1. **Four-Year Terms for Both Houses**

The idea of the term of a Senator being essentially twice that of a member of the House of Representatives had considerable community appeal and was accordingly supported by the Commission. But the idea of extending the term of a Senator from six to eight years, if the term of the Representatives was also extended from three to four, had never been popular. The real reason why four-year terms for both Houses was now being proposed was that it would give the Prime Minister much greater flexibility, and thus greater political advantage, in calling an election whenever it was most propitious to do so. Permanent double dissolutions would also create inherent instability as it would make it much easier for minority parties and individuals to frustrate the political process. This accorded with Labor's long-standing and oft-expressed desire to limit the powers of the Senate at every opportunity. Indeed, for more than half a century, from 1920, Labor's platform included a call for abolition of the Senate.

2. One Vote, One Value

Under this extremely complex proposal Australians were asked if they approved a Bill to provide for fair and democratic elections throughout Australia. This may have been a seductive proposition, but this terminology did not even appear in the Bill. Moreover, the proposal did not apply to the Senate, yet sought to take away the power of State parliaments to make their own arrangements for State elections. It also did not even ensure that electorate boundaries were drawn impartially. The real inspiration for this proposal was borne of Labor's continuing frustration with its performance in Queensland, where the Bjelke-Petersen administration had kept it out of office for over thirty years.

3. Recognition of Local Government

On its face this proposal was little more than a formal acknowledgement of the importance of the third tier of government. In reality, it was a Trojan horse, designed to enable the Federal government, via the High Court, to bypass the States and extend the definition to include a plethora of electricity councils, harbour boards and water trusts.

4. Three Basic Rights: trial by jury; freedom of religion; acquisition of property on just terms

These completely unrelated issues were almost self-evidently unnecessary and, accordingly, this question amounted to little more than pious sloganeering in favour of the status quo.

Trial by jury had never been under threat in Australia, either at State or national level. Similarly, there had never been any suggestion that Australians did not enjoy freedom of religion. Acquisition of property on just terms was already entrenched federally and there was no suggestion that the States did not adhere to this long established principle.

Given Australia's long history of saying No in referendums, especially where there was no compelling need and no bipartisan support from the major parties, the result should not have come as any surprise. Unfortunately, it also amounted to a costly and unnecessary setback for the cause of serious constitutional reform.

Leadership tensions

The internecine battle between John Howard and Andrew Peacock continued unabated and, when it was resolved, for the time being, in favour of the latter in May 1989, I found myself appointed as Shadow Minister for Communications, no doubt in large part based on my studies and writings on the subject of telecommunications, including publication of my Master of Business Administration thesis on Telecom and its Universal Service Obligation, a copy of which I had thoughtfully provided to the Leader's office.

Inside the Senate party room tensions were running high. The then deputy leader, Austin Lewis of Victoria, who had been a strong supporter of John Howard, had allowed himself to be persuaded to vote for Andrew Peacock. This led to a clear majority of the Senate party room signing a letter indicating they would support me for the position of deputy leader. Having only been in Parliament for three years and being somewhat green in leadership challenges, I thought it would be appropriate to let Austin Lewis know that I would be challenging him the next morning. This advice was immediately brought to the attention of the new leader who summoned me to his office and told me in no uncertain terms that I was not to proceed with the challenge. As a result, when Austin stood down after we lost the 1990 election, another Victorian colleague, Jim Short, became deputy leader in the Senate unopposed, and I had to wait until we lost "the unloseable election" in 1993 before assuming the position, which I then held until my retirement from the Cabinet in 2003.

We entered the 1990 election as the underdog. Bob Hawke, having already won three elections, was still in his prime, despite interest rates being high and Victoria being enveloped in a financial crisis. But his decision to go for an extended campaign period assisted the Coalition to narrowly win the two-party preferred vote, but still lose the election, causing the Liberal leader, Andrew Peacock, to resign in favour of John Hewson. Peacock was an attractive retail politician with a flair for publicity. The media loved him but, ultimately, he lacked the policy finesse or political shrewdness to oust Hawke, a master of the trade. Looking back, he was a natural as Foreign Minister and, later, Australia's Ambassador to the United States.

Hewson was an economics professor but a political novice who treated powerful interest groups, whom he generally regarded as rent seekers, with a haughty disdain, oblivious to the damage such treatment could wreak and ultimately led us to the historic election loss in 1993. He was supremely confident that he could sell his brave, but complex, GST proposal but, after he stumbled badly in the unforgettable cake shop incident, where he couldn't explain the impact of the new tax on a simple cake, he lost momentum and never recovered.

I vividly remember the first debate between the two leaders. Instead of answering every question on its merits, Paul Keating, who had ousted Hawke in December 1991, cleverly decided to make every answer an attack on the GST – for example Q: what time is it? A: time to kill the GST. This strategy was a master stroke. It focussed the electorate's attention on one issue – the prospect of a big hairy new tax, never an attractive proposition. The "unloseable" election was a great wake up call for us. Whilst many of the proposals in *Fightback!*, our key policy manifesto, were logical and, in a purely policy sense, long overdue, the project ignored the political vulnerability of putting a series of complex and politically radical proposals before a rampant Keating, an undisputed expert in demolition politics.

This experience showed that it was folly to propose big changes in a number of areas at once and made us acutely aware of the critical importance of doing our homework on the detail.

Learning the ways of the Senate

A fair part of my first few years was taken up with becoming familiar with the arcana of Senate practices and procedures. This was best done by osmosis – in other words, turning up to committees, sitting in the chamber and listening to debate, reading as much as possible, soaking up the atmospherics and seeking advice from the procedure experts in the Senate Clerk's office. There were also invaluable learning experiences to be gained by serving on Senate standing committees, so I spent the best part of my first three years before becoming a shadow minister being involved in the work of both the Constitutional and Legal Affairs and Finance and Public Administration committees. These were not usually intended to be overtly partisan exercises, even if they often turned out to be.

One inquiry into the operations of the Loan Council introduced me to many aspects of the structure of government, which simply did not have any private sector equivalents. One very important committee, which provided me with a whole new perspective on the dark side of the human condition, was membership for three years of the Joint (Senate and House) Statutory Committee on the National Crime Authority (NCA). The NCA was a very powerful body with the capacity to pursue witch-hunts and ruin careers, unless properly overseen by a parliamentary committee.

The committees usually travelled around the country to hear from interested parties, now known as stakeholders, listening to disparate views. This exposed me to both sides of sometimes quite tricky questions and provided the challenge to come up with workable solutions. I also served on special purpose or "select" committees into such issues as Superannuation and Subscription Television (now better known as Pay TV) Broadcasting Services – both highly relevant to my shadow portfolio responsibilities.

Scrutinising the ABC

Later I chaired two important select committees, which provided many opportunities for lively public debate, and invaluable political practice. The first was into the management and operations of the ABC, always a matter of heated political argumentation. The committee's chief recommendations, in a report ironically entitled *Our ABC*, were that there should be regular audits of the impact of external funding on program selection and the ABC Board should reverse the trend towards the concentration of ABC activities in Sydney. It was yet another episode in the long running expectation of ever more funding for the ABC and the recommendation to de-Sydney-fy the organisation has essentially gone nowhere in nearly thirty years.

This committee was also the occasion for an episode of high political drama, which ended in a straight sets victory. The formal public hearings were scheduled to commence in Sydney on a Monday morning. The day before I received a call from a journalist from *The Australian*, asking if I would care to respond to an allegation by a Victorian Labor member of the committee,

LIFE IN THE BUBBLE

Senator Kim Carr, that I had been ringing ABC employees and cajoling them to come along and give evidence "in the national interest". Furthermore, I was told that Senator Carr had already put out a press release to this effect and the paper would be running it in the morning. I immediately rang Senator Carr, told him the story was totally untrue, demanded that he withdraw his allegations and asked him the basis for them. He muttered something about impeccable sources, laughed defiantly, and said: "you just wait until tomorrow." A threat to take legal action was to no avail.

Next morning I was decidedly apprehensive about what could possibly lie ahead but when, as Chair, I came to open the proceedings, I decided to take the bull by the horns. I outlined my concerns for the public record and asked Senator Carr to retract. He simply repeated his earlier threat: "just wait until you hear from an early witness". We did not have long to wait. Senator Carr greeted the arrival of his star witness by breathlessly asking: "Would you now tell the committee how and why Senator Alston required you to attend today?" To everyone's amazement the witness replied: "I have never spoken to Senator Alston – the Secretary of the Committee [a parliamentary officer] asked me to come along, and here I am."

As Senator Carr remained totally unrepentant and refused to apologise, I decided to follow through with my Sunday threat and, in due course, I issued a writ for defamation against him, which was stoutly defended. His solicitors attempted to join the newspaper as a party to the proceedings but, when this ploy failed, they realised they were on a hiding to nothing and, not long afterwards, agreed to pay what was a reasonably significant sum. I always strongly suspected that union money was involved. Ultimately, most of the damages went in legal costs, but the object was never the money.

There was one more bizarre twist left. Usually, when legal proceedings are settled, the parties agree to keep the terms confidential. But when we made such an offer the response was essentially: "No thanks, not falling for that one." So I ended up with priceless bragging rights, which later stood me in great stead in Question Time.

Foreign ownership of the print media

The other select committee was an inquiry into Certain Aspects of Foreign Ownership Decisions in relation to the Print Media. This bland nomenclature was a euphemism for looking into the extraordinary public disclosure by the Prime Minister, Paul Keating, that he had told Conrad Black, then an international newspaper mogul before his fall from grace and subsequent incarceration, that he could have a significant increase in his equity holding in Fairfax on condition that he provided "balanced coverage", by which, he had made clear to Black, he meant not favouring the conservative side of politics.

The matter had erupted following publication of Black's autobiography in late 1993. Black had written that, in the lead up to the "unloseable election" a few months earlier, Keating had told him that, if re-elected, and Fairfax political coverage was "balanced", he would entertain an application to go higher.

Following Labor's re-election, the Cabinet approved Black's application. A few months later, while attending an APEC Conference in Seattle, Keating confirmed that he had told Black: "We'll think about it, but we want a commitment from you that the paper will be balanced. And if there is any notion that, you know, of bias, that is that (you) barrack for the Coalition on the basis of (your) conservative proclivities in other places, then there's no way you would qualify as a kind of owner we would like." When asked if it was appropriate for him to make such judgments about journalistic standards, Keating replied: "Well, I'm the Prime Minister. That's how I become the judge."

Any other official putting forward such a proposition would have immediately been up before the stewards, before incurring a lengthy suspension from practice, but somehow the media simply laughed it off as part of the rough and tumble of politics. We would have none of this, and persuaded the Australian Democrats, then headed by Cheryl Kernot, to support a Senate inquiry.

It quickly became a tour de force, with the vainglorious Black strutting his stuff. Like Gulliver before the Lilliputians, he strode, slowly but imperiously from the back of the hearing room to the witness table, where he proceeded to deliver a series of monologues, primarily designed to demonstrate his peerless memory. I remember something like: "As I told the magistrate at the committal proceeding several years ago – it's all on page 235 of the depositions, let me recite ..." He brooked no opposition or any alternative narrative and simply batted away anything not in accord with his version of events, often with withering disdain. I had already spoken to him on the phone and, having read his boastful autobiography/self-hagiography, I was not at all surprised by this performance.

Ultimately the committee reached the self-evident conclusion that Keating had abused his powers. Well known for his animosity towards the Senate, his only response was, in what I described as "a raspberry from Paris", to raise one finger on television to the committee, but otherwise refuse to debate the matter further.

One other committee meeting, more ceremonial but nonetheless very instructive, was the Federal Executive Council, a body presided over by the Governor-General, which gives legal form to Cabinet decisions and many others. It meets on a regular basis at Government House and ministers take it in turns to attend. Afterwards it is customary to stay behind for an informal chat with the Governor-General on issues of mutual interest.

It was always a pleasure to visit Government House, where we were invited to dinner at least once a year. Similarly, formal and informal dinners at the Lodge were always a highlight. One occasion produced a moment of sang froid. It was hosted by the newly-installed Governor-General, Bill Hayden, hitherto a staunch republican, whom I had accused at the outset of his reign of having taken "30 pieces of Yarralumla silver". To his great credit he greeted me warmly and, throughout his term, behaved impeccably.

Sometimes there were opportunities for backbenchers to represent shadow ministers while they were abroad or on holidays. I well remember a phone call from Peter Reith, who had already made meteoric progress, and went on to be one of our finest performers in government. He asked me to represent him over the Christmas holidays as Acting Shadow Attorney-General. I gleefully accepted and, as it was "the silly season", when there wasn't much happening as far as the media were concerned, I was able to get a good run with a series of press releases. I clearly overplayed my hand, however, as it wasn't too long before he telephoned to say that he was returning early, as he didn't want me stealing too much more of his limelight. I completely understood, but I had thoroughly enjoyed the outing.

Peter Reith was a very shrewd political operator. Later, during an election campaign, when we were still in Opposition, I spent a few days in hospital with diverticulitis. Peter rang to enquire how I was, and I said I hoped to be discharged very soon, and I proposed to put out a press release on the issue du jour. "No", he said, "go home and then invite the media to come around and interview you in your pyjamas". I did, and it worked a treat!

Question Time

Another fundamentally important parliamentary institution is Question Time, which involves questions without notice being asked of ministers by non-government members and friendly questions from the government side to its own. Although there are slightly different rules for the House of Representatives and the Senate, the basic principle is the same: to provide an opportunity for the Opposition, and other non-government politicians, to hold ministers to account, with equal time for the Government to argue its case and return the favour by putting the Opposition under similar pressure.

Unlike the practice in the House of Commons, the mother of parliaments, where Prime Minister's Questions are allocated half an hour once a week when Parliament is in session and other ministers take turns on rotation, Canberra Question Time is often at least one hour, every sitting day (usually four per week) for approximately half the year. It can therefore be very demanding, especially if a minister is under pressure on an issue. In that case every question from the other side could be addressed to the same minister.

Whilst the public expectation is that it should be a fact finding and information sharing exercise, the reality is that both sides use the occasion for point scoring, which can have a deadly impact. This should be seen in context. The proceedings are invariably reported by the media, so any serious ministerial shortcomings are likely to be exposed – to the detriment not only of the individual but their party. Question Time is the closest we have these days to a (thankfully verbal) gladiatorial contest. As each side seeks to put its policies in a favourable light and to embarrass its opponent, it should not be surprising if the best parliamentary gladiators in the land pursue their quest with both intensity and emotion – and sometimes with sarcasm, ridicule and even, most effectively, with a good dose of humour thrown in. In many ways this can be seen as the sign of a vigorous but healthy democracy, where the stakes are high, and the contest is for keeps.

The theatre of the occasion is very important for morale and conveying a sense of relative superiority over opponents. The on-looker is not only to make a judgment about the merits of an argument, aside from the bluster, but also to assess the relative political and debating skills of the protagonists. As it often involves vigorous exchanges, with some purple rhetoric thrown in, and all parliamentarians are present, Question Time has become in the public mind the centrepiece of proceedings. By comparison, other public business is usually quite staid, played out before largely empty chambers, with the media paying little attention despite constant claims of holding governments to account.

Afghanistan

One of the consolations of being in Opposition was the opportunity for international travel during parliamentary recesses.

On entering Parliament in 1986 I had taken the place of Senator Alan Missen, a passionate advocate of human rights causes. One of his abiding interests had been the Afghan community in Melbourne. It then consisted of around five hundred members – a relatively small number, but they had still managed to divide themselves into four distinct groupings, with separate bank accounts, letterheads and office-bearers. These were not factions but basically family clans, with no obvious ideological differences. The dynamic Anglican Archbishop of Melbourne, David Penman, was a dedicated supporter and after Alan's untimely death he encouraged me to take up the reins. David had spent several years as a missionary in Pakistan, where he had worked closely with Afghan refugees. In 1985 he became Chairman of the Australian Institute for Multicultural Affairs and, subsequently, President of the Australian Council of Churches.

I was impressed with the community leaders, their strong family ethos and their spirit of hard work and independence. Many had two jobs and none of the able-bodied was on welfare. I agreed to help form a single body which could unite the groups and co-ordinate their activities. David's sound instinct was to strike a balance between recent arrivals and non-Afghan born supporters. The Afghan Australia Council was duly formed and I became the chairman, ably assisted by people such as Dr Philip Ayres, an academic who had spent time in Afghanistan and subsequently became a superb biographer. But just as we were getting into our stride we suffered a body blow with the sudden death of the Archbishop in July 1989, shortly after I had become Shadow Minister for Communications for the first time.

The demands of my new role meant I no longer had the time to continue as chair, but I still kept in touch with the community, attending weddings, meetings and other civic activities. In 1991, a leading member, Moyen Barjaray, asked if I would accompany him to Peshawar, in western Pakistan on the Afghan border, to meet leading members of the Mujahideen, an alliance of Afghan political Islamists and fundamentalists, formed in the early 1980s to fight the Soviet-backed Democratic Republic of Afghanistan. They were effectively exiled in Peshawar as they plotted their return to their homeland.

As Parliament was in recess, I accepted the invitation and, in due course, Moyen and I arrived in Peshawar, a classic wild west town, where lawlessness seemed to be the way of life. It was not only an administrative centre but a hot bed of intrigue, with Kalashnikov rifles everywhere. There was also a thriving black market, where I paid $3 for a Russian-made watch, which was still going strong ten years later! The leadership of the Mujahideen had emerged from the more than one million Afghan refugees who were holed up in huge UN-supervised camps and had turned themselves into a very effective fighting force. Within twelve months of my visit they had defeated the Soviet Army in Afghanistan.

For several days I was escorted to fortress-style compounds in tribal areas to meet the faction leaders of the seven-party Mujahideen Alliance, all professional warriors clearly willing to die for their cause, and all surrounded by innumerable bodyguards and camp followers. They mostly resided in comfortable and spacious unbaked mud-brick and wooden mansions, located in the various tribal areas on the outskirts of the urban centre. In every instance I was received with great fanfare and feted as a guest of honour at overladen banquets. They were very keen to ensure that I understood every nuance of the complexity of Afghan politics, with its regular factional defections and constantly shifting allegiances.

Peshawar has been an important trading centre since the Mughal era, but is now more a frontier town on the edge of the tribal badlands, and serving as the administrative and economic hub of the Federally Administered Tribal Areas. Its topography is dominated by the massive British-era military cantonment established in 1868, which I visited. The city is also not far from the Afghan border and I needed little encouragement to journey up the fabled Khyber Pass, a key part of the ancient Silk Road linking Central Asia to the Indian sub-continent, via the Grand Trunk Road. After a rugged truck trip through the arid hills I finally arrived at Torkham, the official crossing point and a strategic military location, where I was invited to sign the visitors' book. To my surprise, among recent signatures were those of Margaret Thatcher and my old school friend, Tim Fischer, later Deputy Prime Minister on our ascension to government in 1996. As Tim was a long time devotee of the sub-continent and an avid train traveller, I should not have been greatly surprised.

On return to Peshawar it dawned on me that I had a once in a lifetime opportunity to visit Afghanistan, so I approached the Australian embassy in Islamabad to make the necessary representations. It soon transpired that the only means of ingress was through the UN. Their initial response was that they couldn't fly me into Kabul because they did not have the necessary insurance.

I spent the next few days in Peshawar doing the rounds, visiting the UN compound where we again discussed the possibility of me making a brief trip to Kabul. The UN were also not keen on the idea because of the dangers involved, which I airily dismissed as my problem, but the Mujahideen were not very keen either. So I returned to the administrative authorities to make a formal application, but I was required to cool my heels for some days while awaiting a response. After further persistence on my part the authorities suddenly announced a breakthrough – the President was keen to see me, no doubt because he was then a pariah in Western circles and needed friends wherever he could find them. Accordingly, a special charter flight was commissioned to take me there.

The following morning, flying over the legendary Hindu Kush and the snow-capped Pamir mountains was a thrill in itself, but not quite as exciting as what sounded like rapid machine gun fire as the plane approached the airstrip. After landing without incident I realised that the firing had probably come from an official escort. Before long I had been installed in what was euphemistically described as a guest house but was more like a sprawling ranch, where I stayed for several days, all alone except for about four servants, who looked after my every need. Perhaps my most memorable meal was what looked like a typical Afghan meal. When I politely asked the name of the meat dish I was told, somewhat hesitantly: "ah, well, how you say in English – lamb testicle?"

Next day I met with an impressive and well-informed Afghan Minister for Foreign Affairs and was then taken on a tour of Kabul back streets and markets. This was followed by a quick stop at the Inter-Continental Hotel overlooking the city, and finally a visit to the Red Cross/Crescent hospital, where many landmine victims, minus limbs and other body parts, were housed in primitive but clean conditions – a harrowing reminder of the consequences of war. A few years later Australian de-miners were engaged there in extensive clearance operations in one of the most mine-laden countries in the world. The UK-based Halo Trust estimates that up to 640,000 land mines have been laid in Afghanistan since 1979.

The following day I was taken to the Presidential Palace, where I waited to be ushered into the office of the President, Dr Najibullah. I was acutely aware of the country's bloody history of coups, assassinations and ruthless campaigns of violent repression. Najib had qualified as a Doctor of Medicine but had quickly immersed himself in the labyrinthine cesspool of Afghan politics. After the Soviet invasion of 1979 he had become the head of KHAD, the Afghan equivalent of the Soviet KGB, and had turned it into a brutally efficient instrument of government, engaging in repeated terrorist activities. In 1987, with strong Soviet support, he became President but, when the Soviets decided to withdraw from the country and he had to cope with the subsequent loss of military aid and assistance, he proceeded to de-Sovietise the universities, abandon Marxism and allow the formation of new political parties. Communism was dumped and Afghanistan became an "independent, unitary and Islamic state".

Najib, a big man with dark hair and an imposing physique, quickly put me at ease in his presidential office, which I remember as functional rather than grand. We embarked on a long discussion about democratic systems of government and Third World politics, about both of which he was very well informed. He was calm, polite and thoughtful and, although he showed little interest in Australia, he regarded it as a well-run democracy. There was an eerie quiet in the building and I had the impression that as he had few international friends or allies, he was pleased to be able to have a stimulating excursus on political science and global politics as a welcome diversion from the interminable manoeuvrings of his domestic environment.

Later I discovered that, despite his calm demeanour, he must have been under enormous pressure, having survived an assassination attempt only the year before. A tough and ruthless hardman on his way to the top, once there he seemed to have become very much aware of the need to bring the warring factions together. He was moving away from socialism towards Afghan nationalism and was exploring ways of establishing dialogue with the Mujahideen and other groups. He exuded an air of quiet confidence, quite an achievement as his country was then in the midst of a bloody, three-way civil war.

He had a good grasp of the international political scene and was keen to discuss various Latin American dictators and the chal-

MORE TO LIFE THAN POLITICS?

lenges they faced. He seemed to understand the virtues of democracy in the West, having spent time in Europe, and appreciated the complexities of various voting systems very well. After two hours of a fascinating exchange he thanked me very much for visiting him and, on the way out, a palace assistant materialised from nowhere to present me with a large, wrapped gift from the President. It was clearly an important carpet with considerable naturalistic detail of flora, fauna and animals and an impressive colour mix. Islam does not allow any human representations.

As he was attempting to liberalise a hidebound communist system, the Soviets were abandoning him and the Mujahideen were on the offensive. By the beginning of that year the Government only controlled 10 per cent of the country and, by the end of 1991, the Soviet Union was no more. The new Russian President, Boris Yeltsin, was no fan of Najib – less than a year later he had resigned and Mujahideen forces had overrun Kabul. He tried to flee the country but was thwarted and forced to seek sanctuary in the UN compound. He remained there until 1996 when the Taliban, ignoring the international law conventions of sanctuary and diplomatic immunity, invaded the compound, shot him and his brother, impaled their bodies and left them hanging in public view.

Najib's bloody road to power has, until recent times, resulted in him being seen as a ruthless dictator. The passage of time and the performance of others have, however, led later historians to take a kinder view of him, seeing him more as a nationalist and patriot who strove to put his country on a more secure political and economic footing. Despite the brevity of our association, I am inclined to agree with this assessment.

I left Kabul with mixed feelings. Afghanistan has had an exotic history, as every student of the Great Game of the 19th century can attest, but it also seemed to be a country in constant and perhaps never-ending turmoil.

Back to politics

It was quite a shock to return to more tranquil political waters, but it was not long before my adventure had faded in the face of the constant demands of everyday politics. As Deputy Leader of the

Opposition in the Senate I was in charge of Question Time strategy. Shadows and backbenchers were encouraged to submit questions they would like to ask, and it was the task of the committee I chaired to sharpen them up or re-draft them to ensure maximum effectiveness. It also enabled me to be at the forefront of our daily assaults.

In government, ministers (or their offices) could arrange soft questions for themselves, known as "Dorothy Dixers". These were often accompanied by: "and is the Minister aware of any alternative policy approaches?", thus enabling the Minister to present a stark contrast between the competing parties' views. As Deputy Leader I acquired additional responsibilities, one of which was to have the carriage of our case in proceedings on the historic Native Title Bill in 1993. At the time it constituted the longest time taken for debate on a bill, which saw the Senate sitting almost to Christmas, including the first Saturday sitting in thirty years.

Robert Hill was a calm and capable Senate leader and we worked closely together over my ten years as his deputy. This leadership stability and relative internal harmony served us well. I enjoyed the position of deputy as it allowed me to focus intensively on policy issues while still attending to colleagues' needs. My pastoral duties included offering words of encouragement to new arrivals. Whenever a ministerial reshuffle took place there would be colleagues who felt that their obvious talents had been inexplicably overlooked. It was worse for those who had been displaced – some threatened to resign; others just sulked. All needed and deserved some TLC. One for whom I felt great affection, and ultimately great sympathy, was my good friend, Senator Warwick Parer, the most honourable of men, who ultimately felt the need to resign from the portfolio of his dreams as Minister for Resources over a significant stake he had long held in a coal mine. He had done nothing wrong but, in politics, even a perception of possible conflict of interest can be fatal.

As a minister, I enjoyed my Question Time outings. I undoubtedly benefitted from having been in the Communications portfolio for some years before coming to government, so I was rarely caught out not knowing the detail. A ministerial career can founder on the shoals of bad policy mistakes or by not acting quickly enough to deal with the problems that inevitably arise. The trick was to stay ahead of the curve by being proactive. My love of the arts had taught me the benefits of creativity and my interest in business and its practices, including my father's hard-won small business success, had taught me the virtues of calculated risk taking and entrepreneurship.

A journalist once described me as a "share trading, entrepreneurial politician", hardly how I would have described myself, but I was flattered by the character reference. As I have recounted earlier, I had learned the perils of shareholding in Opposition, when I discovered that, while Shadow Minister for Communications, I had owned shares in Skilled Engineering, which I thought was simply a labour hire company. It was, but its biggest client was Telstra and, if I had then been the minister, it would probably have been treated as a hanging offence because of a "perceived" conflict of interest. I soon saw the wisdom of disposing of my share portfolio, and promptly did so.

It was also essential to "keep your nose clean" in terms of personal propriety, so that there were no peccadilloes, or worse, to provide a platform for easily generated, often faux, outrage. Oppositions like nothing better than to drown out a policy debate by changing the subject to a ministerial scandal or administrative calamity, in the hope of securing a ministerial scalp, the ultimate achievement for an Opposition.

For the ALP, when assailing me in Question Time, privatisation of Telstra was often the only game in town. As I frequently reminded them, "when in Government, they had privatised everything that moved " – to be precise, Aerospace Technologies, AIDC, AUSSAT, Australian Airlines, Moomba-Sydney Pipeline and the Snowy Mountains Engineering Corporation. All these, plus two very big bananas, Qantas and the Commonwealth Bank, after vehemently denying, prior to the 1993 election, that they had any intention of doing so.

This perpetual resistance to privatising Telstra came despite both Beazley and Keating having explored the possibilities on a regular basis when in office. In fact Keating had proudly and publicly proclaimed his interest in selling off key Telstra assets, which we characterised as "death by a thousand cuts" and "privatisation by stealth". I was quick to point out that North Korea and Albania were about the only remaining holdouts on privatisation, so Labor was in good company. I labelled them the "just-say-no party," along with other epithets, but it made no difference.

Labor's privatisation inclinations had long been known, if half-heartedly denied. In the lead-up to the 1996 election Senator Cheryl Kernot had no doubts on this score, as she confided at the National Press Club. The most likely explanations for Labor's stance, which provoked both frustration and bemusement in the corporate sector, were:

- they knew the community was generally unimpressed with the concept of privatisation, so they were keen to ride the wave of public opinion, at least until the next election;
- they knew that most of the mainstream media would not call them out for hypocrisy, but instead sit back and enjoy the contest;
- their crude political assessment was that they would never receive any political dividend from supporting a big, Coalition-sponsored initiative;
- they did not want us to have the benefit of the huge war chest which would accrue from the sale. In marked contrast to our responsible approach of using the bulk of the proceeds to retire debt, Labor's track record demonstrated that it much preferred to use such a windfall for working capital and large-scale vote buying;
- the key unions were adamantly opposed to private sector ownership, based on a well-founded fear that this would result in marked labour efficiencies, that is the loss of many cosy jobs. As a result Labor did not wish to unnecessarily antagonise them or jeopardise their willingness to provide election campaign funding. Instead, they preferred to do the dastardly deed only when they were safely back in government.

I learned an invaluable tactical lesson in Question Time early on – if you started off by criticising your opponents you were likely to provoke an early objection that you were avoiding the question. The better approach was to pay at least lip service to the meat of the question before embarking on a demolition exercise. Interjections from the other side were part and parcel of the contest – the parliamentary counterpart of sledging in cricket. It was rarely malicious, but it could potentially put a minister on the spot by drawing attention to an apparent policy weakness or simply upsetting their concentration. For me it provided an opportunity not only to rebut but to respond, sometimes in spades. I was very flattered when Senator Brian Harradine, the famed Independent from Tasmania, said on my retirement that I had been "really expert at reducing complex issues down to first principles". I learned this skill from John Howard, and it served us both well.

The ALP went along with constant disparagement for quite a while, until they apparently came to the view that they were most likely to come off second best. So, instead of interjecting, as soon as I rose to answer a question, they pretended to talk amongst themselves and treated me with studied indifference. I suppose this tactic proved fruitful in the end, as my decision to retire on my own terms, in some ways prematurely, was in small part driven by my increasing boredom in Question Time, with a corresponding loss of the adrenaline charge.

Senate Estimates

These hearings are often seen as a useful forum, and they can be when a big scandal is underway or there is a particular "project" to be pursued. Most of the time is taken up with backbenchers practising their talking skills and tediously asking interminable questions, many of which could easily be put on notice, if the object of the exercise was genuinely to seek information. I decided early on that I would only attend in Opposition for a specific purpose and, in Government, only under sufferance. As a minister, I unilaterally imposed a strict procedural rule: senators could use the allotted time in any way they liked, but under no circumstances would I allow extra time for unfinished business and certainly no spill-over days. This drove the Opposition spare, but certainly ensured that I had a good night's sleep.

LIFE IN THE BUBBLE

On one occasion, as Shadow Minister for Superannuation, I managed to get senior Treasury officials to concede that they had not done the necessary forward projections and calculations to justify their estimates of how much Paul Keating's compulsory superannuation scheme was likely to cost, and what the savings to welfare might be.

When the press gave me a good front page run the next morning, Treasury went into full panic mode. The resumed hearing was to proceed that night and, about an hour beforehand, a detailed package of information and arguments arrived for urgent consideration that evening. It was clearly a deliberate and carefully calculated move to deny me time to consider all the material. Having immediately smelt a large rat, I sought to have the hearings adjourned so I could get some expert advice, but to no avail. As soon as the hearings resumed, no less a personage than the Secretary to the Treasury, Tony Cole, turned up and endeavoured to retrieve the situation with a clever but obfuscatory one liner: "garbage in, garbage out". It was designed to be the next day's headline, which it duly was, but I knew I had struck a telling blow.

Opposition can be very lonely, as the phone calls and visitations are normally neither frequent nor of keen interest. I remember thinking, after we had lost three consecutive elections during my ten years in Opposition, that, even if we never came to government, it had still been worthwhile, as it opened my eyes to people, places and issues that I would never otherwise have encountered, especially if I had stayed at the Bar. But, when victory finally came, in 1996, it was well worth waiting for. It opened up multiple opportunities, the main one being that of being closely involved in important decision-making.

Fortunately we had not wasted the barren years and, particularly as the 1996 election approached, there was a heightened air of excitement. Howard's ascension to the leadership had transformed our prospects and his steady hand and sound judgment made sure we did not blow our big chance. By then Keating was on the ropes, and he knew it. Courtesy of Don Watson's book, *Confessions of a Bleeding Heart*, we now know that he was also beset by, at times, crippling depression, which may have accounted for his surliness and obvious frustration. Indeed, one of his Labor Cabinet colleagues once told me that when they turned up to Cabinet for a 10 o'clock start he was nowhere to be seen and the emissary sent to his home found him sitting on the edge of his bed listening to his beloved Mahler.

One of my press releases, over which I still chuckle, concerned his February 1993 campaign visit to Ballarat, where he met a group of young singers who had already received a modest government grant. After he heard their rendition of Puccini's *O Mio Babbino Caro*, he effusively promised them a generous government funded top-up. My headline response was *Rack Off Lorenzo*, comparing his actions to the fabulous artistic largesse for which the Medicis of Florence have been forever noted. Years later, at an informal party to pay tribute to the sterling service of Hilary McPhee, as Chair of the Australia Council for the Arts, her then husband, Don Watson, told me that, while Keating's staff had found my jest quite amusing, it had had the opposite effect on the Prime Minister.

With an election imminent, the most important meeting was a two-day high-level council of war in Sydney, attended by all the key players. It was there that the crucial decision to link the sale of Telstra to the establishment of a $1 billion Natural Heritage Fund was made. This not only demonstrated that the proceeds would be put to good use, but also gained us the support of some key green groups, not our natural allies and capable of causing us distraction and heartburn during the campaign.

We entered the campaign as favourites, but not before the Federal Director, Andrew Robb, and I had a very narrow escape from disaster. As our research had shown that our Telstra privatisation proposal was hurting us, we decided to meet fire with fire by alleging that Paul Keating was also effectively proposing to privatise Telstra, but by a slightly different means – by selling off key components, such as mobiles and Yellow Pages. Accordingly we had commissioned some visuals, which we intended to unveil at a specially convened press conference.

When I turned up shortly before the starting time, I was greeted by a frantic Robb, telling me that the legal adviser appointed by the Federation of Australian Commercial Television Stations had ruled that our proposal did not accord with their guidelines, and I had five minutes to persuade her to the contrary. By the time I reached her on the phone the press conference deadline had already passed, but I pressed my arguments as hard as I could before she went away to reconsider. We had to wait for what seemed a minor eternity before she finally came back with a Yes. Andrew Robb and I then nonchalantly fronted the media, apparently without a care in the world.

In Government – after ten long years

Winning government was the thrill of a lifetime. I had only spent ten years in Opposition but a few, like John Howard, had waited out the whole thirteen. I always felt very sorry for David Connolly, who spent the whole time in Opposition as a shadow minister, only to lose preselection at the end, and not be there for the opportunities and satisfactions of government. His consolation was a later appointment as High Commissioner to South Africa, where he served his country well.

We were careful to avoid any overt expressions of euphoria and the PM stressed that it was to be "business as usual". We had learnt from Labor's over-the-top reaction to its lucky victory in 1993 which had given us the opportunity to festoon our polling booths with blow ups of Gareth Evans dancing the night away, sending the potent message that "it was all about them".

But there was one joyful moment which, for me, was very special. A few days after our victory I was accosted at the airport by none other than Ronald Dale Barassi, one of the finest ever Australian Rules football players and coaches and a truly iconic figure to all Melbournians. Ron had always been an enthusiastic Liberal, and at one stage had contemplated standing for State Parliament. It was just so exciting to talk to him and a colleague, who I think was Ian Robertson, a former Carlton stalwart. I subsequently encountered Ron a number of times and sat next to him on one occasion when he was guest of honour at a dinner in Parliament House, hosted by the President of the Senate, Paul Calvert.

The Cabinet process is very much under the control of the Prime Minister and we were fortunate that we had John Howard in the

MORE TO LIFE THAN POLITICS?

chair, as his experience in the Fraser Cabinet was invaluable. The first question was what do we call you – John or PM? He said "either", but somehow it just felt right to call him PM, so we all did. A key to our success was that everyone had ample opportunity to have their say, and the PM often sat back without disclosing his view until close to the end – not always, as there were some matters on which he felt the need to provide guidance.

The decision to commit Australia to the Iraq War in 2003 was undoubtedly the most momentous decision during my time in Cabinet, and it was only taken after the most exhaustive and comprehensive discussion. During my more than seven and a half years around the Cabinet table no one ever felt they had been short changed and, as a result, there were hardly any leaks, certainly none of any substance. Nor were there any factional games and I soon realised that it would be futile to lobby colleagues in advance, as no one could be expected to adhere to a commitment if the debate had changed their mind. There was a great sense of camaraderie and little overt grandstanding. The PM expected ministers to speak beyond their portfolio areas of responsibility and not just reflect the departmental brief, and most did so.

Cabinets will always contain some "big beasts", to use the British term, who become thought leaders, creative thinkers and regular media boosters for our cause. Costello, Downer and Reith were very effective warriors as well as experts in their portfolios. Costello was the premier Question Time performer but, in my view, Peter Reith was the outstanding contributor around the Cabinet table, after the PM. John Fahey brought his considerable craftmanship as Premier of NSW to bear on some tricky issues and I always found him very helpful and sensible. Robert Hill, my long serving Senate leader with whom I worked very effectively, and Michael Wooldridge, each had a keen understanding of the sensitive issues in their respective portfolios of Environment and Health, ones which traditionally we had not owned politically. Tim Fischer and John Anderson were very capable operators and astute advocates for rural Australia, making them a pleasure to work with.

It is worth remembering that the Cabinet of today is nearly

50 per cent larger than the first Howard Cabinet of 15. It is often said that the Hawke Cabinet had some serious heavy hitters, but I think ours were at least on a par. They were smart and experienced and successful outside politics, with good, sound instincts for the "pub test". It was not unusual to allow outside experts, especially from the Defence Force, to address Cabinet, but I still felt it was a coup when I persuaded Bill Gates, who was visiting Australia at the time, to speak on the technology revolution.

I well remember attending a farewell dinner in Sydney for Alex Allan, the outgoing UK High Commissioner. When I apologised for being slightly late as a result of attending a lengthy Cabinet meeting in Canberra, he expressed bemusement at the process. He had served as principal private secretary to both John Major and Tony Blair. He explained that under Blair it was all over inside the hour but with Major it usually took a bit longer, as he was always keen to be updated on the latest cricket scores. It immediately struck me that I should be grateful that, under our system of government, the Cabinet owned the process.

Another key meeting was held at 8 am on every sitting morning in Canberra. The original leadership group consisted of, from the House of Representatives, the Liberal Leader John Howard and his Deputy, Peter Costello, the National Party Leader Tim Fischer and his Deputy, John Anderson, together with the Leader of the House, Peter Reith. From the Senate, there was the Liberal Leader Robert Hill and myself as Deputy. I don't recall anyone ever observing that the Liberal five were all lawyers, but it is worth pointing out that the longstanding convention was that the Senate Party Room chose its leaders in Opposition, but in Government it was the gift of the Prime Minister.

The time of the meeting assumed that we had all read the relevant newspapers and allowed us to consider the tactics of the day, as well as to canvass any other matters of current or looming importance. As we all had offices near the Prime Minister's Office it was not difficult to explore policy matters with the Prime Minister and his office. It is always a matter of judgment what and how to raise matters for discussion, but whenever I felt the need to get a steer on an issue, the PM was always accessible. Extremely quick on the uptake, he never tried to railroad or impose his views. His advice was invariably helpful and he frequently found time for a quick political chat afterwards. His office was also very available and helpful, particularly his highly competent, long serving Chief of Staff, Arthur Sinodinos. If you went to Arthur with a policy idea he always gave you a sympathetic hearing and careful consideration, even if the ultimate outcome was: "Mate, it's a great idea and the PM loves it, but it's a timing issue – we'll definitely come back to it later". Sometimes they even did!

It was a great privilege and experience to have a spacious ministerial office and I took the opportunity to personalise it by importing a number of my favourite Aboriginal works of art. Several ministers were content to display football photos on their office walls, but most relied on Artbank, a government unit which leases works of art, principally by emerging artists, to parliamentary offices, other government agencies and even to the private sector. When we came to office the Department of Finance saw an opportunity to sell off Artbank but was unsuccessful, thanks to the support of our very effective Finance Minister, John Fahey, who carefully analysed the arguments before supporting me. As a result Artbank has remained safely in government hands to this day and continues to provide much needed support and exposure for emerging contemporary Australian artists.

Another very useful and generally enjoyable part of parliamentary duties was to be able to undertake fact-finding trips overseas, which the media generally preferred to label "junkets", for all but the PM, the Foreign Minister, the Treasurer and the Trade Minister. In my case, regular visits to Silicon Valley, at least until the tech bubble burst in April 2000, allowed me not only to meet all the major players, but to study at first hand the magic of the place and see what lessons could be applied in Australia. In all, during my nearly eight years as Federal Commmunications Minister, I led ten trade delegations and made official visits to more than thirty different countries, with multiple visits to the most relevant: the US, the UK and the Asian region.

Particularly important and informative were two trade missions which I led to Israel, with the able assistance of Leon Kempler, the long serving, indefatigable and extremely competent CEO of the Australia-Israel Chamber of Commerce. Israel is home to many exciting IT projects as well as its unique venture capital models, which were clearly world's best practice, and helped to inform our own policy development. In addition I attended four APECTEL ministerial conferences in various Asia Pacific locations, one of which, on the Gold Coast in 1996, I chaired.

In terms of international travel, I took the view that in a fast-moving portfolio like Communications and Information Technology, Australia was a small fish in a much bigger pond and it was important, wherever possible, to stay ahead of the curve by learning from global best practice. There were many examples of where we did this, including identifying from a visit to South Korea that CDMA was the best available technology to replace the first generation mobile network in regional Australia, which Labor had contractually committed to switch off without any agreed replacement.

Unfortunately my burdensome travels became the subject of envy from some of my colleagues, with charming epithets like "the mighty nomad" being flippantly thrown around. They obviously didn't appreciate the workload involved or the technological significance of being the first Australian minister to visit Iceland! It was Peter Reith who first christened me Marco Polo. Naturally outraged, I vigorously defended strictly business-based travel itineraries. My Cabinet colleagues soon joined in the fun, led by John Fahey, until I worked out that the best rejoinder was along the lines of: "How was Bali, or off to Davos again soon, John?"

John was well-qualified to be a regular attender, but it was my lot to attend the annual Davos extravaganza only once. It was a very memorable excursion, marked by two personal highlights, apart from all the politically correct wisdom of the day, even before it became not much more than a celebrity gathering of the great and the good. The first was an informal round table dinner, at which I found myself sitting opposite Jane Fonda. When we were asked what we all did for a living, and I said telecoms and the arts, her immediate response was: "What an interesting combination", to which my rejoinder was: "It means we have the most cultured telcos in the world"!

MORE TO LIFE THAN POLITICS?

As Davos also doubles as a leading ski resort and Sunday was the day of rest, I spent the morning on the slopes, which resulted in acute back strain. The afternoon had already been committed to a trip to watch polo on ice at St Moritz with Geoff Raby, then Australian Ambassador and Permanent Representative to the World Trade Organisation in Geneva. Determined not to miss out, I spent the bulk of the three hour round trip lying on my back peering out a window, while Geoff gave me a running commentary on both the alpine surrounds and the key international issues of the day.

Eventually all good things come to an end and, in August 2003, I submitted my resignation from Cabinet to the PM in person. The final formality before my departure from the Senate was that quaint custom of valedictories, where everyone does their best to say nice things about departing colleagues. They can be maudlin affairs but, on this occasion, I was struck more by the solemnity of my departure, knowing that I was leaving behind forever some of the best years of my life.

I ended up being quite moved by some of the contributions. Several referred to my hard-earned nickname, "the burglar of the ERC" (Expenditure Review Committee). In particular, I was struck by the generosity of Andrew Bartlett, Leader of the Australian Democrats, at whose expense I had occasionally enjoyed myself in Question Time. He graciously acknowledged that I had been instrumental in saving Artbank from the depredations of the Finance Department and, although his Party had been opposed, for successfully reforming laws relating to the parallel importation of CDs, which Labor in government had tried and failed to do. He also generously said that I was not a boring, white bread politician and even detected some charisma in the portrait of me entered for the Archibald Prize. He then quoted one of my journalistic protagonists, Errol Simper, whom I had always admired, for calling me both "colourful and mischievous."

I also appreciated the kind words of one of my successors-in-title, Senator Helen Coonan, who not only described my Question Time exchanges as "always vigorous but never vindictive" with "the ability to make a telling political point with style" but also quoted from some press commentators' assessments such as: "As a juggler of touchy issues Richard Alston had few equals"; and, "From the viewpoint of both sides of politics, Alston's achievements in the area of digital television, for instance, are profound." The one I liked best was, "he wears politics like a cloak." Even my formidable opponent, Senator John Faulkner, who rarely gave an inch, acknowledged, somewhat tongue in cheek, that I "was very expert in the field of Aboriginal art", "the first Australian minister to visit Iceland" and an Olympian record holder for "the number of events attended at the Sydney Olympic Games."

Perhaps the most moving contribution were the words of National Party stalwart Senator Ron Boswell:

> When Richard came in here I was a hard-core, right-wing National Party apparatchik. In fact when I came here one person refused to sit next to me. But Senator Alston and I became great mates. That is how the relationship started with the Liberal Party… (he) increased funding for the ABC so that rural and regional Australia would not lose their news and information services … It fell to Richard to implement the changes that put mobile phones throughout Australia …Then there were the Internet connections that we put right around Australia … I cannot give you any higher accolade than announcing that you are an honorary Nat.

One the joys of being in the Federal Parliament was that you encountered people from all walks of life – not necessarily the political high-fliers but critical to ensuring that Parliament looks like Australia. Bos probably heads the list followed by Senators John Panizza, Bill Heffernan, John Herron, Warwick Parer and Bob Katter in the House, for all of whom I retain an abiding affection.

It was also an occasion for some nice story-telling and some charitable character references. Senator Hill told an amusing tale about how he had once been asked a question about an item on the ABC AM program, to which he had replied that he had missed the AM program because he had been listening to Triple J. The question was then referred to me and I said I had also missed it because I had been listening to Classic FM. It will never be known whether this was an example of our age gap, our different cultural tastes or simply an apocryphal yarn.

By 2003 I had been in Cabinet for nearly eight years. While it had been a wonderful ride and an unforgettable experience, it was also becoming somewhat repetitive. My family had been very patient, and I found myself increasingly wondering when, not if, to call time and how I would cope in my next career. I had observed from my love of sport that most experienced athletes seemed to know when the time to retire is right, and I reflected that there was probably not much more I could accomplish. There is always unfinished business but there are also always others ready and willing to step up. Leaving at a time of my choosing meant I could never have any complaints about my treatment and, ever since, I have looked back with great satisfaction as well as awe at the singular opportunities I had been privileged to enjoy. Even more than sixteen years later many people ask me if I miss the life and the answer is always a firm, No. You must know when it is time to move on – there is so much more to do.

With Megs at Government House, Canberra, after being sworn in as Minister for Communications and the Arts, March 1996

With Amy and Nick, Sydney, 2001

Sheila and Bob Alston picnicking in car park at Flemington, 1970s

Top: MV Gudrun Bakke, *a general cargo vessel, whose crew I joined to sail the Pacific*

Bottom: Gudrun Bakke's *pop-up swimming pool, 1961*

*With Nelson Mandela at inauguration of Thabo Mbeki as President of the
Republic of South Africa, Pretoria, 1999*

Sartorially threatening Gough Whitlam at the Sydney Opera House, 1994

HON. E. G. WHITLAM, AC, QC

100 WILLIAM STREET
SYDNEY NSW 2011

TELEPHONE
(02) 358 2022

FACSIMILE
(02) 358 2753

5 September 1994

Senator Richard Alston
2nd Floor, Iloura Plaza
424 St Kilda Road
MELBOURNE VIC. 3004

Dear Richard

I crave clarification of our Kennedy connection.

Susan's father Clarrie ("Mick") Maddocks was the son of my mother's eldest brother. Margaret and I met her and her husband Michael Kennedy at the Asian Development Bank on 11 February 1974. I was last in touch with her about half a dozen years ago, when her mother died. I believe they have four children, Lizzie, Tom, Anna and Sam. Her father's sister tells me that she is now married to Sergei Alexeroff, - spelling? -, a doctor from Russia.

I must check before I next attend a first night at the Opera in Sydney; I had not previously felt sartorially threatened by a shadow minister for the arts.

Regards
Gough Whitlam

Valued correspondence: Dear Richard . . . Regards Gough Whitlam,
September 1994

With John Howard at Lord's, First Ashes Test, July 2005

John Howard launches the Party's arts policy, Arts For Art's Sake, *during 1996 election campaign*

At RAAF Memorial, Reykjavik, Iceland, 2002, with Helen Williams, Secretary, Department of Communications, Information Technology and the Arts, and David Quilty, Chief of Staff

Dick– I like the later versions of your mobile phone towers better than this one!

— spotted between Coonamble & Gulargambone, NSW — August 2003. Best wishes! John Anderson

Customer feedback from John Anderson, Deputy Prime Minister, August 2003

The fruit of SILENCE is Prayer
The fruit of PRAYER is Faith
The fruit of FAITH is Love
The fruit of LOVE is Service
The fruit of SERVICE is Peace

Mother Teresa

PRINTED AS A GIFT TO THE MISSIONARIES OF CHARITY
BY THE KNIGHTS OF COLUMBUS

*Mother Teresa's business card which she gave to me at Home for the Dying
in Calcutta, November 1993*

North-West Frontier Province, Peshawar, Pakistan, 1991

Goat tree, Marrakech-Essaouira Road, Morocco, 2016

Inimitable warning signs, Bollywood film studios, Mumbai,1998

Painting of a porter in souk, Doha, Qatar

6

Leadership

In the modern era, replete with all forms of mass communication, political leadership is more important than ever. History suggests that it has ever been thus – Pericles, Alexander the Great, Julius Caesar, Queen Elizabeth I, Catherine the Great, Napoleon Bonaparte, George Washington, Abraham Lincoln, Franklin D Roosevelt, Winston Churchill, General de Gaulle, Ronald Reagan, Margaret Thatcher and Pope John Paul II. These were outstanding figures who loomed large over the historical landscape, giving weight to what used to be known as "the great man theory" of history. This holds that history can largely be explained, not by major events, but by the impact of highly influential individuals who use their power in ways that have a decisive impact.

There are, of course, some really bad men of history, such as Attila the Hun, Caligula, Nero, Genghis Khan, Adolf Hitler, Joseph Stalin, Idi Amin and Kim Il Sung – all autocrats who used command and control techniques, backed by fear, to coerce and terrorise their subjects.

Someone like Margaret Thatcher was able to inspire fear and respect in equal measure, but she also projected a grand vision, an iron will and supreme confidence. She was a deeply polarising figure, a hero to many in the more prosperous and reform minded south of the country, a hate figure to others, especially in the struggling north, where thousands of jobs were lost on the altar of reform and restructure of the national economy. It is in the nature of politics that there will always be strong views on either side of a powerful leader. The political judgments and voting behaviour of many citizens are heavily based on their assessment of political leaders, who ultimately become powerful representative symbols of their party and, more broadly, their nation. An American citizen voting in the 2018 mid-terms would think "Trump" before "Republican" every time. The party becomes synonymous with the leader, notwithstanding many underlying differences.

Successful leaders in modern democracies need more subtlety to succeed, and much more than blind ambition. Nowadays, in fully fledged democracies, voters have immediate access, through radio, print, television and social media, to every word and move of politicians. The persona, performance and personality of a political leader are crucial factors; trust is perhaps the most important factor of all. Even those who hate Donald Trump as a person might trust him to stand firm and deliver.

In this touchy-feely age, conviction politicians are at risk of being dismissed as ideologues or hard line right wingers. But voters should not be underestimated. They do have respect for those who stand for something, even if they may disagree with that particular something. Time and again pollsters elicited admiration for John Howard as a man of principle, particularly after his courageous stand on gun control, when he persuaded his National Party colleagues to stand firm on a difficult reform. By his own assessment a major proposal has to pass two tests: it has to be in the national interest and it has to be fair. When he reversed his hitherto staunch opposition to a GST, and duly took it to an election containing a major compensation package, many said: " I don't want a new tax, so why is he, of all people, proposing this"? Answering their own question, they said: "Maybe he's right, it would be good for the country". So, many just held their noses and voted for him.

The successful leader will be one who can reach out and accommodate those who are not necessarily of the same world-view. Since the emergence of the modern political party, most successful leaders have come from the right of both major parties. In the modern Australian era, think Menzies, Hawke, Keating and Howard. This is usually because, unless a leader has a firm grip on economics, and not just social issues, proper consideration will not be given to running a successful economy, the ultimate requirement for sustained political success. Most right-of-centre leaders understand that a sound economy is a condition precedent to the successful funding of major projects like the Gonski education package and the National Disability Insurance Scheme. Wealth accumulation makes effective protection of the environment affordable. It is very easy to advocate ever more increases in welfare programs, but not only is this likely to be counter-productive in policy terms, but in the long run probably unaffordable without higher taxes – not the way to build a sound economy.

Gough Whitlam could be an inspiring orator and a charming companion, but he subsequently admitted that economics was not his long suit and he was marked down accordingly. There are only a few fundamentally moral issues in politics – abortion and euthanasia are prime examples, but it is not an uncommon practice to raise the political stakes by characterising an issue as such. Kevin Rudd's attempt to wrap climate change in a moral cloak is a recent, conspicuous example.

Some leaders have made a career out of attempting to portray opponents as lacking in moral purpose. William Gladstone and Woodrow Wilson come to mind. For those who are fanatics on a subject, almost anything can become a moral issue. These days, when society is increasingly secular and sceptical of organised religion, such calls no longer have the same impact as they might have had a century or two ago.

To some extent the desire for spiritual values has been replaced by the pursuit of social justice issues, which provide endless opportunities for those less interested in economic issues. We are all familiar with the rhetorical excesses of some in the green movement, who constantly claim that we are nearing the end of days unless we completely change our lifestyle, our consumption patterns, our materialist obsessions, but who never acknowledge that the political system is constantly responding to real problems and crises, although it almost always discounts doom and gloom prognostications.

According to *Leadership*, the latest work by renowned American historian Doris Kearns Goodwin, the vital qualities are intelligence, energy, empathy, verbal and written gifts, and skills in dealing with people. A fierce ambition and an inordinate drive to succeed, combined with perseverance and hard work, are also important attributes.

Speechmaking is an ancient art form but, interestingly, Goodwin's checklist does not include any direct mention of oratorical skills. It is easy to be seduced by rhetoric. Barack Obama's book, *The Audacity of Hope: Thoughts on Reclaiming the American Dream*, released in the lead-up to his achieving the Democrat nomination for President in June 2008, immediately became a best seller. But while it may have fulfilled its primary purpose of inspiring his supporters and propelling him to ultimate victory, it is unlikely to be seen as one of his lasting achievements – more a moment than a monument. Rhetoric can be a part of the political armoury, but it should never be its raison d'etre. In politics it is mostly deeds, not words, that count. Ultimately, substance beats emotion, as William Jennings Bryan found out in losing three presidential contests.

The Mesopotamians and early Egyptians both valued the ability to speak with eloquence and wisdom, but the two concepts are very different. In the city state of Athens, birthplace of democracy, effective public speaking was essential for success in public life and the same is largely true today. Both Plato and Aristotle, who saw rhetoric as the art of persuasion, condemned the Sophists for relying solely on emotion to persuade an audience. In early Rome, orators and writers depended more on stylistic flourishes, riveting stories and compelling metaphors. It was the great statesman, Marcus Tullius Cicero, who emphasised the importance of a rounded education, drawing on an extensive knowledge of history, politics, art, ethics, law and medicine.

Skill in dealing with people is particularly important. Don't take your supporters for granted and always be polite to your enemies! It is rare to have real friends while in the political arena. Everyone has their own agenda, and many are ultimately biddable – if treated badly, or just ignored, quite capable of changing allegiances. Ultimately sustained success requires it to be a collegial vocation and it is critical that all pull together, especially as an election approaches. As Bob Hawke once famously said: "If you can't govern yourself, you can't govern the country".

Paul Keating

Keating possessed some admirable qualities. In his prime, mostly as Treasurer, he was an inveterate risk taker and high voltage performer. His command of the cutting, often cruel phrase caused one of his own colleagues to label him "a trained political killer", which was probably close to the mark. Having left school at fifteen, he was an auto-didact with a very quick mind and a fascination for breakthrough policy initiatives. His fatal flaw was hubris and his post-parliamentary reputation has suffered from his having a bad case of chips on both shoulders. I have heard him start to make a very powerful speech only to default to solipsism: only he had achieved anything worthwhile – a giant amongst pygmies. Howard was just minding the shop, which was decked out with Keating trophies. Poor old Bob Hawke had been little more than an interested bystander.

I once had the dubious pleasure of sitting beside him on a one hour flight, having to endure a non-stop monologue about how he had single-handedly invented a flawless superannuation system. Keating often gave the impression that he regarded most of the population, and certainly nearly all of his parliamentary colleagues, as being of relatively modest intelligence, and conspicuously beneath his own high cultural standards.

Bob Hawke

Hawke, on the other hand, thrived on public adulation and was always very much at home mingling with the crowd. His Oxford days will forever be remembered for two things: being a Rhodes scholar and being a fast beer drinker and he put both achievements to good use in later years. Saying after our historic America's Cup victory in 1983 that "any employer who doesn't give his workers a day off is a bum" struck just the right note.

Unlike Keating's saturnine countenance, Hawke had an infectious joie de vivre. I always got on well with him. He was very interested in the battle of ideas. Unlike Keating, who instinctively hated Liberals, he was neither an ideologue nor a tribal warrior. Even before I entered politics, but after he became Prime Minister, his generosity of spirit was exemplified by an endorsement he wrote on a booklet summarising the proceedings of a seminar I had organised on Industrial Relations in my capacity as Chairman of the Victorian Division of the Australian Institute of Political Science: "To Richard With best wishes and many thanks for your consistent contribution to national debate in our country."

The morning after our narrow win in the 1998 election I was at Canberra airport with my colleagues Peter Reith and Peter Costello, having fulfilled our respective media duties in the National Tally Room the previous evening. Hawke, wife Blanche in tow, suddenly entered the room. Bob came straight over to us, happy to join in our informal post-mortem: "You bastards probably deserved to win....", but before he could say any more he was interrupted by a furious Blanche in a strident tone: "Bob, how can you even think of talking to those people today". He began to wave her away, but soon decided that discretion was the better part of valour.

Another time, when Megs and I had come from London for the Melbourne Commonwealth Games, we were in Canberra for a formal dinner in the Great Hall of Parliament House with the Queen as guest of honour. For some unknown reason a small group asked if they could be photographed with me. But before the camera could click, Bob Hawke appeared from nowhere, put his arm around my shoulder, and said: "I'll be in this". He loved mixing with ordinary people and his rapport was infectious.

He clearly had the knack of dealing with all-comers, especially recalcitrant ministers and other thrusters around the Cabinet table, earning himself a reputation as a great chairman of the board. This probably understated his efforts. He entered Parliament late, but he came well prepared, having led the ACTU for many years, been on the Reserve Bank board and a member of both the Jackson and Crawford committees of enquiry.

Even in his later years, long after he had left Parliament, I remember a cartoon which said it all: Bob and Blanche were walking along the footpath when someone on the other side of the road waved to him. He immediately turned to his wife, saying: "Pardon me a moment, Blanche, while I resume my love affair with the Australian people".

The Master: John Winston Howard

John Howard presents a fascinating study in leadership. It does not take long to see that he possessed every attribute on Doris

LEADERSHIP

Goodwin's list. I have had the opportunity to observe him in context at fairly close quarters for over thirty years. During my time in public life I have had dealings with eleven Australian prime ministers, as well as meetings with Thatcher, Major, Blair, Brown and Cameron in the United Kingdom, a few Presidents of the United States and more than forty State premiers.

As we all know, there has been a revolving door of prime ministers since John Howard's departure more than a decade ago. Many reasons can be advanced for this, including general incompetence, treachery and political failure. It is convenient to ignore the fact that Australia's Constitution and political structure were deliberately designed to enable such changes to occur, unlike the US system, where the leader is virtually guaranteed a fixed four year term. It is sometimes remarked that a tax system breathes through its loopholes – in the same way our political system contains mechanisms for injecting some fresh air into the body politic. The Coalition would almost certainly not have won the 2019 election without the belated change to Scott Morrison. Leadership instability is nothing new. The first ten years after Federation saw no fewer than five prime ministers, one of whom had three brief terms. Three of these had held the post for less than a year. The relatively long-serving governments of Hughes, Bruce, Lyons, Menzies, Fraser, Hawke and Howard are the outliers in Australian political history.

The bottom line in each of the recent changes of the guard is that the majority of members of each of the major parliamentary parties considered that they were at serious risk of losing their seats and/or the next election under their current leader. This is an entirely appropriate and necessary basis for readjustment if a party wishes to recover, prosper and stay in government. Parliamentarians themselves are the best judges of who should be their leader as they understand the political dynamics of the process and the consequences of major policy decisions. Allowing the party faithful to make or participate in leadership decisions is not likely to deliver the best outcome, as they are more likely to be influenced by what they hear or read in the newspaper – usually a very unreliable, and certainly only a partial, guide. For example, Malcolm Turnbull's so-called popularity in large measure stemmed from

113

the fact that many voters were very comfortable to have him in situ but did not have any intention of voting for him.

The real reason why Howard ruled for almost 12 years without any serious challenge, until at the very end, was because of how he applied himself to the job. He not only knew what was required, but he enjoyed every moment of it. In contrast, Turnbull seemed to hate every minute of it, except when abroad, and saw himself as above the fray. I knew Rudd reasonably well when he was in opposition and always found him quite sensible and amusing. But clearly the top job went to his head almost immediately and it was not long before his colleagues found him unbearable.

There is always an element of luck and timing in ascending to the top. It is conventional wisdom, but supported by the record, that to become Leader of the Opposition immediately after your party has had a long period in government almost ensures that such person will not lead the party when it next returns to office. Brendan Nelson knew this but was undeterred when he sought the leadership in 2007 following the defeat of the Howard Government, perhaps seeing it as his only chance. Turnbull, on the other hand, was so desperate he would not contemplate passing up any opportunity.

First time around as Leader of the Opposition, Howard was up against a still very popular Bob Hawke, so he was clearly the underdog. Ultimately, however, Howard's great advantage was that he rose to the top not only after a long period of Labor government but when Paul Keating was clearly past his prime. This proposition can be overstated, as it should also be pointed out that Alexander Downer became Opposition leader when Labor had been in office for more than eleven years, but he never looked like succeeding against a ruthless and still energetic Paul Keating.

Howard, on his second attempt, despite the scepticism of the media, impressed with common sense and determination, and some key policies, marking him out as the polar opposite to the flamboyant, but increasingly tired and irritable, Keating. Hindsight had taught his side of politics that, in 1993, it had taken too many quite radical policies to the electorate, which found them too much to digest. In 1996 we narrowed our focus – this was not

LEADERSHIP

what the media liked to dismiss as a "small target" strategy, implying that we were just sitting back, hoping to tip toe into government. Rather, it was the execution of a carefully crafted, calibrated approach.

It was all about offering a digestible number of well-crafted policies with which the public could identify, such as using the proceeds of sale of Telstra for a nation-building roll out of world class rural and regional telecommunications infrastructure, plus a $1 billion environmentally-friendly package. Whilst policies are very important, at the end of the day it is the public's judgment of the character and offering of the putative prime minister that makes the difference. L-plate Latham was just too big a risk.

Many negative epithets and much personal abuse had been hurled at Howard during his almost twenty-two years in Parliament before he succeeded to the prime ministership. Given that he held the position for nearly twelve years, and became Australia's second longest serving PM, the constant stream of abuse and denigration was, in some ways, a re-run of the old refrain: "you'll never win with Menzies," which had dogged our longest serving PM in his wilderness years. In other words, political opprobrium goes with the turf.

Apart from the predictable partisanship involved in the treatment of both Liberal Party giants, the media's reflex action is to criticise. To attract readers, viewers and listeners, it is necessary to provide new and interesting happenings, sometimes quirky and outrageous. They are always on the lookout for failings and weaknesses in politicians and not above blowing up a minor lapse in etiquette, let alone a politically incorrect statement, into "a monumental gaffe". The whole concept of being "telegenic" is also alive and well, so that a big strapping individual will often be portrayed as more authoritative than more diminutive brethren.

Howard could never be accused of using soaring rhetoric, but that was very much to his credit. When he said, on the verge of coming to government, that his aspiration for Australians was "to be relaxed and comfortable," many commentators fell about, jeering that he was displaying an appalling lack of vision. But what he was doing was demonstrating to ordinary Australians that

115

he knew what their priorities were. This was a man they could trust, who would not try to bamboozle them with fancy words and phrases but would focus on what mattered to them. His plain language was not only easy to understand, but sincere and persuasive. It resonated with those who count – the electors, if not the media.

Cicero's canons

It is instructive to consider how Howard performed in terms of Cicero's five canons of classical rhetoric:

- **Invention** – the ability to develop and refine an argument: he did not use big words or flowery language, but he did address the interests of his audience in words they could understand and appreciate.
- **Arrangement** – organising arguments for maximum effect: his narrative flowed carefully, logically, unhastily.
- **Style** – how to present your arguments: his deliberately low key presentation was devoid of soaring rhetoric but full of sensible and persuasive nostrums. He did not preach, he simply sought to persuade. He never talked down to his audience nor made them feel guilty.
- **Memory** – delivery without notes: Howard was a master in this regard. Here, again, Menzies was the exemplar. Apart from formal addresses, I never saw Howard once refer to notes, even in the presence of Royalty. Speaking directly to the audience and maintaining eye contact conveys authenticity – anyone can be the author of notes or use an autocue.
- **Delivery** – the how of speechmaking: he did not rely on gestures or hand waving but rather a measured tone, which did not distract from the content.

After he left office he said that "those who triumph politically are those who have not only superior arguments but also the capacity to present those arguments in a compelling fashion", as he often did. Today this concept is captured in the catchcry about "narrative".

John Fitzgerald Kennedy will go down in history as the deliverer, if not the author, of some elegant phrases, such as: "My fellow Americans, ask not what your country can do for you, ask what you can do for your country." Such inspirational rhetoric strikes a chord with us all, but ultimately weighs lightly in the scales which measure performance. Keating was the master of vitriol which was always lapped up by the media, if not by the public, but his reputational longevity rests largely on his achievements, particularly as Treasurer. Working closely in tandem with his leader, Bob Hawke, they successfully modernised the Australian economy and later, as Prime Minister, he singlehandedly derailed the *Fightback!* freight train and caused us to lose the 1993 "unloseable election". Much in all as it was devastating at the time we learned valuable lessons from that unforgettable experience.

In his own way, Howard uttered words which have had even more enduring significance, and which may well have changed the course of history. I was at the campaign launch in 2001 when he declared: "We are a generous open hearted people, taking more refugees per capita than any nation except Canada. We have a proud record of welcoming people from 140 different nations. But we will decide who comes to this country and the circumstances in which they come."

While the message was steely, no one demurred. These were not meant to be uplifting or inspiring words, but an assertion of the primacy of the rule of law in a democratic society, something which all Australians ultimately treasure. They were also very powerful words, spoken in the heat of an election campaign. They not only went unchallenged politically, but they became a touchstone for the strength of leadership on offer.

Howard is proudly patriotic but understands both Australia's geography and its history. As Josh Frydenberg, both protégé and former adviser, has pointed out, Howard has always appreciated the positive contribution of Western civilisation to our daily life. Howard's assessment that, "Despite what the self-appointed cultural dieticians will tell you, Australia is part of Western civilisation," rings inherently true.

His various adages and aphorisms may be understated by

modern standards of arresting political expression – certainly not in the Keating mould – and did not get wide coverage at the time but are nonetheless critical in understanding his priorities. Some examples:

> The most important civil liberty is to stay alive and to be free from violence and death.
>
> Truth is never disposable in national political life.
>
> I've never believed in lower wages. Never.
>
> The "black armband" view of our history reflects a belief that most Australian history since 1788 has been little more than a disgraceful story of imperialism, exploitation, racism, sexism and other forms of discrimination. I take a very different view. I believe that the balance sheet of our history is one of heroic achievement and that we have achieved much more as a nation of which we can be proud than of which we should be ashamed.
>
> There is much in American society which I admire, but I have long held the view that the absence of an effective safety net in that country means that too many fall by the wayside. That is not the path that Australia will tread. Nor do we want the burdens of the nanny state that now weigh down many economies in Europe.
>
> We spent too much time in the first half of the nineties pondering whether we had to become less European, so we could become more Asian. We had this perpetual seminar on our national identity. I never thought Australians had any doubt as to what their identity was.
>
> And I think we've moved on from all that.

Howard also had some sage political advice for his colleagues, which remains pertinent today: "Leadership of the Liberal Party is a great honour, of which I am profoundly conscious. It is, moreover, the unique gift of the party room". Malcolm Turnbull still has great difficulty in grasping this proposition. This is especially surprising, as he orchestrated the party room downfall of two leaders.

In recent years prime ministers like Rudd and Turnbull have prided themselves on being party outsiders, not beholden to powerbrokers or tribal pieties – more in the Tony Blair mould. But no one could mistake Howard's inner spirit. His upbringing was lower middle class and he was proud of it. In many ways he himself was the archetypal Howard battler. While he was still in his teens his father died of chronic bronchitis, a legacy of fighting on the Western Front in the First World War. The son has been a lifelong adult member of the Liberal Party and remains both proud and respectful of it. No fancy airs and graces and no outsized ego, unlike many of his political contemporaries. Hubris is the ultimate sin in politics, but he has never been boastful or self-important. None of the vainglory of a Rudd or a Turnbull.

Howard ultimately became the epitome of a successful leader, but only after enduring many trials and tribulations. He had entered the House of Representatives during the Whitlam years at the relatively young age of 34, having served time in the organisation, where he had been a vice-president of the NSW Division. His first term as leader (1985-89) during his titanic struggle with Andrew Peacock, the glamorous Colt from Kooyong, was not very successful. The 1987 election campaign was fatally derailed by the "Joh for Canberra" bandwagon, which led to unravelling of the coalition with the National Party, one of the few occasions in the nearly 100 years since the formation of the Country Party in 1920.

After losing the leadership in 1989, he spent some six years out of favour but, still a formidable advocate of Coalition policies in Parliament and the media, he refused to throw in the towel. Unlike others, who couldn't contain their outrage at being unceremoniously deposed, he used his time quietly and constructively, always a team player. With hindsight, we can see that this was the measure of the man. A deep student of Liberal history, he well knew the Menzies comeback story and, indeed, that of Churchill's barren years as a political pariah. He fervently shared Churchill's view of democracy as the worst form of government, except for everything else. He was a quintessentially political creature and would not settle for anything less. Menzies and Howard learned some painful lessons from their setbacks but both were the better for it. An ultra-wealthy American patriarch once told his sons: "Remember that often adversity is a blessing in disguise and is certainly the greatest character builder."

MORE TO LIFE THAN POLITICS?

Persistence is an invaluable attribute, especially in politics, where career setbacks at some stage are almost inevitable. Many aspiring politicians give in prematurely – others just keep on keeping on. Lindsay Thompson, Australia's longest serving Education Minister and later Victorian State Premier, and the finest of human beings, tried at least a dozen times before winning a safe seat. Unlike Peter Costello and John Hewson, Howard was prepared to endure a prolonged period in the political wilderness (not quite as long as Churchill in the 1930s, who did not win an election as leader until he was over 75). After losing the top job in 1941, Menzies could have resumed his glittering legal career, but persisted, and went on to political immortality. As Woody Allen once said: "90 per cent of success in life is just turning up". Well, almost.

Howard's re-incarnation was a revelation, a wonder to behold. Last man standing after Hewson's demise and Downer's resignation, he took over at a propitious time, with Keating's star very much on the wane, even though he was some years younger than his new opponent. Unlike Kim Beazley, who kept coming back simply to pick up where he had left off, Howard had used his time in exile wisely. Always on top of policy, he had now mastered the art of bringing disparate forces together.

People skills are a crucial, but often overlooked, aspect of leadership. The media loves to portray the Liberal Party as riven by almost irreconcilable conservative versus "progressive" schisms. But while diverse ideological impulses are present in all parties, the ultimate success of that party will largely depend on its leader's ability to weave the strands together. Hence Howard's almost-obsession with "the broad church". A leader also has to be prepared to confront emerging problems head on – to lance the boil, as Sir Les Patterson, one of Barry Humphries' best creations, would say.

Once at the top there was a certain calmness about John Howard. His long experience had solidified into political wisdom. He had seen it all, and instinctively knew the right response. This not only inspired confidence in his own followers but fundamentally wrong-footed his opponents, who took a long time to learn that the press caricatures of "Little Johnny" were far from the truth.

120

He was living proof of the desirability of successful leaders having had extensive parliamentary experience before gaining the top job. Sometimes, as in his case and that of Paul Keating, the long wait is enforced by a lengthy period in opposition. Although Scott Morrison had a relatively quick eleven-year rise, he had already held a number of senior Cabinet positions, including, crucially, Treasurer. In stark contrast, Rudd had never been in Cabinet before he became prime minister and Gillard had served in Cabinet for less than three years, but, even then, much of it seemed to be spent polishing her image and plotting for the top job. Neither of them had any serious economic experience.

A standout feature of the Howard Cabinet was the overriding harmony that almost always prevailed. Whilst the broad church contained clearly identified adherents of both conservative and moderate inclinations, I never saw any indication of a factional line being pursued. I had learned early that the sensible approach was to go into the Cabinet room with a preferred line of thinking, but to be prepared to listen to and, if necessary, be persuaded by, the logic of the arguments around the table. Some took a while to learn this. I recall two occasions when newly-arrived Cabinet members made plain, during the course of a debate, their deep disappointment that people they had spoken to beforehand were not supporting them in Cabinet. They were both very fast learners and went on to hold very senior positions in the hierarchy.

There was only one time when I did speak to several colleagues before a Cabinet meeting. This was to seek support for my submission seeking funds to promote the cause of venture capital, private equity and innovation. I knew that the Prime Minister's approach was likely to be subdued because one of his sons was working for a hedge fund. I also knew that Peter Costello, the Treasurer, was likely to be opposed in principle to any proposal to spend money. On this occasion, however, my lobbying was successful. More importantly, there were no leaks to colleagues or the media to the effect that the Prime Minister and the Treasurer had not prevailed. In my view, the main reason why the Cabinet process operated so effectively was that the Prime Minister was in total control, albeit with a light touch, and no one for a moment wanted to disrupt the status quo.

Howard's temperament was a major strength. As he himself has said: "You've got to have the capacity to deal with a whole lot of 'things at once". In my experience, that was part of the joy of the journey. He had a strong work ethic and an innate sense of self-belief. During my seven and a half years in the Parliamentary Leadership Group in Government, I met with him every day while we were in Canberra. I never heard him swear or lose his temper. Indeed, quite the opposite – he was always composed and nearly always had time to discuss policy as well as political matters. He had an uncanny ability to quickly master complex issues and details but was never too proud to seek advice from a range of experts. He had a good sense of humour and never let his ego take over. On the contrary, he was always extremely patient and courteous towards others, and I still have to remind myself not to talk over him.

As Greg Sheridan says of him in *God is Good for You*: "underlying everything (was) a certain courtesy and decency in the way he treats people". My former Senate colleague and good friend, Rod Kemp, recalls telephoning Howard to see whether, as Prime Minister, he would be prepared to be at Sydney airport at 5.30 am to welcome home our special Olympians. Without hesitation Howard agreed to do so. He not only turned up but arranged to have his photo taken individually with each one, after which he made a very moving speech. None of this was for the benefit of the press and has probably remained a well-kept public secret to this day.

Recently a regional newspaper proprietor told me of a meeting of the NSW Country Press Association at which John Howard, as Prime Minister, was the guest speaker. As is often the case, guest speakers are wont to depart promptly for another "pressing engagement". Instead, Howard offered to stay back and discuss any issues of concern. When the vexed issue of the cross media rules arose, instead of a passionate defence of his position, he listened politely before saying: "if you can convince the Communications Minister I am happy to be persuaded".

I was always struck by his unwavering political self-discipline.

LEADERSHIP

Courteous and civil at all times, even to those whom he was entitled to regard as "unhelpful", or worse. He always chose his words carefully, especially in the Party room, which he knew was prone to leak. He could convey his sentiments with a hand gesture or a lifted eyebrow, which made his message leak-proof.

I would often go to his office to get his thoughts or guidance on a pressing matter. After quickly grasping the essentials, he would make a helpful and constructive suggestion before taking the political temperature. His desk was always bare – no paperwork in sight, but newspapers close by. He gave ministers full rein and backed them to the hilt until they self-destructed or otherwise lost their way. On one occasion, when I had unintentionally upset Senator Harradine over a privatisation issue, he called to tell me that he would need to say publicly that he had called me but was otherwise very supportive. Even during my, at times, uncivil war with the ABC, chaired by one of his best friends, Donald McDonald, he never chastised me, nor called me in.

A great measure of his integrity came when I was trying to cajole Mal Colston, the renegade Queensland Labor senator turned independent, to support our second tranche of the Telstra privatisation project. Labor kept running the line that Colston was a serial expenses cheat and, therefore, in good conscience, we should not take his vote. Eventually Howard took the very momentous, and politically disadvantageous, decision not to accept his vote. Labor not only had no compunction in doing so but were serial offenders on this score, as they later proved, when they had no hesitation in taking the votes of the discredited Peter Slipper and Craig Thompson.

A significant example of his complete professionalism was his habit of regularly lunching with colleagues in the Parliament House dining room before Question Time. The rest of his ministers spent the time ensconced in their offices, frantically swotting up on possible issues or preparing clever answers, but he was happy to conduct his preparation earlier, no doubt confident that his prodigious memory would see him through the ordeal ahead. As an avid student of history and politics he had an amazing recall of long forgotten political milestones, events and sayings. I have heard it said

123

that when he and his brothers exchanged Christmas presents they usually gave each other books on history and politics.

Since he left the Parliament following the 2007 defeat (involuntarily in his case) he has maintained the same outlook and demeanour. He remains an invaluable mentor to many of his colleagues, past and present, and, like many others, I continue to seek his advice, invariably given graciously and always extremely helpful. No-one campaigned more diligently for the return of the Morrison Government at the 2019 election.

Looking back on those years it is hard not to feel blessed by time and circumstance. In many ways it now looks like a golden era. Howard turned out to be a magnificent leader and history will certainly recognise his many achievements, among them gun control, waterfront reform (in partnership with a very determined Peter Reith), the GST and the liberation of East Timor. All were contentious issues, hard fought all the way – none more so than his deft dealing with the *Tampa* and children overboard crises and the most momentous issue of all, the Iraq War of 2003. It is worth recording that every member of Cabinet took this grave responsibility very seriously and was given every opportunity to speak up, for or against. Ultimately it was a unanimous decision to commit the nation to stand firm alongside the US and the UK. Based on the information available at the time, it was clearly the correct decision.

Howard's overarching achievement was to pursue a range of economy-related reforms which helped to boost productivity and national income. These included the Charter of Budget Honesty, independence for the Reserve Bank in setting interest rates, a new Work for the Dole scheme, Welfare to Work reforms, private health care incentives, outsourcing of employment services to a new Job Network, and centralising government transfer payments and welfare services under Centrelink. The public service underwent similar efficiency enhancing reforms, such as streamlining government procurement programs and restructuring the Productivity Commission. All of these have stood the test of time.

These initiatives and more put the economy back on a solid foundation, with budget surpluses in every year but one. His commitment at the very outset was forceful and immediately demonstrated his priorities. When we came to government we inherited a $10 billion budget deficit and a national debt of $96 billion. The safe course would have been to commit to gradual and steady reductions, but he knew that the first year of the electoral cycle was the best for hard reform. So he bit the bullet by imposing an immediate 10 per cent cut on the spending of all departments and agencies except Defence. Despite all the confected outrage which inevitably greeted this decision (the loudest squeals of all coming from the ABC, which acted as though it alone had been singled out for special treatment), subsequent polls showed it to be a very popular decision – a just reward for political courage.

By the time the national debt had been fully paid off, Australia was one of only two or three countries to be in the "no debt" position. Howard's foresight and persistence set the country up for its world record run – 29 years and counting – of continuous economic growth, as well as equipping it to withstand the Global Financial Crisis, which materialised barely a year after he had left office.

What I learned from watching Howard in action was that strong leadership is a product of experience, knowledge, intelligence, intuition, belief, commitment and dedication – a rare mix of individual chemistry, which cannot be learned in management courses or plotting in backrooms. It also requires a sturdy constitution and sober personal habits, with the qualification that in politics there are always exceptions to every rule! Good leadership can inspire others to outperform and set standards that can lift all boats. In *Sovereignty in the 21st Century*, Australian expatriate turned Washington strategist, Greg Copley, provides another key insight: the role of the leader is to "create simultaneous disruption and unity" – a delicate, but vitally important, balancing act at the best of times, but one which Howard accomplished with manifest dexterity.

Howard's mission was to haul the Australian economy back to the centre and away from the big spending era of the Labor years. His social and moral conservatism went down well in middle Australia, where the aspirational Howard "battlers" were not into the latest "progressive" instincts and were more than happy to settle for a sound economy. As he often said: "The punters may not always agree with you, but they know where you stand". His ability to relate to ordinary Australians was a crucial asset and critical to his success. More a persuader than an orator, speaking without notes, as he always did, meant that this authenticity and sincerity captured the hearts and minds of many of those who mattered most – the voters.

The apprentices: Abbott and Turnbull

Whilst Tony Abbott was in some ways the architect of a number of his own misfortunes and was still coming to grips with the complexities of the responsibilities of prime minister when he was forcibly displaced, he already had some impressive achievements in policy terms. These included three big ticket items: repeal of both Labor's carbon and mining taxes, and *Operation Border Control.* Stopping the boats – they all said it couldn't be done but, with the invaluable assistance of Immigration Ministers Scott Morrison and, later, Peter Dutton, he did. He also signed off on historic free trade agreements with China, Japan and South Korea. But his first "crash through" budget crashed against an unco-operative Senate cross bench, in the midst of widespread accusations of broken promises. It has quickly become a conventional left wing narrative that he was a very combative and ultimately successful Leader of the Opposition, but that those tactics were singularly inappropriate in government. After all, Abbott himself had said: "Opposition is 90 per cent politics, Government 10 per cent". The reality is that effective leadership requires a steely determination to prevail in what is a remorseless and, at times, brutal contest. It was a Liberal tragedy that his successor, Malcolm Turnbull, utterly failed to appreciate this basic fact and seemed instinctively to shy away from confrontation at every opportunity.

It is one of the great enigmas of the Abbott period in office that, although he studied economics and law at Sydney University and, later, Philosophy, Politics and Economics at Oxford, and was always an ambitious political animal, he was basically not interested in economics or public finance. The culture wars were more his thing. He has a deep spiritual dimension, but he was certainly not the religious fanatic that some liked to claim. While he did not have a woman problem, his refusal to replace Sophie Mirabella (a shadow minister defeated at the 2013 election) with a woman, and later not to include any more in Cabinet, was a basic political misjudgment.

There is no doubt that Abbott admired and respected John Howard whom he rightly regarded as his mentor. But once he ascended to the highest office he found it difficult to seek, let alone take, the master's advice. As an unchallenged statesman and living legend of the Liberal Party, Howard had nothing to prove and no axes to grind, having accepted his forcible dislodgement from Parliament with grace and equanimity. No post-election tears in the manner of Malcolm Fraser who was, at the time he lost office, like Howard, the second longest serving Prime Minister. Howard knew he had had a great run, but he also knew that even great runs have to come to an end. His wise counsel was always going to be objective and designed to be helpful. But Abbott was curiously reluctant, especially towards the end of his tenure, to accept advice on the two most critical personality issues of his two years in office, the roles of his chief of staff, Peta Credlin, and his hand-picked Treasurer, Joe Hockey.

Peta Credlin had worked as a policy adviser for me in the early stages of her time as a political staffer. I found her very capable and easy to work with but, when I saw her in action a decade later, the transformation was extraordinary. She had blossomed into a very impressive and formidable all-rounder. On several occasions I attended small dinners where the PM would defer to her on policy issues, and she was immediately in command of every detail, impressing most, but frustrating others, who had come along to hear the PM's own views. I do not blame her for this – she was simply doing what she was asked to do, and doing it very well. This was not a practice I had ever witnessed before so I quickly realised that he depended greatly on her. But it was an uncomfortable combination for a number of the PM's colleagues who saw her gatekeeper role as a firewall barring access to their leader.

I do not pretend to know the rights and wrongs of the avalanche of media criticism to which she became increasingly subject on an almost daily basis. I suspect the issue was being whipped up by others who were using her as a pawn in a deadly game of regime change. There was no doubt, however, that with the passage of time her position, behaviour and influence became a white hot issue in the media and she was being asked to play a role no staffer should fill. Once the widespread perception of a dysfunctional office took hold firm action was required. The politics of politics is inevitably played out in the media, which is where the punters get their news and views. If the media consistently conveys the impression that you are in big trouble, you almost certainly are.

Being in denial is not a winning strategy. I remember in Howard's first term as Opposition Leader, his chief of staff, Nicole Feely, became almost a celebrity in her own right and she had to go. Similarly, shortly after Howard became Prime Minister, when his loyal and long serving chief of staff, Graeme Morris, became embroiled in controversy, he quickly fell on his sword. Nothing of the sort was ever contemplated by Abbott to cauterise the damage being done to the reputations of himself and his chief of staff. There were a few desultory attempts to withdraw from the limelight, such as no longer attending Cabinet meetings, which had been an unprecedented occurrence, entirely the responsibility of the Prime Minister.

As Federal President of the Liberal Party I met regularly with Tony Abbott as Prime Minister, but when the Hockey name was mentioned he simply went into his shell, not prepared to argue the case for his retention and loath to contemplate any alternatives. He was doggedly determined not to contemplate the two obvious replacements – Turnbull, whom he simply didn't trust – not without reason; or Scott Morrison, who seemed to be the obvious replacement, filling a critical economics knowledge gap at the top. Perhaps he felt guilty for forcing Hockey to deliver a "crash through or crash" budget, always doomed to failure in a hostile Senate. Part of the answer may be that, as Abbott has said of himself, he was not a natural networker, but a policy person who saw himself as a conviction politician.

He cared passionately for his country and the plight of the poor and downtrodden, especially Indigenous Australians. He involved himself in a plethora of worthwhile community activities. He was a very decent and honourable person – admirable in so many ways, but quite guileless in other ways and not overly familiar with, or even particularly interested in, all the machinations and political manoeuvring, unlike his nemesis, Turnbull. He probably took a few people too much at face value and surrounded himself with unreliable courtiers who did not always have his best interests at heart, while sidelining natural allies like Andrew Robb and Eric Abetz.

Abbott was curiously unwilling to confront people head on, preferring to delegate to others. His unwillingness to dispense with the services of a senior organisational figure, after having promised to do so, caused me not only personal embarrassment but wasted countless hours of valuable pre-election planning time. I forgave him because I knew there was no malice involved. Turnbull, on the other hand, simply disdained opponents.

To his own serious detriment, Abbott too often did not follow the Howard playbook, which required keeping in regular direct contact with colleagues, both ministers and backbenchers. He never understood that this important aspect of leadership cannot be delegated to others. Disaffected ministers and even backbenchers can feel slighted if ignored and can cause immense trouble. Howard, on the other hand, had a keen sense of what a leader must do personally and cannot delegate, in matters great or small.

The daily grind of internal politics did not come easily to Abbott – to Turnbull it came not all. In contrast, for Howard it was his daily bread and butter and he lapped it up. He says himself that he loved every minute of it and it certainly seemed that way. He was the most natural politician I have ever seen, and I have seen quite a few.

The Prince Philip fiasco of January 2015 is regarded in some quarters as the high watermark of Tony Abbott's prime ministerial ineptitude, despite the fact that various ministers and editorials at the time supported the award of an honour. The true story has only since dribbled out in a desultory way, when timely disclosure could have caused him much less political grief and almost certainly have cast him in a much more sympathetic light.

It has been a long standing convention that His Royal Highness, the Duke of Edinburgh, is granted the highest honour avail-

MORE TO LIFE THAN POLITICS?

able in realm (Commonwealth) countries. So when NZ re-introduced knighthoods, John Key's Government was happy to oblige in the Duke's elevation. In a complementary move, Canada, which no longer has knighthoods, appointed him to the Privy Council of Canada; and, in 2015, similarly appointed the Prince of Wales. When the matter was brought to Abbott's attention he would have had no idea of the furore his otherwise appropriate action would provoke. He might, however, have had some premonition that his political opponents would disdain the proprieties and seize the opportunity to denigrate him.

When the New Zealand Government went about re-introduction of knighthoods, it did so with somewhat more political finesse than its cross-Tasman cousin. It first offered all those persons who had already had the highest award the opportunity to convert to a knighthood. What was clever about this was that, as the former Prime Minister, Helen Clark, had been in office for almost nine years, most of the beneficiaries had first received their awards under a Labour administration. So when more than 80 per cent quickly made the conversion, the new arrangements effectively received bipartisan support and thereafter it was not an issue.

But when the issue first erupted in the Australian public arena during the January "silly season", and Bill Shorten and company piled in, perhaps clandestinely aided and abetted by friendly fire from within the Prime Minister's own ranks, it quickly became a cause celebre. Abbott was condemned by virtually all and sundry as self-indulgent and hopelessly out of touch. This was in part an own goal because of the ham-fisted way the new rank of knighthood had been re-introduced, without any New Zealand-style softening up process first and, apparently, without any consultation, even with a few senior colleagues.

Not even the elevation of Quentin Bryce to Dame pacified the outraged. But what we now know is that Tony Abbott was doing no more than following protocol in acting as he did, with due respect for the Queen of Australia. Not to have done so would have looked like studied discourtesy.

Sometime later, at a dinner function at Raheen at which I was present, Abbott was asked about the matter and gave a very de-

130

tailed and candid explanation. Shortly afterwards I took the opportunity to discuss the question with someone I knew well, who had in an earlier life been Principal Private Secretary to one of the senior Royals. It became clear that, once the issue took off, the first thing that should have been done was a discreet backgrounding of the media to let it be known where the real responsibility lay. It would not have been proper for the Prime Minister to go on the public record and be quoted, but for his office simply to provide background information would have been in everyone's best interests.

The fact that Abbott, a former journalist, never thought of doing so is quite mystifying. I can only imagine that he thought that it was somehow not the right thing to do and was seeking to protect the Crown. But it is hard to see how the Queen's office would have quarrelled with such facts being known, particularly when the issue was causing such political grief to the Prime Minister.

The Australian Honours System

The Prince Philip affair exposes a wider issue. The Order of Australia is in serious need of review and overhaul. Individuals can self-nominate, but very few do, for obvious reasons. The Order therefore relies on people being nominated by others, who often do not think of doing so. Nominators, in theory, are strictly forbidden to obtain information from the nominee, who is clearly best placed to provide all the requisite information. Needless to say, this stricture is more honoured in the breach.

On the other hand, there are people, particularly with sufficient wealth, who can engage firms specialising in drafting proposals for recognition. It should not be surprising that academics fare so well in the upper reaches of the Order, given their professional skills and experience gained in the perennial and incessant search for grants and funding. In the 2019 Queen's Birthday honours list 6 of the 12 ACs were academics and, of the AOs, the figure was 28 out of 69! Meanwhile, many good people simply fall through the cracks, unnoticed and unrecognised.

There is a certain piety attached to the supposedly necessary requirement for achievement above and beyond the call of "your

MORE TO LIFE THAN POLITICS?

day job," which is usually taken to mean charitable, community or philanthropic activity. But for those directly involved in the voluntary or charitable sector their work alone is often, almost by definition, deserving of recognition. What about someone like Fred Hollows, whose life giving work was an all-consuming passion? Should some additional extra-curricular generosity have to be demonstrated before receiving recognition? Many business leaders, simply by doing their day job well, make a major contribution to the nation's betterment. Is the position of Prime Minister not per se deserving of high recognition unless, like Paul Keating, they decline it?

If charitable giving is a critical factor, then the system is heavily skewed to the wealthy or their inheritors, who can easily afford to flaunt their generosity by setting up a tax-friendly family foundation, or letting their largesse be known. I have been assured by an impeccably well-placed insider, however, that the committee quite often rejects applicants who rely on such foundations alone. It is also noticeable that some awardees get the highest award for philanthropy, when they are doing little more than giving away other people's money. Perhaps, as it says in the Gospel, they have already had their reward. But what about the quiet achievers who often give considerable amounts to worthy causes privately and even anonymously?

A better test might be: "Has the person under consideration made a significant, high or very high contribution to the nation or the community?" This can be judged objectively, rather than simply relying on sometimes fawning references, and can be verified by normal due diligence or direct contact with the nominee, who is often the only reliable source of information, and could be asked to confirm relevant information as part of the assessment process.

Whilst the Secretariat does do detailed and independent research once it receives a nomination, it should be proactive and not simply respond to nominations. It should have systems to identify people whose public achievements are deserving of recognition and undertake the necessary checks and enquiries. It could still take account of submissions. The Constitution of the Order would have to be changed to reflect such an approach but so be it.

LEADERSHIP

The current system is also open to misrepresentation by recipients as some, particularly those with lower honours, can airily proclaim that they have received an Order of Australia. Moreover, because there are only three senior levels in the community section – Companion (AC), Officer (AO) and Member (AM) of the Order of Australia – there is also a significant disparity in the middle category. Some are, on the face of it, clearly in the wrong category. Two current examples are a long serving deputy prime minister and a fabled business success story and very generous philanthropist. For some unknown reason they have each only received an AO instead of the higher level AC.

Under the old system, a knighthood enabled the public to identify those who had clearly been outstanding contributors to the national welfare and deserving of the highest recognition. Much elite opposition to knighthoods seems to stem from the fact that they derive from ancient British orders of chivalry, and the issue quickly becomes enmeshed in the republic debate. No one seems to have been able to come up with a suitable alternative prefix, but it is perfectly within our national competence to retain the current form with an Australian badge, à la New Zealand, or simply devise a prefix of our own.

The integrity of any honours system rests squarely on awards being based strictly on merit – not political favouritism or, worse, correctness – and not being too generously thrown around or otherwise misused for political purposes. Calls for quotas to boost certain categories run a serious risk of undermining public confidence in the system. Britain has had several scandals over the last hundred years. In the 1920s Prime Minister David Lloyd George established a general tariff for titles including peerages (dubbed "bargain baronets") and even permitted the activities of honours brokers who worked on commission. More recently, Tony Blair's principal fund raiser was nicknamed Lord Cashbox for allegedly similar activities. Over the years such outrages have led to intermittent calls to scrap the House of Lords altogether, which the current Opposition leader, Jeremy Corbyn, has promised to do if elected.

We have had no such problems in Australia at national level, but several States have, at times, thrown up some dubious choices. When I was living in the UK I remember hearing an amusing anecdote about Margaret Thatcher being advised that a certain person was deserving of a peerage because of his sterling efforts. Her short answer was: "No, not yet – he might stop working so hard for us".

Ambition and leadership

A fierce ambition is fine, but it cannot be at the expense of everyone who gets in your way. The truly shocking way Malcolm Turnbull persecuted, pursued and ultimately destroyed Brendan Nelson's leadership was a case study in extreme selfishness. The way he constantly undermined Abbott as PM, with a remorseless guerrilla campaign, was highly organised and ultimately fateful in its intensity. His earlier lethal snipes, aimed at making a name for himself while undermining Howard and Costello, were only the warm up act for later perfidy.

On the vexed question of climate change, Turnbull knew that Australia's best efforts at emissions reductions could make no appreciable difference to global output while major emitters, such as China and India, remained totally uninterested in accepting any concrete limitations on their carbon emission levels until at least 2030.

It was never clear what he hoped to achieve by his commitments to very industry-oppressive emissions trading schemes and the like. We all knew he was obsessed with climate change, but he never spelt out his reasons, leaving the punters bemused and unpersuaded, especially when it seemed his main interest was in lower emissions, not lower energy prices.

This was not leadership. It was much more an exemplary display of virtue signalling. At least Labor advocates would mouth pieties about Australia setting an example and leading the way.

I found Turnbull cold, distant, aloof – transactional rather than empathetic. His failure on election night in 2016 to accept any responsibility for a totally inept campaign or, despite specific advice to do so, even acknowledge, let alone sympathise with, his numerous colleagues who had lost their seats, was a classic example.

Once again, it was all about him, and always the fault of others. I well recall his negative assessment of a key campaign official's performance, which came down to a perceived personal slight he had felt, and which he subsequently recited to me on at least three occasions.

Virtually everyone in Parliament acknowledges that they would not be there but for their party affiliation. Not Turnbull, who obviously believed he succeeded entirely by his own efforts and owed the Liberal Party nothing. Given his enormous self-regard, he probably saw the Liberal Party as a hinderance and a handbrake on his own superior personal brand. Why else did his electorate posters for years proclaim "Turnbull for Wentworth," and his 2016 election messages promote only the "Turnbull Coalition Team"? No mention of Liberal.

It is important to parse intelligence. Turnbull, who presumably has a Mensa level IQ, was almost totally lacking in emotional intelligence in his dealings with non-family members. He clearly had an insatiable desire to succeed, or at least get to the top, but very little idea of what he wanted to achieve. He never spelt out his vision or assiduously argued his case on key issues – he seemed to think one speech was enough. Once he had made a big announcement he was happy to move to the next challenge.

Leadership is also evidenced by a capacity to attract fellow high achievers. It is therefore interesting to see who Turnbull's partners in crime were when he mounted his final assault on Tony Abbott. No one of any seniority or significant parliamentary achievement was on his team – shared ambition, but very little professional political experience.

Leadership is a difficult quality to appraise, or even, identify, as assessments are usually in the eye of the beholder. The media will sometimes urge a politician to show "leadership", when what they really mean is that he or she should defy fundamental instincts and those of mainstream voters and go for the latest fashionable issue, such as advocating a republic.

Bill Clinton was an impressive politician, his charisma in stark contrast to the persona of his wooden spouse. I met him on several occasions, as well as when he joined us in Cabinet and later spoke to both houses of the Australian Parliament. When Newt Gingrich's *Contract With America* revolution steamrollered him in the 1994 midterms he reacted quickly, tightened the welfare system and soon got back on track to re-election. When his waywardness ("a hard dog to keep on the porch") became an issue, many Democrats simply rolled their eyes and said: "but despite that" and continued to support him, whereas many Republicans said: "because of that" and thereafter strongly opposed him. But it was his political pragmatism, as well as his instinctive understanding of middle America, which got him through.

Since I reached adulthood in the early 1960s there have not been very many outstanding world leaders. Churchill had long retired and Menzies was coming to the end of his long reign. Ronald Reagan, derided by many as an amiable buffoon, turned out to have a political will of steel, staring down, and ultimately breaking, the USSR. De Gaulle, having retired in 1946, returned to the fray in 1958 and proceeded to dominate Europe throughout the 1960s.

Nelson Mandela, with whom I had the honour of conversing when I attended the inauguration of his successor, Thabo Mbeki, was the first democratically elected President of South Africa. He is now universally revered as a statesman who, having served 27 years in prison (his cell on Robben Island, which I visited, still stands as a stark memorial to his political courage and endurance), was able to turn the other cheek and preside over a most unlikely transition to majority rule.

Perhaps not surprisingly for a conservative politician from a stable democracy, I would not rate Mao, Castro, Pol Pot or other autocrats of the era very highly. Lee Kwan Yew dominated an ostensible, but relatively corruption-free, democracy. His success in transforming Singapore from a seedy backwater to a global entrepot certainly brought him worldwide recognition and near universal admiration, and his governance model seems to be widely regarded as an inspiration in modern China.

Xi Jinping is rapidly emerging as a global player but, given his new status of president-for-life, he represents a very different leadership model. He is clearly of the Make China Great Again school and can point to a number of impressive economic achievements. Whether this will voluntarily lead to an opening up of the political process remains to be seen.

Margaret Thatcher is now recognised, even sotto voce by erstwhile political opponents, as probably the UK's most successful peacetime leader for the last hundred years. She came to office when Britain was widely regarded as "the sick man of Europe" and she essentially transformed the economy by a series of long overdue measures, such as curbing excessive union power and widespread privatisation. The Iron Lady was certainly possessed of iron will power and I have no doubt that awareness of her substantive achievements will long outlast memories of her prickly personality. A fresh faced Tony Blair, essentially continuing Thatcher's modernisation program, made New Labour electable.

In recent years Helmut Kohl and Angela Merkel have dominated German politics but it is hard to say they have played a major role on the world stage. Similarly, John Howard, Vaclav Havel, Stephen Harper, John Key and Benjamin Netanyahu (still) were immensely successful in their own jurisdictions. If we look for leadership beyond the political arena the three giants who stand out for me are Martin Luther King Jnr, Lech Walesa (for his Solidarity efforts, although he later went into politics), and Pope John Paul II.

Perhaps one of the defining characteristics of real political success at the highest level, as opposed to mere longevity, is almost total immersion in the chosen field. FDR radiated confidence and strength and there was an infectious and ill-disguised enthusiasm about Churchill. They had their avocations but commitment to the cause was the sine qua non. John Howard's mind never wandered – he remained a keen student of all things political. Even post Canberra he still misses the game – most of the rest of us are wont to complain from time to time of "a hard day at the office". But for him: "There wasn't any day that I didn't find stimulating and interesting." In part this derived from his upbringing, but it had long since become part of his persona, his political DNA.

There can be no doubting the importance of good leadership – we only have to look at the tragic record of caudillos (authoritarian leaders) in Latin America and kleptocrats in Africa to appreciate the fact. Howard is proud to say: "I left a country that was stronger, prouder and more prosperous than it had been when I came to power" – a fitting epitaph which all leaders should aspire to emulate. Australians are remarkably lucky to be living in a stable, prosperous, fair-minded democracy, in many ways the envy of the world. Long may it continue.

7

Communications, IT and the Media

When I first became Shadow Minister for Communications in 1989, the telecommunications industry was a policy backwater. This was reflected in the lowly ranking of the portfolio, which had always focussed on the media and the perennial Packer versus Murdoch battles.

Telecommunications was simply public sector infrastructure – an engineer's fiefdom with no apparent policy issues attached. Labor, ever wary of upsetting the unions, had tiptoed into the corporatisation of a number of government business enterprises, including Telecom (as Telstra was then known), but any suggestion of serious competition, let alone privatisation, was met with the lazy and self-interested assertion that telephony was a natural monopoly – end of story.

I was simply grateful to be on the bottom rung of the front bench ladder, but I was also excited as the potential for new information and communications technologies (ICT) to transform the sector, and the wider economy, was becoming increasingly clear. The first mobile phone had come into use only two years earlier, a big bulky analogue lump of lead weighing more than half a kilogram – unrecognisable from the lightweight 4G-5G smart phones of today. Text messaging didn't really get going until about twenty years later. Now, in the US alone, there are nine billion messages a day, or 32 per person! Add to this, some 200 billion tweets on Twitter and more than two trillion Google searches per year and you get some idea of our increasing dependence on rapid fire technologies.

It was the portfolio of my dreams. I had taken a keen interest in telecommunications since entering Parliament some three years earlier, where I completed my MBA degree. My major thesis was entitled *Time for Some Real Competition: Is Telecom's Universal Service Obligation Still Relevant?* It had recently been published by

Professor Mark Armstrong (Senior Research Fellow at the Centre for International Research on Communications and Information Technologies, Melbourne) in *Telecommunications Law: Australian Perspectives*.

My researches had convinced me that this was an industry sector that was about to explode and set to transform both the domestic and the global economy. But before I could even get my feet behind the desk I had a rude awakening. The new shadow ministry had been announced on a Friday afternoon, so I went home hoping to receive a few congratulatory phone calls on the Saturday. But, after one or two came through, the line suddenly went dead and, when I realised it was going to stay dead, I went next door and telephoned Telecom.

I explained the technical problem and asked if anyone could come out and fix it ASAP. The answer was effectively NO – "it has to be a genuine emergency and I assume you're not a doctor, we'll see what we can do, we may be able to help, but I'm not sure," etc. Bearing in mind one of Gough Whitlam's better bon mots, "this is no time for false modesty," I proceeded to lay my trump card on the table: "This is quite important for me, as I have just become the shadow minister in charge of your company." After a prolonged pause I was asked to wait until some senior executive came on the line to apologise and explain that they didn't do weekend repair calls because it only encouraged the technicians to defer home visits until the weekend with its double time loading. "However, Sir, in your case, we'll be out shortly," and they were.

Telecoms was just emerging as a policy issue, after years of being something only of interest to engineers and backroom boffins. This was rapidly changing. Governments of all persuasions were coming to realise the increasingly pervasive and game-changing importance of telecommunications, with the emergence of breakthrough technologies such as fibre optics, which enables 100,000 simultaneous voice conversations to be transmitted over a single fibre thinner than a human hair. In the wake of the seminal 1993 Hilmer Review on competition policy, even the Labor Party had started to move down the corporatisation path, by formally acknowledging the status of GBEs. But still, for them, the privatisa-

COMMUNICATIONS, IT AND THE MEDIA

tion of Telstra remained a bridge too far. Nevertheless, national competition policy now underlined the importance of competitive neutrality and the need to eliminate hidden protections and subsidies and any preferential treatment by governments.

As the twentieth century was drawing to a close, Telstra was an ageing behemoth. It had some 95,000 employees covered by 22 different unions, both blue collar and professional and had always considered itself above politics.

I had not long been the shadow minister when I had the temerity to suggest publicly that Telstra might have a conflict of interest by having a seat on the board of its competitor, Aussat, in which it held a 25 per cent stake. I promptly received a very nasty letter from the then Managing Director of Telstra, Mel Ward. In later years I found him very affable and helpful when he was Chairman of the Australian Ballet, but on this occasion the gloves were off. He took great exception to my remarks and threatened legal action, presumably for defamation. Later, I realised that this was a complete try on, but at the time it was sufficient to put the frighteners on a neophyte shadow minister, who wanted to keep his job, and with an election not far away. I made no apologies or promises – I just lay low on the issue.

It was not long before I was able to return fire. In a major speech I drew attention to Telstra's large workforce (now about a third of what it was then) compared to its international comparators and took the opportunity to describe the company as "Australia's largest sheltered workshop". Subsequently I received a complaint from a relevant charity, but the real squeal came when I was attending a Telstra function in Parliament House. Mel Ward sidled up and said: "Richard, I strongly advise you not to use that term again. We have about 90,000 employees and they all have families and none of them will vote for you". I thanked him politely for his concern, and a few minutes later Ros Kelly, the junior Minister for Communications, came up with the same message. By now I smelt a large rat, but it was only when I returned to my room that the penny dropped - this was hurting them politically. Next thing, the phone rang. It was the legendary Peter Harvey, National Nine News, Canberra, who wanted to know if he could come and do a quick interview. "It won't take long", he said, "I just need you to repeat that phrase 'Australia's largest sheltered workshop' a couple of times". I duly complied and, sure enough, it led the Laurie Oakes program the following Sunday morning.

Little did I know that I would go on to be almost a one trick pony, being in the portfolio, in Opposition and Government, for nearly twelve years. Another who did not anticipate my portfolio longevity was Frank Blount, Telstra CEO since the early 1990s. In our first formal meeting he could barely conceal his disdain, as he told me he had already had to deal with (certainly not "serve") five Communications ministers in five years and wondered how long I would be around.

Shortly after I had assumed the portfolio, one Sunday morning Henry Ergas and I went for a six kilometre run around Melbourne's Albert Park Lake. As we sat down afterwards for a well-deserved cup of coffee, Henry, in his most didactic manner, said: "My boy (I was actually a few years older than he was, but never mind) you'll urgently need to develop a Communications policy for the next Federal election (then less than 12 months away), so get out a piece of paper and we'll do some work". He then proceeded to dictate, without notes, a very logical and coherent draft policy document, starting with a mission statement/preamble and then systematically addressing all the key policy issues. In a technically complex area this was a very impressive feat, but I was not really surprised, because I already knew that he was a Renaissance man with a genius for understanding and explaining policy issues. I was forever grateful. I also admired his political courage shortly afterwards, when he forthrightly criticised Telstra at a policy forum, only to learn later that the redoubtable Mel Ward had summarily terminated his consulting contract.

In March 1996, when the Howard Government came to office, there was very limited competition in Australian telecommunications, no government support for regional telecommunications, and virtually no consumer safeguards, while Telstra was in full public ownership. The information economy was hardly acknowledged, let alone seen as a priority, while the Internet was only for academics and geeks. There was no such thing as digital TV, and SBS, the ABC and community broadcasters were far less accessible

COMMUNICATIONS, IT AND THE MEDIA

to the homeowner. Pay-TV was in its infancy, and many Australians resided in TV blackspot areas.

Over the next eight years the telecommunications landscape was de-regulated and transformed. Major achievements included full and open competition, two partial sales of Telstra, world class telecoms consumer safeguards, record funding for regional telecoms services, guaranteed minimum Internet speeds, effective regulation of the Internet and e-commerce, a fully funded National Broadband Strategy, world-leading spectrum planning and auctions, the introduction of digital TV, additional targetted funding for the ABC, a massive extension of SBS TV and community radio coverage, the fixing of over 200 TV blackspots, a permanent regime for community TV, world's best practice venture capital reforms, a new National ICT (Information and Communications Technologies) Centre of Excellence, unprecedented funding support for and commitment to small and medium-sized ICT enterprises, updating of copyright legislation for the digital environment and greater efficiency in the postal sector. Privatisation of Australia Post was then, and remains, a prize seemingly beyond reach, in spite of my intermittent musings on the subject.

Innovation and productivity growth in Australia surged in the 1990s, in large part due to the impact of ICT, triggering tectonic shifts in consumer and business behaviour. Now it's a world of super-fast computers, ubiquitous lightweight portable devices, remote sensors, and smart machines – the Internet of (every) Things. The FAANGs (Facebook, Apple, Amazon, Netflix and Google) of today were barely on the horizon. But we had to start somewhere.

Back then, quality of service obligations on Telstra, as the incumbent, fixed-line telecommunications carrier, were virtually non-existent – consumers could wait for up to 27 months for a telephone connection, with no access to compensation if connection or fault repair times were not met. Competition was highly regulated, and Telstra was still overwhelmingly the dominant player – at least better than being a "natural monopoly". But it would often do things only when it was good and ready, as it still controlled access to the domestic network, and consumers simply couldn't go elsewhere.

143

Here was one of the largest businesses in the country, providing commercial services to millions of people every day, corporatised by Labor, but still retaining an entrenched public sector culture, a highly unionised workforce and an overwhelming emphasis on network engineering rather than consumer service. It continued to be run like a private fiefdom, focussed on maintaining the status quo. Meeting the needs of its customers hardly figured.

A fundamental reason for wanting to see Telstra exposed to competitive pressure from the private sector was that its whole culture was inward-looking instead of customer-facing, representing a very poor return for taxpayers, as the ultimate shareholders. Things began to change when Frank Blount (Telstra CEO, 1993-99), an engineer by training but in practice a very experienced senior telco executive from America, was recruited by Paul Keating, with the clear intention of getting Telstra ready for sale. The corporation, until 1975 part of the Postmaster-General's Department, had always been run by engineers who took inordinate professional pride in building a high quality technical network, whatever the cost, however long the wait. Insulated from market forces and with a cost-plus mindset, they were not accountable to Parliament, government or the market, let alone customers. Government, nominally represented on the board by senior public servants, was little more than a passive observer.

It was not surprising, therefore, that the corporation was devoid of any serious strategic direction. It was run by engineers who saw nothing wrong with "gold plating" the network. They took pride in building the world's best technical quality network and charging the captive customers accordingly. With no competitive pressure, they barely needed to keep up with the latest leading-edge technologies, and the potentially large capital expenditure involved. They could simply collect the millions of dollars that poured in and spend whatever they felt like to future proof the network against any outages or breakdowns – a worthy policy objective, but at the expense of efficiency or any concept of value for taxpayers.

This led to serious productivity problems, such as over-employment, no doubt aided and abetted by union desires for more

COMMUNICATIONS, IT AND THE MEDIA

political clout and more revenue from membership dues. But, as an effective monopolist, it was also protected from the rapidly approaching tsunami of new hi-tech developments which were on the verge of changing everything. Moreover, government audit practices were changing. In 1976 the financial management function had been hived off from Treasury to create a stand-alone Department of Finance and, for the first time, there was a watchdog determined to ensure value for money. Telstra was an obvious target.

Lack of concern for customers reached its zenith in the long-running dispute and ultimately endless litigation between Telstra and the COTS (Casualties Of Telecom), which resulted in very generous and repeated substantial payouts in order to placate many small business people whose businesses had been ruined by Telstra's repeated failures to promptly attend to service difficulties and faults. Telstra's default response was to dig in, happy to run up large legal costs as a deterrent to potential claimants. But this only fuelled more negative publicity so, finally, the new CEO, Ziggy Switkowski, bit the bullet and settled most of the outstanding legal actions – a sensible decision which largely put the issue to bed.

The other serious area of neglect by policy-makers was the long-running acceptance of the notion that, by choosing to live in non-metropolitan areas, country residents were implicitly accepting that they should be content with second class telco services. Regional Australia had never known anything other than second rate telco services (by metropolitan standards), and the fact that Labor did not hold many rural seats, and the unions were not very active in those areas, may also have compounded the felony. To make matters worse, the growing importance of mobile telephony and the Internet had significantly increased the impact of this void between metropolitan and regional services.

This became a market opportunity for the Coalition Government, especially as our many rural MPs, both Liberal and National, had long campaigned on these issues. But even we did not get it right initially. Ultimately it was necessary to require Telstra to establish a separate Telstra Country Wide division, headed by Doug

145

Campbell, a lifelong telecoms man and a classic quiet achiever. We also addressed the politics by appointing two additional rural based members of the Telstra board, including Don McGauchie, later Chairman of the company.

We were very keen to put competitive pressure on Telstra. As I said to the National Press Club back then: "If technology is the engine of hope, then competition is the fuel that drives it." We had anticipated that, by opening up the sector, global players like AT & T would be enticed to our shores, but unfortunately the bursting of the tech bubble in April 2000 largely put paid to these ambitions. Even so, Telecom New Zealand and British Telecom did enter the market.

In government we were especially fortunate to have some high quality departmental advisers led by the wily and whip smart Department Secretary, Neville Stevens. Also conspicuous among them was the highly competent senior telco adviser, Fay Holthuyzen, and Tony Shaw, a key public sector architect of the competition reforms and possessed of a deep knowledge of the more technical aspects of telco regulation, including spectrum management.

Privatisation

Undoubtedly the biggest political issue facing the Government during my entire seven and a half years in the portfolio was the privatisation of Telstra – the media couldn't get enough of it. Years later, while living in London, I noticed that telco issues rarely got a run in the media, whereas in Australia they had been a daily event.

For the Coalition, the business case was overwhelming. The track record of governments running commercial enterprises was unimpressive. Private sector managers had skin in the game, with an incentive to not only make a profit for shareholders, but to enhance value by driving productivity gains via labour market reforms and new technologies. Public servants, on the other hand, were much more inclined to be risk averse. Their jobs and career advancement depended on not making mistakes, not on making profits.

COMMUNICATIONS, IT AND THE MEDIA

Telstra and its predecessors had long enjoyed a cosy, protected existence. With over 90,000 employees, most belonging to one of more than twenty blue collar and professional unions, its focus was on maintaining the status quo at a time when governments around the world were realising that privatisation could deliver a big win for taxpayers, with the private sector, not government, funding large-scale technology-driven capital upgrades. For consumers, it meant more efficiencies leading to lower prices, more innovative offerings, and more customer-responsive services. Already the telecom sector was growing strongly, up 18 per cent in 1995, and the Internet sector was estimated to be doubling every three months, so it was the right time to give Australians the opportunity to have a direct stake in one of the nation's largest and most important enterprises.

Britain, under Margaret Thatcher, had led the way in 1984 by selling off half of British Telecom's shares. When the Howard Government came to office more than a decade later, a multitude of other countries had done likewise. I used to taunt Labor that the only supporters of their "just say no" stance were Albania and North Korea, but they were impervious to both criticism or persuasion. I even took to calling Senator Kim Carr "the member for Albania", and dubbing the Leader of the Opposition "Kim Il Beazley", but to no avail. Privatisation of Telecom New Zealand had already seen significant improvements in service quality and price reductions. Chile had started a wholesale privatisation program in the 1970s and, in the late 1980s, it was Australia's Alan Bond who bought Chile Telecom.

Labor in government had already taken a very valuable, if somewhat timid, preliminary step forward in micro-economic reform when Gareth Evans, as Minister for Transport and Communications in 1987-88, had corporatised all the major Government Business Enterprises, including Telecom, later renamed Telstra after its merger with OTC (the Overseas Telecommunications Commission). The next move was also very positive – the implementation of the Hilmer Review's key recommendation of competitive neutrality, whereby governments, competing with the private sector, should do so on an equal footing.

147

The next logical step in the process was privatisation of government-owned commercial entities. But Labor had stopped short of this final step, no doubt due to strong union objections, especially in the public sector, until after the 1993 election. However, once safely back in office, after unexpectedly winning the 1993 election, they quickly proceeded – without an election mandate – to privatise the Commonwealth Bank, CSL (Commonwealth Serum Laboratories) and Qantas (which by now included TAA, the government-owned domestic airline), with Coalition support, so they well understood the concept. But when it came to Telstra they refused to budge – no doubt the unions would have remained resolutely opposed, but I strongly suspected the real reason was that they wanted Labor, and not the Coalition, to be able to spend the substantial proceeds.

Kim Beazley, Leader of the Opposition after the 1996 election, was always distinctly uncomfortable explaining his opposition to the many business people who reported back to us. He was in the thick of the 1990 Cabinet debate, led by him, when he put forward a proposal for consolidating the sector. In his aptly named book, *Whatever It Takes*, Graham Richardson, who had a ringside seat, wrote: "(Beazley's) wimpish proposal did not satisfy Paul Keating, who wanted to go much further and sell off Telecom into the bargain."

Beazley was also well aware that Paul Keating, as Prime Minister, had openly mused about selling off mobiles, Yellow Pages and other major business units, and we had successfully labelled this as "privatisation by a thousand cuts" in the lead-up to the 1996 election. Only a few weeks out from the election Keating publicly confirmed that he still wanted to sell key Telstra commercial units on the basis that they were not "core business". My immediate press release rejoinder was: "Paul Keating ought to be charged by the ALP with offensive behaviour, for exposing himself in public to this extent." We were, nevertheless, very grateful that he had.

And it wasn't just Keating. In 2000, while Beazley was still Labor leader, Macquarie Bank reported that the ALP was considering selling Telstra's retail business while keeping the network in government/union hands.

COMMUNICATIONS, IT AND THE MEDIA

Our 1996 pre-election approach to the issue was both policy creative and politically productive. From the proceeds of selling one-third of Telstra, with tight limits on foreign ownership and a new Customer Service Guarantee, we would establish a billion dollar Natural Heritage Trust fund, an initiative supported by several leading green groups, thus muting their ability to campaign effectively against the Coalition. We also promised a massive commitment to upgrade rural and regional infrastructure in line with then Opposition Leader John Howard's assurance to the National Farmers' Federation before the election: "The Coalition has long recognised that regional Australia (has been) in the front ranks of the 'forgotten people', when it comes to telecom services," particularly as mobile phones and the Internet were becoming essential consumer items but were virtually unrecognised in a telecommunications regime grounded in the time of fixed line services. We ultimately delivered on all of these commitments together with higher speed access to the Internet and other data services. Like many others, I didn't use emails then, couldn't live without them now – same goes for texts.

Competition

Soon after coming to office I convened a big all day meeting at the Sydney Maritime Museum attended by more than 200 stakeholders in the telecoms industry. The purpose of the gathering was to work through the competition reform bill which had already been introduced into the Parliament by my Labor predecessor, Michael Lee. I personally chaired the meeting and conducted a careful examination, almost line by line, of all the major concepts, so that all participants had ample opportunity to express a view. The event was very successful, not only in crafting a workable schema, but also in demonstrating our willingness to get down in the trenches to drive reforms. Full de-regulation from July 1997 would, and did, mean: no restriction on the number of carriers; no restriction on the services provided; increased industry self-regulation; and a technology neutral approach.

One key policy issue which quickly emerged was when Telstra and Optus decided to go head to head in rolling out competing

149

MORE TO LIFE THAN POLITICS?

hybrid fibre coaxial cables network around the country. We favoured infrastructure-based competition, although some argued that we should carve up the landscape so that each carrier was the sole provider in a designated area. This would have followed the American pattern, simply resulting in a series of cosy geographic monopolies and endless litigation involving access rate (price) disputes – a lawyer's picnic, but certainly not in the best interests of consumers.

As it turned out, the strategy of the two major carriers was not particularly successful. Telstra adopted the purely defensive tactic of simply matching the Optus rollout; Optus itself became convinced that it was not likely to be worthwhile so, after Melbourne, Sydney and Brisbane had been substantially covered, they both laid down their arms.

But not before a real political issue had erupted. Optus had worked out that overhead cables were much quicker and cheaper to roll out, but people soon started complaining that they were both dangerous and unsightly – and damaging to (mainly inner-city) property values, always an incendiary claim. My own local council, Boroondara, in the leafy Melbourne suburb of Kew, had already obtained an injunction to prohibit the practice in its own area, and our backbench was on the verge of rebellion. An up and coming colleague of mine, Tony Abbott, had proposed that Cabinet approve a multi-million dollar package to help fund laying cable underground in certain areas, but we quickly realised that the cost would be prohibitive.

After a number of long and fraught meetings with the backbench committee, the rules governing installation of telco facilities were tightened, so that all types of cabling had to be undergrounded wherever possible. The irony of all this anguish became apparent on a subsequent trip to London, where I discovered that the masses were also revolting around the same issue, but there the objection was the opposite – that digging tunnels was dangerous, inconvenient and unsightly!

In September 1996, for reasons mainly related to longevity and patronage, we announced the replacement of five Telstra directors. One of them was Peter Redlich, a lifelong Labor man and a

COMMUNICATIONS, IT AND THE MEDIA

quality human being. We had known each other since the days
when we had both been Victorian State presidents of our respective parties. He rang one day and said: " Richard, we've both been
around for a while and we know that with a change of government there will be personnel changes, so I'm ringing to say that
I would like to quietly step down from the Telstra board." I very
much appreciated his personal and political courtesy, which was
in marked contrast to that of another lifelong Labor man, who refused to stand down and had to be sacked.

In the same month I hosted and chaired the Second APEC Ministerial Meeting on the Telecommunications and Information Industry on the Gold Coast. This provided the perfect opportunity to
demonstrate our reform credentials to an international audience.

Information technology

In 1997 we created NOIE (National Office for the Information
Economy), with both a high powered ministerial council and advisory board. It was my strong view that, while governments had
an important role to play, corporate Australia had to take the lead,
and they certainly responded positively.

The information economy was very much untilled soil, an inherited policy wasteland. Eighteen months into government, I acquired formal responsibility for it, a logical extension to my portfolio, due to the deep technology crossovers with communications.
It was also another great policy bonus for me, because, in many
ways, the future development of technologies and the policy implications was the best game in town.

We were lucky to acquire the services of Dr Terry Cutler as chair
of our first information economy policy advisory council. With his
extensive first-hand knowledge of Telstra and deep understanding of technology, Terry knew where all the bodies were buried
in the telco sector. He had been deeply involved in the development of the Malaysian Multimedia Super Corridor, a high tech
business district, and was also something of a futurist, so he was
well placed to help map out future directions.

NOIE was first headed up by Paul Twomey, later the inaugural
CEO of the global body that coordinates many of the key func-

151

MORE TO LIFE THAN POLITICS?

tions of the Internet, including domain names. Under John Rim-
mer, who came from running Multimedia Victoria, NOIE became
very active in policy development, and regularly published useful
comparative data to ensure we measured up to international best
practice.

One of my key roles in privatising Telstra was to entice Senators Harradine and Colston firmly into our tent, and I spent a lot of
time doing so. They were both ex-Labor, but for very different reasons. Harradine, for whom John Howard and I had great respect,
was a person of the highest integrity. A former secretary of the
Tasmanian Trades and Labor Council and a long serving member
of the ACTU national executive, he had been expelled from the
ALP in 1975 after a bitter ideological struggle over his fervent anti-
communism and his close association with Bob Santamaria's National Civic Council. Later that year he was elected to the Senate
as an independent, and ultimately became the Father of the Senate
and the longest serving independent senator since Federation. A
fervent Tasmanian (despite having been born in South Australia
and only moving to Tasmania in his twenties), all his requests centred around his adopted home state of Tasmania.

One particular gripe of his was that Telstra officially treated
the island, very dismissively, as the Southern Victoria region.
Frank Blount was a highly capable and experienced telco guy who
served Telstra well. But, as an overseas import, he was reluctant to
get too close to the political culture and tended to be dismissive of
government, no doubt borne of his American experience. So when
I asked him to fix the Southern Victoria problem, he was scorn-
ful: "Why should I have to accommodate a two-bit senator from
Tasmania?" My response was equally blunt: "Frank, if you really
want Telstra to be privatised, you do!" And he did.

Colston, a Queenslander, was a very different kettle of fish.
Elected to the Senate at the same time as Harradine, he remained
an ALP Senator until after the1996 election, when the Labor Party
refused to nominate him for Deputy President of the Senate, a position he had held from 1990 to 1993. In 1997 he resigned from the
Labor Party, which furiously denounced him as a "Labor rat", but
we helpfully agreed to support him, and he was duly elected. He

COMMUNICATIONS, IT AND THE MEDIA

was not always helpful, however, voting against our industrial relations package and the second Telstra sale bill.

We eventually came up with a good package which recognised that Tasmania, as a long time indigent State, had been neglected for too long. The initial one-third sale of Telstra (T1) was accompanied by a $250m Regional Telecommunications Infrastructure Fund, known as Networking the Nation, which was distributed on the basis of the percentage of the population in each State residing outside the capital cities. It just happened that this was particularly advantageous to the home States of Harradine (Tasmania) and Colston (Queensland), the two most decentralised States in the Commonwealth.

In early 1998 we announced the decision to sell the remaining two-thirds of Telstra. Further funding was committed in late 1998 and mid-1999 to facilitate the second 16 per cent sale (T2). This included $40m for development of Tasmania as an Intelligent Island (including the cheekily named TIGERS [Trials In Government Electronic Regional Services] program), the Launceston Broadband Project, funding for mobile coverage on regional highways, including from Hobart to Burnie, funding for telecommunications infrastructure for remote islands such as King and Flinders islands, and funding to help Tasmanian schools go online. So successful was Brian Harradine at using his position of influence to further the interests of his Tasmanian constituents, the oft repeated quip around Parliament House was that, if Tassie received any more funding for telecoms infrastructure, it would sink.

The run up to the mid-1998 vote was crucial. I had to spend a lot of time with Mal Colston, a somewhat surreal experience as he was not particularly interested in discussing policy issues. Instead we talked about personalities, politics in general and the possibility of finding a job for his son in the public sector. Colston had long been under a cloud for allegedly rorting his travel expenses and, once he "ratted", the ALP's vindictiveness knew no bounds. Unsavoury details started to find their way into the public arena. Eventually John Howard was targetted by Labor for taking Colston's "tainted" vote, although Labor itself had no qualms about doing so.

153

The media was happy to run with the Labor line of attack, so eventually we referred the allegations to the Federal Police and thereafter we declined to accept his vote. This was a very honourable decision by the PM, but it later had seriously deleterious political consequences. Colston took great umbrage at this perceived slight and, in the days before the Senate vote on the T2 bill, he became quite distant and hard to find. So we were not altogether surprised when he came into the Senate chamber and did us in. Fortunately he immediately did me a big favour by absenting himself from the vote on the next bill, relating to a pet project of mine, the parallel importation of compact discs, which then just passed.

Following the Telstra defeat and after much internal debate, particularly with our Coalition partners, the Nationals, we announced a staged approach to the further sale, proposing to sell 16 per cent and leaving 50.1 per cent in government hands, with any further sale beyond 49 per cent to be subject to an independent inquiry into Telstra's customer service levels in metropolitan, regional, rural and remote areas. Unless and until the independent inquiry certified that service levels were adequate, after being assessed against performance standards laid down in new consumer protection legislation, Telstra would remain in majority government ownership.

In March 2000, six months after the not so successful T2 sale, we announced a major inquiry, headed by a former eminent civil servant and later a successful businessman, Tim Besley, to assess the adequacy of services in both metro and non-metro areas. The Besley inquiry found that service levels were generally adequate, but more could be done in terms of timely installation, repair and reliability, as well as the provision of better mobile phone coverage at affordable prices. We responded with a $163 million package focussing on improving mobile coverage, Internet speeds and supporting the better use of telecommunications in the health and education sectors. A year later, following the 2001 election and a further inquiry headed by Dick Estens, a well-respected farming identity, another $181 million was committed for further rural improvements. The centre-piece of this initiative was the development of a $143 million National Broadband Strategy, including over $100 million in incentives to enable rural customers to have

COMMUNICATIONS, IT AND THE MEDIA

equitable access to broadband through a Higher Bandwidth Incentive Scheme.

By this time I felt we were winning the battle to convince country voters that the sale of Telstra was also good for them. I fondly remember that, about this time, I went to a little town called Condamine, in the Western Downs region of Queensland, to launch a new mobile phone base station. The hall was filled to overflowing and, after a warm welcome and a short speech from me, I asked if there were any questions. What seemed like a long silence followed, until one bushie, in a languid drawl, intoned: "I rode into town this morning on me horse, when suddenly me phone rang very loudly – frightened the sh.. out of the horse. When are you bastards going to come up with a horse-friendly ring tone?" My instant amusement was followed by the immediate reaction that if that was all they had to worry about, we were on a winner.

2001 was a big year politically, as we were hoping to be elected for the third time, often a tall order. In recognition of the crucial importance which the Coalition placed on competition to drive performance and service levels up, and prices down, we put competition limits on both mobile spectrum auctions and datacasting (now an obsolete term) transmission services, to ensure that no company or associated entity could purchase more than one licence in each licence area. The emphasis on competition reflected our philosophical faith in market outcomes, in marked contradistinction to our political opponents who were often quick to shout "market failure" – a standard excuse to justify ever more regulation and bureaucratic interference.

Whilst our Coalition partners, the Nationals, were very good at keeping us honest in the bush, I found my Liberal colleagues also very committed to a truly national vision for communications, in recognition of the importance that telecommunications and technology played in all our lives. With the 2001 election pending we launched "a telecommunications policy for the 21st century", which provided a $163m package of infrastructure and services in regional and rural areas. It also imposed a further reduction on the timeframe for telephone services to be installed or repaired and required Telstra to provide a minimum effective Internet speed of 19.2 kbps for all Australians, not far short of the then average us-

MORE TO LIFE THAN POLITICS?

age rate. We also committed not to proceed with any further sale of Telstra until we were satisfied that it was providing adequate service to all Australians.

It was also a great time for lovers of creative acronyms, a project sponsored by my senior telco adviser, Paul Fletcher. After leaving my office in 2000 Paul spent eight years at Optus, before entering the House of Representatives. He rose rapidly, culminating in his appointment in May 2019 as Minister for Communications, Cyber Safety and the Arts, a post for which he is the perfect fit.

TIGERS (Trials in Innovative Government Electronic Regional Services) was quickly followed by BITS (Building on IT Strengths) and BARN (Building Additional Rural Networks). At the end of all this exotic wordplay, the cry in the office went up: "please, no more TLAs (three letter acronyms)".

We had a lot of fun in 2001 when Labor released its ill-fated education paper, *Knowledge Nation*, which, thanks to Barry Jones's doodlings, quickly became Noodle Nation. It tried, somehow, to claim credit for our ICT driven productivity gains. But Goldman Sachs got it right in their paper, Australian Productivity: Catching a New Economy Wave: "Australia is ahead of the pack in the use of new technologies."

The main ALP telco policy document for the 2001 election was an intriguing piece of political theatre. Released in the name of the Leader of the Opposition, and headed "Kim Beazley's Plan for Telstra", the major thrust was strident opposition to the full privatisation of Telstra, which we had ruled out two weeks previously. This was pure political cant as it was widely believed that, when Mr Beazley had held the portfolio, he was chafing at the bit to go down the Telstra privatisation path.

On 27 February 2002 we launched a signature initiative – the official opening of NICTA (National ICT Australia) – part research facility, part educational institution, part factory floor, part ideas clearing-house – all in all, commercial premises combined with a dream laboratory. It had been the centrepiece of the Government's landmark innovation initiative of January 2001, *Backing Australia's Ability*, a $3 billion strategy to foster science and innovation and turn great ideas into jobs and income.

COMMUNICATIONS, IT AND THE MEDIA

Backing Australia's Ability was a crucial political initiative. The science community had been becoming increasingly restless and publicly vocal. The internal debate was whether we should try to close the issue down as soon as possible or wait and make a big pre-election announcement towards the end of the year. The decision to go early proved to be a masterstroke. Most critics quickly came on board when they realised the scope and potential of the commitment.

NICTA's mission was to undertake world class research and to link that with industry and community needs. Its establishment reflected our view that Australian universities undertook great research, but too little of it was being commercialised or used by industry to improve Australian competitiveness. I also felt the universities did not have the proper incentive structures in place. I had been very impressed with the Stanford model, which ceded all the intellectual property to the actual inventor, often a young entrepreneurial student. This was a calculated risk but, it quite frequently paid off in spades, as, when some of these researchers hit the jackpot, and made a "mozza", they gave generously to their alma mater. In 2014 the Stanford Endowment stood at $21 billion funds under management. By contrast, Australian universities are much more risk averse, preferring to keep the bulk of the IP firmly in their own hands and reaping lesser rewards accordingly.

The Nationals were becoming agitated, often stirred up by their admirable champion, Senator Ron Boswell from Queensland. He had been such a party stalwart, first, last and always, that he voluntarily stood down from Andrew Peacock's shadow ministry in the run up to the 1990 election so he would not be constrained by joint Coalition policies. As always, the Nats were looking for an opportunity for product differentiation and a bit of tail-wagging-dog politics, which generally we could live with for the greater good. An earlier master stroke had been the appointment of former Deputy PM and National Party legend, Doug Anthony, to head the newly created Regional Telecommunications Infrastructure Fund Board. We also put in place a comprehensive range of consumer safeguards, including the Customer Service Guarantee, the Network Reliability Framework and the Digital Data Service Obligations, as well as the $671 million T2 Social Bonus.

MORE TO LIFE THAN POLITICS?

By 2002 the landscape had changed conspicuously, with increasing recognition of the importance of the looming e-commerce environment and an awareness of how the Internet was transforming businesses, both large and small. In this context, a major collaborator was my National Party colleague, Tim Fischer. As Minister for Trade he kept me fully informed about his splendid efforts in showcasing small businesses that were using the Internet to market their products and open up new sales opportunities around the world. No case study better demonstrated the transformative power of the Internet than Mick's Whips, a small business outside Darwin which, as an early adopter, was able to sell its whips to customers internationally, in no small way assisted by Tim Fischer's personal advocacy and unique story-telling ability.

We also set up another high powered Broadband Advisory Group, which I chaired, bringing together leading thinkers in the broadband arena, such as Ziggy Switkowski, and requiring them to consult with international experts, as I also did personally on a number of occasions.

It was very important to fast track the take-up of broadband, particularly in key productivity sectors such as small business, education, health and community services. We placed considerable emphasis on "future proofing", to ensure universal access to affordable Internet services. This involved the adoption of a suite of measures, including minimum Internet speeds, funding to provide satellite access for rural customers unable to access the Internet terrestrially, financial support through Networking the Nation for Internet Points of Presence (POPs), and subsidies through the Higher Bandwidth Incentive Scheme to provide pricing parity for regional and rural customers.

In 1997 there had been three licensed phone companies – Telstra, Optus and Vodafone. By 2003 there were 89, 40 per cent operating in regional areas. By 1 July 2003 the ACCC found that fixed line call prices had fallen by almost 25 per cent, mobiles by 27 per cent, local and long distance prices nearly 30 per cent and international by 61.2 per cent. Furthermore, the Allen Consulting Group found that competition had led to consumer benefits of approximately $750 per household and that GDP had grown by $10 billion, with an additional 100,000 jobs as a result of telecommunica-

COMMUNICATIONS, IT AND THE MEDIA

tions competition. There is no doubt that emerging technologies had played a part in these very consumer-friendly outcomes, but it had also needed government to keep the pressure on carriers and ensure that cost savings were passed through to consumers, via increased competition.

One of the big policy debates leading into the 2004 election was about the structure of Telstra, which many, including the Government, considered to be too oblique, thus handicapping both its customers and its competitors. Some were suggesting that we should go down the path of full structural separation of Telstra's network and services arms.

The overwhelming weight of international evidence did not favour this extreme solution. Both the *Economist* and the OECD were strongly opposed. The OECD said bluntly: "It is too complex with uncertain outcomes, the benefits of structural separation are uncertain, while the costs are potentially large." The ALP waxed and waned. Their capable spokesman, Lindsay Tanner, eventually conceded that "splitting Telstra into network and services companies is simply too complex and too costly"; he switched to advocating the nebulous concept of virtual separation. Essentially Labor didn't care, as long as the network stayed in government hands, as it harboured a large slice of the blue collar workforce, the bedrock of Labor's union support.

We did not disagree with the experts' assessment, nor the political reality that we had frequently promised to keep Telstra intact as "a going concern", in stark contrast to Paul Keating's proposal to sell off key elements of the business. Accordingly, in mid-2003, after extensive public consultation, we issued a final direction requiring Telstra to implement accounting separation of both its wholesale and retail activities. In terms of current debates about the need for maximum transparency, we were well ahead of the game.

Looking back on the period, the best outcome for the nation was that regional, rural and remote telecoms finally came of age. Thanks to the vast proceeds available from the Telstra sale tranches, we spent well over $1 billion on the bush, hopefully making it feel no longer isolated, and finally able to be part of all that the new century had to offer. We had achieved, in the title of a key book on the telecoms revolution, published in 1997, which I had read several times, *The Death of Distance.*

The media

Both the media and politicians must strike a balance between their unique power and influence on the one hand and their democratic responsibility to be accountable to society on the other. Each operates in very competitive environments, where the core business is winning – sales or votes. They each depend symbiotically on one another. Whether they admit it or not, nearly everyone gets their news and views from the various forms of media – unfortunately, these days, many only from social media. Conversely, without political stories and sometimes screaming headlines, the media would be very different, and much less interesting.

For the media, as fundamentally commercial enterprises, cover price, subscriptions and/or advertising revenue are their lifeblood. Unlike the protected national broadcasters with effectively guaranteed income streams, the commercials must live or die by their success in attracting readers, viewers and listeners. In recent years, the impact of the digital revolution on publishing and advertising has caused traditional print media to suffer enormously and, in the case of the once illustrious Fairfax empire, fatally. They now face existential threats from new digital behemoths such as Google and Facebook.

News outlets may like to present themselves as staunch guardians of the national interest but, in reality, they are pitching their offerings to a particular demographic – older, more traditional voters; young and progressive voters; inner suburban class warriors who thrive on stories of discrimination and inequality. The Internet has dramatically expanded access to publications and enables personalised targetting of groups and individuals. In Australia, outlets such as the *Guardian* service this market with outrage at the status quo and a normative view of the world, full of "if onlys" and, even more, "ought to be's".

A hoary chestnut of the left is that, by August 2001, the Howard Government was heading for certain electoral defeat at year's

COMMUNICATIONS, IT AND THE MEDIA

end until it refused permission for the Norwegian freighter, MV *Tampa*, carrying 433 rescued refugees, to enter Australian waters. To the horror of many commentators, this action won widespread approval from the Australian public. The reality is that although the Coalition's year got off to a shocking start, culminating in the loss of the safe Queensland seat of Ryan at a by-election, John Howard managed to turn things around with an astute cancellation of automatic fuel indexation and a good Budget. By mid-year the Government had won the Aston by-election and was back in front in the polls when the *Tampa* came along.

Notwithstanding, this canard got yet another run in the UK *Guardian* during the London tour of duty of one of my predecessors. When he wrote a letter explaining that the Howard Government was ahead in the polls at the time, they refused to publish it. When he took the matter up with senior management they explained that their readers just loved refugee hardship tales so, effectively, they were not prepared to let the facts get in the way of a good story.

I had a similar experience as Minister for Communications when I had lunch with some senior *Age* newspaper executives. When I asked why they always seemed to run left wing lines they told me they were catering for what was then the Australian Democrat party demographic and they had to be market responsive. News outlets will claim to be objective, but it is not hard to tell by reading vastly different headlines for the same story that they are each catering to their different readership groups. For those with a more market-oriented commercial world view and a genuine interest in economics and business, *The Australian* and the *Financial Review* are there for them. Those who prefer a steady diet of discrimination, embracing inequality and unfairness can go elsewhere.

The media has a delicate role to play. No one wants a government-owned or controlled newspaper. If a presentation is too bland or merely focusses on economic issues it is likely to be dismissed as boring. Too much good news is likely to be largely discounted as mere propaganda and spin. Even if focus groups say they want positive news stories and in-depth analysis, their behaviour suggests otherwise. Some commentators prefer to justify the media's perpetual preference for bad news stories as being "more morally serious." I prefer a more pedestrian and ultimately commercial explanation, based on the human condition. People seem to be hard wired to prefer scandal, shame and humiliation and the free enterprise media stands ever ready to accommodate them.

Media companies must operate within an implicit social licence, providing information, news and, occasionally, excitement, while remembering that they are a vital part of a functioning democratic society. This is a heavy burden. If they go too far, although they may not lose their followers, they are ultimately subject to the dictates of the Parliament and, to a much lesser extent, the sanctions of the Press Council and other industry regulators, including the Australian Communications and Media Authority.

The media has to be careful not to overplay its hand lest it provoke the political class into legislative curtailment of its activities. The UK phone hacking scandal involving illegal recording and subsequent airing of private conversations, via bribery and entrapment exercises, brought down London's best-selling newspaper, the *News of the World*, after 168 years of publication, and nearly ended the careers of leading members of the Murdoch family as well.

Politicians are under even more pressure, subject to high expectations and often suffering serious disappointments and sometimes career ending setbacks. Their core business is winning elections, but they must strike a delicate balance by keeping the dark arts out of sight as much as possible, while offering policy solutions which the majority of the electorate regard as being in their best interests. While politics is the art of the possible, many political compromises are readily portrayed as yet another grubby deal at the expense of the long suffering public. Because it is much easier to question the motives or impugn the political integrity of a political decision-maker than to impartially analyse the merits of the decision, it is not surprising that so many members of the public have a low opinion of politicians.

As fierce competitors in a very tough business, the major politi-

COMMUNICATIONS, IT AND THE MEDIA

cal parties are engaged in a remorseless struggle for supremacy, where failure can mean loss of office, career and reputation. The spoils of office provide unique opportunities to improve the nation's lot. But politicians also have an awesome responsibility for the freedom, safety and prosperity of the nation's citizens.

We know that the hip pocket nerve is often what determines election outcomes – what people consider to be in the best interests of themselves and their families. Why is it that the newspapers and other media are usually full of everything else? Why did gay marriage dominate the media for months on end? Why the constant yearning for a republic debate when most, except a few zealots, regard it as a second order issue? Why is every day another Trump outrage? Maybe they just have to fill up space every day so they go for stories where there are activists on both sides of the argument always ready to stoke the fires of fierce controversy.

Sure, there is always some economic analysis somewhere, but most of the media is usually filled with what it deems "newsworthy material", often related to their targetted demographic. To hold their readers' and viewers' attention the stories must constantly cover whatever is regarded as "new and interesting". There is always a famine or a disaster somewhere in the world and the emotional travails of the participants can be heart rending. But such stories can suddenly fade from sight when another "hotspot" emerges, and the caravan moves on.

The media finds itself on the horns of a dilemma. It is happy to question the motives of almost every politician and will never tell the story the way it is presented to them. This is perfectly understandable, except that media outlets are quick to accuse politicians of spin when they attempt to put a favourable gloss on their story. They would never concede, however, that their default position is to do the same by giving most political stories a negative or, at best, a sceptical slant. This may be an almost universal human instinct, but it is still spin and the public recognises it as such by holding the media in low esteem. One of the great advantages of being a journalist is never having to say you're sorry. Maybe, occasionally, a small sanitised correction, but no similar sized retraction.

At times a politician may be portrayed as dishonourable for

163

seeking political advantage. Time and again politicians are called on to show leadership by advocating something that the public is not particularly interested in, but the media thinks would be nice and controversial, for example, the republic.

The cross media rules

There were two major media policy reforms on which we spent a good deal of time and effort: media ownership and the transition from analogue to digital television. On the first we struggled; on the second we clearly succeeded.

The cross media laws had been put in place by Labor for the stated purpose of ensuring media diversity, although they were not above using them for partisan political advantage. The intent of the laws was to prevent any one proprietor from owning more than one of a newspaper, a commercial radio licence and a free to air commercial television licence in the one market. As then Treasurer Keating famously said in 1986 before the laws were enacted: "they [the proprietors] could be princes of print, and queens of the screen, but not both".

The Howard Government had always taken the view that this law was an arbitrary construct to keep certain proprietors at bay and that normal competition laws – and potentially a whole-of-market diversity test, if necessary – was a more effective way to regulate the media sector. It was also important that any changes to media ownership laws did not favour any particular proprietor and so, in addition to removing the cross media laws, we sought removal of the media-specific foreign ownership laws, which operated in addition to the normal Foreign Acquisitions and Takeovers provisions administered by the Foreign Investment Review Board.

Ultimately our attempts to reform the media ownership laws were unsuccessful, stymied by a combination of an obstructionist Senate and a highly effective campaign by Kerry Stokes's Seven Network, which argued that the changes would give too much power and influence to Rupert Murdoch and the other Kerry. Looking back, the clearest reason for removing the cross media and foreign ownership restrictions was that they were becoming an anachronism in a digital world, where the Internet was increasingly dominant and anyone, anywhere could produce and distribute their own content in whatever format they wished. The lines between television, radio and newspapers were blurring and have arguably now become non-existent, and virtually impossible to regulate. More than twenty years since the election of the Howard Government, it is only now that the remnants of the cross media laws are being removed.

Digital television

The other major media reform issue was the advent of digital television. Around the world, and particularly in Europe and the USA, various models were being pursued. It was always going to be important to ensure that an Australian model built upon our existing broadcasting environment. It had been underpinned by the commercial television networks, with a much later start-up for subscription (Pay) TV compared with the USA and many parts of Europe, where cable and satellite subscription providers dominated the market and the viewership. As with most issues relating to media, all the key players claimed their solutions were in "the national interest" but when you dug deeper, they were remarkably, but quite understandably, aligned with their own commercial interests. I well remember a senior media executive coming to my office, fervently pitching his policy line. When I pointed out that he had come to see me twelve months earlier arguing the opposite case he didn't blink – just pointed out he had then been with a different employer!

For the Government, digital television, like digital telecommunications, was first and foremost a transition from an analogue to a digital environment. As such, it was necessary to assist incumbent players in making the transition, as it would come at a significant cost. There would be a need to simulcast in analogue and digital for an extended period so that viewers were not left in the dark with no access to television. Careful management of scarce spectrum was required, and it was considered reasonable that incumbent broadcasters would not have to pay upfront for the spectrum, as they would have to invest in digital production and transmission infrastructure while continuing to pay annual licence fees. At the same time, provision was made for community television to have access to the digital spectrum and financial support was provided for regional broadcasters who, comparatively speaking, needed to make a larger infrastructure investment without the deep pockets of the Nines, Sevens and Tens of this world.

For the media moguls digital television gave rise to two bones of contention. First, the Murdoch camp saw it as a means of issuing a fourth commercial television licence – preferably without the encumbrances of the media ownership restrictions, which they were, understandably, very keen to get their hands on. Second, the digital platforms had sufficient capacity to enable high definition digital television, or a full array of multiple channels, but not both.

The fourth licence was always going to be a hard ask. The Coalition had made clear that we did not support an additional licence and during the digital transition the additional investment required by the existing licencees was not the right time to subject the market to the further upheaval of a new player. On the question of high definition or multichannelling, the incumbents were divided, with Nine and Ten supporting high definition and Seven supporting multichannelling. In the end, while I always believed there was a strong argument to allow a degree of multichannelling as well, Cabinet opted for high definition.

The reaction from the Murdoch media was primeval, but not without a hint of humour. The *Telegraph* ran a front page lead with a four letter acronym as the headline in the largest possible font – KPTV (as in Kerry Packer TV). The front page lead was augmented by further highly negative pieces on the following pages, as well as the editorial and the main cartoon all reinforcing the newspaper's dissatisfaction that the digital television model favoured the incumbents and would not allow for a fourth commercial television licence. Both the Murdoch media and other media outlets (including the ABC which was allowed to multichannel immediately) focused on the cost of high definition televisions, claiming that the Coalition's policy was destined to be stillborn, due to the considerable cost of high definition TV sets.

These sets were expensive at the outset, as is always the case

COMMUNICATIONS, IT AND THE MEDIA

with the advent of new technologies, and set top boxes initially were the primary way that viewers accessed digital television. Fifteen or so years later, virtually every television set in the market place is high definition and the technology has continued to develop beyond high definition to integrated television sets, which enable access to all sorts of online offerings. Additionally, the capacity of the scarce broadcasting spectrum has increased exponentially, and Australians now enjoy both the highest quality television pictures and sound as well as greater choice through free-to-air multichannelling. In retrospect, I believe we got digital television right for both consumers and the broadcasting sector.

The anti-siphoning laws

There was one other highly sensitive broadcasting related policy issue which absorbed an inordinate amount of time for the Communications minister, and other interested parties, including the Prime Minister. The anti-siphoning list had been invented by the Keating Government to ensure that iconic sporting events remained on free-to-air and were not siphoned off to Pay TV – a laudable objective which the Coalition supported. On many occasions, we reviewed the effectiveness of the anti-siphoning policy and the sporting events on the list. We introduced anti-hoarding provisions to prevent free-to-air broadcasters from purchasing events on the list but not broadcasting them. If this occurred, the events had to be made available to the ABC and SBS.

On the face of it, there were clearly too many events on the anti-siphoning list, making it difficult for the nascent Pay TV sector to come up with an attractive sports offering for their subscribers. Every attempt to make any significant changes to the list was inevitably met by a combination of free-to-air broadcasters crying foul, the politically dangerous prospect of denying the general public free access to their favourite sporting events, and the particular sporting loves of senior political colleagues. Imagine the reaction of the then Prime Minister, a cricket tragic, if the Lord's Ashes Test was no longer available on free-to-air or the then Treasurer, an Essendon tragic, if AFL matches were removed from the anti-siphoning list! I say no more. Over the years the pay networks have

167

sought to whittle away at the regime to the point where, now, the free-to-air channels have first rights but can on-sell to the pay networks.

The moguls

It was my good fortune to be around when Kerry Packer and Rupert Murdoch were still in their prime. They were both larger than life characters, but in very different ways. One normally quietly spoken and thoughtful, the other capable of charm but also bluster. Both were passionate about their core business, and very strategic in their thinking.

Murdoch, an instinctive risk taker, quickly outgrew his domestic ambitions and became, almost certainly, Australia's greatest international business success story. He never quite bet the farm, but he was prepared to pay over the odds for "must have" bolt on acquisitions, such as the *Wall Street Journal* and the National Football League rights. In his long career he has had at least two near death experiences – once in 1990, when crippling debt brought him to the brink of bankruptcy; and, again in 2011, when the *News of the World* scandal nearly had him banned from Britain. On each occasion, his iron determination, his remarkable resilience and his ability to think clearly in a crisis, saw him through. His eclectic ownership of media assets demonstrated his instinct for risk diversification.

The Times (of London) and the *Wall Street Journal* were graphic demonstrations of his commitment to serious journalism. *The Sun* (London) and the *News of the World* were classic examples of money spinners which enabled him to pursue more strategic assets such as DirecTV. Later, despite his lifelong passion for newspapers, he saw the way they were heading in the digital age and moved purposefully into the entertainment sector.

He has always been intensely interested in the political process and in good economic policy outcomes. Industrial relations and tax reform have always been at the top of his list. It has become somewhat commonplace among his detractors to suggest that his backing of certain politicians was opportunistically designed to advance his commercial interests. I prefer a more benign interpre-

COMMUNICATIONS, IT AND THE MEDIA

tation. A close examination of his picks would suggest that he was more concerned to see good leadership prosper. When people and parties ran out of steam, as the Liberals did in Australia after 23 years of Menzies and his successors, Murdoch saw the opportunity for a fresh start under Gough Whitlam. Similarly, after just on 18 years of Thatcher and Major, he saw Blair as a bright new thing, ready to take Britain into a more progressive era.

These endorsements did not mean that he was ever a Labor/Labour supporter, despite his republican instincts, but that he thought the respective countries needed economic reinvigoration. He remained a proudly consistent conservative. He was no doubt subsequently disappointed with the economic profligacy of the Whitlam years, but would perhaps not have regretted his original decision, which he probably saw more like calculated political risk-taking which backfired.

He was a strong admirer of Margaret Thatcher, a fellow big risk taker, and greatly appreciated her support for his breathtaking Wapping coup, which sidelined the short sighted and overly powerful printing unions, but only after a long and bitter battle. In the process he permanently transformed their neanderthal publishing practices. His imagination, courage and persistence – qualities he shared with Thatcher – changed the face of Britain's newspapers and labour relations forever.

He was more cerebral than his more visceral Australian counterpart. I well remember visiting him in New York, where he graciously gave me several hours and spent the time outlining, in quiet but impressive detail, how his global businesses fitted into his overall strategy. Not once did he mention Australian politics or his commercial interests in his native land. He is intrigued by technology but not blinded by it. He is a businessman first and last, and not a geek. His son, James, impressed me as being very tech savvy, but he no doubt realised that strategic business thinking was more important in the long run. As Jeff Bezos of Amazon and Jack Ma of Alibaba have graphically demonstrated, IT competence is not essential for a CEO's success in a digital world – it is commercial smarts that count. Andrew Carnegie did not know much about making steel, but he sure knew a

MORE TO LIFE THAN POLITICS?

great deal about making money. It is Murdoch's business acumen that matters, as was obvious in discussions with him. He never resorted to geek talk – it was all about strategy.

I once asked Lachlan Murdoch how his father managed to have such a global and encyclopaedic knowledge of business – was he involved in endless meetings, did he read constantly? The answer to both was No. The secret to his success was that, blessed with a very good memory, he constantly discussed matters on the telephone and absorbed new information like a sponge. As a result he was constantly regurgitating relevant matters and, like any good politician's stump speech, the logic and persuasion flowed easily.

Both Murdoch and Bill Gates were somewhat slow to recognise the transformational potential of the Internet but quick to capitalise on it when it became apparent. Perhaps that explains why News reacted so badly when the Liberal Government chose a pathway to the Internet based to a significant extent on a detailed submission from the Packer camp. Given their media and commercial experience and success, the views of the key players were vital to a workable policy outcome yet, for some inexplicable reason, News chose not to put in any serious submission, yet acted as if we had put a bullet through their business.

Kerry Packer was a very different character to Rupert Murdoch, but just as driven – his lifelong passion was television. On one occasion at the Melbourne Grand Prix he stood with me in the front row of the grandstand, watching the cars whizz by. After a few minutes he said: "I can't see a f…ing thing – enough of this rubbish, come upstairs." He then took me into a room full of cameras, positioned strategically at all the critical bends and other hot spots, saying: "Why on earth would anyone in their right mind want to watch this stuff live and see only a car flash past, when they can see all the action from their armchair – give me TV any day."

He never accepted that free-to-air was on borrowed time, and he knew the business better than anyone. You could walk into his office and find him busy swapping channels and handing out unflattering character references. He was not to be interrupted.

He was also a visionary risk taker, whose single-handed pur-

170

COMMUNICATIONS, IT AND THE MEDIA

suit of one-day cricket permanently transformed the great game. He was possessed of a mercurial temperament. At times the public saw his tough, even icy, exterior and so did those who had to negotiate with him. But he did have a softer side. I can recall several occasions when, after a very willing exchange and I was ready to make a quick getaway, he walked me to the door with his arm around my shoulder and spoke soothingly about my family and cricket. He was also a very generous behind-the-scenes benefactor of many charities, as well as incredibly loyal to his staff, from the tea lady to the highest executives, from whom he demanded a lot in exchange. He had strong views on many issues in my portfolio, but deep down he knew that politics was the art of the possible, so he gave everything his best shot. One of his betes noires was our high television licence fees, which he said was about the only example of world's best practice in my portfolio.

On one occasion, when I was scheduled for another bout, I mentioned to his son James that I had recently seen a newspaper report that Kerry had lost about $17 million in one night's gambling. James quickly suggested that I not bring it up, which was, indeed, very wise counsel. Another time I had publicly floated the idea of requiring regional television stations to have minimum news obligations, after some urgings from the Nationals on the backbench committee. I heard in advance that he had gone ballistic when he had read this, so I changed tack. I walked in and said: "You can forget about that proposal, I now have a better idea." His scornful reply (expletives deleted) was something like: "Don't think you're going to get away that easily – you can just sit there while I tell you what a shocking idea it is," and he proceeded to do just that. This taught me to let him blow himself out first, and then we could get down to business.

I made it my practice to keep in touch with him. But one time – we hadn't spoken for a while – I was sitting in my office one morning when he rang. We chatted inconsequentially for some minutes and then he said: "I suppose you're wondering why I'm ringing." I didn't deny this, so he continued: "Well, I'm on the golf course with my good friend, Bob Whyte", whom I knew as the owner of one million Telstra shares, which were then under water. I steeled myself for an onslaught, but he just laughed and said: "Bob just bet me I couldn't ring you and get straight through."

We all know he loved a punt – on one occasion he was keen to explain the importance of Kenny Rogers' timeless words of wisdom, "know when to hold, and when to fold." He then asked whether I had liked the film *Oceans 11*, about a series of elaborate robberies at five Las Vegas casinos. When I said I hadn't seen it, he was appalled, and immediately rang his PA and asked her to go out and buy me a copy, which she did. I promised to look at it but somehow it got lost!

In his own way, he loved company, but such are the drawbacks of fame that I suspect he did not get out all that much. One night I was having dinner with James at his Bondi pad when Kerry arrived unannounced and proceeded to stay for the evening. I very much enjoyed James's company – he was very quick on the uptake and had a good strategic sense and an acute understanding of technology. I found him both warm and engaging, and he never asked for anything. He followed public affairs closely and it was once rumoured that he thought seriously about going into politics. I think he was wise not to enter the bearpit – the family's media enemies would have had a field day.

Before leaving for London I heard that Kerry was in hospital, so James arranged for me to go in and see him. But, just as I was heading off for the hospital that morning, James telephoned and said Kerry had discharged himself and wanted to see me in the office. I suspect that his principal motivation was to have a cigarette. He complained about all the medication he was on but was otherwise in good spirits. I knew it would almost certainly be our last meeting, which it was, and I will always have fond memories of a very complex, larger than life individual who left an indelible mark on the community.

At times we seemed to be the meat in the sandwich in the continuing tussle for supremacy between the two media titans. Kerry Packer was fond of jokingly asking: "Since when's it been an offence to hold an Australian passport?" – a none too subtle dig at Murdoch's preference for US citizenry.

On one occasion I was invited to meet Lachlan Murdoch, and

COMMUNICATIONS, IT AND THE MEDIA

the then chairman of News Limited Australia, John Hartigan, at News International offices in Los Angeles. I had understood that the meeting was to discuss the Government's latest proposal for changes to cross media rules. After about half an hour of idle chatter, Lachlan suddenly said: "Dad's in the next room, would you like to come in and meet him?" Naturally I said yes but, as I entered a room full of his top executives from around the globe, Rupert's voice suddenly boomed across the room: "Gentlemen, meet Senator Alston – he gives Kerry Packer everything he wants". In the face of this ambush, I could only smile wanly.

This, however, was not a one-off. John Howard and I attended, as Rupert's guests, a pre-Christmas soiree on the lawns adjacent to the Sydney Opera House. We both got the same treatment, same form of words, as Rupert introduced us to his then wife, Wendy Deng. Although I may have been paranoid, for some months it seemed that the *Australian* newspaper managed to turn every happening into a Howard Government blunder – a level crossing accident in northern Queensland was due to inadequate federal funding. This went on for months, until successive Newspolls showed we were still travelling OK, and the apparent vendetta suddenly evaporated. Fortunately my time in the Murdoch deep freeze was not permanent. Once I took up my London posting, I found myself on the guest list for his annual London soiree at the Serpentine Gallery in Hyde Park.

Certain sections of the media were quick to characterise any government decision affecting the media as caving in to one camp or another. The reality was starkly different. It obviously made sense to be in close and frequent contact with the key players, but this did not mean playing them off against each other, let alone pandering to their every whim. I well remember a vigorous and at times heated debate with the commercial television networks about the merits of allowing them to have additional digital channels for what was then called multichannelling. Kerry Stokes, and therefore Channel Seven, was in favour, but the other networks and pay TV operators such as News Ltd were resolutely opposed.

It seemed to me that consumers would benefit from choice, particularly as it would enable fervent cricket followers like myself to simply change channels to continue the coverage, which was often cut off at a critical stage by the mindless need to go to the news on the hour. Having made the decision to go to Cabinet recommending multichannelling, I subsequently heard about a fascinating post-mortem conversation between good friends Lachlan Murdoch and James Packer. Lachlan was asking why on earth I had been so obstinate, to which James replied that maybe I just thought that it might be good policy!

8

The Arts

Ever since my teenage years I have enjoyed a variety of art forms, from theatre to painting, from rock-and-roll to classical music. I can still vividly remember the shock and pain on discovering that my prized schoolboy collection of classical LPs had been stolen from our house. But books have always been my favourite form of relaxation and inspiration. At a young age I eagerly devoured such international doorstoppers as *War and Peace*, *The Count of Monte Cristo* and *Les Misérables* and, on the domestic front, *The Fortunes of Richard Mahony* and *For the Term of His Natural Life*. In my final year, much to the amazement of my fellow students, I won the Edward Ryan Prize for Modern English Literature at Xavier School.

Great literature has always attracted me – it has stood the test of time – outlasted all the fads, fashions or prejudices of readers and governments. If people are still reading Dante more than 700 years later it must be for very good reason. Same with Shakespeare, who will surely never lose his majestic authority or universal appeal. We continue to learn from the classics, not just from Greece and Rome.

Aboriginal art has long been my favourite painting art form, ever since the late 1970s when I travelled to the Northern Territory, home of Arnhem Land bark paintings. There I acquired a small colourful red and brown piece, the start of my continuing interest in Indigenous art. I also gradually became a collector, mainly of Central Desert dot paintings. Aboriginal art is unique and, like most art forms, not to everyone's taste, but it has certainly graduated from primitive or tribal to fine art status, both in Australia and internationally. The colours can be mesmerising and the iconography a source of continuing attraction, encouraging the viewer to explore the artist's family background and clan heritage as well as to wonder about the circumstances in which it was created.

My visit to the NT was a life changing event, which led to my abiding interest and concern for Aboriginal disadvantage and my deep admiration and support for the work of the legendary ophthalmologist, Fred Hollows, who dedicated his life's work to restoring the eyesight of thousands in outback Australia and, subsequently, in Nepal. His foundation continues Fred's pioneering work in over 25 countries.

In February 1993, together with a Liberal colleague, Bob Baldwin, I paid my last respects to Fred at his Randwick home. He got out of bed specially to greet us. Also present was the famous author of *Power without Glory*, Frank Hardy, who, at Fred's funeral service at St Mary's Cathedral a few days later, told the assembled multitude of admirers, including Prime Minister Paul Keating, that after we had left the house Fred had rasped through his breathing mask: "Nice to see Richard – not a bad bloke, for a Liberal."

I later saw the work of Fred's team in Ethiopia, which I had visited several times en route to Eritrea, for whom I served as an honorary ambassador for a number of years. Later in 1993, together with Senate colleagues Kerry Sibraa and Robert Hill, and Booker Prize winning author Thomas Keneally, I attended the independence celebrations in that benighted country, after an almost thirty year long war with its much larger, but equally poor, neighbour, Ethiopia. In 1989 Keneally, an infectious and irrepressible spirit whose company you could not help but enjoy, had written a powerful novel, *To Asmara*, based on the capital of Eritrea, which explored the cultures and conflicts of the two countries. He remained a strong supporter of the cause.

Opera

Opera is a special favourite, the ultimate art form, with singing, acting, drama, costume and dance all enveloped in lavish production values. The Sydney Opera House, known the world over for its unique architecture, was recently ranked in the world's top ten best opera houses by *National Geographic*.

One especially memorable occasion was when Gough Whitlam and I were there in our dinner suits. The next day he sent me a letter saying that he "had not previously felt sartorially threatened

THE ARTS

by a shadow minister for the arts!" He proceeded to elaborate
what I thought was a somewhat tenuous family connection – his
mother's eldest brother was the father of my sister-in-law. This
apparently amounted to me being almost one of the family, as he
subsequently took to calling me "cuz", sometimes across a crowded room, in his trademark booming voice. On one memorable occasion he did so at the Opera House in the presence of the then
Arts Minister, Michael Lee, who immediately responded: "I think
I can see the resemblance."

Despite our political differences, Gough and I developed quite
a rapport. No more than a fellow traveller with Christianity, he
once joked that if he ever met God he would "treat Him as an
equal". He loved to dilate on religion, particularly the Catholic variety, displaying his usual encyclopaedic knowledge of the subject
matter, with Latin quotes thrown in.

Shortly after my appointment as High Commissioner to the
UK had been publicly announced in the lead up to Christmas
2004, I was lunching in Sydney at Machiavelli's, the favourite
haunt of political junkies, replete with prominent, if rotating,
portraits of the legends of the trade. Some self-important types
are said to remind management when making a booking that a
portrait of their good self was in the storeroom, in order that it
could be prominently displayed for the edification of their dining companions.

On this occasion I noticed that Gough's portrait had pride of
place, although I'm sure management did not need any prompting. When I looked around, there was the "great man" (one of his
famous self-descriptions), with spouse and office staff in tow, enjoying the pre-Christmas spirit. In due course I wandered over, to
be warmly congratulated on my diplomatic appointment. I naturally responded by saying that I hoped he and Margaret would
be able to make an early visit for lunch at Stoke Lodge, the High
Commissioner's residence in London.

He immediately thanked me and said he would love to do so
but, sadly, it would not be possible, owing to Margaret 's precarious state of health (I think she might have been on crutches at the
time). I then proceeded around the table to issue a similar invita-

MORE TO LIFE THAN POLITICS?

tion to Margaret, only to be told that she would love to do so but, sadly, it would not be possible because of Gough's parlous physical condition: "arms, legs, joints – nothing works anymore." When I pointed out that his voice still seemed to be in excellent working order, she sighed loudly and said: "just tell me!"

Over the years I have been fortunate to visit a number of Europe's iconic opera venues, including the Royal Opera House in London (where, on one occasion, I was taken backstage to meet the cast, including Placido Domingo), the Paris Opera, the Staatsoper in Vienna and La Scala in Milan – as well as the Mariinsky Theatre in St Petersburg and the acoustically perfect Dorothy Chandler Pavilion in Los Angeles.

Especially memorable for me were less conventional locations such as inside the walls of the Tower of London watching Donizetti's *Anna Bolena*, not far from Tower Green, where the wretched Anne met her fate, near her burial site in the Church of St Peter ad Vincula, adjoining Tower Green.

In the United States, the Glimmerglass Opera, now the Glimmerglass Festival in the eponymous park in upstate New York, was an entrancing cultural detour for the sports minded, like me, who travelled the extra eight miles to take in the National Baseball Hall of Fame in Cooperstown on the beautiful Otsego Lake. An idyllic venue, the lakeside theatre hosts a wonderful variety of operas and musicals in the summer season. The park itself is renowned for picturesque woodland trails, spectacular wildflowers and wildlife around Beaver Pond.

One of the many summer cultural highlights for comfortably off Londoners is a visit to the unforgettable rural idyll of Glyndebourne, where Megs and I certainly made the most of our bountiful opportunities. Situated some 70 miles due south of London, near Brighton, the performances are carefully timed for early evening to allow diners to crowd into a very modern wood encased restaurant, safe from any unwelcome summer rain.

On a fine day – never guaranteed in the UK – many prefer a picnic dinner in the gardens overlooking that unique English creation, the "ha-ha", a manicured ditch wide and deep enough to separate the patrons from the lowing and grazing herds nearby.

178

THE ARTS

It unobtrusively but effectively inserts a barrier into the landscape which prevents access by unwanted motor vehicles or grazing livestock, while preserving an uninterrupted view of the landscape beyond. The unusual name, "ha-ha", is said to derive from exclamations of surprise uttered by those coming unexpectedly across them.

Glyndebourne has a fascinating and colourful history. The first performances were presented in a 300-seat auditorium and orchestra pit inside a 600-year old house. There is now a free-standing opera house in the grounds. In the 1990s a brand new theatre was built at a cost of £34 million, 90 per cent of which was raised through donations. The modernity of the original manor house, still standing, is represented by recently installed wind turbines which provide almost all of its power needs.

Founded in 1934 by John Christie, it remains in family hands, privately owned with no direct public funding, but nonetheless very successful. It has since been emulated by other pastoral retreats which has led to the thriving genre of Country-House opera in twenty-first century England. It offers the unique opportunity to escape from the quotidian urban reality of our daily lives to be briefly transported to the age of Edwardian opulence. Indeed, Oxford Professor of Music, Suzanne Aspden, recently described the experience this way: "Audiences feel more like guests at a private house party, and therefore dining and picnicking become part of the evening's entertainment."

Another wonderfully romantic opera house setting, until recently, was Garsington, in the rolling Chiltern hills of Buckinghamshire, amidst foppish outdoor structures such as telephone booths, known as "follies", ostensibly useless indulgences of wealthy rural landlords but also doubling as entertaining conversation pieces. Garsington Manor House, built in the 16th century, became the home of the legendary chatelaine, Lady Ottoline Morrell (1873–1938), doyenne of the Bloomsbury Group of writers and artistic cognoscenti such as Bertrand Russell, Aldous Huxley, Virginia Woolf, John Maynard Keynes, W B Yeats and D H Lawrence, who all used to meet at the manor. In 1982 the Manor House was bought by Leonard Ingrams, a banker and music enthusiast, who

MORE TO LIFE THAN POLITICS?

established the Garsington Opera, an annual open-air opera festival, staged each summer from 1989 until 2010. After his death the opera moved to Wormsley Park, Buckinghamshire. The performance space was inside the old house with a warm low ceiling and rustic feel.

But perhaps the most exotic opera location I have visited is the medieval castle of Olavinlinna, built in 1475 and located amid spectacular lake scenery. It was the venue for the Savonlinna Opera Festival, held annually in the eponymous city in waterlogged rural Finland. On the occasion of my visit with Megs, the formalities commenced with a mayoral dinner at which the principal delicacy was reindeer, generically known as venison. As excited as we were at the prospect of this unique local offering, my thoughts quickly turned to the main event, Verdi's *La Forza del Destino*, in the hallowed portals of the ancient castle. Suddenly it occurred to me that the opera was likely to be in Finnish, not one of my long suits. When I politely enquired whether this was so, I was quickly assured that there was no need to worry as there would be surtitles. It was only when the curtain went up that I realised to my horror that there were, but in Swedish.

My favourite style of opera is bel canto, so it was a rare treat to cross paths on several occasions with La Stupenda, Dame Joan Sutherland, Australia's wonderful dramatic coloratura soprano who excelled in the very challenging art of "beautiful singing". First popularised by castrati such as the immortal Farinelli, this difficult and demanding musical form, requiring exquisite vocal agility, had fallen into disuse until largely resurrected in the late 20th century by our Joan (and her husband, the conductor Richard Bonynge), whose renditions of the works of Bellini and Donizetti continue to dazzle to this day.

When we were first introduced she immediately asked if I knew what her middle name was. When I answered in the negative, she was quick to proclaim, "Alston", and suggested I research any links. I was therefore mortified when we next met as she asked if I had done so – all I could do was plead guilty and apologise for this manifest breach of etiquette. I am still not sure whether we are even distantly related – I can only hope so.

Whenever I am in New York my most important port of call is the majestic and opulent Metropolitan Opera where I have never been disappointed and have always come away with the latest recordings of Met performers.

Arts policies and politics

I was delighted to be offered the Arts portfolio, initially in Opposition and later for more than seven and a half years in government. I took to the task with enthusiasm, ably assisted by Fiona Poletti, my Arts policy superstar.

It was a master stroke of Paul Keating's to have the Arts minister, Michael Lee, also the Communications Minister, in Cabinet. In fact it was only because of this structure that I became Arts minister. When Alexander Downer was elected leader of the Liberal Party in May 1994 he convened a meeting in Adelaide of the Leadership Group, himself and Peter Costello, his deputy from the House of Representatives, and Robert Hill and myself from the Senate. Our main task was to choose the new front bench team. Robert became spokesman on the Environment, while I retained Communications.

When we had finished the discussion and allocations, Alexander suggested we should check our list against the Labor team to ensure we hadn't overlooked any key portfolios. When we came to Michael Lee as Communications and the Arts, he suddenly asked: "who has the Arts for us"? A short awkward silence followed when we discovered the oversight, before he asked if I would like it, to match Michael Lee. I jumped at the suggestion and duly scored the jackpot. I had never dreamed of such a prize and I only discovered later that Alexander would dearly have loved it for himself, but graciously deferred.

Once I became Shadow Minister for the Arts in 1994 we quickly put together a cultural policy statement entitled, The Cultural Frontier. It neatly pre-empted Keating's much delayed launch of Creative Nation, which followed 12 days later, in October 1994. We chose Bronte House in Sydney as the venue for the launch, to which Keating responded with the line that this was a sacrilege equivalent to dragging swine through the Vatican.

MORE TO LIFE THAN POLITICS?

One of the strategies developed by Fiona was to identify quality arts journalists, such as Brook Turner from the *Financial Review* and Matthew Westwood from *The Australian*, who were genuinely interested in the subject and good policy, not just the froth and bubble and personality clashes which often bedevil coverage of the sector. As a result we were able to get some of our initiatives on the front page of the leading dailies with some frequency.

Our approach was not to bypass the Australia Council as the conduit for arts funding, which Keating had been doing, openly and loudly. Our stance forced him to reverse his antipathy and get back on board. We emphasised the importance of understanding and integrating the new technologies into multi-media productions, especially in theatre, as well as in the fields of heritage and copyright. Unlike Keating's urban centric preferences, we placed particular emphasis on touring and regional access to art.

Opposition can be very lonely. We had some closet supporters in the arts community, but many were understandably wary of being sent to Coventry by an unforgiving Labor Party if they said something nice about us. We took the view from the outset that it would be a win if we were able to break even with the Labor Party in this important policy area.

We took nothing for granted and made a point of seeking out all the key stakeholders, large and small, to get their views on what policy changes they would like. We kept copious notes and afterwards we went through them all, picking up the key themes. This major consultation process was well received by the arts community, as it demonstrated that we were genuinely committed. As a result some national icons, such as Les Murray, Roger Woodward and Margaret Olley, happily shared their frustrations about an imperious Keating and gave us some useful insights. Margaret Olley was very special. She had always been something of a rebel and was at great pains to tell me she had prospered without government handouts and couldn't see why others couldn't do the same. I had always liked her painting, as did the general public, as she was the subject of no less than ninety solo exhibitions in her lifetime.

THE ARTS

So, for my 25th wedding anniversary present to Megs, I prevailed upon Olley's agent, the charming and vastly knowledgeable Philip Bacon, to acquire one for me for the big day. He then took me to her pad in Duxford St, Paddington, where she invited me to choose from a number of largely completed works. Over the next ten years or so I made a number of visits to her home, which was always warm and welcoming, but with barely a spare square inch to sit down, as the place was bursting at the seams with already completed works and many others under construction, as well as memorabilia lovingly accumulated and retained over a lifetime. I managed to return the compliment in a small way, when she and Philip visited London for yet another exhibition of her works, by hosting them for lunch at Stoke Lodge.

It was very important to burnish the Coalition's arts credentials in the wake of Keating's generally well received 1994 funding extravaganza known as Creative Nation, a $250m package, chock full of cultural goodies and launched in Canberra with a great array of bells and whistles. As the Shadow Minister for the Arts I had attended the historic event.

My most vivid recollection is that one of the highlights involved the presentation of an award to Emily Kngwarreye, perhaps Australia's internationally best known Aboriginal artist. She had previously been a recipient of what were officially the Australian Artists Creative Fellowships, but which quickly came to be known as "the Keatings." They were essentially handouts of up to $300,000 (some, like the Keating family's piano teacher, Geoffrey Tozer, even got two helpings), given to a number of successful and nationally known artists such as actor Reg Livermore, painter John Olsen and jazz legend Don Burrows, ostensibly on the basis that it would enable them to pursue their crafts at their leisure, without having to worry about where the next dollar was coming from. The largesse backfired, however, when Ross Edwards, an eminent composer, said he "felt funny" about taking two grants – and a number of other recipients went public to express their mystification as to why wealthy and successful artists like themselves should benefit at the expense of others much more in need.

The strong suspicion was that, apart from his obvious commitment to the arts, Keating's ambition at the launch was to lure leading lights in the arts community to his political cheer squad ahead of the next election. Emily nevertheless stole the show. Then in her 80s, she had never before been away from her community of Utopia, north-east of Alice Springs. Not surprisingly, she was somewhat overawed by the occasion. As she was being presented with her cheque she looked at it for a while and then said slowly: "This very good – this means I never have to work again". Hardly what Paul Keating had in mind!

Creative Nation set a new benchmark in terms of recognition – and funds – for the arts. But a self-indulgent Keating once more overplayed his hand by attempting to anoint his hometown Sydney Symphony Orchestra, already well endowed, as the national leader, while treating the other State orchestras much less generously. Creative Nation's emphasis on artistic output as a "product" to be delivered by service providers did not make sense to us and, no doubt, if we had adopted such terminology, we would have been castigated by arts leaders for such a soulless, industrial approach. We preferred to concentrate on governance and a business-like approach. We did not want simply bean counters or business types on arts boards – we were seeking arts aficionados with proven business acumen.

Keating launched his 1996 election arts policy at the Melbourne Arts Centre, with many prominent arts personalities there to lend rapturous support. Ours was more modest, at the Australian Centre for Contemporary Art in Melbourne's Botanical Gardens. Fiona had already arranged for us to forego the traditional Liberal Party colours and format in our policy document, cheekily entitled "Arts for art's sake", in stark contrast to Keating's notion of the arts as simply another economic product.

John Howard formally launched our policy. An important statement of intent, it demonstrated that the arts would be taken seriously by a Coalition government. We were pleasantly surprised when people like Albert Tucker and Les Murray turned up, together with most of the heads of arts organisations. Good newspaper coverage next day was aided by a photo of John Howard with a belly dancer – not a party member, to my knowledge.

THE ARTS

Once in government we quickly established a Regional Arts Fund, aimed at enabling local communities to develop their own productions. We also replaced the, by then, notoriously self-indulgent "Keatings" with a Young and Emerging Artists Program for those who really needed help with career development and marketing guidance.

Parallel importation of compact discs – a classic anti-competitive scheme whereby recent releases could only be brought into the country by the local offshoot of the record company – had been a long running policy sore for both sides. Labor knew it was a protection racket designed to keep prices high, but Keating had already tried and failed. The gossip was that Cabinet was heading for a tied vote until Robert Ray voted it down on the basis that he didn't know what a CD was!

We had been regularly told by Emmanuel Candi, the CEO of ARIA (Australian Record Industry Association), that if we even contemplated pursuing this initiative an avalanche of leading artists would come out heavily against us. I was keen to propose it as a pre-election commitment, but several nervous colleagues, presumably sooled on by ARIA, persuaded me to promise to only hold an inquiry, if and when we won office. When we did, we moved quickly and were able to withstand the industry pressures, quite heated at times. Eventually good policy prevailed and, despite the doom and gloom prognostications of vested interests about massive job losses, the industry barely missed a beat and delivered the lower prices we had predicted.

Our success was ably assisted by the Chairman of the Australian Competition and Consumer Commission, Professor Allan Fels, and, despite my fears that the industry might have picked off some key members of Cabinet, we maintained an absolutely united front.

Keating had long since lost patience with the Australia Council and had been openly threatening to close it down. Sensibly, he gave it one last chance by appointing two well respected figures to head the Council – Michael Lynch, a high powered administrator, as General Manager, and Hilary McPhee, legendary co-founder of McPhee Gribble publishers, as chair. Both had solid left-of-centre

185

credentials. Lynch was an outspoken advocate of the republican cause and McPhee was then married to Keating's speech writer, Don Watson.

We made a special effort to de-politicise the relationship and were delighted when they responded warmly, and we were able to work very constructively with them. Michael, in particular, was a forceful and knowledgeable counterparty, and we respected both greatly and were very appreciative of their wise counsel.

After the generally positive reaction to Keating's, Creative Nation, loudly endorsed by some leading arts legends, as well as the usual Labor luvvies, we were understandably apprehensive about the reception we would get from the arts community. Many on our side told me that a scoreless draw would be a great result. But I think we ultimately did much better than that.

We could live with people like Rodney Hall saying that the sky would fall in and the book trade ruined by a GST, but I was far from impressed by my brief encounter with one of Australia's prized luminaries, Peter Carey, who had then just won his first Booker Prize. I had noticed him sitting a few rows from me on an international flight from LA, so, after landing, I introduced myself as the Arts minister and congratulated him on his recent international success. I was taken aback by his response, which was essentially: "If you're from the Howard Government, don't bother."

The acid test came early in our term when we chose to take drastic action to repair our inheritance of Labor's $10 billion budget deficit. This meant a 10 per cent cut in funding for all government departments and agencies, except Defence, so the Arts inevitably took a hit. The arts community could have gone berserk, as the ABC did, acting as though it had been singled out for special treatment. But, instead, a timely call from Hilary McPhee for recognition that the Government was on the side of the arts worked wonders. We were very fortunate to inherit her as chair of the Australia Council. She was widely respected in the arts community and her air of quiet professionalism and authority was very important in helping to negotiate the transition.

One of the great attractions of the Arts portfolio is the opportu-

THE ARTS

nity to meet and work with masters of their craft. These included John Bell, a superlative Shakespearean actor and director, Robyn Archer, an amazing all-rounder, both as artist and administrator, and Graeme Murphy, long time artistic director of the Sydney Dance Company, whom I had great pleasure in subsequently designating one of Australia's finest "national treasures". My father had always been a big Gilbert and Sullivan fan and was delighted when he discovered that Xavier senior school put on a G & S operetta every year. Although my musical talents were not sufficient to get me a part, I quickly became hooked on the genre and, in later years, took every opportunity to refresh my enthusiasm.

It was an amazing experience, a few months after we had won government, to attend Victorian Opera's virtually last production – The Puccini Spectacular, a musical extravaganza, narrated by Dennis Olsen in the role of the great composer. For more than a century the lead G & S roles have been sung by some mighty artists but, for my money, none was better than Dennis Olsen. His perfect diction enables him to get his tongue cleanly around a glorious outpouring of nonsense, but at lightning speed. What makes him stand well apart from his peers is the twinkle in his voice, his ability to vocally trip the light fantastic in a humorous, even cheeky, way which perfectly captures the satire of the lines.

At the interval of the show I was taken underground at the old Olympic Pool to meet some of the performers. Returning through the tunnels I turned a corner and almost ran into the great man. I could not resist the opportunity to pay homage and hopefully have a few words. He was charming and engaging until he looked at his watch, apologised that he was already some minutes late for the resumption of play, but said how much he had enjoyed our chat. I floated back to my seat, safe in the knowledge that I was the only one in the audience who knew the reason for the delay.

Late in 1996, I was invited to participate in an Australia Council international engagement in India and to join a delegation led by its CEO, the highly capable Michael Lynch accompanied by my irreplaceable Arts adviser, Fiona Poletti. In due course we found ourselves in Calcutta where the Australian consular officials arranged a meeting with Mother Teresa, founder of the Missionaries of Charity who have dedicated their lives to helping "the poorest of the poor." This was not only a privilege but an extraordinary and unforgettable experience – to meet someone who was already a living saint. She was formally canonised in 2016, less than ten years after her death, an almost unheard of degree of progress to sainthood in the Church's history. She was not in good health and had to be wheeled in to meet us but she was very friendly and helpful as she explained her great commitment to working in Calcutta with the dying. She then gave me what she described as her business card, which now sits on the desk in my study and bears a message which, over the years, I have found very inspiring:

The fruit of SILENCE is Prayer

The fruit of PRAYER is Faith

The fruit of FAITH is Love

The fruit of LOVE is Service

The fruit of SERVICE is Peace

We were then taken on a very moving tour of the orphanage she also ran nearby.

After two years as the Arts minister, I was fortunate to successively acquire two highly competent junior Arts ministers in Peter McGauran and Rod Kemp. The latter distinguished the portfolio in his own right. Our almost three year tandem act led to me christening him the Minister for First Nights and by his colleagues, particularly after he acquired the sports portfolio, as the Minister for Fun. The division of labour worked a treat – they could service the arts community on a regular basis, while I could be wheeled in for major projects, but their preparation and ground work was critical in getting support and money from Cabinet.

By the 1990s Australia was one of the few countries in the world without an easily identifiable national museum. A big project, and also highly controversial, was our 1996 election promise to "honour Labor's broken promise" and proceed with a national museum on the original Yarramundi site The idea had been around since Federation but, despite repeated promises by the major parties, a vast and diverse collection had been assembled, only to lie gathering dust in the dungeons. In the 1993 election campaign

THE ARTS

Keating had committed to "proceed with the development of the National Museum of Australia." But soon after being re-elected he became increasingly cold on the idea, culminating in his remarks just twelve months later at the opening of the new National Portrait Gallery in Old Parliament House: "I have not always been persuaded that another huge and hugely expensive building on the banks of Burley Griffin ranked high among the things we need for a better national life."

As with his "L-A-W law" tax cuts promise, spelt out in capitals to stress the solemnity of the commitment, once safely back in government he had no compunction in jettisoning a watertight promise – behaviour which no doubt led to many of the voters having serious reservations about the value of his commitments. John Howard quickly realised the national significance of the project, a missing link in our cultural infrastructure. It is also important to acknowledge the importance of the support of a key lobby group, the Friends of the National Museum of Australia, led by the indefatigable John Mulvaney and Winnifred Rosser, who kept their very effective public campaign on foot until victory was assured. They continued to play a vital support role for years afterwards.

There was one last extraordinary twist to the tail, the story of which, until now, has never been in the public arena. As the building was nearing completion an alert departmental officer, to whom we will be forever grateful, noticed some unusual lettering, which he was told was the architect's signature. Suspicious of this explanation, he obtained a book of Braille symbols and discovered that the letters spelt out the word, "sorry", no doubt a reference to the red hot political issue of saying sorry to Aboriginal people for past atrocities. This could have caused an acute embarrassment, with international repercussions, as the Queen was shortly to preside at the official opening. Fortunately the inappropriate message was discreetly covered over and the big day passed without incident.

Another significant initiative was to facilitate more private support for the arts. We had long disapproved of Labor's Australian Foundation for Culture and the Humanities which had started life as a front for advancing the republican cause. Dick Pratt, whom we appointed as chair, assured me that he would keep it under

MORE TO LIFE THAN POLITICS?

control but, by 1999, our patience had run out. We replaced it with a new government-private partnership, the Australian Business Arts Foundation, which proceeded to galvanise many captains of industry in both their personal and corporate capacities and is still going strong, with the new name, Creative Partnerships, under one of my three wonderful Fionas – Fiona Menzies, a graduate of the prestigious Courtauld Institute in London and a dab hand at arts policy.

Allied with this new private sector emphasis, David Gonski, the everywhere arts man, urged, and then assisted, me in devising a new tax regime, which enabled owners of serious pieces of art to gift them to public collecting institutions, retain possession during their lifetimes, and claim an up-front deduction. David's advice on this and on many other fronts was invaluable.

The National Gallery of Australia was another major project. It had been a sheer pleasure to watch and work with Betty Churcher as she wove her magic with hugely successful blockbuster exhibitions. When she stepped down in 1997, after an executive search, I interviewed the final two candidates and chose Brian Kennedy, a beguiling Irishman who had been Assistant Director of the National Gallery of Ireland, with a deep and scholarly background in art history. Brian and I bonded, and I believe we achieved some big breakthroughs together. Not least among these was his idea of allowing free entry to the Gallery on the basis that this would lead to greater sales of merchandise and bigger attendances, an emerging trend that was proving successful with other public art institutions around the world.

I also agreed to an important proposal to raise the spending limit on major acquisitions, beyond which ministerial approval was required. I readily accepted that the minister was not the appropriate decision-maker, no matter how immersed in the arts. The responsibility should reside with the Gallery board of directors, most of whom were highly successful in the fields of both arts and commerce. The issue was controversial because it had become well known that Paul Allen, co-founder of Microsoft with Bill Gates, had not long before offered to pay $100 million to purchase *Blue Poles*, which had caused a public furore when bought

THE ARTS

for $1.3 million in 1973. The board agreed not to accept the offer but only after one of the senior members asked the seemingly heretical question: "so at what price would you be prepared to sell"? This provoked lively and healthy debate which fortunately ended in a no, as the latest valuation of *Blue Poles* is around $350 million!

My opera enthusiasms probably help to explain my willingness to come to the financial aid of Opera Australia, together with my abiding admiration for its CEO, Adrian Collette. He had the difficult task of balancing the perennial Puccini and Verdi favourites to keep the devotees happy against the need to introduce new works, or resurrect old ones that had fallen into obscurity, to keep the aficionados stimulated. Opera Australia was still suffering in Victoria from the much resented "merger" [read take over] of the Victorian State Opera.

Indeed, in 1998 Adrian's recurrent travails inspired perhaps our most important arts initiative, as they made me realise that many of the major performing arts companies were living on the edge – only one box office failure away from disaster, thereby promoting a risk averse culture among administrators when the artists and patrons wanted the opposite. Most companies wisely split the roles of general manager and artistic director, but this could lead to friction when belt tightening was in order.

Opera Australia was only the most prominent example of big arts companies struggling with their finances, leading to the suspicion that they probably needed to review their governance practices and strategic plans, if any. The industry was loudly urging us to review the sector. I knew that this would inevitably mean more money, so I was not keen to go down this path without being confident that a decent level of funds would be forthcoming.

I decided to approach the PM first to seek some assurance. John Howard was not a noted arts patron, but he understood the political importance of the sector, which had traditionally leaned towards Labor. He quickly assured me that, if we set up a high quality review and it recommended a significant increase in funding, he would not leave me high and dry. In the result, Cabinet finally signed off on a Federal-State package of $70m – enough to surprise, and silence, the strongest sceptics.

MORE TO LIFE THAN POLITICS?

When we came to office the Australian film industry was in the doldrums. Beset by the Hollywood leviathan, we were producing art house films beloved by the critics and plenty of films with a distinctively Australian flavour but the target audience was narrow and inward-looking. A welcome exception was *Shine* for which Geoffrey Rush won an Oscar and which had universal appeal. We had launched a number of new Australian releases in Parliament House but with little real success. One of these was *Children of the Revolution*. I had long forgotten about it until one day I was at the London Heathrow Terminal waiting to depart when one of the Qantas staff, dedicated to escorting favoured guests to the gate, came to collect me and then said: "I'll just go and collect Geoffrey Rush." When she duly returned with him I said, almost apologetically: " Geoffrey, Richard Alston – it's a long time since we last met." Without missing a beat he said three things: Canberra – 1998 – *Children of the Revolution*." It was a stark reminder of how good actors must have superior memories and, of course, he is one of the very best.

As a result of our concerns about the film industry, and continued debate about its viability, we commissioned David Gonski to review the health of the sector. David certainly delivered the goods. He downplayed the "screen culture" approach, which emphasised the national identity, and concentrated on its commercial aspects and export potential. He recommended increased funding and incentives, but conditional on improved business efficiency. His insight into the arts as a business struck a chord with me. No one denies that artistic endeavour is core business of all arts companies but, if they are not well managed and do not learn to live within their means, they will either fold or run to government for an urgent hand out, which often merely prolongs the agony.

It struck me that the major arts boards, often lacking critical business expertise, had perhaps devoted too much time to the traditional emphasis on artistic culture and perhaps not enough to business culture, and that it was time to professionalise the sector. Reforming the big companies could hopefully make a major difference to quality as well as setting an example for smaller emerging companies to follow.

THE ARTS

It had been a shock to discover that, of the 31 major performing arts companies in Australia, only one, the Australian Ballet, had substantial financial reserves. Even this was somewhat fortuitous, thanks to its ownership of a veritable cash cow – a car parking station alongside the Arts Centre – in addition to the superior management skills from 1991 to 2002 of Ian McRae, its general manager and a former chartered accountant.

I had vivid memories of how good policy could bring its own political reward. Since 1958, NIDA (National Institute of Dramatic Art) had been the country's premier education and training institute in performance and production for theatre, film and television. Its alumni included a who's who of Australian drama luminaries: actors Cate Blanchett, Judy Davis, Toni Collette, Colin Friels, Mel Gibson, Baz Luhrmann, Garry McDonald, Robin Nevin, Miranda Otto, Richard Roxburgh and Hugo Weaving as well as directors Gale Edwards, Kip Williams and Jim Sharman. Its international standing can be gauged from the fact that, in 2013, NIDA was ranked as the 8th best drama school in the world by the *Hollywood Reporter*, Hollywood's leading daily entertainment trade newspaper since 1930.

For many years NIDA had been petitioning successive federal governments to provide funds for a new theatre. Its pleas had fallen on deaf ears. Its long standing artistic director, John Clarke, was a well-respected industry figure, with no publicly known political affiliations. I recognised that both he and his organisation had made a huge contribution to Australia's outsized international reputation in the dramatic arts. So, in 1998, I accepted his invitation to visit NIDA. His arguments impressed me, the need was obvious, and his timing was perfect, as the newly established Federation Fund was an obvious source for a significant capital sum which would not normally have been available for even the worthiest cultural projects. Accordingly, I made it my business to obtain the necessary funding ahead of the fast approaching 1998 election and I was duly invited to present the good news to several hundred enthusiastic students during the election campaign.

But before I addressed them, John Clarke spoke as follows:

"Many of you here today will shortly be voting for the first time. You may well feel that the ALP is the party of the arts. But although they have done good things in the past I want you to know that the Liberal Party is also our friend. The National Gallery, the Film and Television School and even NIDA came into being on their watch. And today the Minister is to here to deliver something we have been seeking for many years." I could not have wished for a more gratifying endorsement from one of the most respected arts figures and a truly living legend.

It convinced me that we could make a big difference to Australia's cultural life if we believed in ourselves and the sector by taking them seriously and ignored the advice proffered to me by one former respected Arts minister: "forget the nice words – they are only interested in ever more money." This was not my experience – like most administrators and performers they were much more interested in recognition and respect than playing political games. I vividly remember being told by Betty Churcher that she and the arts community valued passion and commitment above all. Thereafter I made a point of not reading my speeches on the arts, whenever possible, and injecting feeling and empathy into my remarks. My excellent departmental speechwriter originally despaired that I was not reading all her well-crafted gems, but I think she also came to appreciate that the medium was the message. Betty Churcher was living proof of dedication to the cause and was almost certainly the most impressive arts administrator that I had the pleasure to work with. I think Paul Keating felt the same.

It was with all this in mind and following the very welcome response from the PM to my request for funds that I started to put the pieces together. I was convinced of the axiom that good policy is good politics, so it was essential to have the review conducted by a team whose members had great business acumen as well as a love of the arts.

The chair of the dream team was Helen Nugent, whom I had known for many years as a very successful merchant banker, a committed academic with a doctorate in Indian history, and a deep love of the arts. The other key members, all equally worthy

THE ARTS

of being appointed chair, were three outstanding business leaders and arts lovers in David Gonski, Michael Chaney and Cathy Walter – appointments beyond reproach. If we had simply appointed business people there would inevitably have been a backlash from those in the sector, most of whom were much more passionate about culture than economics. Each of the members played a very active and enthusiastic role, often sharing ideas and data with me.

They all believed in the vital importance of a vibrant major performing arts sector from which many Australians frequently derived uplifting cultural experiences. They saw the need for a widespread commitment to new works, new productions and new patrons and supporters. They saw rolling triennial funding as a key factor in generating a long term perspective. They took the challenge very seriously and laboured mightily to produce a package of reforms which would put the sector on a much more professional and firmer financial footing.

Their formula for success was very impressive. $70 million would be provided by Federal and State governments and distributed to the companies on a matching basis, meaning they had to raise funds before government would provide an equivalent amount. Triennial funding would obviate the need to live from year to year and not only allow longer term planning but also give them time to recover from the almost inevitable periodic setback. The major arts organisations would also be required to professionalise their operations by submitting a detailed business case to the Australia Council for approval.

It was my singular duty to visit the State government Arts ministers, the majority of whom were also premiers, such as Richard Court (WA), John Olsen (SA), Bob Carr (NSW) and Jim Bacon (Tas) to enlist them to the cause. This was potentially quite a delicate exercise as a number were Labor politicians who might not have been expected to be overly enthusiastic about putting serious money into a Liberal-inspired project. To their enormous credit, I met no opposition, indeed strong support, save for a last minute, futile dummy spit from the Victorian Arts minister, Mary Delahunty.

The real achievement was not the money, much in all as the

media and many commentators often take the lazy option of measuring policy success in financial terms. The game changer was persuading arts companies and administrators that having the company on a sound financial footing gave them much more flexibility. Moreover, building significant reserves and raising funds from the private sector, particularly wealthy benefactors, was a much more reliable long term basis than relying on the vagaries of the political process and the highly variable commitment, enthusiasm and political clout of the Arts minister of the day.

It was critically important for arts companies to develop both a mission statement and a business model which could then be rigorously analysed by what became the Australia Council's Major Performing Arts Board. The Nugent Report also set a goal that all organisations should operate without ongoing deficits, an exemplar of sound business practice, and should also establish an assets base that would sustain them in difficult times – the practical implementation of our "reserves" requirement.

Thus companies and their senior management were forced to address the impact of globalisation, technological change and demographic shifts, as well as improve the organisation's overall performance, particularly by greater emphasis on professional marketing and targetted fund-raising. This enabled them to operate more efficiently and professionally and, by stabilising the ship, to acquire artistic vitality. Thus they would be free of regular government "interference" and could get on with their raison d'etre – high quality cultural performance.

The idea that companies should build reserves was not, as some have alleged, an emphasis on less risk-taking because the primary focus was now to be on "fiscal conservatism". This latter is a loaded term for those who don't want to acknowledge the importance of good governance and living within your means, thereby enabling sensible risk-taking without courting disaster.

The reality is that the "reserves" policy has been an overwhelming success. From only six companies with positive net assets greater than $1 million in 1999, when the Nugent Report was delivered, the 2007 Major Performing Arts Board report stated that this had grown to 16 with a 356 per cent growth in total net assets.

THE ARTS

Moreover, the number of companies with negative net assets had dropped from ten in 1999 to two in 2006.

This bumper result could hardly be used to support the quaint notion that the "capacity of companies to take artistic risk through the presentation of innovative material" had somehow been impaired; quite the opposite – they could now afford to take risks as never before. The responsibility to do so lay squarely with the companies, and any failure could not be deflected to government. Similarly, it is the role of the companies to set prices that reflect their cost structures and the audience's willingness to pay. It is no use saying that if we set prices high we will shut out the less well off. This is a perennial balancing act faced by all companies.

Living within your means should be easy to understand. Balanced budgets should make it easier to persuade government of the need for continuing funding or one-off special project grants. Serial sceptics sometimes suggest that a choice needs to be made between governance and artistic quality and that those of a conservative inclination will always back the wrong horse. This misunderstands the whole thrust of the Nugent Report: if the company first gets governance right, it will then have the means to concentrate on artistic quality. Otherwise, financial worries and poor management can fatally distract it from pursuit of artistic vibrancy.

Once Nugent had been safely and securely bedded down we had got the review bug. In the following year the Cultural Ministers Council commissioned a report into the financial and artistic viability of the small to medium performing arts sector, which resulted in a National Business Development program for small to medium companies. Next cab off the rank was a review of the contemporary visual arts and crafts sector, which we established in 2001. The newly appointed Arts minister, the redoubtable Senator Rod Kemp, quickly seized the moment and appointed Melbourne Myer family scion and arts enthusiast, Rupert Myer, to run the show, which he did in masterly fashion, and the Government subsequently committed nearly $20 million to the cause.

Final proof of the success of the Nugent review for the wider

MORE TO LIFE THAN POLITICS?

arts community is that it became a blueprint for subsequent reviews of other genres such as visual arts and crafts, symphony orchestras, new media, and dance. Professor Jennifer Craik of the RMIT University, in a 2007 monograph entitled *Re-visioning Arts and Cultural Policy*, makes the plausible assessment that, by commissioning the Nugent review, the Howard Government was embarking, in an ostensibly ad hoc way, on a review cycle of major elite cultural art forms.

I prefer to think that, after the Gonski film review, followed by the Nugent review, we had proved that it made sense to professionalise the arts companies – in their best interests, but also so that government could adopt a similarly professional response, based on solid information.

Craik would not seem to have been a fan of the Howard Government, which she says airily "was perceived as anti-arts" without saying when or by whom. She did, however, agree that "its record for injecting extra funds into the arts is impressive, up there with the Whitlam, Keating, Kennett and Dunstan administrations". Again, without being churlish, this assessment falls into the lazy trap of measuring success by quantity, when the arts community would say it is all about quality. While happy to accept the praise, I believe the Nugent review should be measured much more by its success in fostering a more rigorous and accountable ethos in arts organisations, many of which had been mollycoddled, and sometimes repeatedly bailed out, for far too long.

The emergence in recent years of cultural and media studies courses seems to have been accompanied by a severe left wing bias against anything "establishment" – an inherently bad thing – at least until you become part of it. Craik dismisses the major performing arts sector as "the big end of town", funded simply because they were visible, elite-oriented and represented by effective lobbyists. This ideological put-down completely ignores the quality of any of the different offerings and whether they deserve or need public funding. She also ignores the fact that the companies are generally "major" because they represent a vital part of our national high culture. They may not be regularly patronised by the masses, although nearly 50,000 people flocked to the Melbourne Cricket Ground in 1997 to see and hear The

Three Tenors in Concert. But the public surely knows they are a critical part of our cultural identity.

Would the anti-elitists prefer that government largesse be directed to mass culture? Many people, not only the young, have no hesitation in paying a small fortune to attend rock concerts and nostalgia tours – these events hardly need any help from government. The critics have a stronger case in arguing for assistance to emerging artists and the creative industries. Two highly successful Australian artists in Margaret Olley and Ken Done told me in no uncertain terms – Margaret on a regular basis – that you did not need government support to succeed – talent will generally shine through. Then again, commitment and passion are just as important – most artists instinctively know that their career path can be a big gamble, but perseverance is the key.

200

9

Indigenous Art

It was my good fortune to be handed the Arts portfolio at a time when the Indigenous art scene was booming. Paul Keating's Creative Nation, a $252m cultural extravaganza was launched in Canberra in October 1994 with great fanfare. As the Shadow Minister for the Arts I was officially there to witness all the action. Despite the usual personal indulgences of its author, it was a brave and overdue statement of the importance of the nation's culture to its economic and social wellbeing. The Creative Nation package did contain an important initiative, an Aboriginal Centre for the Performing Arts, now located in Brisbane and funded by the Queensland government, offering nationally accredited courses incorporating all performing arts genres, including contemporary dance, music and theatre.

At the same time, Keating was in the process of walking away from his pre-1993 election promise to build a national museum in Canberra. His Cabinet colleagues were understandably not greatly enamoured of this policy back flip and, instead, argued for a Gallery of Aboriginal Australia in Canberra as part of a museum "network". In due course, the Coalition Government proceeded to build the long delayed National Museum, which now has a very popular First Australians Gallery. The National Gallery of Australia also has a dedicated collection of Aboriginal and Torres Strait Islander art.

History

Aboriginal art has been acclaimed as the "greatest single cultural achievement" of Australia's post-white settlement history. According to Wally Caruana, author of the one of the earliest and best books on the subject, entitled simply, *Aboriginal Art*, it is "the world's oldest continuous living culture". The art is centred on storytelling, often primitive morality tales of the land, events and beliefs of the Aboriginal people, carefully handed down through the ages. It is characterised by its iconography of signs and symbols indicating various aspects of daily life and usages – waterholes, animal tracks, honey ants, spears, shields, tracks and meeting places.

It can be found in widely separated parts of Australia. There is evidence in the escarpments of Arnhem Land suggesting that paintings of ochre on rock were being made 50,000 years ago, with a continuous culture dating back even further. Kakadu holds one of the world's greatest concentrations of rock art, with some 5,000 sites recorded, and many more thought to exist. That these paintings constitute one of the longest historical records of any group in the world is one of the reasons why Kakadu is now a UNESCO World Heritage site.

Another place of considerable cultural significance is Quinkin Country, around Laura, in northern Queensland, with rock art dating back some 30,000 years. Wilpena Pound, in the spectacular Flinders Ranges, where Megs and I had a wonderful post-honeymoon holiday many years ago, also has amazing natural ochre rock paintings and engravings. The Kimberley region of northwestern Australia is famous for rock art featuring the so-called Bradshaw figures, named after the European explorer who discovered them. The Kimberley also embraces the vast area of the Wandjinas, the supreme spirit beings and creators of the land and its people. We have a wonderful painting of a Wandjina figure by Jack Dale in our sitting room. Quite recently a team of archaeologists and geochronologists from the University of Western Australia has identified more than 250 rock art sites, with more than 30,000 images, in the Kimberley region alone.

Bark paintings

But it was not just rock art that preceded the 20th century Aboriginal art explosion. Tommy McRae and William Barak were prominent, but conventional, 19th century Aboriginal artists, based in Victoria, who produced interesting contemporary drawings commissioned by European settlers. Produced almost exclusively in the Top End, bark paintings, based on sacred designs, with distinctive rarrk (cross hatching), have long been produced for instructional and ceremonial purposes.

The painting is on the interior of a strip of tree bark. The preferred medium is the bark from Stringybark, a form of gum. It is best cut from the tree in the wet season when the sap is rising, and then excising knots and other blemishes. The subject matter is often either a traditional Dreamtime story or a map, sometimes depicting a particular ancestral journey. On completion, a fixative, usually orchid juice, is added and the bark is splinted at either end to keep the painting flat and avoid curling.

The earliest surviving bark paintings date from the 19th century. Modern barks first appeared in the 1930s, when missionaries at Yirrkala and Millingimbi encouraged local people to produce commercially saleable paintings that could produce income to support the local mission and education facilities. Throughout the 20th century bark paintings were increasingly being made for more commercial purposes, and broadening their appeal so that, in 1929, the National Gallery of Victoria opened the first exhibition of bark paintings held outside an ethnographic museum. In 1963, the historic Yirrkala Land Rights bark petition was presented to the Federal Parliament, protesting the granting of mining rights over land excised from the Arnhem Aboriginal Land reserve.

Until the 1970s the bark paintings of Arnhem Land were effectively the market leaders. But, by the 1980s bark paintings had been accepted as fine art, not just interesting Indigenous handicraft.

The Desert Art movement

Aboriginal bark paintings have the longest history of collectable artworks from Indigenous Australia, but they were ultimately overtaken by a new artistic form which became the central desert dot art revolution.

A major breakthrough occurred in the 1930s when Rex Battarbee, a non-Aboriginal artist, went to the Hermannsburg Lutheran Mission, west of Alice Springs, where he introduced a young Albert Namatjira to the wonders of watercolours and landscape painting.

Namatjira went on to become the first internationally acclaimed Aboriginal artist superstar. His mastery of European techniques had obvious beauty in Western terms, but his subject matter was essentially confined to his ancestral landscapes through which he expressed his personal and spiritual relationship with his country.

Prior to the 1970s watercolours were the primary medium but gradually ochres and bark paintings became commercially sought after and the first art and craft centre was founded at the Ernabella mission in South Australia in 1948.

The genesis of the dot painting of the central desert art movement is generally traced back to 1971, when Geoffrey Bardon, a young, idealistic, white art teacher was sent to Papunya, near Alice Springs, to teach Aboriginal children. He noticed that when the Aboriginal men were telling stories they would draw accompanying symbols in the sand. He then persuaded them to start using Western techniques, painting initially on school walls and then on canvas, which he supplied, together with other necessary materials. Bardon was also instrumental in the establishment of the Papunya Tula co-operative, which still exists today. The first paintings from the Papunya Tula school of painting were never intended to be sold, being created as visual reminders of the artist's own life, land and family storyline. But it was not long before their striking beauty and freshness of style saw them in great commercial demand.

Clifford Possum Kngwarreye was one of the leaders from Papunya of what came to be known as the Western Desert Art Movement. Already an expert wood-carver, he subsequently created works of great beauty and complexity, earning him widespread international recognition. In 2007, one of his works sold for $2.4 million.

It was then that dot painting, as we now know it, took off, and it has never looked back. Just as it often represents the family storyline of the artist, so it also reflects the distinguishing features of the community from which it emanates. Its diversity also came from the colours, ochres and pigments employed. The dot style was often part of an aerial, or bird's eye, perspective, whereby artists imagined themselves hovering over their land (country), observing both the natural and metaphysical aspects of the landscape. The emergence during the 1980s of a profusion of female artists led not only to women-only communities such as Utopia, home of the famed Emily Kame Kngwarreye, but also a wider range of modern colours.

According to *The Amazing Story of Aboriginal Art*, an excellent essay published by the Artlandish Aboriginal Art Gallery of Kununurra in the east Kimberley region, it has since morphed into the most exciting contemporary art form of the 20th century.

With the emergence of the Desert Art mob the Aboriginal art movement exploded and shed its long-standing characterisation as folk art. In the early 1970s, following creation of an Aboriginal Arts Board with discretionary resources, grants were provided to individual artists for professional development and additional funds were made available for promotion, development and marketing. This was accompanied by the sudden emergence of the "new" style of acrylic-on-board at Papunya, which generated considerable excitement, especially in traditional fine art circles.

The 1970s also saw funds deployed for the employment of arts advisers who were directly accountable to the artists. This, in turn, encouraged new forms of art practice as well as the nurturing of younger artists and mentoring by older ones. The success of the arts centre model is the division of labour. Artists can get on with producing art while the professional imports can concentrate on buying and selling, as well as documenting, conserving and transporting the works. Other important tasks include arranging exhibitions, hosting visitors, handling intellectual property issues, administering grants and myriad other duties vital to the success of a commercially run small business.

My travels

In the course of my almost ten years in the Arts portfolio I visited many remote Aboriginal communities and pastoral stations. One of particular significance for rock art was a remote Kimberley cattle station named Fossil Downs, once part-owned by the cattle king, Sidney Kidman, and recently purchased by Gina Rinehart. It is home to fossilised plants and animals found in many of its limestone outcrops. It is an awe-inspiring experience to stand before

MORE TO LIFE THAN POLITICS?

still intact rock face of great antiquity and reflect that Australia's geology includes all known rock types from the Earth's 4.5 billion years of history.

Aboriginal art has been my favourite painting art form since the late 1970s, when I made my first acquisition, a small rectangular red and white bark painting.

In 1978, shortly after I had been elected Federal President of the United Nations Association of Australia, I visited Yalata, a remote South Australian Aboriginal community near Ceduna on the edge of the Victoria Desert, on the southern margin of the Nullarbor Plain. I have an indelible recollection of the small Aboriginal community, whose subsistence consisted of hunting and fishing in open mallee scrub. They were living in appalling Third World conditions. When I said so to the Melbourne *Age*, my observations received considerable publicity and, shortly afterwards, I was invited to join a unique parliamentary delegation to visit Docker River, nearly 700 kms west of Alice Springs on the WA/NT border.

The purpose of the visit was to accompany Ian Viner, the Federal Minister for Aboriginal Affairs, and attend an official ceremony to witness the handover to the local Aboriginal community of the land title deeds to the nearby Petermann Ranges. There were two ALP federal politicians on board: John Dawkins, then a fast rising backbencher from WA, and an avuncular Senator Ted Robertson from the NT. Both were excellent company and warmly welcomed me into the fold. The other important attendee was Paul Everingham, Chief Minister of the NT (1978-84), and later member of the House of Representatives for the Territory. Paul generously invited me to return with him to Darwin and accompany him on some flying visits to outlying communities, which he regularly visited. I have always been indebted to him; he was largely responsible for my introduction to the Indigenous way of life.

The Docker River excursion was a wonderful learning experience. After the formalities, we were bundled into the back of a ute and, after what seemed like many hours, we finally arrived around sunset at a very special ceremonial site with a number of important, but well concealed, water holes. They were not only of sacred significance but were also the life blood of these remote communities. After a very special ritual performance by tribesmen covered in very colourful feathers, we finally slept under the stars, always a mystical experience in the outback, and next day drove to Uluru, then still known as Ayers Rock.

In the course of these peregrinations I bought a piece of Aboriginal art, as previously mentioned, a modest bark, which marked my first major and unforgettable foray into the world of Indigenous politics and culture. Later I aspired to buy more but it was not until my portfolio responsibilities brought me into close contact with some wonderful artists and their works that I was really hooked.

I have continued to enjoy and acquire many more pieces, mainly central desert and Kimberley acrylic-on-canvas dot paintings rather than the Arnhem Land barks of my initial acquisition, which are always at risk of warping and cracking. In recent years lack of space at home and in the office has slowed down my acquisition impulses, to my wife's immense satisfaction. I still await the home delivery of auction house catalogues with considerable, if now largely academic, interest.

Among some very impressive art experts I met was Bob Edwards, who later offered me considerable sage advice. But undoubtedly one of the most interesting and knowledgeable Indigenous arts practitioners I have ever come across is Hank Ebes. His very unconventional career path has led to him being extraordinarily successful but also rather reclusive. He arrived in Australia as a youthful immigrant from his native Holland in 1962. His first career was crop dusting, before moving on to the printing trade, which had always fascinated him. His real breakthrough came as a result of the 1987 recession and the accompanying share market crash. At the time he was running an antique print shop. When the business fell into a hole, completely by chance the legendary Bob Edwards, then curator of the South Australian Museum, walked in. After a chat he offered Hank a job as honorary curator of printing history and technology. Hank decided instead to sell small paintings by Aboriginals to tourists. From that point on he never looked back and quickly immersed himself in the culture and business of Indigenous art.

MORE TO LIFE THAN POLITICS?

Obviously born to trade and commerce, he travelled extensively around central Australia and its many Indigenous arts communities. Over the years he acquired a number of mini masterpieces by leading artists, especially Emily Kane Kngwarreye, for whose work he had a minor obsession. Early on, I became quite a fan of Emily myself and purchased a nice piece from a leading Canberra gallery for $5,000, then a not insignificant amount. Imagine my mortification when, several weeks later, I read in the *Canberra Times*, not only about my purchase, but the amount paid. When I took this up with the gallerist her response was along the lines of, "I didn't think you'd mind". I certainly did, and declined to speak to her thereafter.

Undoubtedly the highlight of Hank's trading career was acquisition of Johnny Warrangula Nyunkunu's dreamtime painting, although in 2007 he sold a Clifford Possum masterwork for $2.4 million which he had bought at auction in 1996 for $39,600. The price far outstripped the first piece of Indigenous art to sell for more than a $1 million – Emily Kngwarreye's *Earth Creation*, for $1.056 million.

I first met Hank when he was running the very spacious Aboriginal Gallery of Dreamings at the top end of Bourke Street in Melbourne. He remained there for 20 years, until forced out by ever higher rents. He was very generous with his time and his encyclopaedic knowledge and acute insights into the Indigenous arts industry opened a treasure trove for me. His vast collection was spread over several floors and he would happily take me around on a guided tour while giving me chapter and verse on the foibles of the artists and the iniquities of the industry.

I bought paintings from him from time to time and, after I had departed from my formal arts responsibilities, he invited me to his newly acquired "aircraft hangar" masquerading as a vast warehouse in suburban Cheltenham. This Aladdin's cave contained the most eclectic array of art acquisitions, including Chinese pottery, tin toys, Japanese art, meteorites, model dinosaurs, burial suits and his beloved printing presses, in addition to his amazing Indigenous art collection. In 2011, after I had returned from London, he asked me to open his Emily Kngwarreye Gallery at Cheltenham and later

INDIGENOUS ART

to launch an auction of a number of valuable and significant Indigenous art works. Once again, showing his usual shrewd judgment, he was selling direct to the public and bypassing the auction houses and thereby their 22 per cent buyer's premium.

Indigenous art can be found in all parts of Australia – notable examples include Cape York (particularly the Lockhart River "Art Gang"), the Torres Strait, and Mornington Island in Queensland and the Pitjantjatjara Yankunytjatjara (PY) Lands in South Australia. The biggest collection of communities and the greatest outpourings of Aboriginal art, however, are to be found in Western Australia and the Northern Territory.

Western Australia
Western Australia has 30 per cent of the nation's art centres and 30 per cent of known Aboriginal artists. Most of the important art communities are in the Kimberley region, which has a long history of involvement with the cattle station movement and land rights.

Warmun
One of the most famous is Warmun, formerly Turkey Creek. One of the great modern Australian artists, Rover Thomas, created a new style of minimalist painting of ochre on canvas which was followed by other members of his East Kimberley School, such as Paddy Bedford Nyukunu, Freddy Timms aka Nharmaliny Gnarrmaliny, Jack Britten (who specialised in painting the nearby Bungle Bungles rock landform), George Mung Mung Lirrmiyarri and his son, Patrick Mung Mung, who is still going strong. Another Warmun legend was a close friend of Rover Thomas Joolama, Queenie McKenzie (Nkarra), with whom I had a prolonged afternoon tea not long before she died. Fortunately, I have a typical piece of her art, as well as those of some of the others, in my Kimberley Corner.

Balgo
My favourite art centre was Balgo (local name Wirrimanu), a small Indigenous community of around 400 in the heart of Western Australia's Great Sandy Desert, adjoining both the Great Sandy and

MORE TO LIFE THAN POLITICS?

Tanami deserts. In my time it had a supermarket, a Catholic school and church and not much else, apart from a rundown art centre. The community had been established in 1939, following the arrival of German Pallottine missionaries but, by 1981, it had reverted to Aboriginal control. Shortly afterwards an arts and crafts program was established, giving the residents their first access to art supplies.

According to a very informative article published by Japinka Aboriginal Art, a Fremantle based gallery: "The Balgo art movement gained momentum when local men painted large cloth banners for decorative use in the church. The calico banners were painted with poster paint, using traditional blacks and browns. Between 1982 and 1984 Aboriginal women also began to participate in painting classes and, in 1986, The Art Gallery of Western Australia displayed the inaugural Balgo exhibition *Art from the Great Sandy Desert*." By 1987 the Warlayirti Artists Co-operative had been formed at Balgo. I can always remember being taken by the predominance of the colour black, which to me was almost a defiant statement in favour of a colour that is not always popular. It was with me.

Japinka also says that in the mid-1990s, about the time I first visited, the resident art co-ordinators (who must have been my friends and mentors, the Cowans) encouraged artists to use brushes instead of wooden dotting sticks, and introduced vivid acrylics in blacks, pinks, greens, blues and yellows. So I was there at the beginning.

James and Wendy Cowan lived in the old mission house which they had already decorated with some wonderful art pieces. I also recall a priest lived nearby. Balgo is one of the most remote settlements, 300 kms from the nearest town of Halls Creek, surrounded by spinifex-covered plains, vast, windy escarpments and bright orange red rocky outcrops. The silence of the desert is profound, and the stark beauty overwhelming. An extraordinary experience, which I repeated several times on subsequent visits, was to spend time in an ancient cave perched on the side of a steep cliff, offering a panoramic view of the hills and outcrops which dotted the valley floor – the perfect place for contemplation. The Desert Fathers of Egypt would have loved it. I was told that, a few years before, a Catholic nun had actually lived there in isolation for more than twelve months. This made sense, as the grotto also contained a rudimentary altar and a statue of the Blessed Virgin Mary.

The Balgo artists' cooperative, which ran the art centre, was founded in 1987 after some of the original members of the Papunya Tula movement were allowed to return to their homelands, bringing with them the latest tools of trade, acrylic on canvas. Some of those who went on to fame, if not always fortune, and revelled in exotic names included Susie Bootja Napaltjarri, Eubena Nampitjin, Boxer Milner Tjampitjinpa, Bai Bai Napangardi, Tjumpo Tjapanangka, Helicopter Tjungurrayi, Sunfly Tjampjin, Millie Skeen Nampijin, Lucy Yukenbarri Napanangka and Wimmitji Tjapangati. Both men and women painted from the outset, but each gender has retained ownership of particular patrilineal or matrilineal links to country. Given Balgo's strategic location at the crossroads between various tribal groups, it is not surprising that there were regular social and ceremonial interactions, and it was not long before the artists' cooperative came to represent artists from the surrounding communities of Mulan and Bililuna.

According to that excellent work, McCulloch's *Contemporary Aboriginal Art*: "Two of the original painters of the Balgo painting movement were Milliga Napaljtarri, who freely translated drawings in sand and on the body by painting directly on canvas with her fingers, and Donkeyman Lee Tjupurrula, whose works included strongly coloured renditions of the classic Tingari (group of ancestral spirit beings) story". Balgo art has a distinctive vibrancy, with lavish use of bright colours, notably black. The artists themselves are an admixture of the contemporary and the traditional, displaying a deep understanding of the stories and ceremonies of the mythical Dreaming, and with a unique ability to combine the abstract with landscapes, the spiritual with a sense of place. It immediately struck me that it was an exciting form of Aboriginal art, unlike anything seen elsewhere. I became a lifelong fan.

Perhaps inspired by the long-standing religious ethic, painting at the art centre was a sociable, communal activity. The Catholic missionaries had an enlightened and sympathetic relationship with the local community: children were not removed from their families and the use of traditional language and customs was encouraged, resulting in mutually enduring links.

The virtual explosion of the new art techniques at Balgo is often explained by the introduction of modern painting materials such as brushes instead of dotting sticks and acrylics on canvas and later Belgian linen. But one critic, Robert Nelson, also gives credit to Sister Alice Dempsey who, in the early 1980s, proposed what he calls "an art commission of genius". It was a new decorative scheme for the church, so that instead of acrylics on canvas, artists were encouraged to produce large banners which, Nelson writes, "had a powerful effect in galvanising the will to make art for spiritual purposes that have belonged to the region since time immemorial".

Balgo is one of the oldest Indigenous art centres and, certainly in my time, one of the largest and most financially successful. There are no pastoral stations for miles around and absolutely no normal employment or other income earning opportunities, which may explain the extraordinarily high proportion of both male and female artists it has produced – a galaxy of self-taught desert art painting talent, with a diverse range of painting styles. It has been fortunate to have a succession of highly capable and visionary arts coordinators, usually married couples, who had made the place hum.

On my first visit, I found an art centre in name only, basically a broken-down timber, corrugated-metal shed. The paintings were unceremoniously piled on tables and the floor was both dusty and dirty. I therefore made it my duty to ensure that the Government's very successful Federation Fund, launched in 1999, not only covered the cost of a substantial renovation, but also enabled the building of a new visitors' cultural centre, replete with large light filled display areas and generous storage facilities. As a result, the conditions for art creation and production were transformed. The new centre also enabled the artists to expand their art forms, and thus commercial opportunities, to include prints, etchings on paper, photography, glass-making, film and music.

On one very memorable visit I was accompanied by Brian Ken-

INDIGENOUS ART

nedy, the charming and irrepressible Irish import whom I had earlier appointed as the Director of the National Gallery of Australia, and Antonia Syme, the wonderfully knowledgeable and long serving Director of Artbank, a very successful art rental program established in 1980 by the Fraser Government, but which had to be rescued from seizure and sale by the Finance bureaucrats early in the Howard years.

We were there to assess progress, but we also knew that Balgo was likely to have some very fine works for sale. Brian was keen to acquire some high-quality paintings for the National Gallery and I hoped to get a few pieces for myself. It was agreed that the rolled up pieces of canvas lying on the dusty floor should be exhibited, one by one, so we could first appraise the entirety of the offering. As they were being laid out, Brian began to set some aside. When I observed that this was occurring with some frequency I realised that, at that rate, I was likely to miss out altogether. After some loud grumbling on my part a truce was called, we reverted to plan A, and we both ended up very satisfied with our acquisitions.

Balgo subsequently became famous for its vibrant colours and dynamic designs. Gabriella Coslovich wrote in 2011:

> Their paintings celebrate the ever-shifting colours of the desert, the rock holes and soak holes where life giving water is found, the bush tucker concealed beneath the spinifex and the curious parallel lines of sandhills that make the Great Sandy Desert like no other.

Capturing this was an extraordinary achievement, given that many of the artists lived in abject squalor. I was once taken to the home of one, where I found a very famous artist effectively locked away in a dark back room and lying on a very dirty floor. He did not seem to be in poor health, but he was certainly not well looked after. The better organised painters were happy to work inside the art centre, dirty and cluttered though it was, but others painted in the desert, often with dogs and children all around and sometimes walking or running over the canvas.

On one occasion we were standing outside the art centre when

213

MORE TO LIFE THAN POLITICS?

a young lad turned up driving a clapped out 4WD. He asked if
we were interested in purchasing some canvases which he had
in the back. Without waiting for an answer, he proceeded to roll
out some wonderful pieces in the sand and dust. We later discovered he was a relative of Helicopter, one of Balgo's finest artists.
Whether he had the artist's permission to negotiate a sale was another matter.

Balgo thrived during the boom years prior to the GFC, with
the top artists earning up to $500,000 a year, from which they
retained 60 per cent, the remainder going to the art centre to buy
materials, pay salaries and attend to the innumerable administrative tasks that keep the business going. But the end of the boom
saw revenue fall by half and, with increased competition from
newly established art centres and the passing of many big names,
plus emerging social problems mostly associated with alcohol, it
became a hard slog. By 2011 the art centre had about 250 artists
on its books – more than half the town's population, although
only about 80 were regular painters. More importantly, the town
had become an alcohol-free zone, leading to a marked drop in
alcohol-related problems.

Warburton

The now defunct Warburton art centre in the south-east of WA
had a long tradition of cultural preservation, collecting and cu-
rating its artists' work. It also had a very impressive historical
collection and a professional glassblowing facility as well. At one
stage it exported its glassblowing skills to Balgo. Unfortunately,
despite claiming to have the nation's largest Indigenous-owned
private collection, then valued at about $6 million, in 2014 War-
burton was forced to close, not long after completing a highly
successful three-year exhibition program through China. Part of
its problem was remoteness. I had always thought of Balgo as being a very isolated community, but I was astounded to discover
that the closest town to Warburton, situated just south of the Gibson Desert in the remote east of Western Australia, was Laverton,
560 km away, almost twice as far as the distance from Balgo to
Halls Creek.

Northern Territory

There are over 90 remote centres in Australia, all run by Aboriginal organisations, with Indigenous boards of directors. The Central Desert Art Movement began in the NT, so it is not surprising, given its success, that the majority of Australian art communities and centres are located there. According to McCullough's *Contemporary Aboriginal Art*, art and craft have been practised at Central Australian communities such as Ernabella, Amata, Fregon, Uluru (Ayers Rock) and Hermannsburg since the 1960s. The main locations are at Yuendumu, Utopia, Haasts Bluff, Lajamanu, Kintore, Mt Liebig and Tennant Creek. I have visited most of them and, at least in my time, they varied enormously in organisational structure and effectiveness.

Papunya

In many ways the community of Papunya was an artificial construct of no inherent cultural significance. It had become home to many different groups of desert Aboriginal people who had been moved there in the late 1960s under a government policy of assimilation. It was not until Geoffrey Bardon's arrival in 1971 that its fortunes were transformed.

As we know, it was at Papunya that the school of acrylic painting on canvas began, with giants like Clifford Possum, and his fire dreaming and honey ant stories, leading the way. Other founding members, a number of whom reached great heights, were Ronnie Tjampitjinpa, Billy Stockman Tjapaltjarri and Long Jack Tjamamarra. The first works painted in the early 1970s were on board and similar hard materials, only later moving to canvas and Belgian linen. Natural ochres were quickly replaced by acrylic paint, a chemical compound, its fast-drying and water-resistant qualities making it a more durable and versatile application.

Recreating traditional transient images on more permanent materials not only enabled them to be preserved for posterity but also provided a means of passing vital aspects of time-honoured culture to younger generations. By 2008 many of the great original artists had died and the population of Papunya had dropped to around 300: many of the core Pintupi artists had returned to their homeland settlement of Kintore and most traces of the original structures gone. The famous school mural, which Geoffrey Bardon had carefully nurtured, had long ago been painted over by insensitive bureaucrats. Notwithstanding, Papunya Tula Artists Pty Ltd, with its large showcase shopfront gallery in Alice Springs, has become the best known Aboriginal arts centre in Australia.

Yuendumu

One of the biggest and most successful communities, Yuendumu art has always stood out because of its vibrant colours and intricate patterns. Even the external walls of the original community arts centre are completely covered by brilliantly coloured murals. Almost all of its more than one thousand residents are of the Warlpiri language group, so that there is an unusual level of social cohesion compared to other more disparate communities.

Utopia

This important art community, some 300 kilometres north-east of Alice Springs, is nowadays best known for the extraordinary artistic talent of Emily Kngwarreye, but the modern history of the region goes back to its days as a collection of sheep stations settled by Europeans in the 1920s, before being returned to Aboriginal ownership in the late 1970s. Utopia's modern art movement began in 1977, when a batik-making fabric workshop was established. This was so successful that, by 1988, the Utopia Women's Batik Group had more than 80 members.

For many years Emily confined her artistic talents to the making of batiks, and it was not until she was in her 70s and she had moved to conventional acrylics on canvas that she hit the big time and went on to be a genuine international superstar, with several of her works selling for more than $1 million. Among her early promoters, and later dealers, were Janet and Donald Holt, owners of nearby Delmore Downs, which I visited on several occasions. Emily was not alone in her artistic success at Utopia, which was otherwise dominated by the Petyarre clan (Ada Bird Petyarre, Gloria Petyarre, Anna

INDIGENOUS ART

Petyarre, Greeny Purvis Petyarre, Kathleen (and her daughter, Abie Loy Kemarra) and Nancy) and the Pwerle clan (Emily Galya Pwerle Atnwengerrp, Minnie Pwerle and her daughter, Barbara Weir).

Ampilatwatja

Just over 100 kilometres north-east of Utopia is another amazing community, established only 20 years ago as an offshoot of the Utopia community. I had the pleasure of visiting it not long after it came into existence. What immediately struck me was the style consisted of traditional Aboriginal art figures on a very recognisable western landscape. It was proof positive that Aboriginal art had the capacity to evolve and to bridge the divide between the contemporary and the traditional. Susan McCullough describes it as "a unique, freshly figurative and naïve style". It is certainly a splendid development and, as a result, I have a number of splendid colour pieces, including several from Jilly Holmes.

Hermannsburg

In the 1920s Hermannsburg was a Lutheran mission station where pioneer missionaries encouraged the local Arrente (then known as Arunta) people to experiment with lacework, embroidery and carving, and it was not long before a school of naturalist watercolour painting was established under the guidance of two Melbourne painters, Rex Battarbee and John Gardner. In 1936 Battarbee gave materials and lessons in watercolour painting to the young Albert Namatjira. By the late 1940s at least ten male artists became known as the Hermannsburg School, painting in the style of the master, many of whose descendants have had successful artistic careers.

In the 1960s, in quite a separate development, a pottery school was established by a mission employee and, after a few false starts, it has continued to prosper to this day, on both the domestic and international stages.

Art centres

Whereas many western artists pursue formal training and work as individuals, most contemporary Indigenous art is created in com-

217

MORE TO LIFE THAN POLITICS?

munity groups and art centres. The art centres have a vital role in promoting economic independence. Today's business managers need to have an ever-wider range of skills including facility with social media. Unfortunately it seems that, like the Indigenous art industry in general, the art centres have struggled badly since the GFC of 2008.

In 2016, the Art Economies Value Chain research project, commissioned by the Co-operative Research Centre for Remote Economic Participation, collected data from 87 art centres and 136 art businesses throughout Australia, "focusing on economic, social and trade issues in the art value chain". It found that earnings in 73 art centres had dropped by 126 per cent over the 12-year period to 2013, despite Commonwealth funding to art centres during the same period of $160 million, constituting 80 per cent of funding to the sector.

A dozen large centres, such as those at Yirrkala and Yuendumu, accounted for about three quarters of total sales. The highest producing region, by number of products and value, was the Western Desert, followed by the Kimberley. More than 80 per cent of all sales were concentrated in the four major art regions: Western Desert, Arnhem Land, the Kimberley and the APY lands of South Australia.

Art centres in those four regions serviced 75 per cent of registered artists and received half of all relevant funding. Half of Australia's art centres, representing almost 4000 artists, produced less than 20 per cent of sales. More than half were not profitable, raising questions about their long-term viability. What this major research demonstrates is that art centres are inherently fragile, depending heavily on the calibre and continuity of competent art centre managers and at the mercy of markets as well as the weather.

The key to success of any Indigenous arts centre, particularly in more remote areas, is to have good art co-ordinators, now called managers. They usually work in pairs, and are often recent graduates with a committed interest in Indigenous culture and lifestyle. There are no formal job qualifications but the skills required are an all-round ability to run a business and relate to people. Demands are constant. Artists need raw materials, a place to paint, and access to reputable urban galleries. They also require help with fi-

INDIGENOUS ART

nancial, domestic, medical, legal and transport needs and, sometimes, protection from avaricious relatives, known in the trade as "humbugs."

Professor Jon Altman from Deakin University argued in 2005 that, although Aboriginal visual art had been a spectacular success for more than 30 years, it remained highly dependent on public patronage and active brokerage between artists and the fine arts market, for which the intermediating influence of arts centres, governed by Aboriginal committees, has been crucial. His numbers are no doubt dated by now, but he asserts that there were then about 1200 discrete Indigenous communities, with an estimated total Indigenous population of 120-150,000 and around five to six thousand artists.

He regards the key participants in the industry as not so much the artists themselves but the mostly white people whose expertise is in the fields of anthropology and Western art. He says that the earliest community art centre was established at Ernabella in the north of South Australia, but the missionaries, not the artists, controlled it. This was not a bad thing as, without their entrepreneurial spirit, it would probably never have happened. Production and sale of art was seen not only as a means of introducing the cash economy in remote communities, but also as a way of demonstrating Aboriginal cultural vibrancy. As a result, by the 1960s there were missionary society shops in Melbourne and Sydney, working closely with arts agents to mediate both collecting and selling.

One of the most successful art coordinator teams was the husband and wife combination of James and Wendy Cowan at Balgo, as described earlier. James had an instinctive feel for how to ensure the adoption of business-like practices whilst also being conscious of the need to have empathy with his charges. I first met James when he was at Balgo in the mid-1990s and we kept in touch for over ten years until his peripatetic nature took him away from my ken. James was a class act, a charming companion and a wonderful raconteur. He had such a wide knowledge of different tribal cultures, having lived extensively in many remote parts of the globe. He was also a very successful writer and author of a number of internationally acclaimed books, including *A Map-*

maker's Dream, winner of the prestigious Australian Literature Society's Gold Medal in 1998.

James subsequently wrote two books on Balgo art and was also an ardent collector. He was especially taken by the works of Eubena and persuaded me to acquire several. I didn't really need much persuading, given Eubena's graphic use of dazzling pinks, reds and yellows.

This period was more than a recrudescence. It was a rebirth of Aboriginal art in the late 20th century. One thing that makes the early generations of the Indigenous art movement unique is that many of the most successful artists, both men and women, came to the vocation late in life. Eubena, one of Balgo's most prolific artists, began painting in her mid-40s and survived to a ripe old age. Her contemporary, Susie Bootja Bootja, was in her mid-50s when she took the plunge to become a full-time artist.

Indigenous women artists

Men predominated as artists well into the 1980s, often as principal custodians of their patrilineal culture and familial customs. There were only a few women such as the Napangardi sisters, Pansy and Eunice, at Papunya working alongside male artists. The Women's Batik Group at Utopia, formed in 1977, created Aboriginal textiles for the fashion market and subsequently provided the springboard for Emily Kngwarreye's rise to international fame. Beginning in 1989, whilst in her 70s, she began painting her Country and Dreaming, developing a unique colourist style and producing over 3,000 works. At Utopia, Emily mentored her niece, Barbara Weir, who in turn encouraged her mother, Minnie Pwerle, to take up painting in 2000.

Not long before I headed to London in 2005, I visited Utopia. I was blown away by the quality of the artwork of many of the female artists. Their business activities, however, were being handled not by a resident art coordinator at Utopia but by a white intermediary based, at least temporarily, in Alice Springs. Shortly after arriving in London, he emailed me, advising that his art affairs were a mess, he was headed for the courts and he could no longer identify which works were mine. Not quite knowing what

INDIGENOUS ART

to do from the other side of the world, I made a few phone calls
to the Northern Territory. Eventually, a very helpful senior officer
from DFAT, based in Darwin, agreed to pursue the matter. Thanks
to her patience and diligence, the matter was eventually resolved
and, in due course, I received five excellent works which are now
on display in our home. What made them so interesting was that
they were colourfully painted by Aboriginal artists but the subject
matter was more in the western landscape style, without any overt
indication of the artist's country or family history.

From the late 1980s female artists began developing distinctive
regional and personal styles, which they linked to their own close
kinship ties and shared creation stories. At Kintore in the 1990s,
women from near Papunya started using a distinctive palette
with brighter colours and loose brushstrokes. They also began to
take on key community leadership roles. In the east Kimberley,
Queenie McKenzie combined the teaching of local women's law
with being an active producer of high-quality art work. For many
years she combined with her kinsman, Rover Thomas, to create
works in gentle colours of soft pinks, browns and yellows.

Meanwhile urban Aboriginal women began to flex their mus-
cles. In 1987 the Boomalli Aboriginal Artists' Co-operative was
formed, with numerous artists working in a variety of contemporary media. These included trailblazers such as Bronwyn Ban-
croft, designer and manager; Brenda Croft, photographer, curator
and writer; Fiona Foley, diverse media and installations artist; and
Tracy Moffat, photographer and filmmaker.

Government support

The Australian community has long recognised that there are certain art forms, such as opera and dance, which, because of fixed
cost structures, limited demand and market volatility will always
require significant government funding. But Aboriginal art is not
just another money-making commercial art form.

It reflects the earliest period of our historic Indigenous culture and
has both artistic and anthropological merit. It has provided a powerful incentive to survive and hopefully thrive in remote communities
where it is often the only sustainable income earning activity.

MORE TO LIFE THAN POLITICS?

This transcendent art movement has helped to strengthen cultural ties in Aboriginal society by reinforcing the values of traditional knowledge which form the basis of Aboriginal art. It is something uniquely Australian of which the whole nation should be proud. Given the unique importance and high international recognition of Indigenous Australian art, governments should not be reluctant to accept comparable responsibilities in this area.

Having responsibility for Indigenous art was both an honour and a pleasure. Apart from the joy of being around some priceless and inspiring works, there was always the awareness that the greater good was at stake. Painting was, for many, a vocation which gave them purpose in life and, often, a sense of significant achievement. But it also provided an escape route from poverty, more than psychic benefits for their relatives, and a lifeline for many communities.

In addition to the guidance I obtained from experts in the field, I also had the invaluable assistance of my Courtauld-trained Aboriginal arts adviser, Fiona Menzies, whose enthusiasm for the project and her close collaboration with my senior arts adviser, Fiona Poletti, gave us a formidable and high-achieving team, for which I will always be very grateful.

David Hockney in his studio in the Hollywood Hills

With David Hockney and Peter Goulds, his agent

David Hockney
"Two Red Chairs, March 1986"
Home made print
Edition 11 of 44
8-1/2 x 11"
© David Hockney
Photo Credit: Richard Schmidt

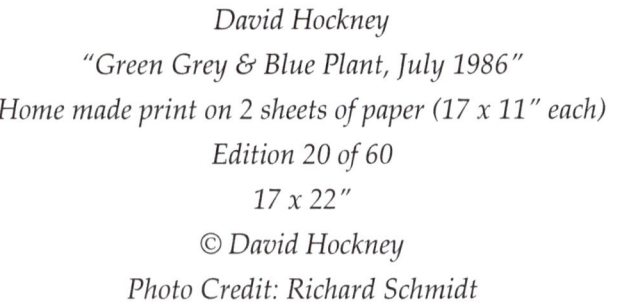

David Hockney
"Green Grey & Blue Plant, July 1986"
Home made print on 2 sheets of paper (17 x 11" each)
Edition 20 of 60
17 x 22"
© David Hockney
Photo Credit: Richard Schmidt

David Hockney
"The Studio March 28th 1995"
Digital inkjet print
Edition 27 of 45
35 x 43-3/4"
© David Hockney

In the study: major aboriginal works by Long Jack Phillipus and Clifford Possum and "one small upright bear" from Whistler, British Columbia

Stella Gimme, Balgo artist, untitled

Jack Dale, Kimberley artist, "Wandjina Woman"

Wilma Ross Ngala, Ampilatwatja artist, untitled

With Dr Brian Kennedy, former Director, National Gallery of Australia (left), and artist Michael Jagamara Nelson (centre)

A soumak (flat woven tapestry) from the Caucasus

Persian silk carpet purchased in Tehran, 2006

10

Whose ABC?

Like most Australians, I have long regarded the ABC as one of the country's leading cultural institutions. I grew up on an unrelieved diet of ABC broadcasts of football and cricket (including staying up until 3 am our time when stumps were drawn in Ashes Tests in England) as well as listening to regular 15 minute on-the-hour news broadcasts. The absence of advertising was a unique feature, making it an irresistible alternative to the commercial stations, especially as in those days the ABC took mainstream sport very seriously.

Political allegiances have become much more fluid over the years since the ABC's establishment in 1932. When I was growing up I never heard my parents, neither of them left-wing supporters, ever criticise the ABC, let alone accuse it of bias. They and their contemporaries had great respect for the organisation and its programs. But it must be said that, even then, leading politicians had a somewhat more jaundiced view. Indeed, the Prime Minister of the day, Mr Menzies, is reported to have observed that, while ever there was an ABC, there was no need for the Labor Party to have a publicity department!

But the ABC seems, especially since the Vietnam War era, to have become increasingly one-sided in its views and coverage. Maybe, like many institutions, it has simply run out of steam. But it is more complicated than that. Back in the days when Talbot Duckmanton was General Manager the direction of the organisation was in firm hands; now it seems to be run by the staff and there is not much the Board or senior management can do about it. As Sir Humphrey Appleby famously said: "Ministers come and go, but we go on forever". But the staff don't really want to run anything. They prefer a cultural takeover, with the organisation being run on their terms and in accordance with their world view.

It is interesting to reflect that, in little more than twenty years since I first became Minister for Communications, almost everything within my then policy purview has changed, often dramatically, sometimes at warp speed, so that many rules and regulations are no longer fit for purpose. What has not changed in the slightest is the political and cultural conceit of the ABC. As a consequence, many recent controversies around funding disputes and unacceptable bias still ring loud bells for me, and are worth considering later in this chapter, alongside a case study of ABC radio's coverage of the Iraq War in 2003.

Chairing a Senate select committee into ABC practices in the early 1990s, combined with my participation in Estimates hearings while in Opposition, gave me some insights into the way the national broadcaster was run. But it was not until we came to government that I saw how chaotic some of its processes were. Three key issues quickly became apparent: the basis and level of its funding; the quality of its content offerings; and the broadcasting standards to which it is required to adhere.

I had always thought that most of its key news and public affairs presenters and commentators had a very different world view, not simply from that of the Liberal Party but, more significantly, from that of the community at large. The ABC is generally insulated from the reality of ordinary lives. The News and Current Affairs department, largely Sydney-centric, probably couldn't help themselves, but I still didn't see it as a deliberate ALP view, rather more of a green, social justice, anti-establishment view, to the left of both major parties. I had little doubt that most would put Labor ahead of the Coalition at the ballot box. On several occasions in Estimates hearings I asked the then Managing Director, David Hill, about the staff's political proclivities, but he always batted such questions away with an airy, "Senator, we would never ask them who they supported or whether they belonged to any political party".

Hill rose to political prominence initially under the auspices of Neville Wran when he was Premier of New South Wales, first as head of what was called the Ministerial Advisory Unit and then as chief executive of the State Railway Authority. Under the Hawke Government he moved to the ABC, first as chairman and shortly afterwards as Managing Director. He later ran as the Labor candidate in the seat of Hughes at the 1998 Federal election.

When I was practising at the Bar, I once asked Dick McGarvie, QC, an icon of Labor and a long standing member of its Victorian executive, what he thought of the ABC. I half expected a vigorous defence, but, more in sorrow than in anger, he told me that when he was growing up, the ABC was the broadcaster of record – now it was anything but.

On one occasion, after I had been pilloried in cartoons portraying me as thumbing my nose at an ABC logo, I was asked if I would repeat the gesture with a smile on my face for the private amusement of a strictly in-house ABC soirée. Trustingly, I did so, only to find that within a matter of hours it was all over the media. And they wonder why at times they perceive an absence of good will!

Coming to government

I had never been in favour of advertising on the national broadcaster, let alone deliberately starving it of funds. But these and many other slurs were immediately thrown at the Coalition when we came to government in March 1996 in a deliberate attempt to muddy the waters. One of our first actions was to commission Bob Mansfield, a successful businessman with impeccable commercial and media credentials, having run McDonalds, Optus and Fairfax, to conduct a review of its operations.

He reported that the ABC could cope quite adequately with $500 million, and they did. Just over 20 years later, with sluggish wages growth for the last half of that time, their annual budget funding now exceeds $1 billion, but the ABC still complains that it needs more! The concept of living within its means seems to be an alien one – much easier to just run a political campaign to embarrass the Government into caving in to its demands and provoke the Opposition of the day to be the good guys by offering much more. The ABC's view appears to be that statutory independence means that governments cannot legitimately quibble with whatever the ABC thinks it needs or even what it would like. No other agency of government, nor any private sector entity, operates in this way.

The Mansfield Report was well received in many quarters, including inside the ABC. Nevertheless this did not stop the so-called "Friends of the ABC" hysterically proclaiming it to be "a step towards the end of the ABC as we know it" – hardly a constructive contribution to public debate, just another "my country, right or wrong" parody, but a good example of the hyperbole that often passes for debate about the ABC.

Its zealously guarded "independence" is mentioned several times in the *Australian Broadcasting Corporation Act 1983*, but it is not defined. The Act makes it clear that the Corporation does not have carte blanche. Under government-wide legislation all public corporations, government business enterprises, agencies and commissions are accountable to the Parliament and the public and have strict obligations in terms of budget and financial management reporting. There is no entitlement to any particular level of public funding. The Government strictly observes the obligation not to interfere in the day-to-day running of the Corporation, but it certainly controls the purse strings and is accountable to the Parliament for doing so.

But any proposal for change, or even a suggestion thereof, by a Coalition government, is met by a barrage of criticism from groups such as the "Friends" and the easily outraged Community and Public Sector Union, together with howls of "political interference", often amplified by recruiting a few big name soft touches, the politically disaffected like John Hewson, or obvious political partisans, and especially some high-profile actors or artists. Labor politicians, while in opposition, can be relied upon to loudly support any and all grievances, at least until they find themselves in office.

Long serving in-house warriors like Quentin Dempster have had no compunction about publicly criticising management if they disagree with the Board's strategy. Employees see nothing disloyal about leaking documents or briefing journalists – conduct which would never be tolerated in the private sector. Staff-elected directors are free to exercise personal judgment about the extent to which Board deliberations are briefed to those upon whom they rely for re-election – a classic conflict of interest which does not prevail in any public company, for very good reason, as it ensures that directors will be very circumspect in their boardroom contributions, lest they be leaked to the media or staff.

Someone once told me in relation to the BBC: "A decision of the Board merely signals the start of the debate". He might as well have been speaking about its Australian next of kin. Employees will fight their corner with little regard for the bigger picture. When the Mansfield Report recommended more outsourcing, the push back was multi-layered and emotional: this could be the death of the good old ABC; steamrollered by a values-free ruthless private sector, etc. The obvious answer was that the ABC would still control the project – do the commissioning, set the values, pay the bills, but the case was never publicly considered on a cost/benefit analysis basis – much easier to run on nebulous concepts of values and precious notions of "independence and freedom", guaranteed to strike a sympathetic chord with those who don't have to worry about value for money.

When management sought to achieve efficiencies, such as Brian Johns' *One ABC* proposal to yield large savings by bringing television and radio together after being under separate management since 1983, there was insider uproar. Brian Johns, Hill's successor as Managing Director, was a very fine human being, and a dedicated servant of public broadcasting, having previously distinguished himself as chief executive of the Special Broadcasting Service (SBS). Alas, he had to contend with considerable high-level internal opposition and it was very regrettable when he was ultimately elbowed aside. It was an honour to speak at his retirement function.

I do hear the occasional call for the ABC to be privatised, but no one I know wants it to be closed down, sold off or emasculated. The Parliamentary Liberal Party has certainly never advocated it. What people want is for the ABC to live up to its obligations, be transparent and accountable, produce high quality content and, like the rest of us, live within its means.

Nor did I ever suggest, despite frequent anti-conservative philippics from Phillip Adams, that Radio National should be closed down. Its suite of quality programs, not uniformly even, but interesting and thought provoking niche offerings, catering principally to educated and diverse audiences, had always impressed me notwithstanding the political rantings of Robyn Williams, the head of the science unit. That is the essence of quality broadcasting, and no other medium could possibly offer such a range.

Classic FM, by contrast, posed more of a dilemma. For many years I had enjoyed, and still do, the UK's Classic FM, a commercial station with the highest ratings in the country, offering essentially middlebrow classical music and some talk back. The ABC version, on the other hand, has too little opera and too much talk. Christopher Lawrence was an outstanding presenter, and he was not alone. But, as there are already community stations offering very similar fare and the ABC's content offering has no unique points of difference, the real question is why does the ABC need to compete in this space?

Funding

The ABC relies almost entirely on the taxpayer for funds, and the Parliament has a duty to ensure that these funds are spent wisely. There are plenty of examples of taps being turned off in the public sector where there has been an obvious case of lavish spending or fiscal negligence. While the Liberal Party ruled out advertising, it did encourage the ABC to adopt a more commercial approach by raising funds from private and philanthropic sources, instead of simply putting its hand out for ever more taxpayer largesse. Unfortunately, the ABC has never had much success at being more commercial. It probably feels it doesn't really need to or is fearful of an internal backlash from those who still think "commerce" is a dirty word.

In the last ten to fifteen years the commercial broadcasting sector has been under enormous pressure, having to change formats, styles and charging regimes just to survive in the new, technology-driven world. As we know, many parts of the print media sector teeter on the edge of bankruptcy, saved only by proprietors with deep pockets. But the ABC, which is under no such pressures, has lowered its standards. There is no longer any supervision of spelling and pronunciation and the line between news and opinion is increasingly blurred – what starts out as a story about the weather quickly becomes yet another scare about the impact of climate change.

WHOSE ABC?

The commercial media is able to put whatever slant it likes on a story, subject to various codes of practice, as it has to make money from advertising and circulation and therefore endeavours to boost audience numbers by judging how best to appeal to them. There is a serious crisis right now in regional media with the closure of many country outlets, both television and print – the survivors struggle on, unlike the metropolitan media, which has the capacity to adapt. The bush desperately requires trusted media sources and the ABC is uniquely placed to fill the emerging gap. But it seems much more attracted to the digital world of the big cities. The BBC in regional areas now shares content with the commercials and sometimes its journalists are even embedded there – the only way to get local stories is to have journalists on the ground. Has the ABC examined this model?

The funding of national institutions does not proceed in a vacuum. If the country is at war, everyone's belt has to be tightened. Where the country is in recession, or there is an urgent need for budget repair, hard decisions have to be taken. The right and proper amount for the ABC is largely in the eye of the beholder, the outcome of protracted negotiation and persuasion.

The ABC acts as if it is a natural monopoly – there as of right, to be respected and appreciated, but never to be scrutinised nor critically questioned. But it should take note of the impact on content of the technological winds of change from which it cannot be immune. In the UK, 860,000 viewers cancelled their TV licences in 2018 – an eight per cent increase on the previous year – due to the "Netflix effect". The ABC budget is like a glorified defined benefit scheme, where you get your reward irrespective of investment performance and the employer's capacity to pay. Such schemes are, these days, very much out of fashion, as it is no longer generally acceptable for other recipients of government funding to have to take their share of the fiscal medicine while the privileged few are insulated at the expense of all other claimants. The argument is not that the ABC budget should be tied to GDP, or the Government's fiscal situation. The argument is that it should acknowledge that is fortunate to be largely insulated from the vicissitudes which confront the rest of the media and society more generally, instead of thinking that its claims should trump all others.

I am reminded of the tariff protection debates in the 1970s and '80s where policy-makers, not least politicians, finally came to realise that protective walls simply encouraged inefficiency, with no need to pursue innovation and value for money. Competition now drives these outcomes. The trouble is that the ABC does not have any direct competitors.

The ABC view on its "unearned income" is therefore a throwback to a bygone era. I will never forget going into bat for ABC senior management for something like a $75 million package to benefit rural listeners and viewers, only to hear them say, when the funds had been safely pocketed, that they would spend the monies as they saw fit. Independence is not licence.

A 2011 book about the ABC by historian and admirer Ken Inglis makes compelling reading. He clearly had access to many ABC staff and happily endorsed their views and the way the ABC sees its finances. He starts by saying that, in 1996, the incoming Finance Director, Russell Balding, later a capable Managing Director, had discovered that, since 1985-86, funding had fallen by 25 per cent in real terms and that "during the last few years expenditure had been allowed to go on rising … if you were running a private organisation you would be ordering serious surgery or closing down". In other words, a private sector organisation in this situation would be on the brink of insolvency. But, instead of heads rolling or systems being overhauled, even in-depth post-mortems undertaken, this became a fiscal crisis that only the Government could solve by, as readers will quickly guess, more money.

The ABC had been grizzling since early in Mark Armstrong's term as Chairman (1991-96) about "a decline in real terms", but instead of accepting that it had to make do with the available funds, it saw the only way forward was to bully the Government to give more. Apparently someone had been asleep at the wheel for quite a while, for it took a new Finance Director to discover that: "for the last few years expenditure had been allowed to go on rising". The ABC's answer, if the Government did not come to the party, was to threaten that its most popular shows were at risk, accompanied by high profile job cuts. This was entirely a political strategy, designed to play out in the public arena, with fingers pointed at the

Government for being fiscally callous – no acceptance of internal irresponsibility, or any mention of internal cost saving proposals. When I was first appraised of the ABC's latest "fiscal crisis", and I understandably asked why it had taken so long to discover the shortfall, Inglis is quick to characterise my response as minatory, in other words, threatening.

On taking office in March 1996 the Coalition discovered, contrary to repeated Labor Government assurances, that it had inherited a $10 billion Budget deficit. The Government took the brave but heroically vindicated decision to fix the problem in one fell swoop by cutting the budgets of every government department and agency, except Defence, by 10 per cent. But this did not stop the ABC and its supporters from screaming blue murder and carrying on as though the ABC alone had been singled out for special treatment, often accompanied by dark implications that this was all part of a secret, pre-determined plot to cut the ABC to pieces. When I announced that the ABC budget for the remaining year of the triennium would remain steady, but thereafter be subject to a $55 million cut at the start of the next triennium, all hell broke loose, and we were repeatedly accused of breaking our election commitments.

My infamous "pre-election" commitment

This particular allegation warrants careful examination. The Coalition had gone into the 1996 election with some specific promises regarding the ABC: "The Coalition will maintain existing levels of funding to the ABC". Taken in isolation this could mean in perpetuity, but it was immediately qualified by the next commitment: "The Coalition will continue to support triennial funding". Implicit in the triennial concept is that every three years the Government would renegotiate the existing agreement and not simply be bound to continue existing arrangements. Otherwise there would be no need for a three-year review. The first commitment was similarly silent on the question of indexation, so "existing levels" on its face meant the same amount, not an increase in real terms (as was afterwards alleged), until the expiration of the then current triennium in June 1997.

MORE TO LIFE THAN POLITICS?

These promises were honoured, but the subsequent furious debate seems to have proceeded largely on the basis of an answer I gave, after the election (so, by definition, not a pre-election commitment). Late on election night, when we were all deep in celebratory mood, Jim Middleton, an experienced ABC journalist, asked a series of harmless questions, before coming to his "gotcha" question. It may not have been intentional, but it certainly suited the ABC's purposes.

His question, taken from a video of the interview, was: "Turning now to your ABC commitment to maintain funding in real terms over the term of the coming Parliament, does that still stand, even if you discover on Monday that the Budget bottom line is much worse than the Government has been saying?" [emphasis added]. My reply was: "Absolutely. John Howard has made it very plain that we want to honour all our commitments". He was clearly purporting to refer to our pre-election written commitment, despite quoting it inaccurately in the preamble to his question. I was just as clearly referring to our actual commitment which certainly did not contain the words, "in real terms", and also included nothing about maintaining funding "over the life of the Parliament".

Our explicit reference to triennial funding, which ran out during the term of the coming Parliament, said quite the opposite. If the question had merely been, "do your pre-election promises still stand, even if you suddenly discover that you have inherited a big Budget deficit?", it would have been not only perfectly legitimate but also very prudent.

But he chose not simply to refer to what we had promised but to add a few extra words giving a different meaning and one much to the advantage of the ABC. Most of it was a legitimate question but, tucked away inside, was a seriously inaccurate statement with potentially damaging effect which might have gone unnoticed in the carnival atmosphere at the moment of victory to add what the ABC wanted, not just what we had promised. It is also significant that, although I repeatedly pointed out the lethal falsity of the excess verbiage, neither apology nor clarification from the ABC was ever forthcoming.

232

Most businesses are constantly under pressure to perform. It is not only small businesses that fail. Look at the list of the ASX 200 over a ten year span and a number of those companies will have fallen or merged. It is even more precarious in the United States. The ABC has been around since 1932. Not many companies are so lucky. Schumpeter's "creative destruction" does not threaten the ABC – it is uniquely privileged. Earning a living for most of us can be very challenging. But the ABC is very different. It doesn't really have to earn a living – taxpayer funds roll in every year with not much volatility. Its funding is not based on performance (in the ABC's case, numbers of viewers or listeners), unlike private sector companies, where dividend streams can evaporate following a bad year. Even BHP's pay-out ratio now varies with performance. But the ABC does not have any shareholders in the conventional sense, so it is much less accountable. It is very hard to be dismissed for underperformance, especially given the thicket of industrial protections in place. Sackings usually only occur when a "financial crisis" (code for bad management), blamed on the government of the day for not agreeing to the ABC's funding demands, compels cost cutting.

The ABC's financial modus operandi is to put public pressure on politicians – a budget tactic not usually available to government departments and other public agencies. Many businesses, especially in the media, are required regularly to review and, if necessary, discard their product offerings. Senior managers are expected to take tough and, at times, unpalatable decisions. With the advent of digital technologies, and the capture of advertising revenues by the digital platforms, traditional media companies in the ABC's core markets of free-to-air TV and radio have had to cut costs, restructure and consolidate – or go out of business. As bonuses or other incentives are not readily available in the public sector, a lower level decision-maker's first instinct is to be risk averse, as a "wrong" decision could damage prospects of promotion or preferment. Things may have changed in recent times, but it used to be standard practice to refer matters up to the next level of management so that only the top layer had to deal with any hard decisions – kicking the can upstairs.

A very good example of cost savings available from the cross-media approach to production arose one day when I was at Eildon in north-east Victoria on Christmas holidays. A crew of at least six from several different ABC radio and television news departments arrived in a helicopter to interview me. When I publicly asked, a few days later, why the one feed could not be shared by others, I was met with aggressive accusations of ingratitude. Senior colleagues had repeatedly asked me the same question: why, whenever they did a press conference, would there be half a dozen or so ABC journalists (plus technical staff) from every conceivable ABC outlet. Some years later, no doubt delayed by classic featherbedding strongly supported by the union, this eminently sensible and long overdue reform was adopted and the same news package began to be disseminated across multiple channels.

Bob Mansfield's suggested sale of the ABC's Gore Hill premises in Sydney, then well past its use-by date, provoked a furious reaction, as did the idea of co-locating television and radio at Ultimo. These changes are now quite uncontroversial, indicating that the original opposition was not soundly based, and yet another example of the default, just-say-no, let's-whip-up-another-ferocious-protest-campaign mentality. I suspect what brought the combatants to their senses was that we finally said we would only give the ABC the $20 million for digital conversion that they sought if they proceeded with the economies proposed by Mansfield.

When we were arguing the case for restraint in ABC spending, Tim Bowden, a middle ranking broadcaster, made a special trip to Canberra to assure me that spending had already been cut to the bone and there was no fat in its budget. When I asked if he was an accountant or involved in setting the ABC budget parameters, he looked at me blankly, apparently believing that I should take his undisguised self-serving, fact-free rhetoric at face value.

This is the same Tim Bowden who once breathtakingly asserted: "Some say the ALP is now to the right of the Liberal Party" (he advanced no evidence to support such a transparent fantasy). But he went on: "If, as Michael Kroger [Liberal Party stalwart] said recently, the ABC is to the left of the Labor Party [Bowden got that

WHOSE ABC?

part right] doesn't that put the ABC smack in the middle, where it ought to be?"

This is desperate stuff. At least it concedes where the ABC ought to be, but the rest of this pathetic defence simply shows the lengths to which its die-in-a-ditch loyalists will go to avoid facing up to reality.

Editorial standards

A major concern, for many observers, was, and still is, the ABC's unrelenting left-wing disposition, more concerned with social issues of poverty, discrimination and social disadvantage but never the economics of how to afford their "obvious" remedies. It took some four years of badgering before it agreed to put on even one economics or business program. This was much more than a party political concern. Whilst its preferred priorities were much more in line with ALP values than those of the Coalition, the ALP in government felt the same frustrations. Indeed, shortly after coming to office, I received a call from a former senior Labor Cabinet minister: "Mate, on the ABC, we're right with you. Don't expect us to say anything in public, for obvious reasons, but go your hardest."

What most people want is for the ABC to uphold the highest standards of public broadcasting, with accurate, fact-based and comprehensive coverage of the news. It is fatuous and disingenuous for the ABC to respond to criticism of specific programs or items by saying that Australians overwhelmingly approve of the organisation. This deliberately conflates the preponderance of its coverage, rarely contentious, albeit of varying quality, with its coverage of politics (which it sanitises by calling it news and current affairs), which is, by contrast, often highly contentious. If these two binary fields of endeavour were to be held in separate entities, the response might be quite different.

Another much favoured line of defence is: "if both sides of politics criticise us, we must be doing something right". This juvenile non sequitur ignores the fact that the ABC critique is always from the left of both major parties. Whilst the ABC should be free to defend itself, there is no good reason why a broad based objec-

235

MORE TO LIFE THAN POLITICS?

tive body cannot be put in place to assess and adjudicate on non-frivolous complaints. In a realm as fraught as politics there will always be stark differences of opinion, real or contrived. But this is no reason why a reputable body of independently appointed citizens could not come up with at least a majority verdict, which all sides of politics can accept. The ABC is required to develop a code of practice, which it must then notify to the Australian Communications and Media Authority (ACMA) and comply with the regulator's directions. Assuming that ACMA has the tools at its disposal, the real question becomes one of enforcement. Raps over the knuckles are easily absorbed and quietly ignored. Financial penalties would have more impact; they should be considered.

What must be understood about dealing with the ABC is that it is intensely political – everything is contestable, every employee seems to have a strong view. The problem is that most have a conscience that tells them that there is so much wrong with the world that is almost beyond repair. As it gives little attention to economics and finance, pursuit of good government, or the priorities of middle Australia, it swiftly defaults to moral outrage – a much easier line to pursue and easily lapped up by the indolent couch lizard. In arithmetic you are either right or wrong, but with social justice the campaign never ends, so everyone's a winner, except, as it happens, the actual victims. But mostly journalists do not have time to ruminate on the real life consequences of social or economic deprivation because the journalistic imperative requires moving on quickly to the next moral outrage.

Most ABC employees have an almost uniform world view, according to which they seek to right every wrong, real or imagined. They like to pretend that they need to "hold governments to account," but this almost always means an obsession with finding endless perceived shortcomings, notwithstanding that thinking listeners and viewers, for whom the ABC likes to think it caters, are also seeking dispassionate analysis. The ABC also seems to think that its job is to bring governments down, always looking for a political barb, instead of analysing policy critically (in the purist sense), sometimes even agreeing or, at least, conceding the complexity of an issue.

WHOSE ABC?

Whenever the subject of ABC bias arises, everyone defaults to the Charter. But the Charter is so vague and open ended as to be virtually meaningless. The ABC seems to take its cue from what Humpty Dumpty famously said to Alice: "When I use a word, it means just what I choose it to mean – neither more nor less".

The Act requires the gathering and presentation of news and information not only with impartiality but with a diversity of perspectives so that, over time, no significant strand of thought or belief within the community is knowingly excluded or disproportionately represented. On its face this means the ABC is required to present both sides of an argument. As Australia's most eminent Chief Justice, Sir Owen Dixon, once said: "A story is good until another is told". In politics there is always another story, valid or otherwise. This is a precept the ABC is yet to learn.

In any case, this formulation once again provides a get out clause wide enough for the mythical coach and horses to pass through. When David Hill was chastised about an obviously one-sided piece, he rarely sought to defend it directly. He relied instead on the weak defence that no doubt it would be corrected "over time". That time never comes, as the ABC is, indeed, notorious for only presenting one side of the picture on many big issues, whether it be climate change, immigration, asylum seekers, gay marriage, the Palestinians or the unspeakable Donald Trump. The most egregious omission in the ABC Charter is that there are no specific guidelines for the most contentious aspects of its activities.

The ABC Act is quite explicit – the ABC has a statutory duty to gather and present news and information that is accurate "according to the recognised standards of objective journalism". Unfortunately that crucial last qualifier is simply there to give the ABC an escape from any suggestions of inaccuracy. Even the reference to "objective" is more honoured in the breach. It is also required to act with impartiality, which certainly, as far as the ABC is concerned, is open to interpretation and, again, who decides?

In order to understand how the ABC sees its obligations, an article by Alan Sunderland, head of television, published on its let-

237

MORE TO LIFE THAN POLITICS?

terhead, offers telling insights: " ' Fair and honest dealing' sometimes permits deception, and a breach of an undertaking might be
justified 'in the public interest' ", presumably self-defined. This is
a Machiavellian admission that the end justifies the means – hardly the highest of ethical standards.

Sunderland pays lip service to the concept of "balance" but
says that "impartiality does not require that every perspective
receives equal time – one of the hallmarks of good journalism
is balance that follows the weight of the evidence." Many interested viewers, irrespective of their views on an issue, are still
interested to hear the counter argument. But, far from providing
factual information that enables viewers and listeners to make
up their own minds, the ABC feels free to freight stories with
whatever slant it decides is appropriate. In other words, if a self-
defined "fair and open-minded reporter" considers that there is
only one side to a story that is worth reporting, that's what the
viewer/listener gets.

Effectively this means it is up to reporters to decide whether the
subject matter, together with the reporter's manner and method of
questioning, is impartial by their own standards – a purely subjective test, whereas any reader of the Charter is entitled to assume
that the test will be objective: "what would any fair minded reasonable person think?" ABC top brass are happy to disparage the
concept of equal time, but history shows that they do not hesitate
to resort to this subterfuge when its suits their efforts to counter
allegations of bias.

During one election campaign in which I was involved a Liberal interviewee was met with frequent, sceptical interjections such
as: "surely you can't believe that?"; the corresponding interview
with a Labor politician was more along the lines of: "would you
like to say any more about that". This illustrates the typical divid-
ing line between a hard and a soft interview, which can graphically demonstrate an interviewer's leanings, but is never acknowledged by the ABC and its defenders. Instead, in this instance, the
ABC response to criticism was to commission a report from a carefully chosen academic content to show that each side had received
equal time.

238

WHOSE ABC?

This is not only a matter of partisan politics – have you ever heard an ABC interviewer stoutly cross examine a refugee lawyer or put a climate change advocate through their paces? A furious debate has been going on for many years over this latter vexed issue and there are many well qualified scientists who frequently question key aspects of ABC reports. The ABC is happy to console itself with the cliché that "the science is settled", when it never is – even Albert Einstein had trouble accepting the then revolutionary new science of quantum mechanics because it didn't accord with Newton's "settled view" of physics. Bias can start well before an item goes to air – when decisions are made about who to interview, what line to take, the blurring of the once black distinction between news and opinion. Not only should the interviewer be balanced – if a panel is loaded towards one side of a hot debate there will inevitably be a slanted outcome.

An increasingly common practice is for one ABC journalist to interview another ABC journalist. Given that most have a similar world view it is a pretty safe bet that there won't be much disagreement forthcoming. This is the lazy but cheap option to doing its own field research and breaking a few legitimate news stories. There is very little evidence of checks and balances. The Managing Director is also supposed to be the Editor-in-Chief – an impossible task to vet any sensitive issue before the event and usually too late to monitor or assess afterwards.

The ABC website dismisses the validity of any commitments to "fairness and balance" which, it claims, have never been recognised as standards of objective journalism. About the only obligation it seems prepared to accept is "accurate and impartial" but, again, its insistence that it should be the sole judge renders this effectively meaningless as a community standard.

It is clear that since I left Parliament nothing has changed as far as the ABC is concerned – never explain, never change and, above all, never apologise. By way of stark contrast, in 2017, when *Quadrant* was guilty of the online publishing of an appalling slur against the ABC, the Managing Director immediately sought and received an unreserved apology – end of story. The ABC is quick to demand apologies from others but notoriously reluctant to re-

239

MORE TO LIFE THAN POLITICS?

ciprocate. I was once told by an ABC insider how the organisation was happy to run up bills of hundreds of thousands of dollars to defend defamation actions because it feared a public apology would simply incite others to complain. Better to settle quietly for big payouts, on non-disclosed terms, than to run the risk of being forced to recant.

In 2009, the supposedly funny *Chaser* team did a very sick skit ridiculing the Make a Wish Foundation, which helps children battling life-threatening illnesses. It concluded with the unbelievably callous words: "why go to any trouble when they're going to die anyway". The ABC suspended the program for two weeks, "removed", or possibly just re-located, the head of ABC comedy, and promised to review its editorial processes. But it is not clear whether any apologies were forthcoming, or any real lessons learned, especially by the perpetrators.

In 2013, another *Chaser* segment showed a photo-shopped image of News Corp columnist Chris Kenny having sex with a dog. Notwithstanding nearly 200 complaints, the ABC not only refused to apologise, but then poured petrol on the flames by stating defiantly that such admittedly offensive material did not breach its editorial policies because viewers had been warned in advance of "potentially offensive content".

This utterly disingenuous response was self-evidently laughable. Offence could be given to all and sundry, as long as some prior, non-specific warning had first been given. As the ABC well knows, no one takes any notice of such self-serving advance pieties anyway. Not knowing what is coming, viewers just sit back and cop it, with apparently no available avenue of redress. Eventually, after the journalist took the matter to court, which many of those offended cannot afford to do, he received a half-baked, generalised expression of regret from the Managing Director. Once again, there was no apology.

Paul Barry, of the ABC's *Media Watch* , for one, was not persuaded: "No doubt the Chaser team's defence is that it's satire. But I can see nothing satirical or clever in the suggestion that Kenny – who is one of the ABC's noisiest critics – has sex with animals."

The *Chaser* team remained utterly unrepentant and refused to apologise. According to the *Guardian*. "The Chaser team marked the apology [by Mark Scott , the Managing Director] by posting a fresh buggery 'joke' online."

Such open defiance of management would not have been tolerated in any other organisation. This sorry episode was brought to an end when ACMA ruled that the ABC was in breach but, again, there was no sign of genuine contrition from any of those responsible.

In 2014 the ABC was caught out over a story which featured asylum seekers with burns they claimed were inflicted by Navy personnel. Faced with trenchant denials the ABC issued a statement of regret, without any accompanying explanation of what, if any, endeavours had been made to verify such incendiary claims.

Another egregious recent example of the ABC's persistent recalcitrance is the case of Andrew Probyn, then a neophyte political reporter who, in a 7 pm ABC national TV news item in April 2018, saw fit to label Tony Abbott "the most destructive politician of his generation". This disgraceful outpouring of vitriol was in the context of Abbott making some dismissive remarks about climate change – a subject, it would seem, close to the hearts of the entire ABC workforce.

Paul Barry, again, was not impressed: "But [Probyn] delivered it on the 7 pm news as the ABC's political editor. And we agree that was a step too far."

Probyn's outburst was condemned as pejorative by ACMA, the broadcast regulator. It found that: "The impartiality provisions in the ABC's own code require it to demonstrate balance and fair treatment when presenting news and avoid conveying a pre-judgment". This was a crystal clear assessment. It also gives the lie to the casuistry practised by the likes of ABC Editorial Director, Alan Sunderland who, some six months before the Probyn episode, had written, as already noted, that fairness and balance have never been recognised standards of objective journalism. At least he, perhaps accidentally, acknowledged that objectivity is a required characteristic, notwithstanding that the ABC's modus operandi, on all things related to bias, is to give paramountcy to their own subjective assessments. There is no evidence that the ABC bothered to report ACMA's finding.

This is a singular example of what happens when groupthink sets in. Moral superiority becomes a rational blindfold. Even Ken Inglis was impressed with an investigation by John Henningham of the University of Queensland who found that journalists in general tended to identify themselves as on the left, with the ABC one of the organisations where this was most apparent. Journalists were only half as favourably disposed to the monarchy as Australians at large, and significantly more sympathetic to trade unions, Asian' immigration, Aboriginal entitlement to traditional land, and gay rights.

Tom Switzer, a lonely member of that rarest of species, a conservative at the ABC, has said: "They just can't imagine that someone could oppose the Kyoto protocol or an Aboriginal apology or a labour monopoly on the waterfront because, to them and their friends, these are self-evident truths". The same can be said for other favourite obsessions of the ABC such as anti-Israelism, the environment, asylum seekers and the plight of women.

These are all important issues, but the case for reform is hindered if only one perspective is relentlessly pursued. Industrial action is virtually always only ever reported from the angle of trade unions, which seem always to be ready to provide footage and accompanying sob stories. Who will ever forget how, during the waterfront dispute, ABC journalists refused to cross union picket lines, preferring to remain embedded with the strikers, whose attitude was essentially the only one reported. Social disadvantage is invariably portrayed as an egregious consequence of lack of compassion, as if governments just have to stop being mean, hand over billions and the problem will go away.

Tom Switzer does not believe all this is deliberate but, equally, "there is little doubt that an entrenched left-wing bias … seriously undermines the ABC's claims to be an impartial provider of news and current affairs." What is most revealing is that no reputable commentator, even on the left, has attempted to refute these arguments on the merits – a few cheap shots about threatening the independence of the ABC, and then it's lie supine under the doona until the next time.

Q&A is a hot bed of the narrow leftist thinking of inner-city

WHOSE ABC?

elites, usually led by a compere who proudly wears his dispositions on his sleeve and never lets a perceived right-wing view go uncontested. Nearly all of its subject matter being alien to middle Australia, the ABC likes to claim the handpicked audience is politically representative. But you only have to watch for five minutes to know it's not – even the loaded youth demographic gives it away. The selection of questions is not spontaneous and more often than not focussed on the ABC's pet subjects, while the panel invariably includes a token "conservative" often subject to audience booing or ridicule.

One solution which might help to break down this fortress mentality would be dispersal of staff geographically along the lines of the BBC's major relocation from London to Manchester a few years ago. Inner Sydney values are quite different to those elsewhere in the country, especially in non-metropolitan areas. Currently the ABC has more staff in NSW than in the rest of Australia combined, with 53 per cent of the total workforce, up more than 5 per cent on the proportion ten years ago. Its centralised news model means no production now occurs in Adelaide or Hobart. The ABC may be more inner Sydney-centric than ever, but does it care?

Climate science is a notoriously complex issue, but dire predictions are often based on desktop, not field-based, projections, and are mere extrapolations which assume neither government policy changes nor technological advances. Many livelihoods depend on its being portrayed as an imminent, if not potentially existential, threat, so conflicts of interest abound. Kevin Rudd was happy to depict it as the biggest moral issue of our time, only to walk away when other more pressing issues popped up. A quite separate debate, thus far largely ignored for more than a decade, properly revolves around the nature and extent of the problem and what to do about it.

These are all legitimate subjects for discussion but, because of the inherent difficulty in explaining complexities in bite sized chunks, the first resort of its fervent adherents is to denigrate opponents as "denialists." Despite the importance of the issue and the need for a sensible assessment of all the implications, the ABC is only ever on one side of this "debate". Almost every weather

243

event can be breathlessly reported as someone, somewhere being concerned that it is a consequence of climate change or global warming, as it used to be known, until the planet basically stopped warming almost two decades ago. As a result the emphasis is now on carbon emissions, which is quite another matter.

The real problem remains the world view, unleavened by any right-of-centre commentators – an offering which has been accurately characterised as "influenced by the narrow middle class values of the Australian secular left". It could be added: "and a determination never to be caught out acknowledging the legitimacy of the largely conservative views of middle Australia", which it seems to equate to the lumpen proletariat of yesteryear. Perhaps it thinks this is what critical journalism demands or, maybe, it is just chasing what sells, what boosts the ratings and what preserves their jobs – after all, outrage can be a great driver of a news story. When journalists of the calibre of Paul Barry and Jonathan Holmes, both of whom would regard themselves as left of centre, are happy to say publicly that the ABC has a left-wing bias you would think this would be a wake-up call, especially when the new chair, Ita Buttrose, has said, somewhat diplomatically, "Sometimes I think we might be biased". Even Charles Licciardello, a member of the *Chaser* team, came clean on one point when he conceded: "I do think the ABC is a left-wing network."

But the new Managing Director, David Anderson, couldn't resist the temptation to warn during the 2019 Federal election campaign that there would inevitably be cuts to staff and services if the Coalition was elected. This is an intervention which would at once have been coolly received by the Coalition and very warmly welcomed by Labor, its friends and supporters, especially as he gilded the lily by using a figure of $84 million as the certain budget reduction instead of acknowledging that it was no more than an estimate, based on an inflation rate double its current level. A head of a government department who barracked in this way wouldn't have lasted five minutes. What is so significant about Anderson's clumsy contribution is the grotesque self-importance and sense of entitlement it embodies – the arrogance of spending much of your working life in an organisation which is not required to compete with others.

WHOSE ABC?

Perhaps the only chance for long term sustainable balance is for ACMA to ensure that the broadcaster is held to the high standard of accuracy and impartiality already enshrined in legislation. Only a few months ago it found that the ABC was guilty of an "unfair" depiction of the Australian beef industry, so it knows the ropes.

The Iraq War 2003

On 20 March 2003 troops from the United States, the United Kingdom and Australia launched a war against Iraq on the basis of a perceived threat of weapons of mass destruction and the possible use of chemical weapons, widely believed to be in the hands of Saddam Hussein. The war lasted 21 days before US forces occupied Baghdad. I had listened intently to the coverage each morning on *AM*, the ABC's flagship current affairs morning radio program. As I did so I became increasingly frustrated with what seemed to be persistent anti-American bias. I decided to address the issue head-on, but through my ministerial office.

Normally the ABC unit in my Department would be the first port of call. The Department generally had very high standards which I greatly appreciated but, when it came to the ABC, it had form. Back in 1996 a highly sensitive Cabinet submission had found its way into the media before I had even seen a copy. It even contained a totally unauthorised and false assertion that "options examined in this submission are inconsistent with government election commitments to maintain ABC funding levels". Predictably, the leaked submission provoked widespread outrage and misinterpretation, as its disclosure was undoubtedly designed to do. Once bitten, twice shy, so I chose not to seek its assistance on this occasion. Instead, a key staffer and I personally drafted a total of 68 questions which we then submitted in writing to the ABC Managing Director, Russell Balding.

Several months later I received a sneeringly dismissive response from the ABC's completely non-independent, one person in-house complaints review executive, grudgingly upholding only two of my complaints. In response to my expression of gross dissatisfaction, the ABC then referred the matter to another body it had set

245

up, the Independent Complaints Review Panel, where it should have gone in the first place. This body found merit in no fewer than 17 of my complaints. I then took the remainder to the Australian Broadcasting Authority, which eventually found in my favour on another four charges – a total of 23 over the 21 days of the Iraq War, or more than one a day!

This substantial vindication notwithstanding, no apology was ever forthcoming, nor even an undertaking to do better. The ABC, as usual, waited for the storm to blow over. Meanwhile, a number of its media acolytes retorted that, as I had only succeeded on about one-third of my complaints, what was the problem? No responsible organisation would bury its head in the sand in this way. The whole complaints handling procedure was carefully designed to make the process as long and complicated as possible, to deter all but the most persistent and resourceful.

The police, and many other authorities, have long since ceased to investigate themselves. The conflict is obvious. Asking a long standing employee to be objective means that they may be required to be critical of their employer or high profile fellow employees – courageous maybe, but not likely to be career enhancing. Some organisations appoint someone to do the job at arm's length from management, or just wait for a higher authority to step in. How can the ABC justify this, especially when it is so quick to lambaste others, like the Catholic Church or, more recently, the banks, for not doing so?

The result of the Iraq War saga, which received massive publicity, mostly along the usual "unacceptable interference" line, was drearily predictable. *The Age*'s Michelle Grattan, however, went further with an almost entirely negative feature article headed, as I recall, "Alston the Terminator", as though we were about to close the place down. There was never any acknowledgment of guilt or lax practices, and certainly no apology nor any proposal for substantive changes to editorial policies or practices. Suffice to say, I have never known any other organisation to be caught red-handed over a major issue and escape totally unscathed.

Content

The ABC's statutory obligations under the ABC Act include provision of "innovative and comprehensive broadcasting services of a high standard" and programs that inform, entertain and educate, and which reflect the cultural diversity of the Australian community. It must also promote the arts in Australia, take account of the broadcasting services of the commercial sector and provide a balance between programs of wide and specialised appeal.

This virtually allows carte blanche – "inform, educate and entertain" pretty much covers anything at any time, especially as there is no guidance as to boundaries or priorities. "Innovative and comprehensive" is again a low bar – why should we expect anything else? Moreover, the requirement is so vague that its assessment is in the eye of the beholder. Notwithstanding that it is required to promote the arts, the ABC is effectively an arts-free space with no dedicated television program other than the funky music, youth-oriented *Rage*. The ABC's obligation is not confined to the high arts and contemporary culture is not excluded. Reflecting cultural diversity should be unexceptional but, again, it is a matter of balance. Unsurprisingly, Bob Mansfield found the Charter too general and too open to varying interpretations.

From a $1 billion plus budget the ABC could, if it chose to do so, find ways to obtain, by commission or purchase, high quality content, be it Australian period drama, history, film remakes of classic or contemporary Australian literature, or major political events. But there always appears to be other agendas, be it digital technology, the youth market or keeping the industrial peace with its large workforce. The unions seem more interested in quantity – number of employees instead of quality programs of excellence.

I once suggested to Quentin Dempster, a long-standing Coalition critic, that the ABC should position itself as "the quality alternative to the commercials". He recoiled in horror. I suspect he thought it was a trap – that if its audience numbers diminished, as a result of concentrating on excellence instead of ratings, this would be used as an excuse to reduce the ABC's budget allocation. David Hill always claimed that the ABC didn't chase ratings – he would say that, wouldn't he – but the populist nature of much of what was on offer suggested otherwise.

The quality problem – the short answer

The short answer to the quality problem could be to look to the UK, where the BBC negotiates a ten-year funding package, to which all sides scrupulously adhere, and continues to be the global public broadcasting pace setter on quality of content. Mansfield's formulation that the ABC should "strive to be distinctive", presumably in an up-market way, was very much in line with my thinking, in stark contrast to the mindless mush that often masquerades as comedy and quiz shows. But any such long term settlement should only be contemplated if the ABC is willing to make serious concessions on other matters such as extended regional and rural coverage or reducing the Sydney component of its workforce.

The world is full of major problems, many intractable, at least in the short term. The ABC knows this better than anyone, as it spends an inordinate amount of time wallowing in the mire. There is rarely any serious attempt to analyse why these problems occur, how possible solutions could be funded, or sometimes even just to explain basic facts. Once upon a time we had *Monday Conference*, where serious issues of political, intellectual, religious and economic significance were pursued relatively even-handedly. Presumably this would now be regarded as tame journalism. The *Big Ideas* program on Radio National could cheaply and easily be translated to the small screen. British success stories like the BBC's *University Challenge* and *Mastermind* could easily be copied, as the latter once was, very successfully, with Huw Evans as quizmaster, (and is now, again, by SBS). Jenny Brockie's *Insight* program on SBS could easily be emulated.

But no, our screens in prime time are clogged up with endless re-runs of pseudo-intelligent quiz shows like Stephen Fry's *QI* and distinctly non-funny comedy and lifestyle shows. This blatant dumbing down is presumably designed to appeal to a younger demographic – the "viewers of the future", as the ABC fondly hopes. Unfortunately, as it never publishes the vital statistics, we don't know whether this is any more than wishful thinking. What we do know is that the viewing public has never been properly consulted. Most of these pedestrian genres can easily be found on the commercials, so what is the ABC's point of difference? Radio National aside, the ABC is an intellectual desert.

Most of what is on offer on the ABC is not politically controversial. When it comes to comedy, it may be low brow, adolescent, or unfunny humour – all that is a matter of choice, even taste. But Australians are entitled to expect that the great majority of its programs, and all its news and current affairs reportage, should be a cut above the commercials, who have to cater to mass markets to earn a living. The ABC should be seeking to elevate, not imitate. Nor should it see itself as a left-wing counterbalance to what it might perceive to be a right-wing commercial offering.

Successive parliaments have not funded the ABC so it can mimic and compete with commercial broadcasters. Indeed, it was established in 1932, before the advent of television, to complement the commercial radio sector. Competition is a matter for the private sector. The Parliament and the people have always expected the ABC to offer something new and different and generally of a higher quality and standard than available elsewhere. The Parliament understands that a civilised society may have to fund, if only in part, expensive services or art forms, like opera and ballet, which will never pay their own way. Economics and commerce inevitably get a run in news and current affairs but are rarely seen or heard elsewhere.

The furore around Emma Alberici's continuing struggle with the finer points of economics initially provoked a similar non response. The blizzard of high level complaints from then Prime Minister Turnbull among others was met with a few quick admissions of undeniable factual errors but otherwise damage control, by keeping her out of sight for a while, but, again, no apology from senior management, let alone the principal culprit or the official editor-in-chief. Her Economics 101 howlers, in particular appearing not to know the difference between revenue and profit, have not led to any recantation or any public acknowledgement of counselling. That the ABC can't manage to recruit an experienced, well qualified economics correspondent from the private sector speaks volumes for how seriously the ABC takes economics which, after all, is the cornerstone for so much serious political debate.

News and current affairs

According to *The Australian* columnist, Nick Cater, the audience for the ABC's evening news and *The 7.30 Report* has halved in Sydney and Melbourne in the past ten years, while the population has increased by nearly 20 per cent. In the face of this serious decline in viewer numbers, down by 100,000, or 12 per cent, in the twelve months to May 2018, the ABC simply proposed more journalist training. The real answer is to get out more and ask the public what it wants. One very important mandate should be that the ABC release, each year, its audience ratings for all major programs and production costs enabling the public to judge what the ABC is spending its money on and whether it is getting value.

But the ABC had already received some cogent advice and sound guidance from an impeccable source, with whom I don't always agree. Almost eighteen months earlier, Paul Keating belled the cat, with a typically withering blast: "The ABC was failing as a news gathering organisation and was letting Australia down". Specifically, he said that its News covered "too many tragic reports, of no broader consequence", and *The 7.30 Report* broadcast "too many hard luck stories. If you want to watch a good news service, watch SBS news, which tells you what's happening in Iraq, what's happening in the US election, what's happening with Donald Trump. What you get on the ABC is: 'A truck has just overturned on the Pacific Highway'. In the case of *The 7.30 Report*, it is a news magazine instead of a hard news breaking operation".

On this occasion, I am in furious agreement with the former Prime Minister. Wallowing in compassion while not offering any policy insights, nor canvassing possible solutions, is not only lazy journalism but an insult to its audience. As usual, there was never any substantive response from the ABC to Keating's outburst. Just as significantly, no one else sprang to its defence.

Keating's principal grievance is the poor choice of subject matter. The ABC has huge discretion as to how and where to spend its money. But it seems more interested in disseminating stories than pursuing them. The wider point of criticism, surely, is the nar-

WHOSE ABC?

rowness of the offering. For many months thereafter the ABC continued to boast about how Leigh Sales had recently done two big – and very friendly – interviews, for which she had travelled all the way to New York City. One was with James Comey, which no doubt helped to promote his book, *A Higher Loyalty*, (or A Higher Hypocrisy, as it was more aptly labelled by the *Wall Street Journal*). The other was with Hillary Clinton, visiting Australia on her global grievance tour – both avowed Trump haters with whom the ABC is no doubt in vigorous sympathy.

My suspicion is that we get all these low grade police rounds reports on the daily news, and journalists interviewing journalists, because they are low cost and only a phone call away. Another increasingly common diet of "scandals" on *The 7.30 Report* is how workers are being maltreated, underpaid and undervalued, always with a trade union spokesperson deeply embedded in the content. These pre-packaged "news" stories are clearly carefully wrapped up and hand delivered to the ABC, presumably on the understanding that no serious alternative viewpoint, let alone rebuttal, is presented. This is the antithesis of the "fearless and balanced journalism" on which the ABC likes to pride itself.

Another prominent community leader, Noel Pearson, is particularly disenchanted with the ABC's unrelievedly negative perspective on Aboriginal disadvantage, and its persistent ranking in importance of the preservation of the environment above Aboriginal advancement and jobs. He feels they would prefer endless welfare to more jobs, so they can continue to decry endemic poverty, but the truth is probably more mundane – just another case of preferencing the inner city green demographic, with whom they are very comfortable. Pearson has described the national broadcaster as "the country's miserable, racist national broadcaster: a spittoon's worth of perverse people willing the wretched to fail". Harsh words, no doubt, but simply further evidence of the narrow myopia of the ABC worldview.

Keating and Pearson are not Liberal stalwarts. They are fierce and clear-eyed voices from across the spectrum. And yet they have never even received a response, let alone reasoned counter argument, from their target.

A way forward

In the face of the ABC's granite determination not to adopt mainstream values, in 2017 the then Minister for Communications, Senator Mitch Fifield, announced a range of transparency and accountability measures, including amending the ABC Charter to include specific mention and board seat representation of rural and regional Australia. More importantly, he also announced that the ABC Act would be amended to include the words, "fair and balanced," alongside the existing obligation for news to be "accurate and impartial."

This proposal has not so far gone anywhere, regretably but not surprisingly. It is a step in the right direction but there is still a long way to go. It is one thing to prescribe, another to enforce. It is to be hoped that ACMA is willing and able to take any such responsibility seriously. The Minister responded after stoically observing the ABC's abject performance over several years. The same can be said for the then Prime Minister, Malcolm Turnbull, previously a stout defender of the ABC, but whose patience was finally exhausted by their dismissive response to his two batches of complaints over the Emma Alberici fiasco and its treatment of his important innovation initiatives.

The ABC should not be irredeemable. It should know by now that it infuriates many of its most ardent followers. If it is prepared to gravitate towards the centre ground we will all be very grateful.

What to do?

Privatisation of the ABC is not a serious option – more of an unnecessary distraction. Nor is a merger with SBS which now has a much better news service that would be at risk of being dumbed down by the bigger partner.

One way of determining popular support for the quality of its news and current affairs offerings would be to structurally separate them from its other activities. Although the ABC is wholly funded by government it resolutely refuses to make public its own ratings surveys which cannot be commercial-in-confidence. No doubt the ABC's general offerings, which are not overtly political, would be viewed in a very different light by the public – and the ABC should not be afraid of such an outcome. Surely the public is entitled to express its approval or otherwise of the programs put before them. If the commercial stations find a program is failing to attract viewers it is quickly axed – in other words they are responsive to public opinion. The ABC always pretends it does not chase ratings. It clearly follows them closely but there is no evidence that it takes account of the views of its viewers. The steep decline in viewers of *The 7.30 Report* has not resulted in any discernible change of direction.

Another approach the Government could take would be to set aside additional contestable funds for quality broadcasting for which the ABC, and other media organisations, could compete for funding for certain types of program streams, as has occurred in the UK. For example, the Government could make funds available for Australian history documentaries. The same might go for investigative journalism. Should there be some minimum level of Australian production?

The Government could also appoint, in consultation with other political parties, a panel of wise men and women, not all with professional journalistic experience, to assess the quality of the ABC and SBS on a periodic basis leading to an annual report to Parliament. The aim would not be a consensus outcome but a vigorous debate and the identification of insights useful in public discussion and encouraging a sense of informed popular opinion. This would certainly make the ABC more accountable to its shareholders.

The Government could also establish a high powered inquiry to decide what the ABC's role should be and what it should offer its viewers and listeners. Should it have a bias towards youth or any other demographic? Should it become the quality alternative to the commercial stations? Should it be duplicating the commercials with low brow comedy or game shows or should it seek to distinguish its programs or genres by an emphasis on quality and elegant production values? Does it need its plethora of TV multichannels, radio networks and digital offerings? Why should it not have a dedicated arts program on television?

The Government should establish an independent, arm's-length complaints mechanism, charged with providing speedy outcomes for consumers, not the current stalling and grinding down of complainants which is the ABC's current approach. As the media regulator, it would make sense for ACMA to have this role, operating in a way that provides timely responses to complainants and with real teeth, particularly concerning alleged breaches of the Act and the Charter, as well as systemic issues.

Perhaps the new $100 million Nielsen journalism fund could devote some resources to emulating the Fraser Institute in Canada and the valuable work it has undertaken over the years to monitor the activities of the national broadcaster. This work could ensure that there is a genuine and expert arm's length qualitative assessment of the ABC's responsibility to be impartial and unbiased in its political coverage.

In order to overcome the Sydney-centric bias and the narrow urbanist world view it produces, the ABC and, if necessary, the Government, should seriously consider adopting the BBC model of geographic dispersal to provide some regional and truly national perspectives.

People have often said to me that it must have been very challenging to have to deal with two media moguls, Kerry Packer and Rupert Murdoch, each still at the top of their game, and a third, Kerry Stokes, waiting in the wings. The reality is that, although they were all tough negotiators who argued their cases forcefully, they (nearly) always treated us with respect and never tried to cut side deals. They certainly didn't leak against us or employ bullying tactics through the media.

My biggest hurdle, without doubt, was dealing with an organisation which considered itself unique and almost a law unto itself, which did not hesitate to leak and intimidate to advance its cause. All of this was deeply disappointing. Without such a no holds barred, adversarial relationship with the Government and a highly protective corporate culture, they would have achieved a lot more.

My concerns should not be dismissed as political, despite the galling nature of the ABC's narrow world view. I am more interested in seeing a thriving and relevant ABC, attracting more, not less, viewers and listeners. If the ABC continues to preference inner city post-industrial urbanists it is likely to lose its previously rusted on viewers, who are much more fluid these days and will simply go elsewhere if they don't appreciate what is being served up. I suspect this is already happening with more 7 pm evening news viewers preferring the much higher quality SBS news. They also run the very real risk that departing older viewers will not be replaced by millennials, who are happy to rely on online news sources.

With the universally applauded appointment of a vastly experienced, high level media executive in Ita Buttrose as its new chair, the ABC now has the unique opportunity to conduct a thorough self-examination of its raison d'etre. Otherwise others might have to do the job for them.

256

11

Life beyond Politics
Before and After

I was a late starter in politics and, with hindsight, I think I was also a slow learner. Both at school and university, politics had passed me sublimely by. But in other ways maybe it wasn't such a bad thing in terms of character development. Plenty of experts had advised that you needed a passion – a fierce, single minded dedication – to succeed in whatever occupation you chose, but somehow I thought having a good all round education with diverse life experiences might also be the keys to the kingdom. Almost subconsciously I was drawn to avocations such as reading, which soon developed into a life-long obsession. But there have been many other pastimes I have pursued which have made my life more interesting. It is also true to say that, politics being a high risk and unpredictable endeavour, it probably wasn't a good idea to have all your eggs in the political basket. Having serious income-earning employment before entering politics can help to keep politicians grounded, and outside interests can keep them balanced, and relatively sane.

Sport and fitness

I have always been interested in sport – both active and passive. My on-field skills were modest, only slightly above average, but I have enjoyed playing and watching sport all my life. One unforgettable sporting event for me was the 1956 Melbourne Olympic Games. I was one of the altar boys at our local Catholic Church, when the parish priest, Father Fennessy, gave us the ultimate earthly reward of tickets to some of the leading events including the dramatic finale to the high jump, in which the runner-up was the Australian, Charles "Chilla" Porter, later Director of the Liberal Party in Western Australia when I was Liberal Party President in

MORE TO LIFE THAN POLITICS?

Victoria. More than forty years later, another thrill of a lifetime was attending many events at the 2000 Sydney Olympics, this time as a Minister of the Crown.

I had a modicum of talent at Australian Rules football, having played a few A grade Amateur games for the school old boys, but I much preferred, and still do, the grace, poise and drama of cricket. A special joy as High Commissioner in the UK was to fulfil my duties by flying the Aussie flag at two days of each of the five riveting Ashes tests in 2005.

We can probably blame the genes as neither of my brothers was much better at sport, although Ian is always keen to remind me that he once kicked five goals in a best on the ground performance in the E grade Amateurs. Bob assured us that he had been a respectable country week cricketer and that his father had been a crack rifle shot but I don't remember seeing any trophies. Mother claimed a modest distinction at tennis but was otherwise totally uninterested in any sport except horse racing, for which she had quite a passion. Her father had been a successful horse owner, keeping her in above average comfort as the family lived in good class Sydney hotels until the Depression wiped him out.

Melbourne has some of the world's best sporting facilities – not surprising for what has always been a sports-mad town, where Aussie Rules has long been a virtual religion. In the post-war years, except for the miniscule number of members of Keith Dunstan's Anti-Football League, everyone had to follow a side. When asked which team she supported mother always said Fitzroy, where her husband's business was located, but I have no doubt she did not know the name of a single player. Incidentally, I suspect that, as a creative journalist, Keith Dunstan's apostasy was probably tongue in cheek, as he was the author of a wonderful book, *The Paddock that Grew*, about Melbourne's world famous sporting arena, the Melbourne Cricket Ground, which still doubles as the home of Australian Rules football.

My serious sporting career effectively came to a halt in my mid-20s when I headed overseas for twelve months. On return, I was little more than a social footballer in winter and a mediocre suburban B grade matting cricketer in the summertime. Neither of these enjoyable past times did a great deal for my fitness, so I started going to the gym in my early 30s, initially at The Oasis, a city gym run by well-known sports trainer and physiotherapist, Stan Nicholls. Not too far from Owen Dixon Chambers, it was the nearest thing to a celebrity gym in those days, frequented by leading tennis players such as Neale Fraser.

In his memoirs Rod Laver wrote about how Stan and Harry Hopman, Australia's legendary tennis coach, devised a strength and conditioning program for him. However, whilst I recognised a few VFL football types, my most notable fellow gym junkie was Daryl Dawson, later a High Court judge. As my involvement in organisational politics grew, Daryl was quick to offer sympathetic advice on a wide range of issues. Thus commenced my lifetime enthusiasm for gyms, mainly the traditional kind, certainly not the wellness centre version. When booking a hotel anywhere, my first requirement has always been that it must have a gym.

I was vaguely aware that health was a key component of happiness and a positive indicator for the longevity to which most of us aspire. But it wasn't until I was in my mid-30s that I took up running – something I have never been good at, but always enjoyed. My discovery of running coincided with reading the *Complete Book of Running* (1977), a best-selling book by James Fixx, who is credited with helping to kick start America's fitness revolution by popularising the sport of running. Tragically, both James and his father died young, of congenital heart conditions. Nonetheless, the legend lives on and I can say, like many others, that he changed the course of my life. I realised that you did not have to be an elite athlete to enjoy running, which is a very pleasant way of exploring new cities and enjoying old ones. We now live opposite Albert Park lake in South Melbourne and I do my best to sporadically jog the majority of the way around its 5 kilometre perimeter track.

James Fixx always extolled the benefits of physical exercise and how it considerably increases our energy levels. His last book, *Maximum Sports Performance*, published posthumously, discussed the physical and psychological benefits of running, including increased self-esteem, acquiring a "high", and being able to cope better with pressure and tension.

His book became my secular epiphany, my sudden realisation that my life and health could evolve in quite different directions – drink too much, eat too much and get lazy, or get fit, get slim and regain vitality. This certainly proved correct as, instead of having a drink after work, a big meal and a night's television, I could go for a late afternoon run or a gym workout and then do a good night's work – at home or in chambers. This habit has persisted so that I rarely watch television, except for news or sport, preferring to read or work most nights. I do recall a time, however, when I took my running instinct too far. I was in Perth and had had a very hectic day of ministerial meetings and interviews. As it got closer to tea time, and I had a commitment to attend the ballet that night, I had to choose between a meal and a run. I chose the latter. At interval, the chairman of Western Australian Ballet Company, Michael Chaney, offered me a glass of beer – I consumed half and promptly fainted. So my reward for a healthy run turned out to be a night in Royal Perth Hospital.

Although there are no health guarantees in life, I became convinced that I should take the healthy option just in case – a variation of Pascal's wager, which argues that just in case a god rather than nothingness awaits, why not take out some insurance and lead a worthwhile life. But it was more than that, as it also delivered a comprehension of the larger essence or meaning of life and strengthened my determination to succeed.

I once asked Gough Whitlam what he did for exercise. He looked at me imperiously for a moment and said: "putting on my slippers." Naturally, he lived to 96. He followed in the footsteps of another nonagenarian, Winston Churchill, who, despite occasional participation in aristocratic sports like polo, relished the art of consuming copious quantities of brandy and cigars, sometimes even for breakfast, and constantly promoted his "never run when you can walk" credo. Not a true contrarian, he admitted the possible benefits of regular exercise and claimed that bricklaying and regular dictating while walking about were the keys to his health success. But his black dog may have been the price he had to pay.

Another great prophet of the fitness revolution was George Sheehan, a medical practitioner, who was also a prolific writer

LIFE BEYOND POLITICS

and speaker on circuit. My favourite quote of his was: '"You may not live a day longer, but you will certainly live a longer day". As you grow older this wisdom becomes even more compelling. His audio tapes got a regular workout in my car and his seemingly inexhaustible stock of one liners made him a great motivator. For example: "The moral purpose of running is not to live longer but to live better, have more energy and self-worth and clarity to do all the more important things in life than run."

I took to reading *Runner's World*, the new bible, for which he was the medical editor and a frequent contributor. He elevated running from a sporting activity to a way of life, preaching in a beguiling way: "exercise, you don't have time not to."

I particularly enjoyed the idea of sweating, which provided a degree of endorphin rush and, more generally, a sense of well-being. Both an earned reward and a satisfying experience, it cleansed both body and soul. I was never even vaguely tempted to try competitive running. I realised that the race was against one's self. I readily adopted George's aphorism: "once you have decided that winning isn't everything you become a winner – just try to be the best possible you."

As he also liked to say: "the competition is against the little voice inside you that wants to quit," an insight that taught the rewards of perseverance. He looked back to the ancient Greeks, for whom sports were essential to their education: "They saw in sports the integration of body, mind and soul, the creation of beauty, the mastering of athletics and the challenge of competition." He compared running to a monastery – a retreat, a place to commune with God and yourself, a place for psychological and spiritual renewal.

I didn't quite succumb to chasing PBs (personal bests), but I was always up for a run, when time allowed. Once, as I was about to embark on a running-sightseeing tour of New Delhi, I was momentarily deterred by an overzealous diplomat who insisted on taking me to the hotel window and pointing out a number of mangy dogs, all of which he assured me were bound to be highly contagious carriers of rabies. I was not deterred.

I continued to run into my early 50s when a dodgy low back

MORE TO LIFE THAN POLITICS?

brought my running to a halt. After a twenty year gap, and endless back strengthening exercises, I was able to resume jogging in my 70s, although by that age there isn't much difference between a fast walk and a slow run. More than twenty years ago, I can still vividly recall that, after completing the 14 kilometre run from Point Lonsdale to Barwon Heads, a spectator was unkind enough to call out: "(Good) On you, Cliff (Young)" – a cheeky reference to a famous, but eccentric, ultra-marathon runner of the day.

My father was always keen on self-help books – we were all given copies of the Dale Carnegie classic, *How to Win Friends and Influence People*, and I have always found biographies of successful people in all walks of life both insightful and uplifting. A recent life of Cornelius Vanderbilt demonstrated that it was possible to start a successful new career in the 70s, as Colonel Sanders had done some years ago. This confirmed my father's determination never to retire, as he added NSW to his Bata responsibilities for Victoria and Tasmania when he was nearly 80. I have endeavoured to follow his example. I have certainly found it physically and mentally rewarding to be actively involved in commercial activities through my 70s. As David Gonski sagely advised: "The key to old age is to remain relevant as long as possible." Gordon Darling, who retired from the BHP board following a record 32 years' service because of declining hearing, assured me that getting older should not mean retirement but simply "doing other things." He subsequently went on, with his wife Marilyn, to do "wonderful things" for the arts in Australia, especially their heroic efforts in establishing the National Portrait Gallery, one of only four in the world.

Another fitness revolution came with the emergence of the aerobics movement, the father of which was Dr Kenneth Cooper. His ideas transformed the fitness regimes of the US defense forces and his teachings quickly gained a wider following, as it came to be appreciated that strength and muscle tone could be daily enhanced without the need for any equipment. It followed that exercises could be performed anywhere and at short notice – at home, in the office, in the bedroom – even in the shower!

Examples of aerobic exercises include cardio machines, spin-ning, running, swimming, walking, hiking, dancing, cross country skiing, and kickboxing. Many of these are now staple offerings in most modern gyms. At home, on rising, it is my invariable practice to do a series of stretches and exercises each morning, primarily designed to strengthen the lower back.

Not everyone is a gym freak – we take our exercise in a great diversity of ways. After three years as High Commissioner, I was fortunate to be able to return to London on a regular basis, including four trips a year as a non-executive director of London-based Chime plc, founded by the original spin doctor, Lord Tim Bell. A key unit of the business was Bell Pottinger, a very successful public relations and corporate advisory arm which specialised in acting for the powerful, such as the US Defense Department, as well as the rich and famous. In the wake of a relatively minor scandal, when investigative journalists posing as potential clients of an out of favour Central Asian republic engaged in yet another of those entrapment exercises in which the media delight, Tim decided on a partial management buyout to take Bell Pottinger private.

This necessitated his resignation as Chairman of Chime and his replacement on an interim basis by the senior non-executive director, Rodger Hughes, a very experienced and astute accountant, who filled the position very effectively and should have been confirmed as the permanent chair. He was also quite trim, so I asked him the secret of his fitness regime. He said that his sole form of exercise was always to walk, rather than stand, up and down the escalators on the London Underground. My regular observations told me that this was in marked contrast to the behaviour of 95 per cent of Underground patrons. I was a regular user of the Piccadilly line, one of the deepest, which serves key parts of central and west London, as well as many of the key tourist attractions, so I soon appreciated the benefits, and have been an enthusiastic devotee of this unique fitness measure ever since.

My Early Extra-Curricular Activities

In 1967, following return from my "grand tour" of Europe, I quickly enrolled at the Bar. The pace of life began to increase but something told me that padding around the lower courts, and probably drinking too much in the process, even if aided and abetted by magistrates, was not the wisest way to get ahead. I decided to undertake further studies, initially as a preliminary for a Master of Arts, in pursuit of my passion for the humanities. But at the end of twelve months my lecturer asked me why I was doing the course and I had to face the fact that it was probably more of an aesthetic indulgence than a career enhancing project.

I enrolled in a Bachelor of Commerce course, with teachers of the calibre of Geoffrey Blainey. A fascinating new adventure, it opened my eyes to hitherto undiscovered aspects of the real world and gave me some invaluable insights into how the economy worked.

It was probably around this time that I started to make up for my years of coasting and to get serious about the future. Combining my studies with a burgeoning law practice and a young family was quite demanding but also satisfying. I didn't think much about it at the time, but a barrister is a sole trader/risk-taker, only one major sickness or monumental failure away from personal and financial disaster. But youth is generally blind to such possibilities, and I was no exception. As a result of my youthful travels, I had developed quite an interest in international affairs and decided to join the Victorian branch of the United Nations Association of Australia, which brought me in touch with people with extensive community interests and contacts, including Cecile Storey, and her husband, Haddon Storey, QC, later Attorney-General of Victoria and Minister for the Arts. They were both very active members of the Liberal Party and encouraged me to sign up, which I did in 1970.

I also became quite extensively involved in the overseas aid field and, in 1978, I became Chairman of ACFOA (the Australian Council for Overseas Aid), the peak body representing all Australian aid agencies. This was a fascinating experience, during which I participated in several overseas missions as part of a Department of Foreign Affairs aid oversight group, responsible for ensuring that project funds for Third World countries were wisely and effectively spent, as was not always the case. Trips to Papua-New Guinea, Sri Lanka, India and Bangladesh, as well as a number of

East African countries, taught me how to deal with high-ranking officials in countries where English was not the first language. I also learnt how to assess the effectiveness of government spending and the appropriate accountability measures which this entailed.

I subsequently chaired a combined agencies national emergency relief fund and attended meetings of the International Council of Voluntary Agencies in Geneva, again, very good training ground in diplomacy, as global policy and politics consistently overlapped in the aid field. Probably the most important learning experience from my involvement in these fields was accepting and accommodating the reality that I was often dealing with people whose political sympathies were not the same as mine.

These were volatile political times. The Indonesian invasion of East Timor late in 1975, which overthrew a popular and briefly Fretilin-led government, sparked widespread demonstrations in Australia. I vividly remember addressing a lunchtime crowd on the steps of St Paul's Cathedral in Melbourne, alongside politicians such as Don Chipp (then Liberal) and Clyde Holding (ALP), the latter never a favourite of mine, but united in a common cause. I was also actively involved in the Australian Institute for Political Science, whose annual conference over the Australia Day long weekend was a gala event on the Australian political calendar, attended by leading politicians as well as luminaries such as Sir John Kerr and Lionel Murphy. As chairman of the Victorian division, I was at a very big national meeting in Hobart where East Timor was undoubtedly the issue du jour, provoking passionate speeches and urgent representations to government. I well recall being lobbied by a leading federal ALP politician to raise the issue with the then Prime Minister, Malcolm Fraser, which I duly did.

Only a few years before, I had been on the fringe of a widespread anti-apartheid movement, which was then in full swing, opposing the 1971 Springbok Rugby tour of Australia, and an upcoming cricket tour, scheduled for 1971-72, which had culminated in the declaration of a state of emergency by Joh Bjelke-Petersen in Queensland.

I learned to be discreet in negotiations and to think carefully before arguing a case or preparing a submission. My activity in non-

MORE TO LIFE THAN POLITICS?

government organisations also taught me how to chair meetings involving highly committed and, at times, fractious professional activists by allowing equal time for both sides of the argument.

I came to realise that a number of ACFOA leaders were aware that a sense of moderation was important in dealing with the government of the day, which just happened to be Liberal. It also helped my elevation to Chairman that I was from a smaller agency, which did not have the powerful and, at times, conflicting, interests of the major players. The final political aspect, left unspoken, was that they seemed to take it in turns to revolve the presidency between supporters of the right and left. My immediate predecessor was Neil Batt, then Deputy Premier of Tasmania and subsequently Federal President of the Labor Party from which he subsequently became disaffected. His predecessor was Major-General Paul Cullen, a staunch Liberal, who had followed the first chairman of ACFOA, Sid Einfeld, a senior minister in the NSW Wran Labor Government.

The guiding force behind the foundation of ACFOA was Sir John Crawford, then Chancellor of the ANU, after a brilliant public service career as an internationally regarded economist. I met Sir John on number of occasions and I suspect his astute behind-the-scenes guidance was largely responsible for keeping the organisation on the rails and not irretrievably hostile to the government of the day. I served as ACFOA chairman for five years – right through my three-year term as State President of the Liberal Party in Victoria. Whether it helped or hindered my political prospects is impossible to know, but it certainly tagged me as a "small l" liberal.

Fortunately, my manifold Liberal Party duties and my dual national leadership roles in non-government organisations did not seem to have a significant impact upon my legal career. In hindsight, given that by then my inclinations were much more towards politics than the law, I probably should have spent more time devising a strategy for entering Parliament, as it was not until some four years after my term as State President had expired that I finally made it into the Senate, after a number of unsuccessful attempts to gain preselection for a House of Representatives seat.

I had finally managed to embrace my father's work ethic and

realised that being busy could be very satisfying. The lesson was clear – success in life was likely to derive much more from hard work than innate ability. As Edison once said: "Success in life is 10 per cent inspiration and 90 per cent perspiration." Or, as someone else said: "The harder I work, the luckier I get."

The greatest sacrifices are made by families and, in this regard, I can only be thankful for the patience and forbearance of my wife, Megs, and children, Amy and Nick, in the face of my prolonged absences and multiple outside commitments, which also included regular visits to Hamilton, Western Victoria, on legal circuit. When I became State President in 1979, our two children were only aged five and three and this inevitably put a heavy and, with hindsight, unfair burden on Megs. At least when I entered Parliament seven years later the children were older but, like all youngsters, they still needed careful and devoted handling and I will always be grateful to Megs for her dedication to this vitally important role.

I was slowly learning that whilst politics demands both dedication and concentration, if it comes to dominate your life to the detriment of family, friends and outside interests, then your political and domestic future is likely to be headed for disappointment, if not disaster.

A political career can collapse overnight, or just peter out, so there needs to be a Plan B. With average life expectancy continuing to expand, most will need to pursue post-parliamentary income earning activity, not just to pay the bills but to engage in productive and socially worthwhile employment and, with it, the freedom to enjoy the fruits of life and the joys of family.

What my experiences taught me was that, whatever the central purpose or cause was, be it the law, politics, business or home life, it required consistent and dedicated application. But it should not preclude the enjoyment of life. One of the defining characteristics of my time as a Cabinet minister was that my Canberra office staff enjoyed themselves. We instinctively did not take ourselves too seriously and a healthy scepticism, but certainly not cynicism, prevailed. This often enabled us to gain productive insights. Similarly, although there were times when we thought that some of our departmental officers were a little too straight laced or politically neutral, as they were required to be, we worked very constructively with them and I made a special point of attending their Christmas party, which I subsequently discovered was quite unusual behaviour for the presiding minister. These occasions usually involved some very enjoyable and entertaining acting performances and send ups of key personnel. One of the highlights was usually repeated references to the fact that we had three Fionas on staff, each seen by the respective departmental officers with whom they dealt as highly intelligent, extremely competent and very personable, as indeed they were. It was sometimes suggested that changing one's name to Fiona would be a guarantee of employment. This was not quite true; being a serious Collingwood supporter was probably more likely to be a fast track to successful engagement! Although, in the case of Danny Rosen, a Collingwood tragic, his silky skill set was almost impossible to ignore.

For most of my years in active practice at the Bar I had straddled organisational politics but, at all times, I was careful to ensure that when I was engaged in my forensic duties they were my absolute priority. The reality is that I managed to run a quite successful, varied and enjoyable practice at the Bar. Indeed, a successful practice can be quite lucrative, especially when on circuit and, if anything, I gave less than the attention that politics normally demands. At the same time I made a conscious decision to expand my horizons beyond the lucrative bread and butter fare of personal injury cases. I learnt about commercial and administrative law, which later provided an invaluable understanding of the workings of both government and the private sector.

I did not consciously follow this course in order to pursue a political career but it certainly proved highly beneficial. The same could be said for my studies in commerce and business administration. From the latter I obtained a generalist overview of the key elements of the workings of the economy. Corporate finance concepts such as the time value of money, embodied in net present value and internal rate of return, made crucial business decisions both rational and understandable and, later in corporate life, assisted considerably in arriving at judicious commercial outcomes.

An appreciation of accounting, statistics, marketing, entre-

LIFE BEYOND POLITICS

preneurship and management analysis was also extremely valuable, not only for my later involvement in the running of businesses, both public and private, but especially in aid of personal investment skills and strategies, which have always fascinated me, but not made me much richer. There is a contrarian investment philosophy which has some parallels in politics. When everyone is adhering to the conventional wisdom and following the herd, it is the brave and often lonely person who is prepared to swim against the tide. But often that is where the greatest riches lie.

Collecting

In recent times my wife and I have developed a particular fondness for all things Italian, especially history, food, culture and architecture. For the last few years we have spent several weeks in Bologna, home to the world's oldest university, dating from 1088. But while Megs has been an ardent devotee of an Italian language school, I have pursued an increasing interest in Dante and his times. In his Purgatorio where, with a little bit of luck, most of us are likely to be headed, what many would probably consider innocent and enjoyable past times are regarded as mere time wasting, when the focus should be strictly on the main game – getting to Paradiso as soon as possible. This wisdom could also be applied to hobbies and collectibles, where the ultimate purpose should not be mindless amusement but a productive outcome.

Collecting, like politics, is much more an art than a science. It entails study, research and calculation, but it also requires willingness to take calculated gambles and exercise sober judgment. Sometimes it becomes an addiction. As there are very few rules it is necessary to define, or at least understand, the boundaries. Budding young stamp collectors, for example, have to decide if they want to collect only Australian stamps or stamps from almost 200 countries and, if so, how. Should they concentrate on current issues or delve into the past, where some scarce prints can be very expensive? Do they seek to acquire issues of famous people or special editions of commemorative events? And who pays for all this? Even doting parents have their limits.

Collecting can be very satisfying. My treasured autograph

book, which I still have in my desk, was originally acquired to memorialise my Test cricket heroes and became a wonderful repository for signatures of star athletes at the 1956 Melbourne Olympic Games.

Maybe that's when I first caught the collecting bug but, like many other parents, I suspect it was only after the children had finished their education, the mortgage had been discharged and we had attained a measure of comfort that collecting assumed a more determined hue or, as my wife likes to say, became a compulsive habit. Private collections can cover an almost infinite range of subjects but mine have principally been in the fields of painting, carpets, textiles, glass and books.

Like most children, I went through an avid stamp collecting phase. As an adult, my first foray into the art world probably began with a modest Aboriginal art acquisition in the late 1970s and later accelerated as my interest grew. As I started to travel extensively, often to developing countries on international aid missions, I acquired diverse examples of local art as permanent mementos of my visits. As a result, paintings of a flooded river delta in Bangladesh, an Arab washing-wallah in Kenya, an art naif village scene from Nicaragua, a porter sitting on his wheelbarrow in Doha, a lonely hut on a hillside in Iceland – all became poignant reminders of my travels to exotic places. I have since continued to see Aboriginal art as my main focus with modest additions of leading non-Aboriginal Australian artists.

David Hockney

One of the great joys of being the Federal Arts Minister is the opportunity to meet some very impressive artistic exemplars. International Australian superstars like Barry Humphries and Joan Sutherland spring to mind. But, for me, none more so than David Hockney, probably the world's most famous living artist and one of the founders of the Pop Art movement amongst a myriad of other credits – certainly one of the most influential artists of the 20th century. In his early 80s, and still going strong, his industriousness, creativity and ability to re-invent himself are legendary.

LIFE BEYOND POLITICS

Some years ago, he declined a knighthood in his home country but was happy to join that most exclusive of clubs, the Order of Merit. Membership, the personal gift of the Sovereign, is limited to 24 living citizens from the currently 16 realm countries of the Commonwealth. John Howard, the former Prime Minister of Australia, is a member.

I first met David when he visited Australia in 1999 to mark the acquisition of one of his masterworks by the National Gallery of Australia (NGA). He was accompanied by Peter Goulds, his Los Angeles art dealer for more than 40 years, a charming and very astute owner of LA Louver Gallery on North Venice Boulevard, who has since become a very good friend of mine. David had two brothers living in Australia, so he already had an affection for the country, especially since one of his opera designs had been staged in Melbourne some years earlier.

The event was also attended by two other internationally acclaimed artists, Frank Stella and Dale Chihuly, whose works formed part of the exhibition and subsequently adorn the NGA. Chihuly not only attended the big event but worked with students at the NGA art school on glass blowing, of which he is a world expert. His water feature and giant window proved very popular and he later described the visit as "one of the most joyful experiences of my working life".

After the official presentation, the Gallery Director, Dr Brian Kennedy, who had masterminded the Hockney coup, put on a very swish formal dinner and I found myself sitting next to David. As he has had a serious hearing problem for many years, we effectively engaged in a very seemly shouting match. His first question was, could he go outside for a cigarette, to which I could only say, "after dinner." Only slightly mollified by this, he proceeded to tell me there were only a handful of restaurants in LA which would allow any smoking on the premises, even outdoors. I later discovered that this was not only a constant bone of contention for him but also a great subject of amusing conversation.

We had an absorbing technical discussion about A Bigger Grand Canyon, the painting to which we were paying homage that night. He had created it in his LA studio entirely from memory in

MORE TO LIFE THAN POLITICS?

1998. The Grand Canyon itself is some 17 million years old, a mile deep, 277 miles long and 18 miles wide. Bigger than the State of Rhode Island, it is notoriously difficult to paint. In 1997 David had exhibited a huge 40 foot-wide version of his 1982 photo-collage of the Grand Canyon, but quickly concluded that the work lacked vibrancy because photographs do not have the luminosity of paint. He revisited the subject matter, adopting a new approach. He would not attempt to convey information about the topography or geology of the canyon, but instead present the experience of space.

The result was the work now in Canberra, then the largest painting he had ever done. It consists of sixty joined-up panels, each with a vanishing point, which lies roughly in the centre-rear of each piece and to which the casual eye is usually drawn, creating a tremendous feeling of space for the viewer. Importantly, multiple panels also mean that if the artist screws up in one part he can simply paint a fresh panel, without any need to adjust the entire work.

The next time I was in LA Peter Goulds arranged the complete package for me – a trip to David's magical Mulholland Drive hideaway and studio, a visit to the LA County Museum of Art which houses a number of his works on permanent display, and then to David's spacious and tidy West Hollywood workshop on Santa Monica Boulevard where, on a later occasion, I met two of his most fervent admirers: the legendary architect Frank Gehry, a close friend of David's for many years and the prominent private equity investor, and Bill Clinton devotee, Ron Burkle, a long-time collector of David's works.

A few months later I led a trade mission to Silicon Valley and, on the way back, together with a staff member and the Departmental Secretary, Neville Stephens, we had the pleasure of inspecting David's outsized studio in the Hollywood Hills where we were shown some tricks of the trade, including some of his most famous props, such as the swimming pool and vivid blue and red outdoor furniture. David was, as always, a gracious host, and, over dinner, he talked about many aspects of painting and current affairs, with only occasional references to his multitude of amazing life experiences.

LIFE BEYOND POLITICS

His versality is amazing. By any standards he is a world class photographer, turning photo-collages into some of his subsequently best known works, such as Pearblossom Highway, compiled from over 700 separate photographs, which David himself describes as a drawing rather than a photographic piece. He hit the big time in the US in the 1960s with his sun drenched portraits of naked boys and rippling swimming pools, especially a 1967 work entitled A Bigger Splash, in which he managed to capture the happening of a split second against a background of a very permanent and unmoving house structure and diving board. By the 1970s he was into colour etching, designing opera sets at Glyndebourne and publishing an autobiography aptly entitled *The Early Years*, which was a huge success. By 1978 he had made his permanent home in Los Angeles which he proclaimed "stunning" and the "world's most beautiful city."

He was constantly looking at new ways to move forward, experimenting with transparent glazes in oil painting. He was among the first artists to make extensive use of acrylic paint because of its fast drying qualities, which perfectly suited the hot and dry Californian landscapes. But, in due course, he moved out of this comfort zone to produce watercolours, sketches, black and white drawings, dry point etchings, abstracts, theatre and opera curtain designs, interspersed with a series of portraits – hardly ever of celebrities (although Barry Humphries was a notable exception), mostly friends, supporters and collectors, who were required to spend three days sitting for him. This series, entitled "82 portraits and 1 still life", has since been exhibited throughout the world, including in Melbourne.

On one occasion, in his west London studio, he was at great pains to show me his newly discovered fascination with Chinese scrolls. What appealed to him was that the Chinese artists painted their work on a continuous piece of rectangular paper which, when later unfurled and read slowly from right to left, created the impression of "walking" through the landscape. He later applied this technique to his modernist works.

In between all this artistic frenzy he managed to write a book, *The Secret Knowledge*, published in 2001. It was almost a detective story. After painstaking research, he advanced the credible thesis that the painting techniques of Old Masters such as Caravaggio, Velázquez, and even da Vinci, had actually involved the use of mechanical devices such as optics and lenses to assist in accurately rendering perspective. His researches indicated that mirrors and apparatus such as the camera lucida were being secretly used by the great masters to create their highly detailed and realistic paintings and drawings.

Alongside his analysis he reproduced hundreds of the best-known and best-loved paintings and also included his own photographs and drawings to illustrate techniques used to capture such accurate likenesses. His research was supplemented by multiple extracts from historical and modern documents and correspondence with experts from around the world. The book caused a popular sensation as well as a scholarly debate which continues to this day. Many would say the jury is still out on Hockney's hypothesis, but his ability to pursue such a potential step change in art appreciation, while frantically busy on a multiplicity of other fronts, is yet another example of his extraordinarily fertile mind.

A unique aspect of his creativity is his enthusiastic embrace of new technologies. With the rapid advances in computers he discovered that video art, via the Paintbox used in graphic design, could be enlisted in his own art work. He also found, very early on, that printers and computers could be linked. The laser copier acted as a camera and the result was what he christened Home Made Prints. This advance enabled him to superimpose image upon image to form a photographic collage. He was fortunate that his sister, Margaret, later showed him how to use Adobe Photoshop, as he quickly discovered it was possible to draw very freely and fast with colour on the computer. This led to various experiments making digital inkjet drawings on paper, which were a mixture of drawing and collage, of which I have one.

With the arrival of the iPhone, he created yet another new art form – drawing on his iPad and later his iPhone with a new Brushes app, with which he could paint anything at hand and complete it in a couple of hours. He was particularly proud that he could draw with his right hand, freeing his left hand to hold a cigarette

LIFE BEYOND POLITICS

"to let me concentrate". He then started sending these to selected addressees, so that I now have more than fifty. I once asked
which was the original; the answer was none, as each one came
out slightly differently, but he insisted that he was still mulling
over the intellectual property implications.

Having lived in LA as a Bradford-born British expat for many
years, David decided in 2005 to move back to Bridlington, in his
native Yorkshire, where I subsequently visited him. It was a town
with which he was very familiar. It had been one of the working class playgrounds of the North, within easy reach of his home
town of Bradford, and his parents would take the family there for
summer holidays.

He quickly embarked on another series of local landscapes
which have since become iconic works around the world. Despite
being the breadbasket of the North, the East Riding is relatively
remote, on a road to nowhere, and largely neglected by serious
artists. One day, after lunch, he took me out into the Woldgate
woods to show me some of his subject materials. While we were
admiring the trees amidst the rural tranquillity, a group of hikers
suddenly approached him. I assumed they had recognised him,
and I wondered how he would deal with the uninvited interruption. But they simply asked him the time of the day and, when
told, went away satisfied, but none the wiser.

To him this was one of the great attractions of Bridlington. After a lifetime of celebrity, fame and fortune and being the constant
cynosure of attention, it must have been sheer joy not to be constantly feted and pursued, and to be able to drive for hours and
scarcely see another vehicle. He was sublimely at peace with his
easel planted firmly in the forest soil.

This led to his next technological innovation, attaching high
quality digital cameras to his motor vehicle and filming his slow
progression through the woods or along deserted country lanes,
while recording the ever changing features of the natural environment. This technique soon evolved into a new art form of digital
film or video drawing to compose a picture. He would return to
the same spot during each of the four seasons for later aggregated
comparisons.

His humour can be both wicked and infectious, and his love

275

of game playing almost inexhaustible. His conversations can also be laced with refreshingly clear-eyed, but gentle, North Country scepticism. Once, when Peter Goulds and I were dining with him at one of his favourite London haunts, the Chelsea Arts Club, despite the refined surrounds, David insisted on regaling us with his earthy views on the shortcomings of government, while I maintained a discreet silence.

Late in 2005, when we were both in London, he called me asking what I was doing on a certain evening. I said that unfortunately I wouldn't be available as I would be attending the Labour Party conference in Brighton, to which he immediately replied: "So am I, that's why I'm ringing. I want to invite you to a fringe event which I will be hosting on smokers' rights". This had come about in response to the Blair Government's planned ban on smoking in public places, to which David had taken furious exception. By then a reformed smoker, albeit a tolerant one, I promptly agreed and, in due course, I entered a semi smoke-filled room in a Brighton hotel with about sixty others.

David ran the show, sitting beneath a huge portrait of Churchill brandishing a large cigar. He suddenly spun around and theatrically pointed to the great man, saying: "Look at that – a good vegetarian product – never did him any harm". Next thing he held up a poster proclaiming: "Death awaits you, even if you don't smoke." But the coup de grace was one of his favourite anecdotes: When Deng Xiaoping died, aged 92, the *New York Times* ran a piece saying, in effect, while he might have undertaken some worthwhile economic reforms, he was really a shocking role model as he was a chain smoker all his life. David promptly fired off a Letter to the Editor saying: "Hitler didn't smoke – was he a good role model?" The *NYT* refused to publish his letter and David has ever since dined out on the story.

According to the second volume of Christopher Sykes's very impressive biography, David has also been known to ask rhetorically: "On D Day Eisenhower smoked 80 cigarettes. Do you think he didn't need them?" Being a bohemian at heart, he also treasures a sign saying "Thank you for Pot smoking." In 2002 he agreed to sit for a portrait by Lucian Freud, but on one condition – he should be allowed to smoke.

The smoking story I like best of all, as told by Christopher Sykes, goes as follows: "When Tate Britain gave a party for Hockney's seventieth birthday, Nicholas Serota, the director, announced after dinner that they were going to make an exception and turn off the smoke alarms for 10 minutes so that David could enjoy a cigarette. It was an honour that would have been granted to no one else".

For nearly sixty years David Hockney has brought great joy to millions with his colourful artistry, spread over many cultural art forms. He remains a larger than life character, witty but with serious intent. His relentless industriousness and determination to remain relevant make him a model for us all. I am fortunate to own half a dozen smallish limited edition prints, his originals being only for those who inhabit the financial stratosphere.

Books

Of the almost infinite number of collectible items, book collecting is, for me, one of the most satisfying. But the pursuit of books, especially first editions, has many pitfalls for beginners.

Given his prolific output and immortal status as the gold standard for humour, collecting the UK first editions of P G Wodehouse seemed an obvious place to start. It proved remarkably easy at the outset, as there were quite a number available at respectable prices. I quickly learnt that these were usually the later ones, of which more copies had been printed to meet increased demand as his fame had spread around the world.

Acquiring earlier works was quite a different matter. When a writer is just starting out as a relative unknown, publishers are often only prepared to risk small print runs. These works proved not only hard to acquire but were often very pricey. Tales abound of ultimately very famous authors whose first books were summarily rejected by a multitude of publishers. Receiving a negative chit was almost a rite of passage for many. Acquiring that elusive first book was often a major challenge for even the most assiduous collector.

It was not until I was out of politics and firmly ensconced in London that I became serious about book collecting. My odyssey was to a degree prompted by repeated expressions of concern on the domestic front. My art collection, consisting primarily of Aboriginal and modern Australian art, had developed apace during my years as a minister and my good fortune in occupying large offices in both Canberra and Melbourne which had provided substantial wall hanging space.

Departure from office meant the collection now had to be largely accommodated at home and it was not long before Megs was complaining that the place was bursting at the seams, even after the garage walls, and even the floor of my study, had been enlisted to handle the overflow. Barry Humphries once told me that his architect had warned him that "one more paperback and the joint will collapse". I wasn't quite at this stage, but what it meant was that the collection of items requiring substantial display space was at an end, with a few occasional, irresistible exceptions.

I eventually realised that collecting books, especially rare and intriguing assemblages – a noble hobby pursued by famous men such as Thomas Jefferson, Jerome Kern, Maynard Keynes, Ian Fleming and Larry McMurtry, to name but a few – was a much less intrusive and space demanding activity than art collecting, particularly as large bookcases could hold multiple layers of books. There are many esoteric, sometimes almost obscurantist, aspects to book collecting, such as the history of rare books (for example, incunabula – books published before 1501), libraries and outstanding private collections, illustrations, graphics, quizzes, and movie tie-ins – interesting, but a bit narrow. I preferred to align my collecting with my reading interests, with perhaps a minor thought for later value. As with art, if you buy only with a view to making a profit instead of buying what you like, you have missed much of the joy and turned the exercise into just another mundane commercial pursuit.

A significant derivative of book collecting is book lists and book prizes, reminders of which great books have stood the test of time. No infallibility is involved, quite the opposite. Critics and readers alike will furiously disagree with the opinions of experts, as they have every right to do. My experience is that the winner of the Booker Prize is quite often not my first choice, and I have also observed that the wrong book of an author can win the prize. For example, *Atonement* by Ian McEwan is now a latter day classic, but in 2001 it failed to beat Peter Carey's *True History of the Kelly Gang*, which has since sunk without trace. While in London I sometimes attended a Guardian Book Group, where famous authors were interviewed. After Graham Swift, winner of the Booker in 1996 with *Last Orders,* had spoken, I had the temerity to say to him that I thought his earlier work, *Waterland,* was a better book. Sheepishly, he replied: "plenty of people tell me that".

The contents are the sine qua non and, given that I will be lucky to read another two thousand books before I die, I decided some years ago only to read good books and to evaluate quality and learning potential carefully before mindlessly opening the covers on a friend's recommendations or some pundit's latest monthly special. Sporting autobiographies are tempting, but many are ghost written and packed with moral pieties, presumably to make its subject appear more virtuous. While there is always much to be gained by keeping abreast of current affairs and reading the thoughts and experiences of successful people, I am not about to forsake the pleasure of a lifetime, so I will always read fiction or, preferably, literature.

My reading pursuits have passed many phases, starting in adolescence with the Russians: Tolstoy, Chekhov and Dostoyevsky; the French: Alexander Dumas, Victor Hugo, Gustave Flaubert and Honore Balzac; the British: Walter Scott, Dickens, Thackeray, Thomas Hardy and many great Australian novels such as *For the Term of His Natural Life, The Fortunes of Richard Mahony, On Our Selection, We of the Never-Never, Childhood at Brindabella, Coonardoo, The Harp in the South, Kings in Grass Castles*; in addition to many works by great Australian authors such as Alan Moorehead, Morris West as well as Thomas Kenneally whose books I appreciated well before we spent time together in Eritrea.

In my teens I read many books about 20th century Latin American politics, not immediately relevant but providing a window into global politics. I also found that if I read a good book by an impressive author I quickly moved on to others in the oeuvre. As a result I have read all the works of modern authors such as Da-

MORE TO LIFE THAN POLITICS?

vid Lodge, Malcolm Bradbury, William Boyd, Barry Unsworth, Jane Gardam, Brian Moore and Nevil Shute, together with most of the works of Yukio Mishima (inspired by visits to Japan) and 2010 Nobel Prize winner, Mario Vargas Llosa. I had always admired both the the man and his work, especially for his courage in entering the political fray as a serious, but ultimately losing, presidential candidate in his home country of Peru. It was a great pleasure to converse with him when he visited Parliament House, Canberra.

I have also enjoyed reading many of the works of Philip Roth, Saul Bellow, John Updike, Joan Didion, Larry McMurtry, Graham Greene, Somerset Maugham, Theodore Dreiser and Joseph Roth. I was likewise a great fan of writers about late 20th century English politics and social mores such as Anthony Sampson and Bernard Levin. I have long had a particular interest in translations, especially from the Spanish. I have already acknowledged Mario Vargas Llosa, and I have read nearly all the works of a number of contemporary Spanish writers such as Javier Marias and Javier Cercas.

Many of the greatest works of European classical literature have only come to us through translation – Cervantes' *Don Quixote*, Proust's *In Search of Lost Time*, Camoes' *The Lusiads*, Dante's *Commedia*, Bocaccio's *Decameron*, the works of Petrarch, as well as Virgil's *Aeneid* and other Greek and Roman classics. One of the very finest of contemporary translators is Margaret Jull Costa, a British translator who has won many prizes for her renderings of works by renowned writers such as the Portuguese Saramago and Eca de Queiros and the Spaniard, Javier Marias. It is a glaring omission that, while there are some specialist national awards for translation, it has never been recognised as a category for Nobel honours. If the 2017 Nobel Prize judges can contort "outstanding contributions in literature" to include a song-writer in Bob Dylan, just after the 2015 Literature Prize had gone to Svetlana Alexievich, an investigative journalist and non-fiction prose writer, then surely a way could be found to include translation, still a seriously underrated skill.

As a teenager I devoured a number of mighty works which

have stood the test of time: *War and Peace, The Count of Monte Cristo* and *Les Miserables*, as well as much of Dickens, Hardy and Trollope. Unfortunately, it was not until very recently, courtesy of extended European holidays, that I read *Don Quixote*, which some claim to be the first real novel, as well as Dante's *Divine Comedy*, Boccaccio's *Decameron* and works of Virgil and Petrarch.

A good story line is always important, but the joy of good literature is that the craftsmanship transports the reader to another place. I first came across the term, "clerisy", when I was reading the works of Robertson Davies, a wonderful Canadian writer, but also a very successful playwright, critic and journalist. He uses the term to refer to people who like to read books, who read for pleasure, not for idleness, who love books, but do not live by books. I am proud to belong to this select group. E M Forster once defined a humanist as one who is possessed of curiosity, a free mind, a belief in good taste and a belief in the human race. Davies says these attributes, allied with a genuine love of literature, are the marks of the clerisy.

It is often said that when we get to the pearly gates the gatekeeper won't want to know how many books we have read. It would be quite right for that question not to be asked, as it relates to quantity, when our lives and our reading habits should be about quality. Ralph Waldo Emerson was right when he wrote: "The purpose of life is not to be happy (that would be selfish unless it derived from helping others). It is to be useful, to be honourable, to be compassionate, to have it make some difference that you have lived and lived well".

I will be forever grateful that my father, a non-practising Presbyterian, acceded to his wife's wishes for their three boys to have a first class Catholic education. I never tire of visiting the many breathtakingly beautiful Catholic cathedrals throughout Europe. By contrast, some other religious places of worship often lack a conspicuous aesthetic component. Religion has always played an important part in my life, not as a consolation but as an inspiration. It helps to keep setbacks in perspective and has given me peace of mind and made me focus on the beautiful and worthwhile things in life and to have regard to the welfare of others, when we can be all too ready to develop solipsistic tendencies and get caught up almost obsessively in our own world of career advancement, personal wealth and happiness. On that point, however, despite Jefferson and his fellow drafters of the American Declaration of Independence seeing Life, Liberty and the Pursuit of Happiness as the height of human endeavour, experience strongly suggests that, if this does not include the happiness of others, we are doomed to fail.

A recent exhaustive study of Chief Executive Officers found that the most successful were not the extrovert alpha males but rather the quieter, more reflective types, lacking in hubris but fired by a fierce determination to succeed. If we can lead a worthwhile and moral life there will be little anger, resentment or remorse as we navigate the ups and downs which inevitably beset us all as we journey through life. "Being the best possible me" takes the envy out of aspiration and makes us grateful for all the wonderful things that life has to offer. Its inherent optimism helps us to cope with the inevitable setbacks and crises. Having a loyal and generous nuclear family also gives much joy and contentment to life and I am grateful for my good fortune in this regard.

Being ever conscious that there is a higher authority certainly helps to put a dampener on hubris, but it also gives purpose to life. Taking a broader historical perspective, Ferdinand Mount, in *Prime Movers*, observes that: "As Christian faith began to wane, its causes were largely taken up, if not taken over, by the new religion of humanity." For me humanism is not a substitute for religion – one is about the here and now, the other is about the life both now and the eternal hereafter, which, for me, is much more important.

During my 18 years in Parliament I was fortunate that I was able to turn off from the pressures of the day as soon as I reached the sanctuary of home. Once inside, it was my almost invariable practice to read, mostly literature, for an hour before turning out the lights. I understand former Labor giant, John Button, did likewise. Even at that stage of my busy life I was reading an average of two books a week. Now the average is close to three – I know this, because for the last six years I have recorded the names, authors and dates of all the books I have read. This simple reference point allows me to keep track of what, and when, and even helps avoid unwitting duplication.

The Booker Prize

For some years I had been interested in the Booker Prize, now awarded annually to the best original novel written in the English language and published in the UK. One day I decided to see how many I had read of those books shortlisted for the Prize since its inception in 1969. By 2000 the shortlisted number was around 185, of which I had read about half. As a special project, I set about reading the balance, as well as the six more which come out each year.

But it was not until I arrived in London, the home of the Booker, that I decided to go one further. I learnt that it was quite common for enthusiasts to collect first editions of the winners. That struck me as a trifle mundane. Why not collect all shortlisted books and, even better, why not all signed? – that is with the author's signature flat signed on a page of the book and not merely on a bookplate pasted inside. This would be much harder to accomplish, but would be a much more satisfying, and perhaps valuable, achievement. I soon discovered that some signed first editions were extremely hard to get, meaning that, even if they turned up, they could be quite expensive.

The key was to identify relevant booksellers, but I soon found that there were, and still are, only three real experts: David Rees, a bookseller in Hay-on-Wye, Wales, who specialises in Bookers and has been very helpful; a legendary publisher named Peter Straus, who has had a lifetime obsession with the Booker; and Chris Connolly, an expat Australian living with his family in Bath, who has an encyclopaedic knowledge of all things Booker and assiduously attends book fairs and Booker events. In this quest, Chris's enthusiasm, guidance and expertise have been indispensable.

Peter Straus, a friend and adviser on the project, is sui generis in the book trade. Some years ago he accumulated virtually all shortlisted UK-signed first editions of shortlisted Bookers and then sold the collection to the J P Morgan Library in New York. Known in the trade as a completist, he also acquired voluminous author correspondence and other memorabilia.

MORE TO LIFE THAN POLITICS?

But his real claim to fame, and perhaps Booker immortality, came in 2010, when he realised that in 1969 and 1970, the first two years of the Prize, the shortlisted books had been those which had been published the year before. But in 1971 the rules were changed so that, henceforth, the shortlist would consist of books published in the same year as the award. This meant books published in 1970 had not been considered, so he inspired a special Lost Man Booker Prize, ultimately awarded to *The Troubles* by J G Farrell, selected by three expert judges from a shortlist chosen by public vote.

My real collecting breakthrough came when I was told about a husband and wife, trading as St John of God, booksellers, in Bolton, Manchester. They had been appointed joint executors of the estate of an eccentric neighbour with instructions to sell his entire collection of signed UK first editions of books shortlisted for the Booker Prize. They had started out with little knowledge about the books, let alone the Prize, and the experts advised me that their asking prices were too high.

I had by then realised that there was no one right price to be paid for any collectible book, other than perhaps the minimum price for which a seller was prepared to sell. I had been born in Perth at St John of God Subiaco Hospital, so I had an added, somewhat quirky, attraction to pursue what I quickly realised was a unique opportunity as long as I was not too fussy about price.

Accordingly I promptly arranged to visit them the following weekend. I took the train to Manchester, hired a car and drove out to see them. They had already disposed of quite a few of the collection, but still had a fair number left, and I had little hesitation in buying something like 60-70 books and piling them into the boot. The condition of each book, so important to an expert, was only a minor consideration for me. Most were, in any case, in very good condition. Even then I came partially unstuck as the cover of an early Booker Prize winner was in a manifestly inferior state, so I declined to purchase, only to find that another signed copy took some years to find. It was both a fortuitous and fortunate meeting with two wonderfully friendly people, who had come to regard their own experience with the Booker as a priceless adventure.

LIFE BEYOND POLITICS

This sizeable acquisition was a master stroke, as it gave me the impetus to get serious about the chase and I began to visit rare and antiquarian booksellers. It quickly became apparent that it was going to be a largely fruitless exercise, as the Internet was fast becoming the main game, offering even obscure and hard-to-get works from around the world much faster and more effectively. This became my main source of supply but, as my wanted list has shrunk, it has become a hard, slow slog.

Now, after thirteen years of pursuit, despite no additions in the last three years, I only need four to complete the official collection. This, I am assured by those who know, gives me the largest collection in private hands in the world, but I have no great confidence that I will reach my goal. So, with the invaluable aid of Chris Connolly, we are now chasing the long list (an additional 160 as at 2019), which has only been published since 2001. To fill the gap I have also been collecting signed UK first editions by some of my favourite contemporary English authors such as Ian McEwan, David Lodge, William Boyd, Brian Moore, Barry Unsworth, Nevil Shute and Penelope Fitzgerald.

Carpets

My interest in oriental rugs began when I was a minister and travelled with an Australian Government Arts delegation to India. I bought a few big woollen pieces, nothing special, but it was a start. I quickly discovered that the spiritual home of carpets was Iran and I resolved that one day I would go there. Later, when we were living in London, I visited warehouses which resembled Aladdin's cave as they imported rugs from all over Central Asia, the Middle East and the Indian sub-continent. My growing fascination inevitably led me to the Victoria and Albert Museum (the V&A), founded in 1852, with the world's largest museum of decorative arts and design. Its permanent collection of more than 4.5 million items includes the famous Ardabil carpet, which I have had the pleasure of inspecting several times.

The original Ardabil carpets were a pair of carpets dating back to 1539, initially designed for a shrine in Ardabil, not far from Tabriz, in north western Persia, in honour of Shaykh Safi, a Sufi mys-

285

tic who died in 1334. He is the spiritual father of the mighty Safavid Empire, named after him, which ruled Persia from 1501 until 1736, during which time it became the apotheosis of Persian culture.

These two carpets are now considered to be among the finest in the world. Whilst one of the originals, restored, but reduced in size, resides in Los Angeles, the other is on permanent display in London at the V&A, which bought it in 1892 on the urging of William Morris, the famous English textile designer, who described it as being of "singular perfection."

The entire surface of the Ardabil carpet is covered by a single integrated design, with a border of four parallel bands, surrounding a huge rectangular field. Displayed in a vast open area, under a tent-like structure, with glass walls, it is lit up for ten minutes on the hour and half hour to preserve its rich colours.

I was soon led to the amazing story of the Pazyryk carpet, excavated in 1949 along with a number of superbly preserved textiles from the frozen tomb of a Scythian nobleman in burial mounds in the Pazyryk valley of the Altai Mountains in Siberia, due east of Moscow. Whether it was made in the region or came from elsewhere remains a matter of contention. It measures 183cm x 200cm and its fine weaving and elaborate pictorial design are indicative of an advanced, state-of-the-art carpet weaving industry at the time of its production.

Its central field is a deep red colour with two frieze borders of animals proceeding in opposite directions and accompanied by guard stripes. The inner main border depicts a procession of deer, with men riding, leading horses. The design of the carpet already shows the basic arrangement of what has become standard oriental carpet design: a field with repeating patterns, framed by a main border with elaborate design and several secondary borders.

Radiocarbon testing indicates that it was woven in the fifth century BC, making it the oldest known carpet in the world. The importance of the rug is that it proves that pile-weaving is an ancient craft.

This extraordinary carpet now resides at the Hermitage Museum in Saint Petersburg. Megs and I once spent a magical weekend in what is often dubbed "the Paris of the north" for its cultural and historical sophistication. We did the grand tour of some majestic churches, including Our Saviour on the Spilled Blood, built on the spot where Emperor Alexander II was assassinated in 1881 by revolutionaries, who threw a bomb at his royal carriage. We also saw a performance at the famed Mariinsky theatre, visited Dostoyevsky's home, and ate at sumptuous hunting lodges.

But the Hermitage is the must see. The State Director who showed us around was at pains to say that even if you only spent fifteen minutes in each of the 400 rooms it would take several months to see the whole collection. The complex contains innumerable masterpieces from all over Europe. In one room I noticed a large painting lying unframed against the wall. When I asked why it did not have a glass frame to protect it from the sun I was told that there were not enough days of sunlight to make much difference! Unfortunately, I was not aware at the time of our visit that among the myriad treasures of the Hermitage was the priceless Pazyryk, but at least it is a good reason to go back. Some years ago, in London, I bought a small replica of the Pazyryk, and even now it is a joy to behold.

Iran

One of the great advantages of London is that so much of Europe is only a few hours away. One weekend, after I had finished a board meeting, I decided to explore Poland, an important swing country in Europe, which both Russia and Germany had tried to wipe off the map during the Second World War. Being under communist oppression for so long has had the ironic effect of moving it closer to the US and mainstream economic policies, and away from the European "social model" of welfare state paramountcy which was slowly suffocating Europe. As a result, Poland was becoming somewhat of a contrarian member of the EU. My long weekend was a revelation. On an earlier occasion, accompanied by my son, Nick, I had visited Krakow (the home town of Pope John Paul II), with side visits to Auschwitz and the Wieliczka underground salt mine. This time I travelled to Warsaw and Gdansk (formerly Danzig).

This remarkable experience inspired me to think beyond Paris and Barcelona, so it wasn't long before I realised that Tehran was "eminently doable". The Persians, among the pioneer weavers of the ancient civilisations, initially catered for utilitarian uses such as floor, entrance and bed coverings. They progressively moved up market to meet the needs of kings and nobles. Within the group of Oriental rugs produced by countries of the so-called "rug belt", the Persian carpet stands out by the variety and elaborateness of its manifold designs.

Carpet weaving is still an essential part of Persian culture and Iranian art, and Iran remains the undisputed champion of silk carpets. Moreover, because of the country's relative isolation from Western countries, the prices it can command are quite modest. It was therefore the perfect place to begin my exploration of the new world of silks.

I was able to enjoy two separate weekends, about twelve months apart, at the Australian Ambassador's residence in Tehran and from there travelling, via the holy city of Qom, to Isfahan, once one of the largest cities in the world, a vital stopover on the Silk Road and Persia's capital during the fabled Safavid dynasty.

Isfahan's amazing Royal Square encompassed one of the world's biggest maidans, large open spaces, used in India for simultaneous cricket matches as far as the eye could see. More importantly, the quadrangle was surrounded by covered bazaars and stalls, many stocked with carpets of all shapes and sizes – and prices. Bargaining could be a real trap. If the opening bid is too high, you are doomed to overpay. But where to start? Fortunately, the Australian Embassy provided me with a carpet expert as a guide, who kept me in affordable territory. A few years later, in Morocco, I learned how to bargain – the seller will quote a high figure hoping your first bid will come close. But, instead, you offer only one third – he will feign outrage and you may have to walk away. But eventually he will settle for half of the original asking price. Maybe not infallible, but at least you are bargaining with a professional purpose.

Persian carpets and rugs of various types were woven in parallel by nomadic tribes, in village and town workshops, as well as royal courts. They represent different, but simultaneous, lines of tradition, and reflect the history of Iran and its various peoples.

LIFE BEYOND POLITICS

Town manufactories like those of Tabriz have played an important historical role in reviving the tradition of carpet weaving after periods of decline.

I had long wanted to visit Tabriz, a large city to the west of the capital. It has been the centre of carpet production for centuries and the home of so-called picture carpets. This unique art form portrays life-like "photographs" of people, animals and places. Tabriz has the largest covered bazaar in the world and, since 2010, has been a World Heritage site. Unfortunately, my flight from Tehran was cancelled at the last minute, due to inclement weather, so I had to content myself with acquiring a picture carpet of a tiger in Isfahan.

During the 16th century Tabriz had been the capital of the Safavid Empire, which ruled an area covering today's Iran, together with parts of Turkey and Georgia. The Empire was founded by Shah Ismail of the Safavid brotherhood, originally a Sufi order which strives for perfection of worship. Sufi orders trace many of their original precepts from Muhammad through his son-in-law, Ali, the inspiration of the Shia religion. Under Safavid rule eastern Persia became a great cultural centre, with textiles and carpets reaching new heights of perfection. The carpets woven in the Safavid court manufactories are famous for their elaborate colours and artistic design and are treasured in museums and private collections the world over.

Rugs woven by villagers and various tribes of Iran are distinguished by their fine wool, bright and elaborate colours, and specific, traditional patterns. Nomadic and small village weavers often produce rugs with bolder and sometimes more coarse designs. These are considered the most authentic and traditional rugs of Persia, in contrast to the artistic, pre-planned designs of the larger workplaces. Gabbeh rugs are the best-known type of carpet from this line of tradition. In my cross-country travels by bus there seemed to be looms everywhere – in service in rural houses and for sale in town stores. Carpets were often laid out in the street for washing or airing and there was no shortage of carpet shops in the big cities catering for both rich and poor.

Given the images we have in the west of morals police on every corner, rigidly enforcing the "promotion of virtue and the prevention of vice", it was surprising to see, especially in restaurants, young women in western garb with no head coverings. I even managed to strike up conversations in English, which assured me that most of the population had no animus towards the US, despite huge billboards and building walls proclaiming "DOWN WITH THE USA". I also heard of many wealthier middle class people who shopped in Dubai at weekends and returned home with all manner of western clothing and accoutrements, presumably for domestic display only.

The art and craft of carpet weaving has gone through periods of decline during times of political unrest, or under the influence of commercial demands. It particularly suffered from the introduction of synthetic dyes during the second half of the 19th century. While carpet weaving still plays a major part in the economy of modern Iran, it may be a dying art, as fewer women and children are willing to risk their eyesight for very modest wages. Modern production is characterised by revival of traditional dyeing with natural dyes, reintroduction of traditional tribal patterns, and invention of modern and innovative designs, woven in the centuries-old technique. Hand-woven Persian carpets and rugs have been regarded as objects of high artistic and utilitarian value and prestige from the first time they were mentioned by ancient Greek writers, until today.

Just as chemicals in food products are now being replaced by organics and Aboriginal art is moving away from acrylics and back to natural ochres, so there has been a revival of traditional natural dyes in modern carpet production. This renewed interest has extended to commercial enterprises which commission carpets from tribal village weavers to whom it can provide a regular and welcome source of income. The modern era has seen the reintroduction of traditional tribal patterns, as well as the invention of modern and innovative designs, albeit woven using centuries-old techniques.

Revival of natural dyeing has had a significant impact on rug production. Initiated in Shiraz in south central Iran during the 1990s by some master dyers, village-woven rugs of coarse quality and medium size, such as gabbeh, raised much interest when they were first presented at the Great Persian Exhibition in 1992. Woven for home use and local trade and coarsely knotted with symmetric knots, the colours initially seen were mostly natural shades of wool. But with the revival of natural colours, gabbeh are now produced in a full range of colours. They meet the growing western demand for primitive, naïve folk art in preference to elaborate commercialised designs, and have gained increasing popularity.

In commercial productions the gabbeh rug patterns remain simple but tend to show more modern types of design. Corner articulations are a particularly challenging part of rug design. The ornaments have to be woven so that the pattern continues without interruption around corners. This requires skilful advance planning, usually not done with village or nomadic rugs and, as a result, such discontinuities can help distinguish rural or nomadic from workshop rugs.

Silks

My abiding interest in carpets gradually morphed into a preference for silk, a relatively expensive material with particular tensile strength. Silk, a versatile natural fibre, can be added to woollen and cotton combinations to highlight the design and, when used for warp threads, produces a strong foundation. Silk on silk is of superior quality as it retains soft pliancy. Very fine knots can be made with silk. Silk pile carpets are often exceptionally fine and, being less resistant to mechanical stress, are often used as wall hangings or pillows; a particularly fine piece has pride of place as a floor covering in my study. Piles are much shorter since the 1979 revolution in Iran, thus saving silk.

My interest in silks had first been piqued by a small piece which I picked up in Peshawar. Once home, however, and on inspecting it more closely, I noticed that the top half was a slightly different colour to the bottom. I then found that this was not uncommon, and it was a function of abrash, the appearance of slight deviations within the same colour. This is usually explained by the likelihood that the weaver did not have the time or resources to prepare a sufficient quantity of dyed yarn to complete the rug, so that only small batches of wool were dyed from time to time. When one string was used up, the weaver continued with the newly dyed batch, but the exact hue or colour was rarely able to be replicated.

A colour variation can also suggest a village or tribal woven rug, which is appreciated as a sign of quality and authenticity. As a result, abrash is sometimes introduced on purpose into a newly planned carpet design.

The carpet seller had claimed that my silk came from Hereke, a village near Istanbul in Turkey, world famous for the quality of its silk carpets. For over 150 years its intricate weavings had been known for producing some of the finest hand-knotted carpets in the world. In my naivete I accepted the stated origin of my carpet. Later I had reason to be more dubious, as I heard wild stories of Chinese merchants buying the best weavers from Hereke and taking them to China. It turned out that the true story was quite different, but just as outrageous.

At the same time that Turkish authorities had officially closed the Hereke municipality, due to declining population numbers, a giant industrial zone was being constructed in China where silk carpets were being machine manufactured under the newly registered trademark brand name of "Hereke". By naming the complex the "Hereke Industrial Zone", Chinese companies were legally able to tag their carpets, "Made in Hereke." The carpets were being sold in the Turkish market to unsuspecting tourists keen to acquire the fabled Hereke carpets and, at the same time, displacing 90 per cent of the local Hereke market and blowing away Turkey's original master craftsmen, who had previously constituted 25 per cent of the $2 billion Turkish carpet market but were now virtually all out of business.

The original Hereke carpets were made through a painstaking process of hand-made knots, taking many months or years to complete. They could not possibly compete with machine made Chinese imitations. Moreover, it was also alleged that the material that they were being made from was not real silk, but it was impossible to tell the difference. As a result, they were being sold for the same price as domestic hand-woven carpets. Adding insult to injury, in Bursa, another leading silk carpet town in Turkey, the carpets were now being made using much cheaper Chinese silk. Because silks are more expensive than other carpets they are often not on display in carpet shops, so more detective work and perseverance is required. There is probably no substitute for visiting Iran – a big ask, but potentially a very rewarding one.

Although the term, "Persian carpet", most often refers to pile-woven textiles, flat-woven carpets and rugs like kilims, soumaks, and embroidered fabrics like suzanis are part of the rich tradition of Persian carpet weaving. Kilims are quicker and less costly to produce than pile carpets. Generally identical on both sides, the obverse side is usually ragged and not fit for display, but the recto or "up" side is simpler and more straightforward than knotted carpets. Originally made by tribal groups and designed principally for indigenous use, kilims were traditionally seen as cheap and inferior to pile carpets. Their bold and colourful designs have made them increasingly collectible, and we have several in the home as very attractive floor coverings, often on varnished floorboards. Kilims don't have plush piles like most rugs or carpets – this means they are thin and not as soft to touch. Kilims have become a popular choice amongst Australians as they are especially suited to our understated tastes and harsh conditions. Their slight but sturdy construction makes them particularly versatile and easy to maintain.

Suzanis are highly decorative tribal textiles, delicate and often very colourful. They usually have a cotton fabric base embroidered in silk or cotton thread, which gives off a characteristic metallic sheen. The name derives from the Persian word, suzan, for needle, but they originate from the Uzbek communities of Central Asia. London, fortunately, has a Turkmen gallery where I recently bought one. They also make very good wall decorations.

My interest in carpets extends beyond Asia. Once, when attending a conference in Phoenix, Arizona, I drove about 200 kilometres to Sedona, a magical small town surrounded by glowing red rocks and steep canyons, which had proven to be the perfect place for the site of filming of many early westerns. Megs and I had visited the town a few years earlier en route to the south side of the Grand Canyon. The purpose of my visit, in part inspired by time spent inspecting Dale Chihuly's extraordinary collection of over 700 North American Indian blankets, was simply to purchase a Navajo rug – a beautiful red, white and black Mexican serape blanket, of stepped and wedge-edged design. It now adorns the floor in our sitting room.

Glass

David Hockney's LA dealer, Peter Goulds, just happened to be the agent for another famous artist, glass sculptor extraordinaire, Dale Chihuly, one of whose distinctive outdoor creations had accompanied Hockney's A Bigger Grand Canyon to the NGA in 1999. Chihuly has been credited with "having revolutionised the potential of glass as a medium" and as having "become an institution by creating a bridge between the decorative and the fine arts".

At the beginning of his career he worked, studied and learned the art of teamwork in glass-making at the world famous Murano glass factory in Venice. By the mid-1990s he and his team had installed his blown-glass creations over the canals and piazzas of Venice.

By 1999 Chihuly was an established international glass sculptor and designer, an innovator in the process of transforming the conventional understanding of glass making as an art form with his new concept of mega environmental artwork. He now has large works in leading casinos, the Victoria & Albert Museum in London, the Western Wall in Jerusalem, and many other large-scale outdoor venues. I once accompanied his assistant on an inspection of an exhibition of his outdoor works, strewn through London's Kew Gardens. Very impressed, I readily succumbed to his blandishments, and bought a five-piece set from his Seaform series, which now has pride of place on our mantelpiece.

A few years later I happened to mention to Peter Goulds that I was on my way to visit Bill Gates and Microsoft in Seattle. He immediately arranged for me to visit Dale Chihuly's spacious studio there. I was fortunate to have a decent chat with the normally reclusive artist, sporting his famous eye patch, a legacy of an eye lost in a youthful automobile accident. His studio at the Boathouse, closed to the public, is situated just north of the Seattle CBD. A long rectangular room overlooking Lake Union contains a 25 metre long table made of a single timber piece, which I was told had accommodated Microsoft board meetings. The design and manufacturing area was more like a medium sized business, with about eighty employees. Apart from the glass making complex the building also housed the artist's spectacular collection of North American Indian rugs. He had studied weaving in his youth and this led to a lifelong infatuation with textiles, particularly Pendleton blankets, whose designs he has, at times, managed to incorporate into his glass pieces.

I had assumed that Chihuly was a glass specialist but, after closely inspecting some of the more exquisite glass pieces, I was pleasantly surprised when his assistant suddenly asked me if I would like to see Dale's paintings. He then took me into a special room, where there were about ten very colourful abstract works on display. I expressed serious disappointment when he told me that they were not for sale; he thought for a moment and said: "I'm sure Dale won't mind if I make an exception". I was, of course, pathetically grateful and, as a result, I now have the perfect permanent reminder of a very special day.

Perspective

Looking back on my life, I feel that I have been very fortunate in so many ways – lucky to be born healthy in Australia, a safe and prosperous country with a good climate and a sensible system of government, and to live in a city regularly voted the world's most liveable. None of us knows how our lives will turn out. We may have our dreams, but there is always the hand of fate hovering over our every move – ready to harm our health, even our life span, our family, our career, our life style. Life is a lottery, and there is not much we can do about many aspects of it, other than do our best with the opportunities which come our way, work hard, have the right value system and something and someone(s) to believe in.

On all fronts I have much to be grateful for. On one view mine was a conventional middle class upbringing but, by many standards, I was privileged – a good private school, the first in my family to go near a university – again, one of the best – a career path that suited my skills and temperament and, most importantly, a loving nuclear family all of whom have made their mark and lived good lives.

MORE TO LIFE THAN POLITICS?

My wife, Megs, has been a great support to me in many ways – never comfortable with the life style of a politician but adapting and living her own very worthwhile life, with a strong interest in social justice issues. She has had a very interesting career, starting out as a lawyer before gaining a Diploma of Education after our children were born and moving into teaching. She then embarked on a decades long commitment in the international aid field. For many years she worked with Australian Volunteers International as well as other international NGOs, including as a board member of a large international organisation, Action Aid Australia. Over the last 20 years she has devoted much time and energy to East Timor having visited there a number of times. She is currently the chair of Friends of Suai, a local government-based friendship group connecting the communities of the City of Port Phillip, Melbourne, and Suai, Covalima, a remote district in East Timor.

She has also been an amazing mother, ever solicitous for the welfare and well-being of our two children, Amy and Nick, now both in their 40s and carving out happy family lives and career paths, both as corporate lawyers at this stage, but capable of doing many other worthwhile things. Whilst they both have a keen interest in politics, they have never contemplated entering the arena. This is despite the fact that when Amy was born and Megs had the choice of her first name, and I the second, I opted for Anne on the basis that she would then have a triple A rating but also, if she went into politics, a good chance of picking up the donkey vote!

One of the great attractions of continuing to work post politics is the opportunity to travel, learn about new business sectors and practices, and meet interesting people. A special joy for me has been my involvement with Matt Collard, a senior mining executive with whom I have worked on an almost daily basis on an ironsands project in Fiji and strawberry farms in Victoria and Queensland. Neither of these businesses, both of which I chaired, would have been successful without the backing of Kenny Zhang, who started a very successful paint manufacturing operation in Australia over twenty years ago and has been very successful in a diverse range of activities.

12

London – My Duty

Being High Commissioner

It was the thrill of a lifetime to be asked to represent Australia at The Court of St James's, the sovereign's royal court, as the nation's 21st High Commissioner to the United Kingdom. It is one of those quirks of British diplomatic protocol that, as Australia is one of only 16 members of the Commonwealth which recognises the British sovereign as head of state, it has a separate status as a "realm" country, and ambassadors to and from Commonwealth member countries are known as High Commissioners, a term originally used to describe envoys of the Imperial government.

The role of Australian High Commissioner to The Court of St James's has a long and distinguished history. However, its importance has diminished somewhat over the years, particularly after the abolition of Imperial preferences forced Australia to become less reliant on the "mother country."

The United Kingdom encompasses Great Britain and Northern Ireland, and the post has been traditionally regarded as one of the top five diplomatic postings, along with Washington, Beijing, Tokyo and Jakarta. One of our most pre-eminent diplomats, past or present, once told me that Indonesia was the most challenging and most interesting, because there we carried the most weight and were looked up to by both the British and the Americans.

By contrast, we have so much in common with the British that I was often tempted to say that if the relationship had been any closer, it would have been indecent, but that would have been undiplomatic. In my time, there were only a few big issues, involving the EU (European Union), which did, however, take a considerable amount of time and required a degree of finesse and persistence, before achieving a satisfactory outcome. One was a proposal to introduce a complex scheme called REACH (Registration,

Evaluation, Authorisation and Restriction of Chemicals), which would have required non-European companies such as BHP and Rio (then Rio Tinto) to submit to endless testing of every batch of chemicals imported into the EU. Ostensibly a health measure, it was one which also happened to provide considerable commercial protection for local competitors.

The other important issue involved Australian company Adsteam. The EU had suddenly and unilaterally changed the basis for taxing foreign tug boats, leading to a massively increased tax bill for the Australian company. It was clear from the outset that this was little more than a thinly disguised non-tariff barrier to trade. Even these two examples were enough to convince me that the EU was an unaccountable body, run by bureaucrats with little popular or parliamentary accountability, amounting to a massive "democratic deficit".

Much of the bread and butter work in the High Commission involved staying in touch with members of Parliament, and I therefore spent considerable time talking to ministers and their Opposition counterparts. Three different Labour Cabinet ministers told me that far too much of their time was taken up with routine "meet and greet" appointments with heads of mission and, if I hadn't been a former politician, they would not have bothered to see me. The idea was that politicians generally speak the same language and can therefore read the scene quite effectively. It was also clear that many of them had great respect and, indeed, admiration for Australia, and were keen to be invited to visit.

Another very important aspect of the role was regular interaction and visitation with the various British national security agencies with whom we enjoyed a close and high level information-sharing relationship. John Howard and I visited Eliza (now Dame Eliza) Manningham-Buller, the Director-General of MI5, the UK's internal counter-intelligence agency, and I subsequently entertained a number of senior military and security personnel at Stoke Lodge, as well as enjoying reciprocal hospitality, as guest of the heads of the military forces. It was not all business. I well recall a dinner with Anne, the Princess Royal, and her husband Tim (now Sir Tim) Lawrence, then a senior British naval officer, where I received an extensive and high powered impromptu lesson on the respective virtues of Scottish single malt whiskies.

Much of the High Commissioner's time is spent on ceremonial activities, many very enjoyable, but for those who have spent a number of years in the cauldron of Federal politics, not quite as taxing, even if often as exhausting.

Part of the job description involves playing host on a frequent basis to dignitaries, visiting senior Australian ministers, leading business people and assorted "friends of Australia", intermingled with interesting locals, including frontbenchers from both sides of the Parliament, and the occasional Royal. One trick I identified, early in the hectic summer season, was that elderflower was a good wine substitute to get through a sometimes long night, as it was not readily recognised as a non-alcoholic drink.

One elegant evening brought together two members of the peerage and provided a classic example of the unparalleled British capacity for understatement. I asked one of them how he thought David Cameron was travelling. He replied, in gushing tones, that he thought that the then Leader of Her Majesty's Loyal Opposition was doing splendidly and proceeded to trot out some broad achievements. I then asked the other Lord, nominally of the same political persuasion, for his assessment. There was a long pause before he quietly said: "I'm not sure I completely agree with every word my good friend has just said." This answer was later translated for me by a local to mean: "It's complete BS!" Lynton Crosby later assured me the response, "it's very interesting", had the same connotation.

And it is not only our compatriots who enjoyed Aussie hospitality at Stoke Lodge. We have a well-earned reputation for being refreshingly forthright. So it was that when Doug McClelland was High Commissioner, he invited the then Prime Minister Margaret Thatcher for dinner, ahead of her upcoming visit to Australia. During the course of the evening she asked if there was anything she could do while Down Under. Doug immediately seized the moment: "Well, yes – the Government is proposing to sell this residence, and we don't know how to head them off." The formidable PM didn't hesitate: "Outrageous, what an appalling suggestion.

This is one of the nicest homes in London – leave it to me!" Shortly afterwards she apparently rang Bob Hawke and said: "Prime Minister, tell me it isn't true that your Government is thinking of selling Stoke Lodge, because if it is I won't be coming." There was a pregnant pause before the cagey Hawke replied: "Ahhh, must be that idiot, Peter Walsh, my Finance Minister. Don't worry, I'll fix it for you." And he did.

Since the position was first established in 1910 as Australia's first diplomatic mission, the incumbents have included four former prime ministers, starting with the first three: Sir George Reid, Andrew Fisher and Sir Joseph Cook, each for more than five years. The most influential was undoubtedly Stanley Melbourne Bruce, later Viscount Bruce of Melbourne – the first Australian to sit in the House of Lords. He was in harness for 13 years, and would gladly have stayed forever. He subsequently became chairman of an important specialised agency of the newly established United Nations Organisation, the Food and Agriculture Organisation, from 1946-51 and continued to live in London until his death. Until 1975, every High Commissioner was a former minister and member of the Australian Parliament.

In 1912 the Australian Government bought freehold title to a large vacant island site at the east end of the Strand, and Australia House was built, overcoming wartime exigencies, throughout the First World War. It was officially opened by King George V in 1918 and is now the longest continuously occupied foreign mission in London. Still a remarkable building, it has wonderful statuary by expatriate sculptor Sir Bertram Mackennal adorning the pediment over the front entrance, and a similarly wonderful stone carving on the stairway to the High Commissioner's office. This spacious room in itself is grand, and even imposing, especially when reflecting on its previous illustrious occupants. The building has a very impressive downstairs ballroom cum dining/entertainment area, with an elegantly decorated high ceiling, where, on several occasions, we witnessed mini opera and concert performances. I personally commissioned a painting of the exterior of the building in autumn, by a renowned urban artist, Emma Haworth, which now adorns our home.

LONDON – MY DUTY

It was, for many years, the place where a passing parade of touring Australians were wont to head. I have fond memories of going there in the 1960s to read the newspapers from home, as international phone calls were prohibitively expensive, especially for young tourists. How else could they be expected to keep up with the football scores. At its peak in the 1950s it was home to more than 300 workers, mainly on immigration duties, but it now houses only around 100. It is not overly functional, but it is heritage listed and treasured by all who work and visit there.

Shortly after our arrival we had our first opportunity to attend an official commemorative event outside London, at the historic memorial at Runnymede. It is in a very prosperous part of the commuter belt near Windsor, but it was once the site of the signing in 1215 of the Magna Carta, one of the most famous documents in English history, by which King John entered, under some duress, into a power sharing arrangement with the rebellious barons of his time. It is still regarded by many as the birthplace of constitutional democracy. Standing there, it is hard not to be lost in reverie at the thought of its significance.

Such visits to historical sites around Britain were a constant reminder of the amazing journey on which the country has travelled – from the Druids and the Roman occupation, through the Norman Conquest, a civil war, regicide and suspension of the monarchy, to the Glorious Revolution, the long ascendancy of the British Empire, the dark days of two world wars, the Battle of Britain, the Blitz and, finally, V-E Day. And, despite no longer ruling the waves, Britain is still the fifth largest economy in the world, a permanent member of the UN Security Council, and about to break the shackles of the EU and assert itself yet again.

It would have been reasonable to expect the first six months of our posting to be a relatively tranquil settling-in period. This was not to be. The UK general election was held in May 2005, as usual on a working Thursday, unlike Australia's non-working (for most) Saturday. The Labour Party, again led by Tony Blair, won its third consecutive victory. As a retired politician, I was greatly looking forward to witnessing proceedings, so the High Commission quickly arranged for ringside seats at the tally room. I was accompanied by Dennis Richardson, one of Australia' s most distinguished public servants, then on his way to take up the role of Australian Ambassador in Washington and, while politically neutral, a keen follower of all things political. The quality of analytical coverage was vastly inferior to what we were accustomed to in Australia. We stayed late, but it was a bit of a damp squib. At home the overall result is usually known by 10 pm. By the time we departed around 2 am, they had managed to meander through results from less than half the seats, interspersed with long and repetitive constituency speeches from candidates of all stripes.

A few months later, on 6 July 2005, London was busy celebrating the news that it had just won the bid to host the 2012 Olympics Games. Prime Minister Tony Blair was busy at Gleneagles, Scotland, hosting the G8 summit, also attended by leaders from Canada, the European Commission, France, Germany, Italy, Japan, Russia, and the US.

Terrorist attacks in London

All the euphoria turned to ashes within 24 hours, in the early morning of 7 July.

I was in my office around 9 am when someone came in and said I should be watching the television news. At that stage three bombs had been detonated within seconds of each other, on different moving underground trains which had recently departed King's Cross. The news coverage was somewhat incoherent, as at that stage no one knew exactly what had happened. About an hour later a fourth bomb was detonated on the top deck of a double-decker bus travelling through Tavistock Square.

By this time a number of staff members were congregated around the television set, all in a state of shock, while confusion and chaos prevailed on the streets of London as police, reporters and politicians tried to make sense of it all. Our first reaction was to designate staff members to contact all major hospitals to ascertain if any Australians had been killed or injured. It later transpired that 52 people, all UK residents but of 18 different nationalities, had been killed, and more than 700 injured. The number included one Australian killed and nine injured.

LONDON – MY DUTY

Our emotional response was normal and perfectly understand-able, but the reaction from another Australian expat, at his May-fair office that morning, was remarkably different. Greg Coffey, a young and very successful hedge fund trader was at his desk, watching the television while talking to a colleague on the phone. The news that the Underground had been disrupted by a power surge did not disturb him, but when he learned of a second surge he sat bolt upright, put down the phone, and began buying enor-mous amounts of US Treasuries – a graphic illustration of how financial success can function. That night approximately one mil-lion people still took the tube home as usual, a classic demonstra-tion of British bulldog courage and pragmatism.

London was on tenterhooks for days thereafter, and all sorts of preventative measures were activated to protect the public, in-cluding removing all waste bins from railway stations. Gradually it dawned on people that, with police and security swarming the streets, there was most unlikely to be a repetition. Things settled down and for the next two weeks we were busy preparing for the official visit of our own Prime Minister.

But first, a rare thrill – the traditional late afternoon formal wel-come at Australia House for the Australian cricket team, a few days ahead of the Lord's Test, which just happened to coincide with the PM's visit. The place was packed out, principally with Australian supporters, but also with some of the local UK cricket hierarchy. It was a very enjoyable occasion, everyone filled with anticipation, with speeches all round, including some very nice words from the captain, Ricky Ponting. The cricketers mingled freely, and were enjoying themselves so much that, when Steve Bernard, the team manager, asked me to encourage the players to retire, several said: "not until I've finished this beer."

The PM duly arrived the next day for what would be his only visit to London during my tenure. We started with briefings at the High Commission, ahead of a big day on July 14, which started normally. The grand plan was to see the Chancellor of the Excheq-uer in the morning, then lunch at Downing Street, followed by the afternoon at Lord's watching Day 1 of the first Ashes Test – all that a cricket tragic politician (both of us) could ever ask for. We saw

303

MORE TO LIFE THAN POLITICS?

Gordon Brown in his Treasury office, where he was keen to tell us that he walked in the shoes of John Maynard Keynes, who had held court in Treasury for several years. As I recall, the Chancellor did most of the talking, but we did have a very instructive discussion on economic events, and the state of the books.

Lunch at Downing Street was very special, with about eight or ten around the table. About half way through the meal an aide appeared at Tony Blair's side and whispered an urgent message, after which the British PM told us of what sounded like another terrorist bombing. It had apparently just occurred, and the circumstances were not at all clear, especially on the matter of casualties. As the meal proceeded, he announced that he would address the downstairs media throng, which had materialised from nowhere, and asked John Howard to accompany him. The journalists, as is their wont, were understandably hungry for some hard facts, which, in view of the still sketchy information to hand, Tony Blair felt he was not in a position to provide.

When he said this several times, there were audible groans and the press turned to John Howard for his reaction. He proceeded to steal the show by flying the flag of defiance and talked about the individual and collective heroism of the British people. He cited the dark days of the Battle of Britain and the Blitz and the need to again defy those who would seek to destroy us. This went down a treat and, if I recall correctly, even drew a round of applause, in my experience an unheard of response from hard-boiled journalists. Some years later I had the honour to speak at a function at the National Gallery of Victoria to honour John Howard's wonderful leadership over nearly 12 years. I recounted how he had seized the moment on that fateful day in London and outshone his British counterpart. When I had finished, the organisers immediately put on a tribute video from a number of prominent world leaders eulogising him. One of the first was from none other than Tony Blair, who proceeded to confirm what I had just said, in very generous terms.

Given the gravity of the events, before heading for Lord's, we decided it was important to get a clearer idea of what had happened, which turned out to be a failed attempt to replicate the bombings of 7 July – three at Underground tube stations, and one on a bus. Fortunately, only the detonators of the bombs exploded, with no serious injuries. The suspects fled but, after what the Metropolitan Police Commissioner described as "the greatest operational challenge ever faced" by the Met, the bombers were eventually apprehended, brought to trial, convicted and sentenced to forty years imprisonment.

We eventually made it to Lord's, arriving not long before stumps. Immediately several journalists asked a seemingly innocent question: " Greetings, Mr Howard – enjoying your day at the cricket?" Acutely aware of the insensitivity trap it contained, he made it clear that we had just arrived. While not in the same league as the life and death drama outside the ground, it had also been a day of high drama at Lord's. 17 wickets had fallen in a day and Australia went on to record a convincing win, but eventually lost the series in what is generally regarded as the best Ashes series ever.

After the day's play, we were taken inside the holy of holies and shown around by John Buchanan, the Australian coach. I fell into conversation with a very warm and friendly Brett Lee, with a knapsack on his back. When I asked why, he said: "Mate, that's where I keep my baggy green – can't trust anyone around here – there's no lockers in the change room!" It is ironic that, even after "the greatest Ashes series ever", a number of friends and compatriots insisted on blaming me for the ultimate result, despite the fact that I had done my duty to fly the flag at each of the five Test matches. Aussies like winners!

The next day the PM decided that we should pay some hospital visits to Australians injured in the July 7 bombings. Two I will never forget. Gill Hicks, an Australian expat who had lived in London for many years, was a miraculous survivor. Boarding the Underground at King's Cross, she found the suicide bomber standing several metres from her. 26 people in the carriage died, but Gill managed to use her scarf as a tourniquet and saved her own life.

The last to be rescued alive, she lost both legs to amputation below the knee, and was not expected to live. But, when we saw her in St Thomas' Hospital, some two weeks later, she was in an incredibly positive mood, which she has retained ever since.

She has since become an inspirational speaker, writer and supporter of worthwhile causes around the world, including her own MAD (Making A Difference) for Peace project. Gill Hicks became a classic example of how to look on the bright side of a catastrophic and life changing event, and we remained in regular contact with her as she fought her way back to a productive life. She has since spoken to young people who have become radicalised, and believes her story has made an impact, even on hardened extremists. Like Nelson Mandela, she felt no animosity towards her persecutors, only absolute pity for the misguided young extremist, who also died in the bombing, aged 19.

The other Australian, who was not seriously injured, but obviously harboured political grievances, constantly complained about everything, particularly money and compensation, and expected the High Commission and others to do all sorts of favours for her. When we visited her in hospital she couldn't resist the opportunity to berate John Howard over the Iraq War and other things, and subsequently went on television to complain, yet again, about her treatment. The contrast with Gill Hicks was extraordinary.

On the following day, after we had spent some time with John Reid, then the Secretary of State for Health, the PM, ever the political/historical buff, was keen to re-visit the Cabinet War Rooms, to which the Churchill War Rooms had recently been added. Located beneath the Treasury building in Whitehall, this fortified complex served as a strategic command centre throughout the Second World War. Most people can't get enough of the Churchill legend, and the PM was no exception. He was particularly keen to point out to me a primitive hearing device, with which he no doubt identified, given his own longstanding hearing disability.

The War Rooms are now under the jurisdiction of the Imperial War Museum, founded near the end of the First World War, for the purpose of recording Britain's civil and military war effort and sacrifice, as well as to promote the study and understanding of the history of modern warfare and wartime experience. Now based in Southwark, it also has responsibility for Duxford, an historic airfield in Cambridgeshire, Trafford Museum in Greater Manchester and the Royal Navy cruiser HMS *Belfast*, now permanently moored in the Thames. I also served as an ex officio member, along with other Commonwealth colleagues, on the governing Board of Trustees.

When the time came for the PM to head for home after an unforgettable few days, I accompanied him to the airport where, as he was departing, he confided that he would be making a surprise stopover in Afghanistan, a detour that has become almost commonplace in later years for subsequent PMs. It had certainly been an unforgettable highlight of my time in London. As always, John Howard did his country proud.

The Commonwealth War Graves Commission

Another very enjoyable part of my duties in representing Australia was serving as a member of the Commonwealth (originally Imperial) War Graves Commission, an august body with a distinguished history. Established by Royal Charter in 1917, it honours the 1.7 million men and women of the Commonwealth who died in the First and Second World Wars. It is responsible for building and maintaining cemeteries and memorials at 23,000 locations in more than 150 countries and territories. Three eminent architects, including Sir Edwin Lutyens, were chosen to begin the work of designing and constructing, and Rudyard Kipling, whose only son had been killed in the War, was appointed as literary adviser to recommend appropriate wording for the inscriptions. He was subsequently responsible for choosing the wording used for the Stone of Remembrance, and the immortal words, "Known unto God", for the headstones of unknown soldiers around the world.

The Commission's task and accomplishments have been enormous. By 1918 some 587,000 graves had been identified, and another 559,000 casualties were registered as having no known grave. Prior to the Great War, individual commemoration of war dead was often conducted on an ad hoc basis and was almost exclusively limited to commissioned officers. But the sheer scale and dimension of this slaughter required a fundamental re-appraisal. Repatriation of bodies became a burning public issue and, in due course, the subject of heated parliamentary debate. Ultimately the Commission's view against repatriation was accepted, as well as the decision that uniform memorials should be used to avoid class distinctions.

I served on the Board of Commissioners for three years, together with High Commissioners from New Zealand, India, Canada and South Africa. The President is traditionally a Royal, currently the Duke of Kent, and the chairman is a serving minister but, by a very English convention, neither is expected to attend meetings, which are chaired by the vice-chairman. In those years it was former RAF head and Falklands hero, Sir Peter Squires, with whom, a few years later, I spent the day at the Oval watching Australia get belted. Other distinguished colleagues were the eminent British historians, Sir John Keegan and Sir Hew Strachan.

A special privilege was travelling as a team each year to visit important battlefields and cemeteries. My visits were to the Somme in the beautiful region of Picardy, to northern England around Harrogate, and Arnhem, the site of one of the most famous battles of the Second World War and immortalised in the film, *A Bridge Too Far*. Walking around Arnhem town, I was struck by how close the German and Allied forces must have been to each other, as much of the engagement involved door to door street fighting.

Visiting the Somme is an extraordinarily moving experience, brilliantly captured in Sebastian Faulks' bestseller, *Birdsong*. 1 July 1916, the first day on the Somme, was the worst day in the history of the British army, with almost 60,000 British casualties, including nearly 20,000 dead. More than three million men fought in the battles, which continued for another four and a half months. Standing silently, amid the stillness of the rolling chalk uplands and gently undulating fields, it was hard to comprehend its close proximity to England, where the sounds of large artillery guns and explosions could regularly be heard. The trenches were no longer there, but it was impossible not to be overwhelmed by the thought of the scale of the suffering and devastation.

We also visited Thiepval, a key village taken by the Allies, where there now stands a very large Memorial to the Missing, including more than 70,000 British servicemen who died in the Battles of the Somme. This imposing structure, designed by Sir Edwin Lutyens, has been described as "the greatest executed British work of monumental architecture of the twentieth century". Its dedication reads: "For the dead of the Battles of the Somme of the First World War with no known grave."

Another very moving memorial, built and since maintained by the War Graves Commission, is the Menin Gate at Ypres, Belgium, dedicated to British and Commonwealth soldiers killed in the Ypres Salient and whose graves are unknown. Every evening since its opening in 1927, save for when it was in German-occupied territory during the Second World War, the Last Post has been played and, on a subsequent visit, I participated in the service and laid a wreath.

Political party conferences

The political party conference season was an annual occasion not to be missed. I made a habit of attending both the Labour and Conservative conferences each year but, unaware that the Liberal Democrats would one day help to form a coalition government, I gave them a miss. Both sides traditionally hold their extravaganzas in key regional cities outside London. Manchester, Birmingham, Brighton and Blackpool were particular favourites. They are usually set-piece performances, providing the opportunity for rising stars to speak at myriad side events, while the "big beasts" (leading Cabinet ministers) get first prize on the main stage. Thousands attend and are catered for by many special interest groups and commercial business stands in what has now become "a nice little earner" for both parties.

Whilst Blackpool, in its prime a cheap seaside resort, was culturally fascinating, Labour Party conferences at Manchester and Brighton had a special fizz, as they were then the party in power, meeting in great English cities with powerful political pedigrees. Some years later, together with Karl Morris, Federal Vice-President of the Liberal Party, and Party Treasurer, Andrew Burnes, I attended the Conservative Party Conference in Birmingham. It was quite a performance – there must have been several hundred stalls and stands featuring all sorts of worthy causes as well as a

MORE TO LIFE THAN POLITICS?

number of commercial enterprises and food and clothing offerings – even a great pop-up political bookshop. All the leading politicians were there – for speeches and interviews or just to meet and greet the many hundreds of party faithful.

Art at the Vatican

A personal highlight during my London assignment was an invitation for Megs and me from Michael (now Sir Michael) Hintze, a leading London-based expat and phenomenally successful hedge fund founder and Chief Investment Officer of CQS LLP, to travel to Rome for the day on a private jet. Michael, an amazing all-rounder, had been, and continues to be, a great supporter of the High Commission's activities in London. Not only was he a Conservative Party donor and patron, but he was also a very generous philanthropist and supporter of the Catholic Church. A few years earlier, he had agreed to fund restoration of priceless Michelangelo frescoes in the Pope's private chapel. The trip was to inspect progress, make a call on the CEO of Vatican City, and visit the Vatican Museum, before returning to London – all in the one day.

After some procrastination on the part of DFAT, we got the all clear for what proved to be an unforgettable day's adventure. I will always treasure the memory of climbing the scaffolding and being permitted to touch the most dazzling pieces of art. Michael was subsequently appointed to the board of the powerful, wealthy and mysterious Vatican Bank by Pope Francis in a heroic attempt to clean up the Church's finances. After my posting had ended, Michael appointed me to his international advisory board, where I had the good fortune to be involved with some very impressive business and military leaders for some seven years – a wonderful learning experience which has led to my maintaining continuous involvement with hedge funds for many years.

Belfast

Another very important and moving part of my tour of duty was visiting Belfast a number of times. This was part of my bailiwick, as the UK is shorthand for the United Kingdom of Great Britain (England, Scotland and Wales) and Northern Ireland. In my time we had an Australian consul based in Edinburgh so it was important to visit Belfast to fly the flag in one of the most delightful (apart from the weather) literary and historic cities in Britain. I had been to Northern Ireland in the 1960s as the internecine warfare was just getting underway but, although there were then some non-violent civil rights protests and competing green (Republican) and orange (Ulster) marches, there was little hint of the deadly pattern of violence to come.

On one occasion I stayed at Hillsborough Castle, a magnificent two storey mansion dating back to 1797, which serves as the official residency of the Royal Family in Northern Ireland and slept in what I was assured was the Queen's bed. On another visit, early in 2007, for the official celebration of the opening of the Northern Ireland Assembly, I met both Martin McGuinness and Ian Paisley, neither in firebrand mode, as well as veteran US Senator, Ted Kennedy, whose family had always been strong supporters of the Irish cause.

In many ways a visit to Belfast was a trip through blood spattered living history. I had read of many of the atrocities perpetrated over the almost thirty years of the Northern Ireland conflict, often referred to euphemistically as The Troubles. Whilst the Provisional IRA (the Provo's) are deservedly much criticised for their ruthless and unrelenting guerrilla campaign, one only has to read books like *Mad Dog* and *The Shankill Butchers* to get a sense of the fanaticism of the Loyalist protestant paramilitaries, who embarked on indiscriminate, cold-blooded killings of Northern Ireland Catholics in the name of God and Ulster.

It is extraordinary how close to the central city are the two former opposing hot beds of extremism, divided by the inaptly named "Peace Wall." Even after the official end of the Troubles, with the signing of the Good Friday Agreement in 1998, the key streets were still filled with constant reminders of what people had lived and died for.

Falls Road, a Republican stronghold, is the main road through west Belfast. A predominantly working-class community, with a strong socialist tradition, it was the site of some of the worst violence. The British army maintained a constant and substantial presence throughout the period to counter IRA hit squads based in the Upper Falls. Walking it is an eerie experience as there was a sense of underlying danger, mixed with unsettling memories of the horror of the relatively recent gruesome killings. I certainly would not have done the same at night. The murals to Bobby Sands, who died in 1981 while on a hunger strike in the Maze prison, the Garden of Remembrance, the Solidarity Wall, with messages of support from like-minded international supporters, such as Cuba, all appeared designed to avoid closure. The ubiquitous Irish flag was also hardly a peace offering, but a symbol of defiance. It was hard not to feel that there were still hatreds lurking not far beneath the surface.

Shankill Road, another strongly working-class bastion, had been a centre for loyalist paramilitarism, giving birth to the Ulster Volunteer Force and later the Ulster Defence Association. It copped its share of pub bombings and shootings by republican paramilitary forces. A similar sense of unease accompanies the visiting walker.

IRA outrages, extending to London and beyond, reached a peak in the Provisional IRA's attempt to assassinate Prime Minister Margaret Thatcher and her Cabinet while attending the Conservative Party conference at Brighton in 1984. The IRA claimed responsibility the next day and promised to try again. The passage of time may ease the tensions but, as long as the United Ireland project remains unresolved, mutual resentments are likely to linger.

Charitable causes

A highlight of my work in London was involvement with various charitable causes, especially those with an Australian flavour, such as Friends of the Australian Flying Doctor Service. I'm not sure who came up with the idea, but it proved to be a blockbuster – a grand (black tie, 500 tickets at £500 a head) fund raising event at Lord's, with Shane Warne as guest of honour, interviewed by the very polished friend of Australia, Mark Nicholas. Once advertised it sold out in two hours.

We decided to hold a big-ticket auction, for which, in due course, we were given some wonderful works of art, from the likes of Ken Done, internationally famous for his brightly coloured iconic images of Australian landmarks such as Sydney Harbour. These have been enduringly popular and, as a result, he is sometimes disparaged for being too commercial. He is actually a very serious as well as a very versatile artist. On one occasion, when we were out to dinner in London, I invited him to donate a painting to be auctioned for a charitable cause. He responded enthusiastically and donated a unique Japanese-style painting of two girls at a window. In due course I bought it myself, as it was so different to his usual output, but a great example of his superior craftsmanship.

For the same auction I also approached Rolf Harris, whose response was fundamentally different. These were pre-disaster times for him and I was very aware from my gallery visits that his paintings were very expensive. He once boasted to me that his art work earned him more than a million pounds sterling a year. Yet his first response was that his agent wouldn't let him. When I persisted he sent a few cheap plastic Groucho face masks.

For the Lord's gala auction it was my designated duty to see if Warnie would donate an hour of his time to coach a child, hopefully of one of our wealthier attendees. I duly rang his agent, James Erskine, but when I politely put the proposition to him it provoked a strong reaction: "Shane is sick to death of this type of request – it's not on, the answer's NO". When I ignored his protestations, he said: "Well, you can have half an hour", which I immediately described as an insult. After a short pause he said: "OK, but don't tell Shane – just spring it on the night."

The night was a great success – the highlight was undoubtedly the role played by the inimitable Lord Jeffrey Archer, a fan of Australia, and a regular MC at charity auctions. When the coaching item came along, the bidding was brisk, and quickly reached £16,000, with two fathers slogging it out. At which point auctioneer Archer held up his hand and said: "Shane, wouldn't it be a shame if one of these two had to miss out – his son would be devastated. What about we split it, and they can each have an hour's worth for £16,000 each?" Warne was speechless – clean bowled by an unplayable Archer googly.

Another trick I picked up in London was of particular pertinence to those of us who have had to make speeches for a living. It is usually very prudent to compose your thoughts before delivering them in an organised manner, as John Howard regularly demonstrated. But it took a master of global strategy to take the art of speechmaking to new heights. The occasion was a select group around the breakfast table of a leading London hotel, with Henry Kissinger as guest of honour. After the MC had welcomed him and announced that his special subject would be current affairs, he simply sat there and said: "Rather than me talking on what I think is important, I would prefer to address your priorities, so fire away with your questions". It was a masterly presentation, without all that unnecessary preparation. He told me afterwards that he frequently saw John Howard, for whom he had great admiration, when the latter was passing through New York. I assured him the respect was reciprocated.

Another very important duty was attending the Australian War Memorial at Hyde Park Corner on special occasions such as Anzac Day and, likewise, the opening of a New Zealand memorial nearby in late 2007. Our memorial had been officially opened in 2003 and consists of a downwards grass slope facing a semi-circular wall of grey-green granite slabs, inscribed with the names of more than 23,000 birthplaces of the 102,000 Australians who died in the two World Wars. Every visit is a moving experience.

The Residence

The experience of coming to live in London, not simply passing through, was very exciting despite the snowfall which greeted us on our arrival. My second London sojourn, this time with Megs, was decidedly more up market than the first. On arrival, we quickly took up residence at the stylish but understated official residence, Stoke Lodge, 45 Hyde Park Gate (HPG), built in the 1830s. It is "owned" on a long lease by the Australian Government, whose favoured tenants, the High Commissioners, have been in occupation for nearly seventy years. A splendid haven of tranquillity, it has hosted many of the great and the good as well as the rich and famous. The spacious garden, fitted out with a kangaroo topiary and some Lord's sacred turf, as well as many Australian native plants, provides the perfect summer setting for outdoor receptions. The garden has recently been added to, with the commemorative planting of a tree in recognition of the outstanding contribution of HRH The Duke of Edinburgh, Patron for nearly fifty years of the Britain-Australia Society.

The house also came with a permanent butler, cook, and a day-time-only house maid, the first two living on the premises in separate houses. We became firm friends with all of them and were very sorry to eventually leave them behind. The garden also came with a mangy fox, which was not allowed to be disposed of, but, somehow, one day, it suddenly disappeared. A dedicated driver was also available, although I much preferred the flexibility of self-drive. It was also a good way to get to know London, especially as I got comprehensively lost on my first solo effort, en route to the chancery (Australia House) in the Aldwych.

Royalty

The Queen ascended the throne in 1952, when I was still in primary school. As I was growing up, the Royal Family was part of the Australian social fabric – respectful treatment by teachers, overwhelmingly favourable newspaper coverage, accompanied by regular sell-out Royal visits, fanned by recently arrived black and white television – and no hint of republican sympathies.

But, as the years went by and the golden couple moved into middle age, the visits became less frequent, with a commensurate waning of public fervour. Family scandals and a less fawning media led to more scrutiny of their activities and their cost to taxpayers – standard media fare but calculated to diminish their public standing. By the time I became a minister I had mild republican inclinations. To his credit, this did not deter John Howard from appointing me to London as High Commissioner. I went without any strong views on the future of the Crown in Australia, but with a keen sense of history and anticipation at the opportunity to study the Royal phenomenon from a privileged ring side seat.

I was not disappointed – the first meeting with Her Majesty was a revelation. It was not preceded by a coach ride in top hat and tails, as befits ambassadors from non-Commonwealth countries for their formal accreditation. For those from the 16 Realm countries like Australia, who recognise the monarch as their head of state, it was a more demure reception, but just as exciting. Buckingham Palace was a maze of corridors and the official section was somewhat tired and a trifle dilapidated – not surprising given the constant stream of visitors.

Megs and I waited in a relatively undistinguished ante room for a good twenty minutes, until the President of a Balkan country finally emerged. Once ushered inside, we had barely exchanged formalities before the Queen could contain herself no longer: "That man! What am I meant to do about 2000 years of his country's history? He just went on and on and on – and his wife just sat there, saying nothing." This ice breaker quickly segued into a warm and wide ranging discussion about current events, before she bowled up an almost unplayable curve ball: "So, what do Australians think of Rupert Murdoch?"

It was clear where this was heading – having lived in London for twelve months on and off in the 1960s and having made regular visits thereafter, I knew that the intrusive journalistic techniques of papers like *The Sun* and *The News of the World* were outrageous invasions of privacy but were still addictive fare to millions. The Royal family had been patient and long suffering victims, constrained from public retaliation and inevitably harbouring a strong pent up resentment, which allowed little room for a relaxed attitude to the notion of freedom of the press, which we all recognise, albeit grudgingly at times, as being an essential requirement of a healthy and fully functioning democracy.

Founded in 1843, *The News of the World* had been at one time the biggest-selling English-language newspaper in the world and, even at closure, it still had one of the highest English-language circulations. It had been bought in 1969 by Rupert Murdoch, who transformed it into a tabloid in 1984 and, together with its sister paper, and another red top, *The Sunday Sun*, concentrating on celebrity-based scoops and populist news.

As all these thoughts raced through my mind I quickly concluded that I should do as the British expect of Australians: tell it

LONDON – MY DUTY

as it is. So I proffered the following: "You probably won't want to hear this, but I suspect that most of my countrymen and women recognise Rupert Murdoch as Australia's most successful ever businessman on the world stage." Understandably this did not go down very well, but ultimately proved to be little more than a hiccup in an otherwise highly enjoyable and memorable first encounter. Ultimately the Royals got their revenge when, in the heat of a major phone tapping scandal, *The News of the World* was forced to close down in 2010.

I came away greatly impressed by the Queen's warmth and humanity, as well as her admirable knowledge of current affairs. Whilst it was not uncommon for higher education to be seen as an unnecessary accoutrement for young girls of her era, it is still surprising that it was not thought important for a future monarch. Undeterred, it was clear that her life's work had been characterised by an autodidactic determination, an awesome sense of duty and a fierce commitment to give her all for a greater cause.

In this noble enterprise she has had the perfect partner, Prince Philip, who has stamped his own distinctive mark on his Royal role. It would have been much safer to tag quietly along behind the Monarch and politely meet and greet the great and the good, as well as the humble and the unknown. Instead, he chose to liven things up a bit, to the delight of the media, always ready to pounce. He once told me that on arrival in a southern African country an English journalist quickly introduced himself and proceeded to follow him everywhere. But, after a few days, the journalist came up to say goodbye as he had been recalled to base. When Prince Philip asked why, he said: "I was sent down to report back on your gaffes, but you've let the side down, so it's home to London for me."

On another occasion he arrived at Australia House in his decoy Volkswagen to attend the centenary celebrations of the Australian Life Saving Association. It was not clear to either of us why the event needed to be held in London, but he dutifully did the rounds and met all the guests. As we were going up on to the stage to say a few words, he asked if I knew many of the guests. When I replied, "none", he laconically responded: "Oh, typical Aussies – just came along for the grog!"

Possessed of spartan discipline and keeping himself in impeccable physical condition, he also knew that merely exchanging banalities with all and sundry was likely to be both boring and forgettable for both parties. He made every effort, while staying within the bounds of decorum, to say and do things which would provide a memorable experience. On one special ambassadorial occasion at Buckingham Palace, the Royal couple were formally introduced by me, as the head of mission, to several of our leading embassy lights and their spouses. Having introduced Her Majesty, before I could do the same for her consort, he confronted the Australian Head of the Defence Force, poked him in the chest and brusquely asked why he was sporting a ribbon of one of the British regiments. Upon being told he had been seconded by them for a second time, the Prince promptly asked: "Are your people trying to get rid of you? " This totally unconventional but quirky exchange left us all both relaxed and amused.

Like all working Royals, he is a patron of innumerable worthy causes, in his case a number to do with the environment. But this was not simply lip service. I once attended a packed house where, as head of The Royal Society of Arts, he spoke passionately, at length and essentially without notes, in quite erudite terms and argued an eloquent case.

His seemingly gruff exterior notwithstanding, he could also be both thoughtful and reflective. On one occasion he recounted to me, with moving nostalgia, the delights of Malta, where he had been posted in the navy and where he had spent his honeymoon.

Despite their rigid public adherence to political impartiality, as the ultimate figureheads of the establishment, they had, in times gone by, been regarded with suspicion by sections of the Labour Party. In large measure stemming from their dedication to being "above politics", there was never any evidence of tension displayed by Tony Blair or Gordon Brown, the two Labour prime ministers on my watch. Blair had, indeed, played a pivotal healing role in the wake of Diana's death in 1997, as the Royal Family struggled to come to terms with the public expression of their emotional reaction to the tragedy.

After three years of semi-regular interaction, I finished my posting with enormous admiration for the Queen and the Duke of Edinburgh as strong characters with a fierce devotion to duty and an unswerving regard for the importance of the institution, as the vital glue that unites an increasingly diverse citizenry. They will both be hard acts to follow.

The Prince of Wales

Prince Charles attended many Australian events in London during my time and was always keen to remind me of his abiding affection for Australia, having spent part of his formal education at Timbertop, the essentially outdoors campus of Geelong Grammar School in north-eastern Victoria. He has been an indefatigable and life-long campaigner for many worthy causes but he is already over seventy years of age and has been entitled to succeed since his mother ascended to the throne on 6 February 1952, some 67 years ago. He has already become the longest serving heir apparent (an heir whose claim cannot be set aside by the birth of another heir) in modern history, having overtaken Edward VII, who was born when his mother had already been on the throne for four years. Unlike Charles, he only had to wait 60 years until his mother's death in 1901 to become King. The Queen may perhaps emulate her mother's feat in reaching 101 years of age.

Stability and committed Royal figureheads have been important factors in consolidating public affection. But, behind the scenes, scrupulous attention to detail by skilled advisers and consiglieri has also been critical in handling the media. Hiring a PR firm would certainly not cut the mustard – there are many small but important policy judgments to be made and the media have to be handled with great finesse. Whilst they are almost always in "gotcha" mode, they are also acutely aware that there are red lines which, if crossed, can lead to pain, fines or even closure, as happened to the Royal family's bete noir, *The News of the World.*

In 2017 a French court ordered *Closer* magazine to pay damages and fines for publishing pictures of a topless Duchess of Cambridge while on holiday in Provence in 2012. And who can forget the intrusive role of the paparazzi, who chased Princess Diana to her death in a Paris car crash in 1997.

MORE TO LIFE THAN POLITICS?

When Ron Walker was Chairman of the Organising Committee for the 2006 Commonwealth Games – the greatest Commonwealth Games ever – we made a number of visits to Buckingham Palace for a range of meetings, principally with then Sir Robin, now Baron, Janvrin, Principal Private Secretary to Elizabeth II from February 1999 to September 2007. On our first visit we were upstaged by Australian supermodel, Elle McPherson. Ron subsequently claimed that the Queen said something to him like: "you are almost part of the family." I can't vouch for the accuracy of his hearing, but there could well be a grain of truth in the proposition as he was tireless in keeping the Royals up to date on the progress of the Games.

The relationship of the Royal Family to the memory of Princess Diana was clearly a fraught issue which needed much constant care and attention from within. Commemoration of the the tenth anniversary of Diana's death at the Guard's Chapel was a classic assemblage of the great and the good, which found me sitting next to Sir John Major, who was next to Gordon Brown and Tony Blair. As we solemnly filed out, I followed three more knights of the realm – Richard Branson, Cliff Richard and Elton John, the latter having been a particular source of comfort and solace to Diana and whose tribute threnody, *Goodbye England's Rose*, has sold 33 million copies, more than any other recording in musical history.

Just as the Queen, urged on by her husband, is determined not to abdicate prematurely, so her son is undoubtedly also determined not to stand aside for the next in line, his son William.

The Duke of Cambridge has not put a foot wrong since his marriage in 2011 to Kate Middleton. Happily married and clearly enjoying their Royal duties, they are graceful, outgoing and down to earth, and very popular with the public. The saving grace for William is that his wait for primacy will be very much shorter than that of his father.

13

My London – a Tribute

In the spirit of Dr Johnson's pithy aphorism, I have never tired of London. Indeed, I have visited it more than fifty times in my life, and more than thirty times since my term as High Commissioner to the Court of James's expired early in 2008.

London is unceasingly impressive, especially for those with an Anglo-Saxon upbringing. History everywhere, architecture at times breathtakingly beautiful. The blend of the traditional (Westminster Abbey, Buckingham Palace) and the modern (the Gherkin, the Shard) works well. The population mix makes it the perfect melting pot. The masses of tourists are a constant reminder of the grandeur and the glory that characterise this mighty city.

The streets of London

Many spend an inordinate amount of time trawling along Regent Street or Oxford Street, visiting famous department stores such as Marks and Spencers, Selfridges, John Lewis and, in Knightsbridge, Harrods. The more up-market and fashionable stores include Fortnum and Mason, food store par excellence since 1707 and currently grocer to the Queen, Simpson's of Piccadilly, Harvey Nichols (of Ab Fab fame), and Liberty's. For gentlemen seeking high quality and often quite expensive clothing and other fashion accoutrements such as hats, shoes, shaving equipment and colognes, Jermyn Street is a must. Winston Churchill's father once lived there, as did Isaac Newton. Beau Brummel, that immortal dandy, did not, but nevertheless has his statue there in recognition of his status as the epitome of clothing elegance. Many of the buildings on Jermyn Street are owned by the Crown Estate, but it is justly famous for its high-quality shirtmakers, shoe and boot makers.

But, despite intense competition, the grandest street of all remains Piccadilly. It was a great pleasure to be able to walk from the official residence of the High Commissioner in Kensington to

Hyde Park Corner and then along the great thoroughfare towards Piccadilly Circus. In medieval times it was known as "the road to Reading," adorned by numerous bars and inns. Following the Great Fire of London in 1666 and the establishment of Green Park on the south side several years later, many stately homes were built on the northern side including, adjacent to the famous Burlington Arcade, Burlington House, the home of the Royal Academy of Arts. Former Prime Ministers William Gladstone and Edward Heath also lived nearby, as did King George VI, prior to his accession to the throne in 1936. Several members of the Rothschild family had mansions at the western end near Hyde Park Corner, leading some wags to nickname the street, Rothschild Row. St James's Church, designed by Christopher Wren, was consecrated in 1684 and, aided by the development of Mayfair, Piccadilly quickly became one of the busiest streets in London.

Like most urban areas, it has had its ups and downs. From its genteel beginnings as a place for the sale of piccadills (Tudor-style lace collars, also known as ruffles or "ruffs"), in the 20th century it became infamous for being at the heart of the capital's illegal drug trade, with long queues forming outside unscrupulous chemists. It has since largely regained its traditional lustre, with famous hotels such as the Ritz, Park Lane, Athenaeum and Intercontinental in amongst luxury shops and offices.

In the late 18th century it was a popular area for booksellers. Hatchards, now the oldest surviving bookshop in Britain, opened its doors there in 1797 and has since seen a constant procession of literary, political, artistic and social lions pass through its portals. Despite gloomy predictions of the demise of traditional books with the emergence of e-books, Hatchards has continued to prosper and still retains the loyal patronage of those interested in quality offerings, especially of literature and culture. As the holder of three Royal warrants, Hatchards is, indeed, a unique British institution and always one of my first ports-of-call whenever I visit London. On the other side of the street is the flagship of its owner, the now more down-market Waterstones book group.

Other great cities have their charms but, for an Australian brought up on the cultural and historical links that bind our two countries, not to say regular games of Monopoly, there is a true sense of "going home", a term often used by the English-born, Australian-resident parents of an early girlfriend of mine.

Even in this globalised age, the UK, especially London, retains a unique pulling power. It is a very civilised place. Sure, like other vibrant democracies, it has at times bitter political contests, bombing outrages and minor social upheavals. Politics will always be a messy business. But to visit the modern cradle of Western civilisation is to be reminded of the structural foundations of an effective and relatively prosperous democracy based on the rule of law and the distinctive roles of parliament, executive government, and the judiciary.

Why do avalanches of money continue to flow into UK coffers? Its status as a mini tax haven with lenient treatment for non-domiciles no doubt plays a part. But the main reason is its well-earned reputation for its safe and stable political system founded on the rule of law, an independent judiciary and legally enforceable contracts.

Some years ago, the renowned scholar, Isaiah Berlin, said: "England, above all lands, stood for settled democracy, humane and peaceful civilisation, civil liberty, legal equality, stability, toleration, respect for individual rights and a religious tradition founded as much on the Old Testament as the New."

In a more modern idiom, renowned economic historian, Niall Ferguson, has identified six killer apps underlying the success of Western civilisation. All are found in abundance in the UK: competition, science and technology, property rights, Western medicine, the consumer society and the work ethic.

Most Australians and Britons tend to take these vital requirements for granted, notwithstanding the views of some leading commentators that our brand of democracy is in need of fundamental repair. They warn that we are at risk of falling behind countries with less democratic, more centrally controlled polities which, unburdened by democratic constraints, are currently achieving an impressive degree of economic progress for their citizens. I prefer to maintain a more positive outlook.

London is an historian's dream assignment, crowded with palaces, abbeys, cathedrals, bridges and monuments, all dating back centuries. The list goes on: historic theatres, rare book shops, famous hotels, restaurants and art galleries, the Houses of Parliament, Buckingham Palace, the Tower of London, the Mall, Park Lane, Hyde Park, Piccadilly Circus and Hyde Park Corner. But these are mostly for tourists – to live in London is to have the opportunity to dig deeper.

Parks and gardens

Most tourists don't have the time to notice there are green squares and gardens all over town. The residential square is a unique feature of London life, unmatched anywhere else in the world. Indeed, squares are a defining feature of London. They have been described as London's first suburbs, being built around grand estates and designed as self-contained communities. The first to be called by the name was Bloomsbury Square, laid out in the 1660s, but it was not until the following century that Lincoln's Inn Fields and Leicester Fields were converted to gardens. There are still some hundreds dotted around Greater London. Some, like Trafalgar Square, were always public open spaces but many remain restricted to use by adjoining residents; others are still firmly in private hands.

In addition to these invaluable green spaces, London has some wonderful public areas in which to frolic or simply to amble, such as Holland Park, Hampstead Heath, Wimbledon and Clapham Commons. I have enjoyed visiting each of them but especially the eight stunning Royal Parks consisting of some 110 square kilometres of parkland and gardens and over six million trees. Hyde Park, Kensington Gardens and the Serpentine formed part of my regular early morning runs from the residence. Green Park and St James's Park close to Buckingham Palace are hard to miss but a visit to the largest, Richmond Park, where deer still abound, or Greenwich Park, a former hunting park, is well worth the effort.

Law, crime, prisons and executions

London is a lawyer's paradise, with the four Inns of Court dating back to the 14th century now housing several thousands of barristers. Each of Lincoln's Inn, Inner Temple, Middle Temple and

MY LONDON – A TRIBUTE

Gray's Inn is a substantial complex with a great hall, chapel and libraries, based on the Oxbridge model. They are characterised by ancient flagstones, picturesque squares, tranquil cloisters and glorious gardens. Their history is extraordinary. The Temples are named after the Temple Church, dating from 1185 and built by the soldiers of Christ, the Knights Templar. Shakespeare's *Twelfth Night* had its first outing in the Middle Temple and the exquisite stone church has also more recently featured in the film, *The Da Vinci Code*. Since 1620 the Inns have all ranked equally. But there are other more macabre aspects of the law, which have a special fascination for lawyers, and I made sure that in my allotted time I visited many of these unique sights.

One of the most appealing tours, especially to the younger brigade, and many Australians, is the Harry Potter Tour which takes in Australia House. The wonderful marble interior, and its accompanying crystal chandeliers, served as the interior for Gringotts Bank, run by the goblins in the Harry Potter films.

A trip to Tyburn, on the site of modern day Marble Arch, can be a sombre experience. It was the location for public executions for almost 600 years. It is where Oliver Cromwell's exhumed body was symbolically hanged in 1661. Prisoners to be executed would begin their last day at Newgate Prison, from whence they were brought through the streets in a horse and cart.

A few hundred yards down Bayswater Road from Marble Arch is Tyburn Convent, where a Catholic Order of Benedictine nuns has established a Martyrs' Shrine to honour more than 350 Catholic martyrs executed in England after the Reformation, including 105 at the nearby Tyburn Gallows. It is a moving reminder of how ferocious and deadly the religious wars of the 16th and 17th century were and it has an eerie parallel in the plaque in the centre of Broad Street, Oxford, which marks the site of the burning at the stake in 1555 of Anglican bishops Hugh Latimer, Nicholas Ridley and the Archbishop of Canterbury, Thomas Cranmer, after being convicted of heresy.

Tyburn is only one of a dozen notorious execution sites around London. William Wallace, Scottish knight and independence leader, was hanged, drawn and quartered at Smithfield, later Lon-

325

don's major meat (thankfully, no longer human) market, where he paid the supreme penalty for defeating the English at the Battle of Stirling Bridge in 1297.

Some other very famous guided walks are Shakespeare's London and the Jack the Ripper Tour through Whitechapel. This is built around one of the most mesmerising and terrifying unsolved multiple murder mysteries of all time, as Megs and I discovered – we were still shaken hours afterwards. The tour moves from Aldgate through the sinister alleyways of the East End, evoking visions of the gaslight and fog in 1888, which were of inestimable assistance to the Ripper as he preyed on drink-sodden ladies of the night.

Gory and gruesome are always fascinating but a Dickens' London tour is special. It passes Fetter Lane, the site of a distillery destroyed in the anti-Catholic Gordon Riots of 1780, graphically described in *Barnaby Rudge*. In those same riots, the infamous Newgate Prison, the principal place of incarceration for serious criminals and scene of many public executions, was burnt to the ground. It was rebuilt and lasted until 1904, when it was replaced on the same site by the Old Bailey, the Central Criminal Court.

More than half the population of England's prisons in the 18th century was there because of debt. Marshalsea was a privately run, for-profit debtor's prison in Southwark, immediately south of the Thames. In 1824, aged 12, Charles Dickens went to visit his father, who was briefly imprisoned there. It left an indelible mark on him. He was almost morbidly fascinated by prisons, describing Newgate in no fewer than four of his novels. Not a liberal prison reformer, in his later years he was a frequent voyeuristic visitor to prisons and even morgues, both at home and abroad.

The prison of all prisons is the Tower of London, where Anne Boleyn and the pretender, Lady Jane Grey, were executed on Tower Green, and Thomas Cromwell and St Thomas More breathed their last on nearby Tower Hill, now commemorated by the Hung Drawn and Quartered pub on Great Tower Street. The Tower is also infamous as the presumed last resting place of the two princes in the Tower, imprisoned on the orders of King Richard III and never seen again.

London's single most significant execution site was undoubtedly the Banqueting House, then part of the Palace of Whitehall, and still visitable today. This was where, in 1649, Charles 1 lost his head on a temporary scaffold, after being convicted of high treason by a specially established High Court of Justice, which sat in Westminster Hall. It is not far from the Old Palace Yard, the grounds in front of the Palace of Westminster, where, in 1606, Guy Fawkes went to his final reward. It is ironic that executions, intended to be a deterrent to crime, did not discourage widespread pickpocketing at these events, which attracted huge crowds.

I found the Charterhouse historically irresistible. The area, located between the Barbican and Smithfield market, first became notable in the mid-14th century as a graveyard and plague pit for victims of the Black Death. It was soon converted to a Carthusian monastery, which it remained until the Dissolution of the Monasteries in 1537. Its next incarnation was as a luxurious mansion house until, in 1611, its wealthy owner endowed a hospital on the site and, in his will, bequeathed funds to maintain a chapel, an almshouse for lonely and needy male pensioners, and a school. The hospital steadily developed a reputation for excellence, as did the school before re-locating to Godalming in Surrey.

The swinging sixties

My first taste of London came in the mid-1960s. Carnaby Street – "the embodiment of the swinging sixties, the epicentre of culture and lifestyle" – was in full flight. England was about to win its one and only soccer World Cup – on home turf. Harold Wilson was Prime Minister, not that I noticed or cared – we were there to see the sights, soak up the ambience, imbibe the weak beer.

Shortly after arrival, and with no fixed place of abode, a number of us from the good ship *Fairstar* dossed down in a big rambling house near Hampstead Heath. I was just getting to sleep, well after midnight, when the lights came on and Joe, a cricket groupie, called out: "Who wants a game of cards?" When he was told to ["get lost"], he said: "Well, does anyone want to meet Garfield Sobers?" This provoked quite a different response, and I soon found myself in the close vicinity of the great man – if I recollect correctly, with a cigarette in his hand. We played cards for a while, until Joe announced that as Gary was required to resume his Test innings at Lord's the next morning, he had better get some sleep. It turned out that he was 121 not out overnight and went on to finish with an unbeaten 163.

I had hoped to earn a respectable living as a solicitor, but my hopes were quickly dashed as the barriers to entry were impregnable, and the prospect of £10 a week as a lowly law clerk was not appealing, and certainly insufficient to maintain even a modest tourist lifestyle.

Having been inexplicably rejected as a film extra, I applied to be a temporary "supply" teacher with the Inner London Education Authority. While waiting, I commenced employment with Multibroadcasters, a TV rental firm, as a repossession agent. Radio Rentals were the giants in the field of coin-in-the-slot TV rentals, in the days when most TV sets were hired rather than bought. The remuneration, although still modest, was certainly a vast improvement on any alternative. The real attraction was that you got to take home a little two-door van, with wire netting across the rear back door. This provided unparalleled freedom to travel around London, for both sightseeing and party purposes, without having to rely on the Underground or taxis.

I did, however, have to endure an occasion of serious trepidation when I knocked at the door of a delinquent TV set hirer. Finding the door unlocked and apparently no one home, I quickly entered to retrieve the merchandise. Suddenly I noticed that the walls of the unit were adorned with many photographs of clearly one of London's leading pugilists. Deciding that discretion was the better part of valour, I immediately retreated, only briefly stopping to enter "no one home" in my note book.

London in those days was an exciting place, despite the general lack of environmental awareness, best exemplified by "pea souper" fogs which regularly engulfed the capital and had been around since Dickensian times. The Thames was an unhygienic cesspool of filthy water and vast amounts of casually discarded rubbish. All this was forgotten, shortly after our arrival, by the euphoria surrounding the soccer World Cup in July 1966, culminating in an unforgettable Wembley final and England achieving a glorious 4-2 victory, after extra time, against West Germany. The locals were understandably ecstatic, and we had no hesitation in helping out with the celebrations, joyfully mingling amongst the vast crowds who filled the streets that night, and for days after.

Our general game plan was to spend two months in London, followed by two months on the road – a long one which included travels through Scandinavia, Eastern Germany and the Middle East – across the Syrian desert to Damascus and on to Baghdad. I vividly remember travelling out to the site of the Hanging Gardens of Babylon – the gardens were barely recognisable as such, being a few overgrown terraces on either side of a dilapidated and broken down ancient bluestone "highway". Nearby, there was a little desolate sand and windswept village, with a few mud houses. Suddenly, a young boy emerged and, seeing us, immediately shouted: "Bobby Moore! Bobby Moore!", the name of the captain of England's World Cup winning team. This was proof positive that soccer was a world game.

On return to home base my licence to become a supply teacher came through, so I quickly seized the opportunity to earn some serious money. As Britain was chronically short of relief teachers, the wages were tax-free, amounting to some four times what I would have earned as a law clerk, and probably more than as a solicitor. It was not without its thrills and spills. The idea was that you could be required at short notice to go wherever there was a vacancy, usually for a few weeks at a time. I could find myself teaching French one week, and Religious Knowledge the next. My first assignment was a co-ed comprehensive school in Hackney, near E R Braithwaite's iconic school portrayed in the famous film, *To Sir, With Love*. I later discovered that the school was "right in the middle of the murder mile," according to one of its most famous past pupils, Ronny "Chopper" Harris, then captain of Chelsea FC.

The concept of a comprehensive school, in contrast to a grammar school, was just becoming widespread, having been introduced after the War on an experimental basis. Unlike the grammar school emphasis on merit, comprehensives offered a broader curriculum, catering more for those who needed vocational training, and practical subjects like design and technology. This was probably appropriate in the more poverty stricken East End. My classes consisted mainly of West Indian boys and girls who were generally very bright, often tattooed, and totally undisciplined. As they could leave school at 15, their parents were keen for them to do so in order to contribute to the modest family coffers. Most saw no point in being artificially kept out of the workforce by a killjoy school system. They vented their frustration by being as difficult as possible in the classroom. It was not unusual for a pupil to jump up on the desk or throw around picture cards and sometimes homemade knives. Only speaking when spoken to was unheard of.

Teaching even basic French, despite having studied it at university level, had its pitfalls. After I had struggled gamely through one class, the ultimate indignity befell me when one keen student asked quizzically why I didn't speak in real French. No doubt a reflection on my refined Australian accent, but a valuable lesson in later life, as I decided that attempting to speak in French only encouraged the natives to speak quickly and often in dialect, seemingly to deliberately humiliate.

One particularly memorable episode involved a white English boy who suddenly re-appeared after having been absent for over a week. He handed me a note in childlike handwriting which he said was from his mother. It read: "Please excuse John for not coming to school. I recently received some distressing news, so I kept him home for a while." My first suspicion was that the boy had written it himself, but when he vigourously denied it, I asked around the staff room at the break if anyone knew the family? The response was quick: "His father is a contract killer who was sentenced to death in South Africa recently". I decided not to press the point with the lad.

I soon became enamoured with the theatre, especially in the West End, where big names, both local and international, were always performing. I well remember seeing Jane Asher, former fiancée of Paul McCartney, in *The Tempest*. I also became fascinated with Theatreland. The numerous (around forty), mostly privately-owned West End theatre buildings are of great historical and

architectural significance. Often small and cramped, most are replete with grand facades, elegant and ornate interior design and
decoration, and bursting with theatrical memorabilia. The first
West End theatre, which opened in 1663, was the Theatre Royal,
Drury Lane, followed by Sadler's Wells, twenty years later, but
only offering opera, as it was not then licensed for plays. In my
second London incarnation, I was present at Drury Lane (which is
not in, but merely backs onto, Drury Lane) to watch an AFL concert, organised by the ubiquitous Eddie McGuire, complete with
Charles and Camilla lookalikes.

Drury Lane was followed shortly afterwards by the Haymarket
and the Royal Opera House, Covent Garden. The Savoy Theatre
in The Strand, built by Richard D'Oyly Carte specifically to accommodate the timeless Gilbert and Sullivan comic operas came
along in 1881. Agatha Christie's *The Mousetrap*, the longest running production in the world, has been performed continuously
since 1952. I finally succumbed to its lure a few years ago and was
not disappointed.

My first sojourn in London, fun though it was, and eye-opening
in many respects, was ultimately a rite of passage with a finite
ending. Some of my erstwhile playmates had already departed
the scene. As I entered the school staff room each morning, my
thoughts increasingly turned to the future and the itch soon became too strong to ignore.

Accordingly, in mid-1967, I boarded a Qantas flight for Australia via Tehran and Hong Kong. I vividly remember thinking
that the all-male flight attendants (then known as stewards) were
taking the mickey out of me, so broad were their Aussie accents.
Intercontinental flying in those days was not the consumer com-
modity it is today, but as ships still took some five weeks, and a
new career at the Bar beckoned, I felt I had no time to lose.

Stoke Lodge: residence and neighbourhood

The High Commissioner's residence in ritzy Kensington is known
as Stoke Lodge (or, as Ron Walker was fond of calling it, Stoke
House, presumably after a smart Melbourne waterfront restaurant
until it burnt down). It was a very comfortable, if somewhat up-

market, five bedroom family home, with a downstairs kitchen, a large rectangular conservatory and an outsized garden. Not many houses in inner London could afford the luxury of a large garden, as opposed to the pocket handkerchief sized specimens sometimes seen in adjoining areas.

Stoke Lodge has had a fascinating history. It has been the official residence of the Australian High Commissioner since 1950. The present 76-year lease expires on 24 June 2064. The property is owned by the Campden Charities Trustees, founded by endowments in the wills of Baptist Viscount Campden and his wife who died in 1629 and 1643 respectively. The endowments were "… for the good and benefit of the poor of the Parish forever …" and "… to put forth one poor boy or more to be apprentices …" The Charities' area of benefit remains the old Parish of Kensington. In the will of Viscountess Dowager Campden she left a further £200, which was used to purchase land, called Butts Field, which includes the 0.6-acre site of Stoke Lodge.

The present house was built between 1838 and 1840 by Robert Thew, a Major in the East India Company's Artillery. He subsequently bid successfully for the lease of the site for a term of 98 years at an annual rent of £20. Thew himself never lived in Stoke Lodge, preferring instead to reside in a modest adjoining house, which was later converted into a staff cottage.

In 1851 the house was occupied by a celebrated Italian prima donna, Giulia Grisi, daughter of one of Napoleon Bonaparte's Italian officers. In 1861 new rooms were built on the west side, the verandah was extended and, on the east side, a kitchen and other rooms were added. In 1871 the house was occupied by Sir James Stanfield, MP for Halifax, who stayed for 36 years.

After the First World War the house was occupied by Commander Norman Douglas Holbrook, VC, an Englishman and the first submariner to be awarded the Victoria Cross. In 1915 the name of the New South Wales Eastern Riverina town of Germanton was changed to Holbrook to honour him. In 1975 the sloping roof at the front of the house was removed and the elevation raised to provide full height internally to the front rooms on the second level. At the same time a terrace was formed at the second-floor level and the conservatory was extended in depth, only to be demolished and re-built in 1989. The residence and grounds are now estimated to be worth in the region of £45 million. Just around the corner from the Royal Albert Hall, it adjoins a very exclusive terraced street called Gloucester Gate, once the site of a work house, a public institution in which the able-bodied destitute of the parish received board and lodging in return for work.

At our end of the street where we lived there were really only two very substantial residences, Stoke Lodge and Cleeve Lodge, both pleasant and spacious Regency homes, with large gardens. While Stoke Lodge had a constant flow of visitors, Cleeve Lodge, with the same complement of three full-time staff, was eerily silent. Just when I had finally concluded it was deserted, but certainly not derelict, I returned one evening to find a number of black belt karate types, walking up and down outside the premises, punching their fists into their palms, in a deliberate attempt to intimidate and deter. We were later reliably informed that it was privately owned by the ambassador to Spain from one of the Gulf States, who visited for one week each year, and refused to be driven from his private jet airport, instead preferring to take a helicopter to Battersea Park, and thence travel by motorcade to his residence.

Kensington, in west London, is a blue ribbon area, not only politically. A stone's throw from Stoke Lodge is Kensington Palace Gardens, one of the wealthiest streets on the planet, long known as Billionaire's Row. It was built in the mid-19th century on part of the grounds of the Palace which currently houses Prince William, the Duke of Cambridge, second in line to the throne, and his family, together with a number of minor Royals. During the Second World War, the military intelligence unit, MI 19, used one of the houses as an interrogation centre for German POWs. Several embassies are now located there, along with mega-mansions owned by oligarchs such as Chelsea FC owner Roman Abramovich and Indian steel tycoon Lakshmi Mittal. The presence of the Israeli embassy gives it a somewhat unsettling feel, protected as it is by armed police checkpoints, crash barriers and bollards. The Royal Garden Hotel, where the Australian cricket team usually stays, is a street away.

MORE TO LIFE THAN POLITICS?

As Palace Gardens is essentially a private street, with no out-side vehicles permitted, my early morning runs around Hyde Park took me up the broad walk on the other side of the Palace, where the gates were often garlanded with flowers in memory of the people's princess, Diana, who, in happier times, had resided there with her family. Opposite the Palace, and on the other side of Kensington Road, where a toll gate once stood in the mid-19th century, is Palace Gate which, inexplicably, becomes Gloucester Rd further down.

At the top end of Palace Gate, we discovered an imposing Vene-tian Gothic residence, allegedly expressly commissioned by Queen Victoria, housing a delightful Italian restaurant named Da Mario, which proclaimed itself "Princess Diana's favourite pizzeria". It was separated from Stoke Lodge by a small private lane, which, together with Hyde Park Gate, had its own Residents' Associa-tion – yet another very exclusive grouping. Diana also frequented another elegant Italian establishment in nearby Beauchamp Place, where Ron Walker insisted on taking me on several occasions and where he was well known to the management.

Incidentally, Beauchamp is one of the those many street names which are not pronounced phonetically – try Beacham. I often came across other egregious street and place examples such as Ca-dogan (Ka-duggan), Beaulieu (Bewley), Marylebone (Marlabone), Leicester (Lester), Chiswick (Chissick), Southwark (Suthick), Tot-tenham (Totnam), etc. But the one that got me thinking was Hol-born, which our cockney driver always pronounced phonetically, when others insisted it was Ho-b'n. It gradually dawned that it was a class thing, by which the "well educated" upper classes could embarrass their "higerant" lower class brethren. I then re-membered some of Wodehouse's snobbish (but, as the Brits say, "in the nicest possible way") creations, such as Psmith (Smith) and Featherstone-Haugh (Fanshaw). The Master must have acquired the habit from his family, as his surname, as we all know, is pro-nounced Woodhouse.

Another classic language eccentricity is the family divide over pronunciation of the name Powell. Lord Charles Powell, former key foreign policy adviser to Margaret Thatcher, in line with the

334

MY LONDON – A TRIBUTE

wonderful high Tory author Antony Powell, prefers "Pool", while his brother Jonathan, former Chief of Staff to Tony Blair, opts for the phonetic "Pow-ell." Only the British ... But, then again, it may be a political class thing.

The British penchant for giving the same street different names reaches its zenith in the area. The Residence is located in the middle of a circular cul de sac (colloquially known as "the frying pan"). Our version of Hyde Park Gate (HPG) runs into Kensington Road which, although continuous, becomes Kensington High Street to the west and, to the east, Kensington Gore, before becoming Kensington Road again, and finally converting to Knightsbridge, until it expires at Hyde Park Corner. No doubt these eccentricities are designed for the amusement of local councils and the confusion of visitors.

Our section of HPG runs parallel to a nearby street of the same name, although they have sequential house numbers. To make matters worse, the south side of Kensington Road, which connects the linking HPG pieces, is also called HPG. Apart from my eminent predecessors, our street sector has no notable former residents. In stark contrast, the other main HPG has a veritable multitude of blue plaques commemorating houses where once lived: Winston Churchill, who also died there; Lord Baden Powell, founder of the Boy Scouts and Girl Guides; Sir Jacob Epstein, sculptor and painter; Sir Leslie Stephen, scholar and writer with several of his offspring, including Vanessa Bell and Virginia Woolf; Lord Nigel Lawson, former Chancellor of the Exchequer, and his daughter, Nigella; and Enid Bagnold, prolific playwright, author of *The Chalk Garden* and *National Velvet*, and great grandmother of Samantha Cameron, wife of the former Prime Minister, David Cameron.

Blue plaques are another London original. It is one of the great joys of walking London streets to enjoy an instant informal history lesson and to be reminded of London's magnificent antecedents, linking heroes of the past with the buildings of the present. There are now close to one thousand plaques throughout the capital. The scheme was established by the Society of Arts in 1867 and is the oldest in the world. Similar schemes now operate

335

around England and, indeed, many other countries, but I have to say that Australia has not yet taken up any scheme of comparable significance.

The first London blue plaque commemorated the birthplace of Lord Byron in Cavendish Square. In 1879 the City of London assumed responsibility for erecting plaques within its boundaries. More recently, since 1986, the original scheme has been run by English Heritage. The design was modernised in 1938 and the clean circular blue format has been the standard ever since.

The eligibility criteria for an English heritage blue plaque in London are strict. The famous person must:

- have been dead for twenty years or have passed the centenary of their birth;
- be considered eminent by a majority of members of their own profession and have made an outstanding contribution to human welfare or happiness;
- have lived or worked in that building for a significant period;
- be recognisable to the well-informed passer-by or deserve national recognition.

I learnt at a young age that it is important to have a football team to follow. When I was still a sub-teen my father's team was Melbourne, then a powerhouse in the Victorian Football League, so I promptly barracked for Collingwood. Then, as now, they were often the underdog, despite winning plenty of flags before I was born, including four in a row in the late 1920s. Later I watched Melbourne come close to emulating this magical feat, only to be stopped by "the Pies", so I felt vindicated.

When I arrived in London I had to choose a team. My favourite club from the 1960s had been West Ham, whose origins like Collingwood were very working class – and which had three of the best players in England's winning World Cup team of 1966. This time I decided to go for the locals, Chelsea, as I remembered that Ron "Chopper" Harris, Chelsea Captain during my first London stay, and who still holds the Chelsea record of 655 for the number of club games played, had attended the east end Hackney

MY LONDON – A TRIBUTE

school at which I had taught. Chelsea had last won the first division premiership in 1955. As a typical London eccentricity, the football club is not located in Chelsea but in Fulham, which has its own Premier league football team, alongside Chelsea.

The area of Chelsea forms part of the only Royal Borough of Kensington and Chelsea. In the 1830s it was a country fishing village and had earlier been, according to Charles Dickens, a dangerous place where "few would venture, unarmed and unattended." Dickens was married at St Luke's Church, now known as Chelsea Old Church, where Sir (St) Thomas More is buried, and the funeral of American-born novelist, Henry James, was held. Not far away is the house, built in 1703, of Thomas Carlyle, author of *The French Revolution: A History*, and Dickens' principal guide and mentor. I visited the house several times to soak up the history.

My favourite church, in Cheyne Row, was the Church of the Holy Redeemer and St Thomas More, the patron saint of politicians, who made the supreme sacrifice for his principles. It is a beautiful place of retreat, with discreet statues, lush but tasteful tapestries, a fine oaken, but now disused, pulpit and a sense of calm and majesty.

Other important places for Catholic worship in west London include Westminster Cathedral, which John Betjeman called "a masterpiece in striped brick and stone". It houses the Catholic Archbishopric of Westminster, where I once visited the incumbent, Cormack Murphy-O'Connor. It is not on quite the scale of Lambeth Palace, the London home of the Church of England's Archbishop of Canterbury, but is nonetheless comfortable.

Brompton Oratory, a large neo-classical Italian baroque edifice, is a striking building. The Jesuit Church in Mayfair, fondly known as Farm Street, and to which I have been an occasional visitor, has a high altar designed by famed 19th century architect, Augustus Pugin, and described by respected author, Sir Simon Jenkins, as "Gothic Revival at its most sumptuous." The significance of these places is that, while they are now thriving, the faith that they represent was illegal for several hundred years, from the reign of Queen Elizabeth I (1558-1603) until the *Roman Catholic Relief Act 1829*, the culmination of Catholic Emancipation throughout Britain.

Gentlemen's clubs

One of the great things about London is its many places off the beaten track, but tourists rarely stumble upon them. A prime example is Gentlemen's Clubs, members-only private establishments, originally designed to cater exclusively for 18th century upper class denizens. Before we left Melbourne, Peter Harvie, a thoughtful friend and particular devotee of London's Cav(alry) and Guards Club in Piccadilly, presented me with a wonderful coffee table book entitled *The Gentlemen's Clubs of London*, which enabled me to hit the ground running. Clubland can be a rather nebulous term, sometimes used loosely to apply to entertainment venues such as nightclubs, or even adult entertainment centres. It is not broad enough, however, to include the fictitious Drones Club, frequented by Bertie Wooster of P G Wodehouse fame.

Traditionally the term, "clubland," has applied to the general area of West London, particularly in the general vicinity of St James's Square and along Pall Mall. But "clubs" can also encompass privately owned commercial clubs, some quite modern and well decked out and as comfortable and welcoming as traditional gentlemen's clubs, which are usually owned by the members. The gentlemen's club, which has been described as "another country from another time", to some extent displaced the coffee shop, which had been the principal haven for gossip and scandal in an earlier age. The first clubs, such as White's, Brooks's and Boodle's, were refuges for the aristocracy and allowed gambling, which was otherwise illegal.

Another very special one is the Groucho Club in bohemian Soho, founded in 1985 in response to Britain's then draconian licensing laws of the time, when pubs were closed in the afternoons. White's Club first opened its doors in 1693, making it one of the oldest and most exclusive clubs in London. This male-only, members-only institution has been described as a haven of serenity and counts a number of Royals, including Prince Charles, as members. However, the best I could do in the VIP-spotting contest was to have lunch at a table next to the then Prime Minister, David Cameron, and his wealthy stockbroker father, a former chairman of the club.

MY LONDON – A TRIBUTE

Several of the older clubs have interesting political antecedents. Brooks's was first established in 1762 as a private society, and its alumni include a long-serving Prime Minister, William Pitt the Younger, and anti-slave trade campaigner, William Wilberforce. The Reform Club was first formed in 1836 as a meeting place for Radicals and Whigs, following passage of the Great Reform Act of 1832. True to its progressive roots, in 1981 the club was one of the first to admit women, the only vital qualities still required being "character, talent and achievement".

The Carlton Club had earlier been founded by Conservative Party peers, MPs and gentlemen in 1832, as a place to plan a counter attack on the Great Reform Act. Boodle's, founded in 1762 by future PM, Lord Shelburne, was also aristocratically inclined; originally Whig, it still retains a strong Conservative following.

The British aristocracy often displays a penchant for the eccentric and the flamboyant, as evidenced in 1910 by the decision of Winston Churchill, then Liberal Home Secretary, and F E Smith (later Lord Birkenhead), a leading barrister and Conservative MP, to found The Other Club. It soon became a political dining society and forum for vigorous debate, in protest at being rebuffed by another venerable dining club on the grounds that they were "too controversial". Even at the height of the Blitz in 1941, Churchill insisted on attending and the club continues to meet fortnightly at the Savoy Hotel when Parliament is sitting. Others were more project-specific, such as The Travellers Club, founded in 1819. It has long prided itself on being "a sanctuary of refinement for travelling gentlemen", which presumably includes antipodeans such as myself.

The most exotic is the Garrick Club, a haven of bohemian tranquillity, with a seven year waiting list, festooned with a priceless art collection and a Garrick theatrical library. Named after David Garrick, one of history's most famous Shakespearean actors, since 1831 it has catered primarily for theatrical practitioners and literary lions. Its alumni list reads like a roll call of London artistic society: Charles Kean, Henry Irving, Herbert Beerbohm Tree, Arthur Sullivan, Laurence Olivier, Stephen Fry and John Gielgud. From the literary world came writers such as Charles Dickens, H G Wells, J M Barrie, A A Milne, and Kingsley Amis. The visual arts have been represented

MORE TO LIFE THAN POLITICS?

by painters such as John Everett Millais, Lord Leighton and Dante Gabriel Rossetti.

The club itself is very impressive, the building redolent of its illustrious history. My abiding memory is of oak panelling, narrow winding corridors and scads of theatrical memorabilia. Lord Tim Bell, who later invited me to join the board of his publicly listed public relations, advertising and corporate advisory company, Chime plc, once took me there for a meal. I had previously dined there as a guest of Ian Callinan, QC, former High Court judge, novelist and playwright. The guest of honour that evening was famous Shakespearean actor and Australian expat, Keith Michell.

Another famous club for arts aficionados is the Chelsea Arts Club (1891), where I once dined with David Hockney and his principal agent, Peter Goulds, founder of leading Los Angeles Gallery, L A Louver, and a very good friend for almost twenty years.

John Howard and I once had drinks at the East India Club (1849), when we were in Opposition, after we had both attended a Lord's Test Match (from memory the famous day in 1993 when Taylor, Slater and Boon all scored centuries, while Mark Waugh only managed 99. John Howard, by then PM, attended another famous Test Match at Lord's in 2005, in very different circumstances – the day of the failed bombings. In later years I stayed at the club, founded by members of the East India Company and commissioned military officers, but I found it somewhat stuffy and anti-technology.

Another club, very conveniently located on the edge of west London, and very relevant for someone like me, whose Scottish heritage can be traced back to Dunfermline, is the warm and friendly Caledonian Club (1891) in the heart of Belgravia. I have stayed there several times.

One of the most unusual clubs is the Royal Thames Yacht Club, founded in 1775 and located in Knightsbridge, nowhere near the Thames, but which boasts of being the oldest continuously operating yacht club in the world. Shortly after my arrival as Australia's official representative, I had the pleasure of addressing a packed house, mostly Poms, anxious to confirm that we still bore no grudges, having safely emerged from the long darkness of our relatively civilised colonisation.

Livery companies

The livery company is another unique institution which remains relevant today, despite its principal function having been transformed from commercial to philanthropic. The companies evolved from the medieval guilds, with power to regulate and control wages, labour conditions and industry standards. Many have origins which predate the Reformation and still retain their historic religious associations but, these days, members are free to follow any religious calling, or none. There are currently 110 livery companies, comprising both ancient and modern trade associations and guilds, almost all styling themselves as Worshipful Companies. Some of the extant companies have distinguished histories and still perform useful professional functions related to their original purpose. The Scriveners Company admits members of legal and associated groupings, while the Apothecaries' Company awards post graduate qualifications in some medical specialities. The Hackney Drivers' Company represents licensed taxi drivers who have passed the very demanding "Knowledge of London" test, worthy successors to the Worshipful Company of Carmen, whose origins date back to 1517, when they obtained Royal permission to control the cartage trade. Their motto was Scite, Cite, Certo, Latin for Skilfully, Swiftly, Surely. With the demise of carts they remain a charitable and ceremonial institution with over 500 liverymen.

Livery companies still play a significant part in the life of the City of London, offering both charitable and networking opportunities, as well as voting rights to senior civic offices such as the Lord Mayoralty (with knighthood attached) and the City of London Corporation. They were quick to embrace senior Australians in my time, so I was duly invited to participate in some arcane rituals and even now, many years later, I am still on several mailing lists in case I would like to visit again.

Away from London

Travelling beyond London's boundaries, especially at weekends, provides some of life's great scenic joys and history excursions. The countryside is littered with castles, cathedrals (and minsters), ancient market towns and modern farmers' markets. The Cotswolds and the Chilterns exert a magnetic pull but one of my first destinations is usually Shakespeare's birthplace, Stratford-upon-Avon, where one or more of his plays is always being performed.

There are so many famous places, particularly the university towns of Oxford and Cambridge, where I once spoke to the local branch of the Britain-Australia Society.

Afterwards I was presented with a fine book on the nearby Fens, an ecologically rich marshland which I visited on several occasions.

But for me the most interesting times, and towns, were off the beaten track – across the Yorkshire Dales to spa towns like Buxton; Durham, with its Romanesque cathedral and Norman castle; and Lincoln Cathedral, which houses the grave of Matthew Flinders. Once, years ago, during my youthful school teaching sojourn in south London, we took a weekend excursion to the rugged and desolate Yorkshire moors, the setting for *Wuthering Heights.*

Yorkshire, the largest county in the north, is famous for its dour cricketers (Sutcliffe, Hutton and Boycott) and its working class history, as recounted in George Orwell's *Road to Wigan Pier* (leading to a colliery, not the seaside, as the town is well inland). I once spent half a day underground inspecting a defunct coal mine in Yorkshire, which, until the 1960s, had been the beating heart of the UK's energy supplies and the realm of the powerful President of the National Union of Mineworkers, Arthur Scargill, until Margaret Thatcher saw him off. Employment in UK coal mining has fallen from a peak of over a million in the 1920s to around 2,000 today.

Despite the grit and grime, Yorkshire has some very scenic rural vistas and pretty towns, none better than Harrogate, a large tourist spa and theatre town, on the edge of the Yorkshire Dales, famous for Yorkshire Tea and consistently voted the "happiest town in Britain to live". It also has the third largest fully integrated conference and exhibition centre in the UK, and one of the largest in Europe.

Manchester, still a powerhouse city, with two of the greatest football teams, is a must-see for its history, both past and modern. To the west are Anglesey island and Liverpool, home of the

MY LONDON – A TRIBUTE

Beatles, and to the east the hiker's paradise of the Peak District. Birmingham, heart of the Midlands, is close to London and now a regular venue for Conservative Party conferences, which I attended most recently in 2016 as Federal President of the Liberal Party.

Visiting the islands is a very popular pastime, particularly the Inner and Outer Hebrides, as I did on several occasions. The Isle of Man, a self-governing British dependency with strong Celtic and Viking roots, is a unique experience, with its rugged coastline, medieval castles and rural landscapes. Just south of the Scottish border lies Carlisle, an early Roman settlement which became an important military stronghold and later a densely populated mill town, with its 12th century cathedral and its even more ancient castle. Nearby Hadrian's Wall, built to mark the northern border of the Roman empire, is not far from the gorgeous Lake District, where a few years ago Megs and I joined a group of expat Australians on a four-day ramble.

One of the most interesting historical locations is Ironbridge in Shropshire, home of Blandings Castle, of P G Wodehouse fame. Ironbridge is popularly regarded as the "Birthplace of the Industrial Revolution" due to the process of smelting iron with coke being perfected in the area in the early 18th century. The industrial sites of the Severn Gorge, together with its very educational museum, now have UNESCO World Heritage status.

Nearby is Bridgnorth, on the Welsh border, one of the Midlands' main Royalist strongholds during the Civil War. Across the border in Wales is the book lovers' haven of Hay-on-Wye. The Brecon Beacons mountain range, where we once hiked, is not far away: a photo adorns our kitchen.

Living in London provided ample opportunities to visit places like Cecil Court, a street still owned by the Cecil family of long-serving Prime Minister, Lord Salisbury, and now a booklover's haven, known as Booksellers' Row, near Leicester Square. It was always a personal fascination to attend "affordable art fairs" (variously defined, but usually referring to works priced under £3,000), which were, to me, an irresistible feature of the local scene. I also managed to attend some of the not so affordable art auctions at famed auction houses Christie's, Bonhams and Savills. These plac-

343

es reeked of unstated wealth but also offered some relatively modestly priced paintings of both the traditional and modern style of English and Scots artists such as John Lowrie Morrison.

A most enjoyable outdoor activity, even in the long and gloomy winters, was my semi-religious devotion to a run around Hyde Park and the Serpentine. For variety, I included the nearby streets, past many blue plaques signifying former illustrious occupants, such as JFK, who lived for a while (1939-40) with his Ambassador father in the US embassy in Princes Gate. I was also a regular devotee of two gym chains, Fitness First, opposite Australia House and close to the London School of Economics, and LA Fitness in South Kensington, close to home. Walking there took me down Sloane Street, past the Cadogan Hotel where Oscar Wilde was arrested in 1895 after losing his libel case.

But what I enjoyed most of all were the rich cultural characteristics of London and, by extension, Britain. Blake's *Jerusalem* never fails to stir me nor Kipling's *If* to move me. It is impossible to forget the indelible impact of the two great wars – just to read Rupert Brooke's "The Soldier", as I have done many times, published a year before his death, is to appreciate the enormity of the young soldiers' sacrifice and to understand what they forsook. Roy Strong, the art historian, says that England has always been defined by its countryside and the rural idyll and still entrances the millions who visit national parks, stately mansions and country homes and gardens. But the fact remains that London is where it all happens and always will be.

People would sometimes say to me that Australia is a great place, but it's so far away. My reply was usually along the lines of: "if it was just around the corner, Britain would be deserted." Somewhat of an overstatement to be sure but both countries have their distinctive qualities – Australia's sunburnt life style and economic success are legendary but, notwithstanding the weather, London remains the centre of the world for many, and its vast range of historical, cultural and scenic attractions as well as its stable polity will ensure that it remains an irresistible magnet for generations of Australians to come.

Acknowledgements

This book could not have come together in the way it has without the superb editorial assistance of the redoubtable John Nethercote. I always believed I had an interesting life story to tell but John made it come alive by unrelenting discipline and tight wordsmithing, picking up even the smallest editorial and sometimes factual peccadillo.

I am also very grateful to the publisher, Anthony Capello of Connor Court; to Michael Gilchrist for his skills in type-setting and layout, and a remarkable patience; and David Furse-Roberts for preparing the index when time was running short.

Two other friends who were invaluable to the project were John Roskam, CEO of the Institute of Public Affairs; and Nick Cater, CEO of the Menzies Research Centre, both of whom offered every encouragement and consistently sound advice.

I am most grateful to David Hockney Inc for assistance in inclusion of photographs of various works by David Hockney in this book.

Thanks are due to the Copyright Agency for permission to use photographs of paintings by Stella Gimme, Jack Dale and Wilma Ross Ngala and thanks to the Aboriginal Artists Agency for permission to use photographs of paintings by Long Jack Philippus and Clifford Possum.

I have no doubt that one of the secrets of any success that we may have had in government was the calibre of the office staff. I suspect this was, in part, because Communications became a very interesting and attractive portfolio so we were able to entice many high-quality people including the recently anointed Minister for Communications, Cyber Safety and the Arts, Paul Fletcher, first, as telecoms adviser; and later Chief of Staff.

David Quilty was not only very valuable in Opposition but, after a short detour via the Prime Minister's Office, came back to be a universally admired Chief of Staff, with a great instinct for both good policy and effective politics. David was responsible for building a very strong working culture in which people were able to enjoy themselves while pursuing significant policy ideas. I was never aware of any serious office politics or internecine disputes and I was always struck by how enthusiastic everyone was.

I was exceptionally fortunate to obtain the services of Sarah Ryan. Having already worked as an international translator she came to Australia on her travels and quickly found her niche as personal assistant in the Canberra office. I cannot speak highly enough of her warmth, dedication and all-round capability and will always remember her, and her wonderful Irish lilt, very warmly.

Indispensable stalwarts were the three Fionas – Cameron in Broadcasting, and Poletti and Menzies in the Arts – Creina Chapman, Annabelle Herd and Peta Credlin also in broadcasting, David Kennedy and James Shaw in telecoms and Andrew Jackson and David Masters in information technology.

Impressive all-rounders included Karim Barbara, Chris Faris and Tamir Maltz. Dan Rosen had a special place in my heart, being not only an avid Collingwood supporter but also possessed of an excellent brain as well as a great musical touch. Although I did not always stick to the script, I fondly recall Virginia Cook from the Department for her gifts as arts speechwriter.

My ten long years in Opposition would not have been much fun for staffers who had to endure the inevitable loneliness and disappointments of three losing elections. Some made light of the situation and contributed enormously in helping to put together some good policies.

Far and away the most valuable was Fiona Poletti, who helped enormously with child care policy, and later the arts, before rising to even greater heights when we were in government; I will be forever grateful to her. She remains an enormously impressive and dedicated arts aficionado, with an amazing network of friends and colleagues.

Another who was very helpful in Opposition with the challenging shadow portfolio of Social Security was Michael

Backman. Barely out of university, but possessed of a lightning quick mind, he went on to be a very successful foreign policy author and later a London art dealer. I should also pay tribute to Renata, followed by Annette Walsh and Anita Simmons, all of whom served me long and well as receptionist/personal assistants.

Press secretaries play a key role for any minister and I was ably assisted by Ashley Manicaros, Terry O'Connor, Sasha Grebe and Simon Troeth during my seven and a half years in the job.

Neville Stevens, long serving secretary of the Department of Communications, while maintaining departmental neutrality, was a tower of strength in suggesting sensible and sometimes novel solutions to difficult problems. We all benefited greatly from his calmness and expertise.

We were also very well served by Dr Ian Watt and Helen Williams as secretaries of the Department. Ian went on to greater heights in the Canberra bureaucracy, ultimately becoming Secretary to the Department of the Prime Minister & Cabinet; while Helen was a trailblazer in a number of portfolios.

To everyone who was part of the team, including those whom I have not included by name, I genuinely appreciated their dedication and camaraderie and thank them for their contribution. I hope they all had an experience none of us will ever forget.

Index

Abbott, Tony, 126-31, 134-35, 150, 241

Abetz, Senator Eric, 129

Afghan Australia Council, 88

Afghanistan, 87-92

Alberici, Emma, 249

Alston, Amy (daughter), 267, 296

Alston, Ian (brother), 5, 18

Alston, Megs (wife), 34, 52, 112, 178, 180, 183, 202, 267, 269, 278, 286, 293, 296, 310, 314, 316, 326, 343

Alston, Nick (son), 14, 267, 287, 296

Alston, Philip (brother), 4,18

Alston, Richard

  Appointment to the Senate, 68-69, 87

  Career at the Bar, 31-45

  Early career in London, 28-30

  Education, 7-12, 19-28

  Federal President of the Liberal Party, 59, 343

  High Commissioner to the UK, 47, 54, 177, 258, 263, 297, 299-300, 315

  Minister for Communications and the Arts, 161, 181, 224, 270

  Shadow Minister for Communications, 139

  Ship's crew, Pacific Ocean, 21-26

  Sporting career, 12-15

  State President of the Liberal Party (Victorian Branch), 35, 48, 54-55, 57, 60, 62, 67-68

Alston, Robert Bruce "Bob" (father), 1-4, 7-8, 11-17, 21, 29

Alston, Sheila (mother), 1, 4, 7, 13-18, 258

Anderson, David, 244

Anderson, John, 100-01

Anthony, Doug, 67, 157

Anti-siphoning laws, 167-68

Archer, Lord Jeffrey, 312

Arts policy, 181-99

Australia Council for the Arts, 98, 182, 185-87, 195

Australia Post, 76, 143

Australia-Israel Chamber of Commerce, 103

Australian Broadcasting Corporation (ABC), 60, 82-83, 105, 123-125, 142-43, 166-67, 186, 223-55

Australian Council for Overseas Aid (ACFOA), 52-53, 264, 266

Australian Council of Trade Unions (ACTU), 112, 152

Australian Democrats, 56, 84, 104

Australian Honours System, 131-34

Australian Labor Party (ALP), 4, 20, 37, 41, 57, 95, 98, 103-104, 114, 139-40, 144-45, 147-54, 156, 159, 164, 169, 181-82, 185-86, 191, 195, 223-26, 231, 234-35, 238, 244

Ayres, Philip, 88

Backing Australia's Ability, 156-57

Bacon, Jim, 195

Bacon, Philip, 183

Balding, Russell, 230, 245

Baldwin, Bob, 176

349

Balmford, Justice Rosemary, 28
Barak, William, 202
Barassi, Ron, 99
Bardon, Geoffrey, 204
Barjaray, Moyen, 88
Barry, Paul, 244
Bartlett, Senator Andrew, 104
Batarbee, Rex, 203
Beazley, Kim, 94, 120, 147-48, 156
Bell, Lord Tim, 263, 340
Benetti, John, 20
Besley, Tim, 154
Birrell, Mark, 41
Bishop, Julie, 59
Black, Conrad, 84
Blainey, Geoffrey, 264
Blair, Tony, 101, 113, 119, 137, 169, 276, 301-02, 304, 318, 320, 335
Blamey, Sir Thomas, 41
Bland, Dave, 5
Blount, Frank, 142, 144
Bond, Alan, 147
Booker Prize, 176, 186, 278, 283-85
Books, 277-81
Boswell, Senator Ron, 105, 157
Bowden, Tim, 234
Britain, 31, 133, 137, 147, 168-69
Brown, Gordon, 61, 320
Bruce, Stanley Melbourne, 113
Bryan, William Jennings, 110
Builders Labourers Federation, 21
Burnes, Allan, 37
Burnes, Andrew, 309
Buttrose, Ita, 244, 255
Byers, Sir Maurice, 77-78

Cain, John, 37, 41
Cairns, Jim, 17
Callinan, Ian QC, 340
Calvert, Senator Paul, 99
Campbell, Doug, 146
Canada, 25, 117, 130, 254
Candi, Emmanuel, 185
Capes, Tony, 13
Carey, Peter, 186
Carnegie, Dale, 15
Carpets, 285-87
Carr, Bob, 195
Carr, Senator Kim, 83, 147
Cater, Nick, 250
Catholicism, 7, 62, 69, 177, 246, 281-82
Chaney, Michael, 195, 260
Charles, Prince of Wales, 319-20
Chihuly, Dale, 271, 293-95
China, 50, 126, 134, 136, 214, 292
Chipp, Don, 56, 265
Churcher, Betty, 190, 194
Churchill, Winston, 107, 120, 136-37
Cicero, Marcus Tullius, 110, 116
Clark, Helen, 130
Clarke, John, 193
Clinton, Bill, 76, 135
Clinton, Hillary, 251
Clubs, London, 338-40
Coalition (Liberal-National government), 66, 76, 80, 84, 95, 113, 119, 135, 145-46, 148-49,154-55, 157, 166-67, 184, 201, 224-226, 231, 235, 244
Colette, Adrian, 191
Colman, Geoff QC, 13

INDEX

Colston, Senator Mal, 123, 152-54

Commonwealth Bank of
Australia, 76, 94, 148

Communications, Department of,
245

Connolly, Chris, 183

Connolly, David, 99

Constitutional Referendum
(1988), 77-79

Cook, Captain James, 52

Cook, Sir Joseph, 300

Coonan, Senator Helen, 104

Cooper, Dr Kenneth, 262

Costello, Peter, 100-01, 112, 120-21,
134, 181

Court, Richard, 195

Cowan, James and Wendy, 210

Cowen, Sir Zelman, 27

Cowper, Bob, 13

Craik, Jennifer, 198

Crawford, Sir John, 266

Crean, Frank, 55

Credlin, Peta, 127

Crockett, Bill, QC, 35

Crosby, Sir Lynton, 62, 299

Cross, David, 40

Cuba, 52

Cutler, Dr Terry, 151

Dale, Jack, 202

Darling, Gordon, 262

David, Albert, 29

Dawkins, John, 206

Dawson, Daryl QC, 259

Delahunty, Mary, 195

Dempster, Quentin, 226, 247

Derham, Professor David, 47

Diana, Princess of Wales, 319-20,
334

Digital Television, 165-67

Done, Ken, 199

Dowling, Michael QC, 44

Downer, Alexander, 100, 114, 181

Duckmanton, Sir Talbot, 223

Duke of Edinburgh, Prince Philip,
129, 131, 315, 319-20

Dunn, Philip QC, 34

Dunstan, Keith, 14, 258

Dutton, Peter, 126

Dyson, Sir James, 69

East Timor, 124, 265

Ebes, Hank, 207, 208

Edwards, Bob, 207

Ellicott, Bob, QC, 53

Elliott, John, 20, 55, 56

Ergas, Henry, 75

Estens, Dick, 155

Evans, Senator Gareth, 77, 99, 147

Everingham, Paul, 206

Fahey, John, 100, 102, 103

Faulkner, Senator John, 72, 105

Fels, Allan, 185

Ferguson, Niall, 323

Fifield, Senator Mitch, 252

Fischer, Tim, 89, 100-01, 158

Fisher, Andrew, 300

Fixx, James, 259

Fletcher, Paul, 156

Fonda, Jane, 103

Ford, Professor Harry, 27

Fraser Government, 53, 56, 100,
113, 213

351

Fraser, Malcolm, 10, 48, 127

Fry, C B, 13

Frydenberg, Josh, 117

Gallagher, Norm, 21

Garland, Sir Victor, 54

Gates, Bill, 101

Geldof, Bob, 50

Gilbert, Dr Bob, 25

Gillard, Julia, 59, 121

Gladstone, William, 109, 322

Glass, 294-95

Gobbo, Sir James, 14, 28

Goldberg, Alan QC, 42

Gonski education package, 108

Gonski, David, 190, 192, 195, 198

Goods and Services Tax (GST), 81, 108, 124, 186

Goodwin, Doris Kearns, 109, 112-13

Gorman, James, 42

Gorton, Sir John, 66

Goulds, Peter, 271-72, 276, 294, 340

Grattan, Michelle, 248

Greer, Germaine, 51

Guest, Justice Paul, 28

Guilfoyle, Margaret, 68

Haigh, Gideon, 13

Halfpenny, John, 76

Hamer, Sir Rupert "Dick", 48, 55, 77

Hanson, Senator Pauline, 67

Hardy, Frank, 176

Harper, Stephen, 107

Harradine, Senator Brian, 96, 123, 152-153

Harris, Rolf, 312

Hart, Archbishop Denis, 12

Harvey, Peter, 141

Hawke Government, 77, 101, 224

Hawke, Bob, 80-81, 108, 110-14, 117

Hayden, Bill, 74, 85

Heath, Sir Edward, 322

Heffernan, Senator Bill, 105

Herron, Senator John, 105

Hewson, John, 66, 76, 80, 120, 226

Hicks, Gill, 305-307

Hill, David, 224, 237, 247

Hill, Senator Robert, 47, 93, 100-01, 105, 176, 181

Hilmer Review on Competition Policy (1993), 140, 142

Hintze, Sir Michael, 310-312

Hockey, Joe, 127-28

Hockney, David, 270-71, 274, 277, 294, 340

Holding, Clyde, 265

Hollows, Fred, 132, 176

Holmes, Jonathan, 244

Holthuyzen, Fay, 146

Hong Kong, 23, 25, 30

Howard Government, 114, 140, 142, 147, 160-61, 164-65, 173, 186, 198,

Howard, John, xii, 66-67, 76, 79-80, 96, 99, 101, 108, 111, 112-125, 127-129, 134, 137-138, 142, 149, 152-53, 161, 173, 184, 189, 191, 232, 298, 303-305

Hughes, Billy, 113

Humphries, Barry, 120, 270, 273, 278

India, 134, 187

INDEX

Indigenous Art, 175, 201-222

Indigenous Australians, 128, 176, 189, 202, 215

Information and Communications Technologies (ICT), 139, 143, 156

Information Technology, 151-60

International Women's Year 1975, Mexico City, see World Conference on Women

Iran, 285, 287-91, 293

Iraq War, 100, 124, 224, 245-46

Israel, 102-03

Japan, 3, 24-25, 126

Jinping, Xi, 136

Johns, Brian, 227

Katter, Bob, 105

Keating, Paul, 64, 81, 84-85, 94, 97-98, 108, 110-11, 114, 117-18, 121, 132, 144, 148, 164, 167, 176, 181-85, 189, 194, 198, 201, 250-51

Kelly, Ros, 141

Kemp, Dr David, 67

Kemp, Senator Rod, 72, 122, 188, 197

Kempler, Leon, 103

Keneally, Thomas, 176

Kennedy, Dr Brian, 190, 212, 213, 271

Kennett, Jeff, 41, 198

Kenny, Chris, 240

Kernot, Senator Cheryl, 84, 95

Kerr, Sir John, 265

Key, John, 137

Keynes, John Maynard, 179, 304

King George VI, 322

Kissinger, Henry, 314

Kngwarreye, Emily, 183, 205, 208, 216, 220

Kohl, Helmut, 137

Korean War, 33

Krathammer, Charles, xii

Lachlan, Murdoch, 170, 172-74

Latham, Mark, 115

Lazarus, Jack, 36

Lee Kuan Yew, 25, 136

Lee, Michael, 177, 181

Letwin, Sir Oliver, 61

Lewin, Ben, 34

Liberal Party (of Australia), 17, 35, 47-48, 50, 54, 56-59, 62, 67, 76, 80, 99, 101, 105, 115, 118-20, 126-28, 135, 145, 155, 169, 170, 176, 181, 135, 145, 155, 169, 170, 176, 181, 184, 194, 224, 227-28, 234, 257, 264, 266, 309

Lincoln, Abraham, 107

Linton, Robert, 1, 21

Linton, Sir Richard,1

Little, John, 22

Llyod, Edward "Woods", QC, 35

Lynch, Michael, 183, 185

Lynch, Sir Phillip, 57-58, 65

Lyons, Joseph, 113

MacArthur, General Douglas, 3

Magna Carta, 301

Major, Sir John, 101, 320

Malone, Paddy, 21

Mandela, Nelson, 136

Mansfield, Bob, 225

May, Theresa, 59

McClelland, Doug, 299

McGarvie, Richard "Dick", QC, 40-41, 225

McGauchie, Don, 146

McGauran, Peter, 188

McInerney, Sir Murray, 28

McPhee, Hilary, 98, 185-86

McPhee, Neil QC, 33

McRae, Ian, 193

McRae, Tommy, 202

Menzies, Fiona, 190

Menzies, Sir Robert Gordon, 27, 67, 108, 113, 115-16, 119-20, 136, 169, 190, 222, 223

Merkel, Angela, 137

Michell, Keith, 340

Middleton, Jim, 232

Miller, Bob, 20

Missen, Senator Alan, 68, 87

More, Sir (St) Thomas, 337

Morris, Karl, 309

Morrison Government, 124

Morrison, Scott, 66, 113, 121, 126, 128

Mother Teresa, 187-88

Murdoch, Rupert, 139, 162, 164, 166, 168-70, 172-74, 254

Murphy, Senator Lionel, 33, 265

Murray, Les, 182, 184

Najibullah, President Mohammed, 90, 91, 92

Namatjira, Albert, 203

National Gallery of Australia, 190, 194, 201, 213

National Museum of Australia, 188, 189, 201

National Office for the Information Economy (NOIE), 151-52

National Party (of Australia) Nationals, 67, 101, 105, 108, 119, 154-55, 157, 171

Nelson, Dr Brendan, 114, 134

Netanyahu, Benjamin, 137

New Zealand, 130, 133

News Limited, 173

Nimmo, Sir John, 53

Norfolk Island, 52-53

North Korea, 95, 147

Nugent, Helen, 194

O'Donovan, Fr Thomas, 12

O'Sullivan, Michael, 10

Obama, Barack, 110

Olley, Margaret, 182, 199

Olsen, Dennis, 187

Olsen, John, 195

One Nation, 67

Opas, Philip QC, 39

Opera, 176-181

Packer, James, 174,

Packer, Kerry, 32, 139, 166, 168, 170, 172-73, 254

Panizza, Senator John, 105

Pannam, Cliff QC, 28

Papua New Guinea, 52

Parer, Senator Warwick, 93, 105

Patterson, Les, 120

Patterson, Senator Kay, 68, 76

Peacock, Andrew, 79-80, 119, 157

Pearson, Noel, 251

Penman, Archbishop David, 87

Philippines, 3, 25

Phillips, P D, 27

Phillipus, Long Jack, 215

Pitt, William, 33

Poletti, Fiona, 187

Ponting, Ricky, 303

Pope John Paul II, 107, 137

Possum, Clifford, 204, 215

Pratt, Richard "Dick", 10, 189

Privatisation, 55, 64, 75-76, 94-95, 98, 123, 137, 139, 143, 146-48, 156, 252

Probyn, Andrew, 241

Qantas, 76, 94, 148, 192

Queen Elizabeth I, 107

Queen Elizabeth II, 73, 112, 130, 189, 315-16, 319-21

Queen Victoria, 334

Raby, Geoff, 104

Radio National, 227, 248-49

Ray, Robert, 48, 185

Reagan, Ronald, 107

Redlich, Peter, 150

Rees, David, 283

Reid, Elizabeth, 51

Reid, Sir George, 300

Reith, Peter, 58, 77, 85-86, 100-01, 103, 112, 124

Robb, Andrew, 98, 129

Robertson, Senator Ted, 206

Roche, Ken, 8

Roosevelt, Franklin D, 107, 137

Rosanove, Joan QC, 36

Rudd, Kevin, 66, 109, 114, 118-19, 121, 243

Rush,Geoffrey, 192

Russell, Alathea, 54

Ryan, Ronald, 40

Sales, Leigh, 251

Santamaria, B A "Bob", 152

Schneider, Karl, 14

Sharwood, Professor Robin, 27

Shaw, Tony, 146

Short, Senator Jim, 80

Sibraa, Senator Kerry, 176

Silicon Valley, 102

Silks, 291-94

Simper, Errol, 104

Sinodinis, Arthur, 102

Snedden, Bill, 40

Special Broadcasting Service (SBS), 142-43, 167, 227, 248, 250, 252-53, 255

Squires, Sir Peter, 308

Staley, Tony, 57

Stevens, Neville, 146

StockmanTyapaltjarri, Billy, 215

Stoke Lodge, 333

Stokes, Kerry, 173, 254

Storey, Cecile and Haddon QC, 264

Straus, Peter, 283

Street, Tony, 10,

Stuart, Rupert Maxwell, 36

Sutherland, Dame Joan, 180, 270

Switkowski, Ziggy, 145, 158

Switzer, Tom, 242

Syme, Antonia, 213

Tanner, Lindsay, 159

Telstra, 64, 94, 98, 115, 123, 139, 141-56, 158-59, 171

Thatcher, Margaret, 107, 113, 134, 137, 147, 169, 299, 312, 334, 342

Tjampitjimpa, Ronnie, 215

Trump, Donald, 108, 163, 237, 250-51

Tucker, Albert, 174

Turnbull, Malcolm, 58, 63, 66, 113, 114, 118-19, 126, 128-29, 134-35

Twomey, Paul, 151

UNESCO, 49, 202

United Nations, 47-49, 53, 65, 206

United States, 24-25, 33, 49, 51, 78, 80, 113, 178, 233, 245

University of Melbourne, 39

Van Baer, Ludwig, 11

VFL (Victorian Football League), 6, 13, 20

Victorian Bar, 31, 34

Vietnam War, 20, 48, 223

Viner, Ian QC, 206

Walker, John QC, 34

Walker, Ron, 320

Wallace, William, 325

Walsh, Senator Peter, 71, 300

Walters, Cathy, 191

Ward, Mel, 141

Warne, Shane, 312

Washington, George, 107

Watson, Don, 98, 186

Whitlam Government, 47, 119

Whitlam, Gough, 17, 77-78, 109, 169, 176, 198, 260

Whitlam, Margaret, 51, 177-78

Williams, Peter, 8

Williams, Robyn, 227

Wilson, Woodrow, 49, 109

Woodward, Roger, 182

Wooldridge, Michael, 100

World Conference on Women (1975), 51

World Health Organisation, 49
World War I (Great War), 27, 119

World War II, 3-4, 24, 48

Xavier College, 7, 9, 11-12, 19, 22, 26, 37, 175, 187

Yeltsin, Boris, 92

www.ingramcontent.com/pod-product-compliance
Lightning Source LLC
Chambersburg PA
CBHW042117300426
44117CB00021B/2976